EYEWITNESS TRAVEL

# FAMILY GUIDE

## WASHINGTON, DC

EYEWITNESS TRAVEL

# FAMILY GUIDE

## WASHINGTON, DC

**Penguin Random House**

**MANAGING EDITOR** Aruna Ghose
**EDITORIAL MANAGER**
Sheeba Bhatnagar
**DESIGN MANAGER** Kavita Saha
**DEPUTY DESIGN MANAGER**
Mathew Kurien
**PROJECT EDITOR** Divya Chowfin
**EDITOR** Sushmita Ghosh
**PROJECT DESIGNER** Vinita Venugopal
**DESIGNER** Rupanki Arora Kaushik
**PICTURE RESEARCH MANAGER**
Taiyaba Khatoon
**PICTURE RESEARCH** Sumita Khatwani
**SENIOR DTP DESIGNER**
Azeem Siddiqui
**DTP DESIGNER** Rakesh Pal
**SENIOR CARTOGRAPHIC MANAGER**
Uma Bhattacharya
**ASSISTANT CARTOGRAPHIC MANAGER**
Suresh Kumar
**AUTHORS**
Paul Franklin, Eleanor Berman
**PHOTOGRAPHY**
Paul Franklin
**CARTOONS**
Julian Mosedale
**ADDITIONAL ILLUSTRATIONS** Arun
Pottirayil, Stephen Conlin, Gary
Cross, Richard Draper, Chris Orr
& Associates, Mel Pickering,
Robbie Polley, John Woodcock
**DESIGN CONCEPT** Keith Hagan at
www.greenwich-design.co.uk

Printed and bound in China

First published in the United States
in 2012 by DK Publishing,
345 Hudson Street, New York, NY 10014.
A Penguin Random House Company

**Reprinted with revisions 2014, 2016**

17 18 10 9 8 7 6 5 4 3 2

MIX
Paper from
responsible sources
FSC
www.fsc.org   FSC™ C018179

# Contents

*Children at the entrance of the
Smithsonian's National Zoological Park*

Visitors on Segways outside the
United States Capitol

# How to Use this Guide

This guide is designed to help families to get the most from their visit to Washington, DC, providing expert recommendations for sightseeing with kids along with detailed practical information. The opening section contains an introduction to Washington, DC and its highlights, as well as all the essentials required to plan a family holiday (including getting there, getting around, accommodations, health, money, insurance, media, and communications), a guide to family-oriented festivals and events, and a brief historical overview.

The main sightseeing section in the book is divided into areas. A "best of" feature for every chapter is followed by the key sights and other attractions in the area, as well as options for where to eat, drink, play, and have more fun. At the back of the book are detailed maps of Washington, DC.

## INTRODUCING THE AREA

Each area chapter is opened by a double-page spread setting it in context, with a short introduction, locator map, and a selection of highlights.

**Locator map** locates the region.

**Brief highlights** give a flavor of what to see in the area.

## THE BEST OF...

A planner to show at a glance the best things for families to see and do in each area, with themed suggestions ranging from history, art, and culture to gardens and games.

**Themed suggestions** for the best things to see and do with kids.

## WHERE TO STAY

Our expert authors have compiled a wide range of recommendations for places to stay with families, from hotels and B&Bs that welcome children to self-catering apartments.

**Easy-to-use symbols** show the key family-friendly features of places to stay.

**Price Guide box** gives details of the price categories for a family of four.

# SIGHTSEEING IN WASHINGTON, DC

Each area features a number of "hub" sights (see below): pragmatic and enjoyable plans for a morning, afternoon, or day's visit. These give adults and children a real insight into the destination, focusing on the key sights and what makes them interesting to kids.

The sights are balanced by places to let off steam, "take cover" options for rainy days, suggestions for where to eat, drink, and shop with kids, ideas for where to continue sightseeing, and all the practicalities, including transport.

**Introductory text** focuses on the practical aspects of the area, from the best time of day to visit to how to get around using public transit.

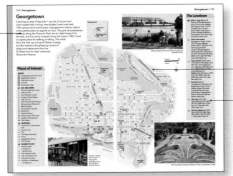

**The hub map** identifies the sights featured in the chapter, as well as restaurants, shops, places to stay, transport, nearest playgrounds, supermarkets, and pharmacies.

**The Lowdown** gives all the practical information you need to visit the area. The key to the symbols is on the back jacket flap.

**The hub sights** are the best places to visit in each area. Lively and informative text engages and entertains both adults and children.

**Key Features** uses illustrated artworks to show the most interesting features of each sight, highlighting elements likely to appeal to children.

**Kids' Corner** is featured on all sightseeing pages (see below).

**Find out more** gives suggestions for downloads, games, apps, or films to enthuse children about a place and help them to learn more about it.

**Eat and drink** lists recommendations for family-friendly places to eat and drink, from picnic options and snacks to proper meals and gourmet dining.

**The Lowdown** provides comprehensive practical information, including transport, opening times, costs, activities, age range suitability, and how long to allow for a visit.

**Letting off steam** suggests a place to take children to play freely following a cultural visit.

**Next stop...** suggests other places to visit, either near the key sight, thematically linked to the sight, or a complete change of pace for the rest of the day.

**More sights** around each hub, selected to appeal to both adults and children, are given on the pages that follow.

**Kids' Corners** are designed to involve children with the sight, suggesting things to look out for, games to play, cartoons, and fun facts. Answers to quizzes are given at the bottom of the panel.

**Places of interest** are recommended, with an emphasis on the aspects most likely to attract children, and incorporating quirky stories and unusual facts. Each one includes a suggestion for letting off steam or taking cover.

**The Lowdown** provides the usual comprehensive practical and transport information for each sight featured.

*One of the popular double-decker buses offering tours of the United States Capitol and other attractions*

# Introducing
# WASHINGTON, DC

# The Best of Washington, DC

The city of Washington, DC is perfect for families – small enough to get around easily, but with enough fun attractions, cultural events, and one-of-a-kind experiences to keep everyone entertained. The National Mall is full of quality museums and theaters, and beyond it, the city and its environs include a range of kid-oriented attractions, from one of the world's best zoos to the remarkable interactive exhibits at George Washington's Mount Vernon Estate.

### Amazing art in gorgeous galleries

Start at the **Corcoran Gallery of Art** *(see p126)*, where signature pieces from the Corcoran collection of historical and contemporary American art are displayed in its Legacy Gallery, along with artworks from the National Gallery of Art. Then head to the **National Gallery of Art West Building** *(see pp76–9)*, which offers an audio tour designed for kids. Walk to the **National Gallery of Art East Building** *(see p80)*, stop at the Children's Shop on the lower level, and ride Villareal's walkway, *Multiverse*, as many times as you want. Don't forget to check out Alexander Calder's mobile and Andy Goldsworthy's *Roof* in the atrium.

For lunch, head to the Pavilion Café in the **National Sculpture Garden** *(see pp80–81)*. Let the kids run in the garden afterward, but make sure they see *Typewriter Eraser, Scale X,* and *Thinker on a Rock.* Next, stop at the **Freer**

*Top right* Washington Monument rising above Constitution Gardens *Below left* Facade of the Supreme Court *Below right* Visitors at the National Air and Space Museum

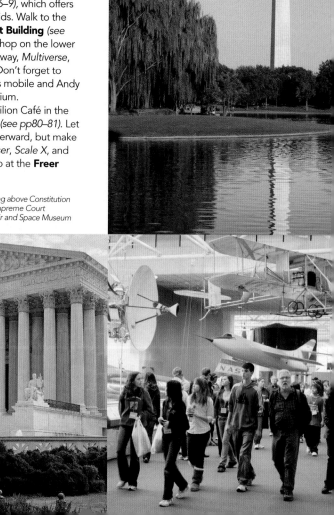

The series of paintings entitled Voyage of Life by Thomas Cole in the National Gallery of Art West Building

**Gallery of Art** (see p66) to see some wonderful Asian art and Whistler's legendary "Peacock Room." An underground passage links the Freer to the **National Museum of African Art** (see p64), which is full of exciting stuff like primitive drums, ceremonial weapons, and masks.

For a break, head to the **Smithsonian Castle** (see p64) for snacks and then on to the Mall so the kids can ride on the historic carousel. Head to the **Hirshhorn Museum** (see p62) and let the kids go wild in its Sculpture Garden.

## Marauding through museums

Begin your day by taking flight – at the **National Air and Space Museum** (see pp56–9). Get in and out before the crowds arrive, but be sure to see the Wright *Flyer*, Apollo 11, the Moon rock, and the "Spirit of St. Louis." Dash across the Mall to the **National Museum of Natural History** (see pp72–5). Don't miss the Hope Diamond and the forensic re-creations of our ancestors in the Hall of Human Origins.

The **National Museum of the American Indian** (see pp60–61) offers a chance to meet modern Native Americans and to enjoy Native-inspired dishes at the Mitsitam Café. Walk across to the **Newseum** (see pp136–9) on Pennsylvania Avenue, where kids will surely want to make their own broadcast in front of a TV camera.

Saving the best till last, the **International Spy Museum** (see pp144–5) is filled with interactive goodies geared for children. Create a cover, see historical and modern spy gear, try breaking a code, and visit the re-created bunker where the US spied on East Germany during the Cold War.

## Check out the government

Those interested in the workings of the American government can watch the US Senate and House of Representatives in action at the **United States Capitol** (see pp104–105). When

the **Supreme Court** (see pp112–13) is in session, you can step into the gallery to watch the Justices debate the legal issues of the day.

Also worth a stop is the **National Archives** (see pp140–41), where the Constitution and other key documents on the founding of the American state can be examined. The **Newseum** has many exhibits that highlight freedom of the press, while a tour of **The White House** (see pp122–3) and the **White House Visitor Center** (see p124) offers insights into the US presidency.

## The great outdoors

Washington's planners had gardens and green spaces in mind when they laid out the city two centuries ago. Start at the **Washington Monument** (see pp84–5) and walk northwest through the pretty **Constitution Gardens** (see p88). For a longer walk, head southwest around the **Tidal Basin** (see p94), which is lined with shady cherry trees, and then back east along the south side of the Mall. Behind the Smithsonian Castle, **Enid A. Haupt Garden** (see pp64–5) has manicured lawns and some quiet, hidden nooks.

Stroll east to the **US Botanic Garden** (see pp106–107) and explore 3 acres (1.5 ha) of flowers and paths in the National Garden, but also pop into the conservatory to check out the orchid collection and the Jungle with its waterfalls and second-story catwalk. Younger kids will enjoy the Children's Garden.

For lunch, head to Georgetown's **Washington Harbour** (see p158) and dine at Tony & Joe's Seafood Place. Walk south to the **Thompson Boat Center** (see p156) to rent kayaks for a paddle on the Potomac, or hire bikes and head north on the **C&O Canal** (see pp156–7) towpath. End your day with a stroll along the green trails of **Theodore Roosevelt Island** (see p191) after visiting the memorial statue of the 26th president, one of America's best-known conservationists.

## Washington, DC on a budget

Washington, DC is one of the best cities in the US in which to have a great time without spending too much money. This is because admission to almost every attraction on the Mall, including all memorials and Smithsonian museums, is free (although there might be a charge for guided tours and special exhibits). Some other free sights on the Mall include the **US Botanic Garden**, the **US Capitol**, and the **National Gallery of Art**. Tours of **The White House** (arranged well ahead of time), the **National Archives**, and the **Library of Congress** (see pp110–11) are also free.

There is free stuff away from the Mall too. Admission to the **Smithsonian's National Zoological Park** (see pp168–9), **Washington National Cathedral** (see pp172–3; cathedral tours: $10 adults, $6 kids), **US National Arboretum** (see pp178–9), and **Kenilworth Park and Aquatic Gardens** (see p180) is free.

Attend one of the free performances that take place at the Millennium Stage in **Kennedy Center** (see p37) at 6pm daily. In summer, the **Sylvan Theater** (202 315 1313) on the Mall hosts free music and theatrical performances, and free movies are shown at the **Screen on the Green** (see p37) on Monday nights. Free guided walking tours (gratuity requested) are offered by **DC by Foot** (see p23).

## Washington, DC by season

Washington turns into a riot of pink and white in springtime, when thousands of cherry trees burst into bloom. The **National Cherry Blossom Festival** (see p17) in late March and early April is Washington's largest celebration, filling the city with special events, concerts, and family- and kid-oriented events. The biggest thrill, however, is simply strolling around the **Tidal Basin** or along the roads of **East Potomac Park** (see p95) under hundreds of cherry trees blanketed in bright blossoms. The Blossom Kite Festival is also held at the same time, filling the sky above the Mall with fluttering color and excitement.

Also in spring, a sea of azaleas in the **US National Arboretum** is in bloom, and at the White House, the annual **Easter Egg Roll** (see p17), for which tickets are distributed via an online lottery, is open to kids everywhere. Every year, thousands show up for a day of music, activities, and, of course, Easter eggs.

Summer brings the **Smithsonian Folklife Festival** (see p17) to the Mall, highlighting homespun art and crafts from around the globe. On the Fourth of July, the Mall becomes one big family picnic as crowds gather for music and fireworks celebrating American independence.

Fall is the time for the **National Book Festival** (see p17), which brings music, food, books, and fun activities for kids to the Mall. During this season, DC restaurants line Pennsylvania Avenue with tents and booths offering every type of delicious food imaginable in the annual **Taste of DC Festival** (www.thetasteofdc.org).

Winter brings the lighting of the **National Christmas Tree** (see p17), and in February, Chinese New Year lights up the neighborhood of **Chinatown** (see p149). Throughout this season, kids and adults flock to the **National Sculpture Garden** to ice-skate to beautiful music on the big rink surrounded by the classic buildings of the Mall.

*Below left* Equestrian statue of Washington, Mount Vernon
*Below right* The Great Hall in the Library of Congress

**Left** *Sculpture of a lion at the entrance to the National Zoological Park* **Right** *Azaleas in bloom at the US National Arboretum*

## Three days in Washington, DC

On the first day, head to the **Washington Monument** with your morning, timed ticket and take the ride to the top early. Then stroll to the **World War II Memorial** (see pp86–7), and walk through the lovely **Constitution Gardens** on the way to the **Vietnam Veterans Memorial** (see pp88–9) and the **Lincoln Memorial** (see pp90–91). Grab a taxi to the **Capitol Visitor Center Restaurant** (see p108) for lunch, after which take the tour of the **United States Capitol** and admire the Rotunda and the view of the Mall from the balcony. Walk down to the **US Botanic Garden**, tour the conservatory and National Garden, then walk across to the **National Museum of the American Indian**.

Start your second day at the **National Air and Space Museum** as soon as it opens, then head to the **National Museum of Natural History**. Walk one block west and one block north to **Elephant & Castle** (see p122) for good pub food in a kid-friendly atmosphere. In the afternoon, walk east and south to the **National Archives** to see the Constitution and the Declaration of Independence. Spend the rest of the afternoon looking at masterpieces at the **National Sculpture Garden** and the **National Gallery of Art** across Constitution Avenue.

Head first to the **Smithsonian's National Zoological Park** on your third day. Arrive early, as the animals are more active in the cool morning air. Spend a couple of hours here and then head to the **Washington National Cathedral** and take its self-guided tour. Have lunch at the fun and funky **2 Amys** (see p168), then drive or take a ferry from the southwest waterfront to **George Washington's Mount Vernon Estate** (see pp186–7) and spend the afternoon learning about George Washington on his riverfront plantation. Have dinner at the **Mount Vernon Inn** (see p187) and then get back to the Mall to watch the sun set behind the **Lincoln Memorial**. Walk to Tidal Basin, then stroll past the **Franklin Delano Roosevelt Memorial** (see pp92–3) and get to the **Thomas Jefferson Memorial** (see pp96–7) just in time for the evening lights.

## Theatrical Washington, DC

Washington has a wealth of stage and theater options. The **Kennedy Center** is the city's largest venue for theater, symphony, opera, and popular music. It also has a regular schedule of children's plays and entertainment.

Another large and varied venue, **Wolf Trap National Park for the Performing Arts** (see p37) is home to the 7,000-seat Filene Center, which hosts over 90 music, theater, comedy, and dance performances during the summer season. The Barns at Wolf Trap hosts a variety of local and special interest acts, and there are also regular children's performances at the Theatre-in-the-Woods.

Elsewhere around DC, **Ford's Theatre** (see pp142–3) offers a year-round roster of classic family entertainment, while the **National Theatre** (www.nationaltheatre.org) presents a wide range of Broadway and popular plays. The **Arena Stage** (see p37) specializes in American plays, while the **Woolly Mammoth Theater** (see p37) offers avant-garde and cutting-edge modern stage productions. The venerable **Folger Shakespeare Library** (see p37) presents classic Shakespeare plays and the **Shakespeare Theatre Company** (www.shakespearetheatre. org) performs both Shakespearean and contemporary plays.

# Washington, DC Through the Year

Each season brings its own reasons for parades and festivals in Washington, DC. The city shines in spring with clouds of cherry blossoms along the Tidal Basin and kites flying high above the Mall, while summer means Fourth of July fireworks and food festivals. Fall brings theater and music performances to the Kennedy Center, and the lighting of the National Christmas Tree kicks off the holiday season. Major League sports draw cheering fans in all seasons.

## Spring

Washington is at its very best in spring, when the city is blessed with mild weather, abundant flowers, and endless festivities to herald the season. No photo can capture the full beauty of the cherry blossoms that canopy the **Tidal Basin** (see p94) in clouds of pink and white each year, inspiring DC's largest festival. Most of these trees were a gift from the mayor of Tokyo in 1912.

### MARCH

The **DC St. Patrick's Day Parade** starts the fun, filling Constitution Avenue with floats, bagpipes, costumed dancers, and "the wearin' of the green." The **National Cherry Blossom Festival** includes a lavish parade, fireworks, and a street festival showcasing Japanese performances, arts, crafts, and food. Festivities kick off with the Blossom Kite Festival in the grounds of the **Washington Monument** (see pp84–5), showing off the skills of kite-makers from across the world. Events include kite ballets and demonstrations, a young kite-makers' competition, and a "hot tricks showdown" featuring amazing flight patterns to music. Activity tents offer kids the chance to learn origami and make a wind sock or a kite.

The **White House Easter Egg Roll**, for which tickets are issued via an online lottery, is a tradition dating back to 1878. The president and his family preside over the South Lawn while children listen to stories and search for the 24,000 wooden eggs that are hidden on the grounds.

### APRIL

**Filmfest DC**, an 11-day international film festival, showcases top cinema from around the world with over 100 feature films, documentaries, and short films. The **Smithsonian Craft Show** draws the best contemporary artisans in the nation to show and sell their works.

The ceremony for **Jefferson's Birthday** includes a military color guard, wreath tributes, and the sounding of "Taps" at the **Thomas Jefferson Memorial** (see pp96–7), while **Shakespeare's Birthday** brings Elizabethan costumes, dances, songs, and a cake to the **Folger Shakespeare Library** (see p112).

Baseball fans look forward to hearing the opening words: "Play Ball" as the Washington Nationals begin their season at **Nationals Park** (see p41).

### MAY

Everyone looks forward to **Passport DC**, a month-long event saluting the city's rich international culture with street festivals, open houses,

**Below left** The colorful kite-flying festival in the Washington Monument grounds
**Below right** Fireworks over the US Capitol during Independence Day festivities

and embassy events that showcase art, music, dance, and food from around the globe. The highlights are tour days, when embassies and international cultural centers open their doors to visitors. As part of the festival, the **Meridian International Center** and the **Ronald Reagan Building** stage festivities for kids featuring music, dance, and films from across nations.

Also on the May agenda are the **DC Dragon Boat Festival**, with colorful races on the Potomac, and the **Fiesta Asia Street Fair**, with live performances by musicians and martial artists, a lion dance, Pan-Asian foods, and a multi-cultural marketplace.

Washington marks **Memorial Day** with a big parade paying tribute to America's war veterans and a National Symphony Orchestra concert on the **Capitol Grounds** (see p108). **Twilight Tattoos** are popular free outdoor events held by the US Army and feature a military pageant.

## Summer

There are many good reasons why so many tourists stream into Washington in the summer. During this busy time, the city offers a feast of outdoor entertainment. Free concerts by

different military bands take place nightly at the Capitol Grounds, and the Navy Band holds weekly concerts at the **US Navy Memorial** (see p142). The Carter Barron Amphitheater in **Rock Creek Park** (see p170) offers films and music shows. Many other events, from fireworks displays and festivals to sports, make it well worthwhile to join the crowds.

### JUNE

Kids love the **Greater Washington Soap Box Derby**, when racers aged 8 to 17 come careering down Capitol Hill in motorless cars. The three-week **Source Festival** premieres new works from theater, dance, music, film, puppetry, and poetry.

The **National Capital Barbecue Battle** fills Pennsylvania Avenue with competition between BBQ chefs, plus demonstrations, tastings, and kids' activities, while the **DC Caribbean Carnival Parade** is known for its masqueraders in costumes dancing down Constitution Avenue. The **Smithsonian Folklife Festival** fills the Mall with free performances, crafts, cooking demonstrations, and storytelling.

### JULY

Washington is the place to be on America's **Independence Day** as bands, floats, military units, and

giant balloons parade along Constitution Avenue, followed by a free evening concert by the National Symphony Orchestra and spectacular fireworks over the Washington Monument grounds.

The 18-day **Capital Fringe Festival** offers edgy theater, dance, music, and puppetry in venues around the city.

### AUGUST

Tennis fans eagerly await the **Citi Open**, when top names compete in a major tournament at Rock Creek Park, while food mavens look forward to the city's biannual **Restaurant Week**, when the best restaurants in town offer bargain-priced lunches and dinners.

## Fall

The **Labor Day** weekend marks the traditional end of summer and the National Symphony Orchestra gives the season a fine send-off with the last of the outdoor concerts in the Capitol Grounds. Fall days bring some of the year's best weather, and the city's parks and hiking and biking trails are all the more appealing amid fall foliage. Summer crowds thin out, also making this an ideal time to take in the city's many monuments and museums.

*Below left* The cake-cutting ceremony celebrating Shakespeare's birthday at the Folger Shakespeare Library
*Below right* The colorful and vibrant National Cherry Blossom Festival parade

**SEPTEMBER**

The two-day **National Book Festival** attracts book lovers to the National Mall to meet famous authors and illustrators, including writers of best-selling kids' books.

September is synonymous with the start of the Washington Redskins football season and brings cheering crowds to the impressive **FedEx Field** (see p41).

**OCTOBER**

Cheer on 30,000 or so runners at Washington's **Marine Corps Marathon** as they run past the **United States Capitol** (see pp104–105), the Smithsonian museums, the famous memorials, and **The Pentagon** (see p190), before winding up in Arlington. Kids aged 5 to 12 are invited to sign up for the Healthy Kids 1-mile (1.6-km) run, held the day before the big race. This race is not timed and all kids receive a medal, T-shirt, and a goody bag.

There's no better way to celebrate Halloween than the **Boo at the Zoo** at the **Smithsonian's National Zoological Park** (see p168–9). Kids can come in costume and enjoy encounters with a spooky crew of bats, spiders, and owls. There are also haunted trails and festive decorations, and candy and snacks

are available from more than 40 treat stations.

October brings sporting excitement to the **Verizon Center** (see p41), where the professional Washington Wizards basketball team and the Washington Capitals hockey team can be seen in action.

**NOVEMBER**

**FotoWeek DC**, held at the former Spanish Ambassador's residence (2801 16th St NW, 20009), features photography exhibitions and competitions, displaying thousands of entries from both professional and amateur photographers, and experts offering tips at workshops.

# Winter

Washington winters are chilly, but only a few days dip below freezing and there is still plenty of life in the city, especially during the gala holiday season. The lighting of the **National Christmas Tree** on the Ellipse by the nation's first family is a beloved American tradition and includes entertainment and a visit from Santa. The tree is lit until 11pm every night through January 1, and free nightly performances are held around it. Colder days also see the opening of the ice rink at the **National Sculpture Garden**

(see pp80–81), an exceptional setting surrounded by beautiful sculptures. If you would rather watch than skate, **Pavilion Café** (see p81) at the National Gallery of Art offers a panoramic view of the scene.

**LATE NOVEMBER–DECEMBER**

During this holiday season, festive music can be enjoyed in December at the **Washington National Cathedral** (see pp172–3). The **Norwegian Train Display** at **Union Station** (see p115) has a handmade model train that winds through replicas of the mountains and fjords of Norway.

**ZooLights** at the Smithsonian's National Zoological Park lights up the night with animal-shaped light exhibits. This event features a special train ride for kids, zoo-themed model train displays, entertainment, talks by keepers, and a contest for the best gingerbread creations.

Christmas at **Mount Vernon** (see pp186–7) finds George Washington's estate aglow with decorations, traditional chocolate-making demonstrations, a gingerbread model of Mount Vernon, and even a Christmas camel, just like he had on the grounds for Christmas in 1787.

*Below left* Ice-skating at the National Sculpture Garden, outside the National Gallery of Art
*Below right* A biker performs at the International Motorcycle Show

**JANUARY**

The **International Motorcycle Show** displays the latest in bikes, cruisers, and All-Terrain Vehicles (ATVs), and includes a stunt show and prizes. The **Washington Auto Show** features some 700 sleek new makes and models, and offers giveaways, kids' activities, and entertainment.

**FEBRUARY**

Washington's Chinatown celebrates the Chinese New Year with a **Lunar New Year Festival**, featuring a parade with music and dance performances, the traditional Chinese dragon dance, crafts, face painting, lion dancing, and tai chi and kung fu demonstrations.

    **Lincoln's Birthday** is marked with the laying of a wreath and a moving reading of the "Gettysburg Address" at the **Lincoln Memorial** (see pp90–91).

    The liveliest **President's Day** celebration is at Mount Vernon, where visitors can sample George Washington's favorite breakfast of hoecakes (small cakes made of cornmeal) cooked over an open fire, chat with a costumed Washington re-enactor about life in the 18th century, and view a parade with fife and drum corps, early American music, and heritage breed animals marching past the mansion.

# The Lowdown

## Spring

**DC Dragon Boat Festival**
www.dragonboatdc.com

**DC St. Patrick's Day Parade**
www.dcstpatsparade.com

**Fiesta Asia Street Fair**
www.asiaheritagefoundation.org

**Filmfest DC** www.filmfestdc.org

**Jefferson's Birthday** Apr 13;
www.nps.gov/thje

**Meridian International Center**
www.meridian.org

**National Cherry Blossom Festival**
www.nationalcherryblossomfestival.org

**Passport DC** www.culturaltourismdc.
org/things-do-see/passport-dc

**Ronald Reagan Building & International Trade Center**
www.itcdc.com

**Shakespeare's Birthday** Apr 22;
www.folger.edu

**Smithsonian Craft Show**
www.smithsoniancraftshow.org

**Twilight Tattoos**
www.twilight.mdw.army.mil

**The White House Easter Egg Roll**
www.whitehouse.gov/eastereggroll

## Summer

**Capital Fringe Festival**
www.capitalfringe.org

**Citi Open**
www.citiopentennis.com

**DC Caribbean Carnival Parade**
www.dccaribbeancarnival.org

**Greater Washington Soap Box Derby** www.dcsoapboxderby.org

**National Capital Barbecue Battle**
www.bbqdc.com

**Restaurant Week**
www.ramw.org/restaurantweek

**Smithsonian Folklife Festival**
www.festival.si.edu

**Source Festival** www.sourcefestival.org

## Fall

**Boo at the Zoo** www.nationalzoo.si.edu

**FotoWeek DC** www.fotoweekdc.org

**Marine Corps Marathon**
www.marinemarathon.com

**National Book Festival**
www.loc.gov/bookfest

## Winter

**International Motorcycle Show** www.
motorcycleshows.com/WashingtonDC

**Lunar New Year Festival**
www.ccccdc.org

**National Christmas Tree**
www.thenationaltree.org

**Norwegian Train Display**
www.unionstationdc.com

**Washington Auto Show**
www.washingtonautoshow.com

**ZooLights** www.nationalzoo.si.edu

## Public Holidays

**New Year's Day** Jan 1

**Martin Luther King, Jr.'s Birthday**
3rd Mon in Jan

**Lincoln's Birthday** Feb 12

**President's Day** 3rd Mon in Feb

**Memorial Day** last Mon in May

**Independence Day** Jul 4

**Labor Day** 1st Mon in Sep

**Columbus Day** 2nd Mon in Oct

**Election Day** 1st Tue in Nov

**Veterans Day** Nov 11

**Thanksgiving Day** 4th Thu in Nov

**Christmas Day** Dec 25

*Below left* A traditional dragon dance during the Lunar New Year Festival, Chinatown
*Below right* The National Christmas Tree across the street from the White House

# Getting to Washington, DC

One of the most popular destinations in the US, both for business and pleasure, Washington, DC welcomes some 15 million visitors each year, well over a million of them from other nations. Served by three airports and a busy rail terminal, the city offers excellent connections to the rest of the US and the world. Knowing what to expect on arrival, and having all necessary credentials ready, including the kids' passports, will make entry easier.

### US entry requirements

Citizens of 36 nations, including most European countries, Australia, and New Zealand, do not need a visa to enter the US, but must apply for the I-94W form via the Electronic System for Travel Authorization (ESTA) in advance. Canadian and Mexican visitors need only valid passports. The **Transportation Security Administration** is the best source for security regulations.

Before landing, overseas passengers need to fill in a **Customs and Border Protection Agency** form with their passport details, flight number, an address in the US, and the value of any gifts being brought in. Passengers are allowed to carry $100 in gifts without tax.

On arrival, you need to have the I-94W and customs forms initialed. The departure half of the I-94W form needs to be presented when leaving the country. Photos and fingerprints of non-residents over 14 years are taken as a security measure.

### Arriving by air

Washington has two international airports, **Dulles International Airport** (IAD) and **Baltimore-Washington International Airport** (BWI). **Ronald Reagan National Airport** (DCA) serves only domestic flights. US carriers like **American Airlines**, **Delta**, **US Airways**, and **United Airlines** offer regular flights to Washington, while international lines include **British Airways**, **Virgin Atlantic**, **Air France**, and **Lufthansa**. An hourly air shuttle service operates on Delta and US Airways between Boston or New York and Reagan.

Fares are generally lower midweek and lowest during off-season (Nov–Mar). Apex and Superapex fares are usually the lowest, but check the airlines' sites for special rates too.

Luggage carts can be rented at all airports; machines require exact change but credit cards are also accepted. Porters are available to help with baggage for a tip. All airports have currency exchanges, ATMs, and luggage storage.

### Airport transfers

All airports have counters that can book transport. The average driving time from Dulles and BWI into the city is about 45 minutes, and about 10 to 15 minutes from Reagan.

From Dulles, the taxi fare to central Washington is $57–61, while **SuperShuttle** shared vans cost $29, with a reduction for more than one passenger. A **Silver Line Express** bus ride from Dulles will bring you

**Below left** *Passengers on a platform of the Metrorail station at Ronald Reagan National Airport*
**Below right** *Travelers waiting at Baltimore-Washington International Airport*

to the Wiehle-Reston East metro ($5; $10 roundtrip) and from there to downtown, a journey of about 90 minutes. The Metrobus 5A to the L'Enfant Plaza metro station costs $6.

BWI has a train service to Union Station for $15–30, and the **MARC** commuter train to Union Station runs from Mon to Fri ($6). The taxi fare from BWI is about $90, SuperShuttle shared vans cost $37, and Metrobus B30 will cost $6. From the Ronald Reagan National Airport, take the metro directly into the city, or a taxi for $15–20.

A limousine service from **Carmel Car Service** or **Airport Commuter** is available at all airports for about $10 more than the taxi fare. As with a cab, one limo fare covers the family. Reserve with a car service at least 24 hours in advance, and ask for a van if you are traveling with strollers.

## Arriving by rail

Washington is a major destination for **Amtrak**, the national rail system in the US. When arriving by train from US destinations, there are no security procedures to slow your arrival, and cabs are usually plentiful outside the station. Book online in advance for discounts, and check for weekly specials and multi-trip travel pass details on the website.

## Arriving by bus

**Greyhound** is the largest intercity US bus line, with a slow but economical service. Their newer buses are comfortable, with ample legroom and electrical outlets. The Greyhound North America Discovery Pass available to foreign visitors is the cheapest way to travel. Purchase tickets online in advance and check for family discounts and other offers on the website. All long-distance buses arrive at the bus depot, from where cabs can be hired. However, porters are not always available here.

The newer and more comfortable **Megabus** or **Bolt** buses from New York, Boston, or Philadelphia arrive at central locations, including Union Station. Fares average $20.

## Arriving by car

Public transportation in the city is excellent, but those who want to drive can rent a car at the airport. However, traffic is heavy, particularly during rush hours. On-street parking is hard to find, and parking garage or hotel rates are high. Some travelers choose to stay in nearby Virginia and Maryland towns with metro stations, where rates may be lower. US currency is required for any bridge and tunnel tolls when driving into the city.

# The Lowdown

**US entry requirements**
**Customs and Border Protection Agency** www.cbp.gov
**Transportation Security Administration** www.tsa.gov

**Arriving by air**
**Baltimore-Washington International Airport**
800 435 9294;
www.bwiairport.com
**Dulles International Airport**
703 572 2700;
www.metwashairports.com/dulles
**Fare Comparison Websites**
www.cheaptickets.com
www.expedia.com
www.kayak.com
www.priceline.com
www.travelocity.com
**Metropolitan Washington Airport Authority**
www.metwashairports.com
**Ronald Reagan National Airport**
703 417 8000
www.metwashairports.com/reagan

**Airlines**
**Air France** www.airfrance.us
**American Airlines** www.aa.com
**British Airways** www.british airways.com
**Delta** www.delta.com
**Lufthansa** www.lufthansa.com
**United Airlines** www.united.com
**US Airways** www.usairways.com
**Virgin Atlantic** www.virgin-atlantic.com

**Airport transfers**
**Airport Commuter** 888 876 1777;
www.airportcommuter.com/washington_dc_baltimore
**Carmel Car Service** 866 666 6666;
www.carmellimo.com
**MARC** 866 743 3682;
www.mta.maryland.gov/marc-train
**Metrobus** 202 637 7000;
www.wmata.com
**Silver Line Express** 888 927 4359;
www.washfly.com
**SuperShuttle** 800 258 3826;
www.supershuttle.com

**Arriving by rail**
**Amtrak** 800 872 7245;
www.amtrak.com

**Arriving by bus**
**Bolt** 877 265 8287; www.boltbus.com
**Greyhound** 800 231 2222;
www.greyhound.com
**Megabus** 877 462 6342;
www.megabus.com

**Below** Aerial view of aircraft docked at the Baltimore-Washington International Airport

# Getting Around Washington, DC

Washington, DC's metro is one of the cleanest and most efficient subway systems anywhere in the world, and covers a large part of the city and its surroundings. If the metro doesn't get you to your destination, the DC Circulator or a city bus probably will. Taxis are easily available, though more expensive. Some areas of the city are walkable, and ample sightseeing services add to the options.

## Finding your way

The city is divided into quadrants, with the **US Capitol** *(see pp104–105)* as the center. The quadrant, NW or SE for example, is included in every address. The streets are numbered and named alphabetically, and most avenues are named after states. Pennsylvania Avenue is the main artery between the Capitol and the White House, and Massachusetts Avenue is the city's longest thoroughfare. The street plan is simple to follow, but a map is needed to see how the avenues cut across the grid. Refer to the map at the back of this book, or print one from the **Destination DC** *(see p27)* website.

## Using the metro

The Metrorail is by far the fastest way to get around the city and it covers almost every main sightseeing location except for Georgetown, where bus connections are needed. Metro stations are clearly marked with a post bearing a large letter M and color strips showing which of the five color-coded rail lines serve that station. The Metro Pocket Guide, available at the station manager's booth, has a Metrorail system map, locates points of interest near metro stations, and gives information on system hours, fares, and passes. It can also be downloaded or ordered in advance from the **WMATA**. The metro runs from 5am to midnight on weekdays and from 7am to 3am on weekends.

Farecards for metro trains are sold at all stations and may also be ordered online in advance. Machines accept both credit cards and cash, and fares are calculated according to zone. The basic single-journey fare in the central zone, where most sights are clustered, starts at $1.75. Fares go up to $1.95 during rush hours (5–9:30am and 3–7pm), and from midnight to closing on weekends. Twenty cents are added for "peak-of-the-peak" weekday periods (7:30–9am and 4:30–6pm). A 1-day pass, excluding morning rush hours, costs $14.50. For longer stays, it is best to buy the 7-day basic pass, unlimited except for rush hours, for $36. Unlimited 7-day passes for all hours are $59.25. Up to two kids (under 4s) ride free with a paying adult; over 4s pay full fare.

For frequent subway or bus travel, the rechargeable SmarTrip card is best. It costs $2, and gives a 25-cent discount on each ride. A SmarTrip card is needed for free transfers between buses and a 50-cent discount on the fare for transfers between Metrobus and Metrorail. Signs at the track entrances identify

*Below left An easily identifiable, energy-efficient Metrobus in the city center*
*Below center Interstate road signs in Washington, DC*

trains by color and their final destinations, and the five lines intersect at several stations for easy transfer. The busiest transfer points are Metro Center, serving Red, Blue, and Orange lines, and L'Enfant Plaza, serving all except the Red line. The way to each line's tracks is clearly marked by signs.

All Metrorail stations and rail cars are accessible by wheelchair users, and signs indicate the accessible elevator entrance. The information pylon outside each station includes information in Braille and raised alphabet. Each station entrance has an extra-wide gate for wheelchairs.

## Using Metrobuses

The Transit Authority is phasing in sleek new energy-efficient buses in place of the older models. The fare is $1.75 with a SmarTrip card. When using the SmarTrip, transfers between buses are free within 2 hours. Metrobuses operate 24 hours a day, 7 days a week, but service is reduced on weekends and holidays. As with Metrorail, up to two kids (under 4s) ride free with each paying adult; those above 5 pay full fare. Buses may be boarded only at designated Metrobus stops, which have red, white, and blue signs that show which lines use that stop. Time

tables can be found at the WMATA website. Some stops give the time of the next bus via cell phone or PDA if you call the metro helpline and type in the seven-digit number posted at the bus stop. The 32 and 36 Pennsylvania Avenue lines (weekends only) double as sightseeing tours as they travel to Georgetown from the L'Enfant Plaza stop.

Most buses have an electronic screen inside that announces the next stop. When you want to get off at the next stop, pull one of the yellow cords along the sides of the bus. A "stop requested" sign will light up at the front for the driver.

Most buses are wheelchair accessible, and either have a low-floor ramp or are lift-equipped. Wheelchair securement areas are near the front of each bus and include tie-downs and lap belts for safety. Disabled persons pay half fare.

## DC Circulator

Washington's second bus system, the red and gray **DC Circulator** buses, travel across several convenient routes in the city for a $1 fare. Pay with exact change or a SmarTrip card. Among these routes are Union Station to Georgetown, Union Station to Navy Yard via Capitol Hill, and the DC Convention

Center to the SW Waterfront. The route map can be downloaded from the website. Buses run about every 10 minutes from 7am to midnight on weekdays and up to 2am or 3:30am on Friday and Saturday.

Transfer rules are the same as for Metrobus – free within 2 hours with the SmarTrip card and a 50-cent discount on Metrorail fares. Red and gold signs mark the bus stops. All buses are disabled accessible.

## Using taxis

Taxis are plentiful in Washington. Although convenient, they can be costly, especially when traffic is heavy and the meter keeps ticking.

You can hail a cab anywhere you spot one. Several taxi companies serve the city, and while some may be painted the familiar taxi yellow, there is no uniform look to the cars. Taxis tend to congregate outside hotels and at train and bus stations. When hotel doormen hail a cab for you, a $1 tip is customary. A taxi can accommodate four to five passengers, depending on its size. The meter begins at $3.25 and increases by 27 cents every 1/8 of a mile (every 200 m approximately). The fare is for one person, plus $2.16 for each extra passenger, except children under the age of 6.

**Below center** Tree-lined, traffic-filled Pennsylvania Avenue at night, with the US Capitol lit up in the distance
**Below right** People outside the centrally located Smithsonian metro station on the Mall

An extra 50-cent fee is added for every bag handled by the driver after the first one. If you phone for a cab, an additional $2 dispatch fee is charged. A tip of 15–20 per cent at the end of a trip is standard. Rates are regulated by the **Taxicab Commission** and any complaints should be addressed to it. Another convenient option is **Uber**, which provides private drivers on demand. Rides can be requested using iPhone and Android apps or on *www.uber.com*. Payment is by credit card.

## Driving

Driving is the least efficient way to get around Washington. Gas stations are few, traffic is heavy, and street patterns, one-way streets, and traffic circles can be confusing.

If a car is necessary, rentals from agencies such as **Hertz**, **Avis**, and **National Car Rental** are available at all airports and many other locations. To rent a car, you must be at least 21, have a valid driver's license, and a major credit card. Be sure you are properly insured for both collision and personal liability; travelers from other countries can buy insurance from the rental company. Street parking is metered and scant, and commercial parking

lots and garages are expensive. Metered parking can be paid for by coins or by credit card, using the phone number on the meter. Rates are $2 per hour in prime central areas, 75 cents per hour in other areas. Overnight parking in a hotel can run as high as $50. Contact the **District Department of Transportation**, which is responsible for any parking-related issues.

## Cycling

While Washington's busy streets are not ideal for bicycles, especially with children in tow, recreational paths in **Rock Creek Park** *(see p170)*, the Capital Cresent Trail from George-town to Bethesda, and the towpaths along the **C&O Canal** *(see pp156–7)* are fine places to bike. Guided bike rides by companies such as **Bike and Roll** or **DC Tours** are a fun way to see the monuments and other sites on the Mall. Bike rentals are readily available; you can pick up a bike at numerous stations around the district via the **Capital Bikeshare**.

## Walking

Though Washington is spread out, neighborhoods such as **Embassy Row** *(see p171)*, Georgetown, and the Penn Quarter are compact and

quite walkable. The museums and monuments on the National Mall are all within a 2-mile (3-km) area, and are easy to cover on foot. Just be sure to bring comfortable shoes that have been broken in at home.

## Sightseeing tours

Washington has some popular sightseeing options to help you make the most of your time. **Big Bus Tours** operates open-air buses that offer live narrated tours of DC's museums and monuments. Live historical tours of Arlington Cemetery *(see pp192–3)* are run by **ANC Tours by Martz Gray Line** and take you through the cemetery on a tram. Check the website for details.

Other popular hop-on, hop-off tour options include the **Old Town Trolley Tours**, while double-decker bus tours are offered by **City Sightseeing**. You may find discounts if you book ahead online.

Walking tours are an excellent way to explore places like Embassy Row or Georgetown. **Washington Walks** hosts interesting tours of Arlington Cemetery and a lovely Monuments by Moonlight walk. **DC by Foot** offers tours that are free, except for whatever tip you want to give the guides. **Cultural**

**Below left** *One of the open-top double-decker buses offering tours of the city*
**Below right** *Visitors exploring the National Mall on Segways*

Tourism DC also sponsors free neighborhood walking tours for two weekends during "Walkingtown DC," usually late September and early October.

Operators such as the **Potomac Riverboat Company** offer sightseeing cruises of the city's monuments along the Potomac River. Another scenic option is to see the city via Segway tours, a popular family activity, offered by agencies such as **Capital Segway**.

## Day trips

**MARC** commuter trains from Union Station can take you to historic destinations like **Frederick** (see p201), Maryland, or **Harpers Ferry National Historic Park** (see pp198–9), West Virginia. Commuter trains provide restrooms but no food, so bring your own snacks or buy food on arrival. **Amtrak** trains travel south to **Fredericksburg** (see pp206–207) in Virginia, or north to **Baltimore** (see pp218–19), Maryland, all close enough to explore in a day.

Take a cruise on the Potomac to **George Washington's Mount Vernon Estate** (see pp186–7) or the water taxi to **Old Town Alexandria** (see pp188–9) for a great day's outing from the city.

## Intercity travel

Washington is also well located for travel to other major cities on the East Coast. Amtrak trains from Union Station can have you in Philadelphia in about 2 hours and in New York in 3 hours and 30 minutes. **Greyhound** buses also serve these cities, but bus lines such as **Bolt** or **Megabus** are more economical and comfortable. These travel to Boston, Baltimore, and Philadelphia for as little as $15 each way, even less with special offers. Many buses leave from the conveniently located Union Station.

## The Lowdown

### Public transportation
**DC Circulator** 202 567 3040; www.dccirculator.com
**Washington Metropolitan Area Transit Authority (WMATA)** 202 637 7000; www.wmata.com

### Taxis
**Taxicab Commission** 855 484 4966; www.dctaxi.dc.gov
**Uber** www.uber.com

### Driving
**Avis** www.avis.com
**District Department of Transportation** 202 673 6813; www.ddot.dc.gov
**Hertz** www.hertz.com
**National Car Rental** www.nationalcar.com

### Cycling
**Bike and Roll** 866 736 8224; www.bikeandroll.com
**Capital Bikeshare** www.capitalbikeshare.com
**DC Tours** 888 878 9870; www.dctours.us

### Sightseeing tours
**ANC Tours by Martz Gray Line** 202 488 1012; www.graylinedc.com
**Big Bus Tours** 877 332 8689; www.bigbustours.com
**Capital Segway** 800 979 3370; www.capitalsegway.com
**City Sightseeing** 877 332 8689; www.city-sightseeing.com
**Cultural Tourism DC** 202 661 7581; www.culturaltourismdc.org
**DC by Foot** 202 370 1830; www.free toursbyfoot.com/washington-dc-tours
**Old Town Trolley Tours** 888 910 8687; www.trolleytours.com/washington-dc
**Potomac Riverboat Company** 703 548 9000; www.potomacriverboatco.com
**Washington Walks** 202 484 1565; www.washingtonwalks.com

### Day trips and intercity travel
**Amtrak** www.amtrak.com
**Bolt** www.boltbus.com
**Greyhound** www.greyhound.com
**MARC** www.mta.maryland.gov
**Megabus** www.megabus.com

*Below left* Boat tour of the Chesapeake Bay Maritime Museum, St. Michaels in Maryland
*Below right* Cyclists biking along the Chesapeake and Ohio Canal

# Practical Information

Families visiting Washington, DC will have access to high-speed Wi-Fi, good cell phone coverage, conveniently located ATMs, excellent health care, and all other modern conveniences that the city offers. Travel insurance, especially for medical emergencies, is a wise investment for visitors from other countries. As with any other large city, it is sensible to follow a few safety precautions.

## Insurance

The high cost of medical care for non-residents in the US and the difficulties of lost luggage or air travel delays mean that travel insurance is a good idea. The cost of insurance varies with the coverage, the length of the trip, and the number of people covered. The most important features to look for in a policy are emergency medical and dental care, trip cancellation coverage, baggage and travel document loss, and transportation back home in case of an emergency. Your travel agent or insurance company can recommend a reputable firm. If you have coverage at home for loss of personal property, check to see that it is valid when you travel.

Medical insurance in other countries is not valid in the US, and since medical care is expensive, be prepared for a hefty fee. Some physicians and dentists may accept credit cards, but they are more likely to want payment in cash. Hospitals usually accept credit cards.

## Health

Be sure to carry any prescription medications in their original containers with pharmacy labels so that they will pass easily through airport security. It is also wise to pack medicines in your carry-on baggage. Notify officials about any special needs, such as supplies for diabetics. Unused syringes will be allowed when accompanied by insulin or other injectable prescription medication. Bring along general medicines for headache, allergies, and stomach upset, and don't forget sun protection. All of these supplies can also be bought at supermarkets or pharmacies.

### MEDICAL EMERGENCIES

Hotels can usually recommend a doctor if you need medical treatment. Alternatively, you can use services such as **Inn-House Doctor**, whose members will come to your hotel. Dial 911 for an ambulance.

Locations of hospital emergency rooms can be found in the DC yellow pages. The main hospitals with emergency care are **Howard University Hospital, George Washington University Hospital, Children's Hospital National Medical Center**, and **Georgetown University Hospital**. Simple medical issues can be handled by a walk-in **CVS Minute Clinic**, found in many CVS pharmacies across the city.

### FOOD ALLERGIES

Wheat, milk, and butter are mainstays in American cooking, so be sure to ask if you have special

**Below left** *Take care of your personal belongings in crowded places*
**Below center** *The charming building of the Sun Trust Bank on M Street, Georgetown*

food needs. Restaurants often are very good about substitutions, including vegetarian dishes and gluten-free foods. Nut allergies should definitely be mentioned in advance. It is best to keep emergency medications with you.

## Personal safety

Like any other bustling, cosmopolitan city, Washington has its share of petty crime, and it pays to stay alert. If you are unsure about whether a neighborhood is safe at night, ask your hotel concierge or clerk before venturing out. Avoid wearing flashy jewelry or carrying expensive smartphones or tablets that might attract muggers. Keep your wallet in an inside pocket, carry purses in the crook of your elbow, and place them in your lap in restaurants.

Spread your IDs or money across different pockets and keep your passport and other valuables in the hotel safe. Keep your hotel room locked when you are inside, and don't leave the "make up the room" sign when you leave. Make sure that you get a receipt for stored luggage, and that you never leave your belongings unattended at airports, taxi stands, or in hotel lobbies. Call 911 in case of a problem, and if

valuables are lost or stolen, get a copy of the police report for your insurance claim at home. Contact the embassy of your home country in the case of a lost passport.

### LOST AND FOUND

If you leave your belongings on the metro or a bus, contact **WMATA** (Washington Metro Area Transit Authority) to report the loss. Items left in a taxi should be reported to the **DC Taxi Commission**. There is a lost and found department at **Union Station** *(see p115)* as well.

## Money

If you want to change foreign currency to dollars, banks and bureaus such as **Travelex** can be found at airports, at Union Station, and at various points across the city. ATMs are widely available, and most are part of the worldwide Plus or Cirrus network. These offer the best exchange rates and a lower fee than bureaus. Bank machines also accept popular credit cards such as Visa, MasterCard, and American Express, though if you get cash advances with these cards you will have to pay interest. To guard against crime, use an ATM inside the bank rather than one accessed from the street.

### CURRENCY

The basic unit is the dollar, which equals 100 cents. Coins come in one cent (penny), five cent (nickel), 10 cent (dime), and 25 cent (quarter) denominations, and each is a different size so it is easy to tell them apart. The $1 coin is rarely used. The most common bills are $1, $5, $10, and $20. Bank machines mostly give out $20 bills.

### CREDIT CARDS AND TRAVELER'S CHECKS

Major credit cards – such as American Express, MasterCard, and Visa – and debit cards are widely accepted throughout the US. They can be used for everything from movie and theater tickets to dining and hotel bills. Large purchases are also best paid for by credit card. Traveler's checks, though still accepted, are slowly being replaced by prepaid, reloadable travel cards issued by Visa or MasterCard. They are as readily accepted as any other credit card and are just as secure, since they are also protected by a PIN and/or signature.

## Visitor information

**Destination DC**, the city's tourism office, operates a central information center in Penn Quarter.

*Below right A ranger checking the tickets of visitors awaiting a tour of the Washington Monument*

## Media

The city's major daily newspaper, *The Washington Post*, covers international and local news. *Washingtonian Magazine*, a monthly, is helpful for restaurant reviews and a calendar of events.

The four major TV networks in Washington are CBS, NBC, FOX, and ABC. Dozens of channels are found on cable. The two main US cable news outlets are CNN and Fox. Kids will enjoy Disney, Nickelodeon, and Cartoon Network, while sports enthusiasts can watch ESPN.

Washington is served by dozens of radio stations, including an all news and weather station, WTOP (103.5 FM). The National Public Radio outlet with news and classical music is WAMU (88.5 FM).

## Communications

All phones within the District of Columbia use the area code 202. In Virginia the area code is 703 and in the Maryland suburbs the area code is 301 or 240. Toll-free calls are prefixed by 800, 866, 877, or 888. Area codes must be dialed first to reach any number. Dial 0 to reach an operator and 411 to get numbers from information (for a fee). To call overseas directly, dial 011, plus the country code, city area code, and number. For operator-assisted calls, dial 01, then the country code, city code, and number.

### CELL PHONES

Public telephones are rare around town, and are found mostly at train stations and airports. Hotels add a hefty charge for phone calls so it can be convenient and economical to use a cell phone. Check with your carrier at home if your phone is compatible with US services, although you may encounter roaming charges. If your present phone cannot be adapted, you can rent a phone from firms such as **Cellhire USA**. Phone cards are available at most newsstands.

### INTERNET AND EMAIL

Most hotels offer Internet access and/or Wi-Fi connections, some free, some for a fee. Ask before you book as fees can be high. Free Wi-Fi is available in all public libraries and at many bookstores and cafés. Outdoor hot spots with free access are found on the sidewalk and plaza in front of the **Supreme Court** (see pp112–13) and portions of the sidewalk and front steps of the **Library of Congress** (see pp110–11), at Freedom Plaza/Pershing Park, and from 3rd Street to 14th Street. The city has only a few Internet cafés.

### POSTAL SERVICE

Many hotels sell stamps and will mail your cards. Otherwise, head for a centrally located post office, as mailboxes are not easy to find.

## Disabled facilities

Washington's metro is one of the most accessible public transportation systems in the US and offers a free downloadable guide to accessible transportation options in and around Washington, DC. Nearly all of the Metrobuses have wheelchair lifts and "kneel" or tilt toward the curb. Disabled travelers can obtain a Metro Disability ID card that entitles them to discounted fares if they apply at least three weeks in advance.

The Washington **DC Access Guide**, available in print and on the website for a fee, is a good source of accessibility-related information for DC, Virginia, and Maryland.

## Restrooms

On the Mall, all of the Smithsonian institutions and the **National Gallery of Art** (see pp76–80) have free admission and offer restroom facilities. Elsewhere, Union Station, hotels, chains like Starbucks and McDonalds, and stores like Barnes & Noble have facilities for patrons.

**Below left** *A big clock at Baltimore's Inner Harbor showing Eastern Standard Time*
**Below right** *The United States Park Police badge*

## What to pack

While many hotels greet families with games and coloring books for kids, it is best to bring along your kids' favorite books, crayons, and games. If you are traveling with infants, bringing a supply of nappies and formula will avoid emergencies.

## Opening hours

Business hours in Washington are usually 9am–5pm. Most stores open at 10am and close at 5 or 6pm Mon–Sat, though some may stay open until later; Sunday hours vary. Banks hours are generally 9am–3pm Mon–Thu, and until 6pm on Fridays. Saturday hours are usually 9am–noon. Most museums are open 10am–5:30pm daily, though it is best to check individual listings.

## Electricity

The standard US electric current is 110 volts. An adaptor is necessary for European appliances.

## Time

Washington is on Eastern Standard Time (EST), 5 hours behind London and 3 hours ahead of California. Daylight Savings moves the clock up 1 hour from spring to late fall.

## The Lowdown

### Medical emergencies

**Ambulance, Police, Fire** 911

**Children's Hospital National Medical Center** 111 Michigan Ave NW, 20010; 202 476 5000

**CVS Minute Clinic** www.cvs.com/minuteclinic

**Georgetown University Hospital** 3800 Reservoir Rd NW, 20007; 202 444 2000

**George Washington University Hospital** 900 23rd St NW, 20037; 202 715 4000

**Howard University Hospital** 2041 Georgia Ave NW, 20060; 202 865 6100

**Inn-House Doctor** 202 218 9100; www.innhousedoctor.com

### Lost and found

**DC Taxi Commission** 202 645 6020; www.dctaxi.dc.gov

**Union Station** 202 289 8355

**WMATA** 202 962 1165; www.wmata.com/about_metro/lost_found

### Money

**Travelex** 1800 K St NW, 20006; 202 872 1428; www.travelex.com

### Communications

**Cellhire USA** 1001 Connecticut Ave NW, 20036; 800 423 4805

**Embassy Information** www.embassy.org

**Post Office Locations** 1050 Connecticut Ave NW, 20036; 800 275 8777
1700 Pennsylvania Ave NW, 20006; 800 275 8777

### Visitor information

**Destination DC** 901 7th St NW, 20001–3719; 202 789 7000, 800 422 8644; www.washington.org

### Disability information

**DC Access Guide** 301 528 8664; www.disabilityguide.org

**Discount Fares** 202 962 1558

**Metrobus and Metrorail** 202 962 1245; www.wmata.com

## Etiquette and tipping

Washington is a favorite family destination and kids are welcomed almost everywhere. Everyone from hotel clerks to bus drivers usually has a friendly smile for young visitors. However, parents should ensure that kids are polite and respectful. If noisy squabbles or loud crying occur in public places, thoughtful parents will take their children outside until the storm subsides. A 15–20 per cent tip is expected for waiters, taxi drivers, and hair stylists. Room service tips are often added to the bill. Hotel bellhops should receive around $1 per bag, hotel maids $1–2 per day, and coat checks $1 per garment. When waiters or others are especially helpful with children, a small extra tip is always appreciated.

*Below left* Customers can access free Wi-Fi services at the Center Café in Union Station
*Below right* A regular United States Postal Service mailbox

# Where to Stay

As expected of a world-class capital city and tourist magnet, Washington, DC offers hundreds of hotel choices. Along with politicos and diplomats, families make up a large proportion of the city's many visitors, and are welcome everywhere, from five-star luxury lodgings to budget motels. The numerous all-suite properties afford extra space and many hotels offer swimming pools and other features that are especially welcomed by families.

### Where to look

Washington has many attractive neighborhoods, but staying within walking distance of the National Mall is ideal, as the majority of the attractions are located in this area. Even if accommodation is a bit more expensive, you save on transportation time and costs.

Hotels in the Penn Quarter or near the White House are also very convenient for families, but the Georgetown neighborhood, although charming, is less suitable because it is not served by the metro system and requires taking a bus or an expensive cab. Choosing a hotel near a metro stop is always a good idea.

Note that bus services tend to slow down considerably during the evening rush hours, which may be just when you want to get back to your room.

### Getting the best deals

During off-season, the best hotel rates are found from December to early March (excluding the February holiday period). Spring, when the city is most popular with tourists, is when room rates are highest. However, it is possible to get good deals, even in spring and summer, and particularly in August, when many families tend to travel.

Hotels are busiest during the week when Congress is in session, so good packages may be available on weekends. Check with booking sites such as **Visit DC**, a free local reservations service that offers discounts. **Destination DC** has many good deals posted on its website and you may find savings with national online discount services. Also check hotel websites for special packages and discounts.

### Hidden extras

When calculating the cost of hotels, be aware that there is a 14.5 per cent room tax in Washington. Tips can add to the tab; expect to tip porters at least $1 per bag when you arrive and depart, and pay the maid $1–2 per day. Many hotels offer only expensive breakfast choices, add high fees for phone calls and Internet use, or charge extra fees for older children or for the use of a cot. Choose hotels that include free breakfast, Internet (see p26), and at least an in-room refrigerator. Using a cell phone (see p26) instead of the room phone also helps.

### Hotels

Space and cooking facilities are two important points to consider when choosing a hotel. Suite accommodations may have a

*Below left* The lobby and café of the Hyatt Regency Washington on Capitol Hill
*Below center* Open-air seating at Café du Parc in the elegant Willard InterContinental hotel

full-sized or queen bed and a double or queen-sized sofa bed. All-suite properties offer that desirable extra space, plus a kitchen, and sometimes two television sets to please both generations. Read the hotel listings carefully, as many hotels also provide microwaves and small refrigerators in the rooms. This is a money-saving bonus and allows for inexpensive breakfasts and snacks.

Check the availability of cots or cribs – if they are free or for a fee – and whether a kids' menu is offered. Most large hotels have a list of reliable babysitters, but it is best to ask about this in advance.

Given Washington's heat in summer, hotels with swimming pools are especially recommended, and pools are a great outlet for restless kids, regardless of the season. A number of hotels have outdoor pools, but indoor pools have the advantage of being weatherproof, and are especially helpful on a rainy day.

## Apartments

Unhosted, furnished apartments are a good option for families. They are often cheaper than hotel rooms, and provide more space. Sometimes these are flats whose owners are away, or apartments set up for this purpose. Apartments generally have full kitchens, but no maid service. These lodgings are available in all neighborhoods, and can range from studios to three-bedroom properties. Book them through agencies such as **Airbnb**, **Vacation Rentals by Owner** or **DC Vacation Rentals**.

## Bed and breakfast

Washington has a selection of small bed and breakfast inns and some lodgings in private homes. While these can be good, they may not allow much privacy and can be tight quarters for children. It is therefore best to be specific about your needs. Bed and breakfast inns are best booked through agencies such as **Bed and Breakfast DC**, which has apartment listings too.

## House-swapping

Many families report success with house swaps. If you live in Europe, for example, a Washington family might be happy to swap their home for one based overseas, saving each of you a considerable amount of money. Swaps are arranged through specialized agencies such as **Home Link** and **Home Exchange**. For a small monthly fee, prospective swappers sign up as members and list their homes. Members can scan listings for the places they want to go, click on listings, and send a privacy-protected e-mail directly to the owner. It is always a good idea to exchange e-mails, talk on the phone, ask questions, and trade home photos before signing an agreement.

## The Lowdown

### Visitor information
**Destination DC** 202 789 7000; www.washington.org

### Bookings and rentals
**Airbnb** www.airbnb.com
**Bed and Breakfast DC** 877 893 3233; www.bedandbreakfastdc.com
**DC Vacation Rentals** 800 472 9704; www.dcvacationrentals.org
**Vacation Rentals by Owner** www.vrbo.com
**Visit DC** 800 847 4832; www.visitdc.com.
**Comparison Websites**
www.kayak.com
www.expedia.com
www.hotels.com

### House-swapping
**Home Exchange** www.homeexchange.com
**Home Link** www.homelink.org

*Below center* Bright and plushly furnished lobby of the Hotel Monaco Washington DC
*Below right* Entrance to the Marriott Courtyard Washington Convention Center hotel

# Where to Eat

The city's many politicos, eminent visitors, and international residents are well served by numerous fine-dining and ethnic restaurants. Families are also catered for by the many casual, reasonably priced choices. Reserve ahead at popular restaurants, and dine early to beat the crowds. Well-behaved kids are welcome everywhere. Prices given in this guide are based on lunch for a family of four. A 10 per cent sales tax is added to dining tabs.

## Opening hours

Formal restaurants are generally open from 7 to 10am for breakfast, 11:30am to 2pm for lunch, and from 5:30 to 10pm for dinner, but families can easily find many dining choices serving food all day in areas such as Penn Quarter and at the popular food courts. Museum cafés keep the same hours as the museums, and are convenient options if you can avoid the lunchtime rush.

## Breakfast

Washington has ample choices for a great breakfast – waffles at **Lincoln's Waffle Shop** (see p148), chocolate banana French toast at **Bread & Chocolate**, and fried chicken with waffles and eggs at **Founding Farmers** (see p87). **Market Lunch** (see p113) is a favorite for pancakes.

## Local and ethnic fare

Washington has access to a bounty of seafood from nearby Chesapeake Bay, and proximity to Virginia means excellent southern-style eateries serving ribs and barbecue. The city's ethnic dining places offer a range of cuisine, most at reasonable prices. **Full Kee Restaurant** (see p147) offers Chinese food, **Lebanese Taverna** has Middle Eastern specialties, and **Mitsitam Cafe** (see p61) serves Native American dishes. Try Ethiopian fare at **Meskerem**, and check out 18th Street in the Adams Morgan area for more ethnic choices.

## Food courts

From Cajun-style dishes and tacos to pizza and sandwiches, the city's food courts serve something for everyone. Excellent examples include the food courts at **Union Station** (see p115) and **Ronald Reagan Building & International Trade Center** (see p75).

## Children's favorites

Even the pickiest eaters will be happy at some of the city's burger and pizza joints. The most popular places for burgers are **Five Guys Burgers and Fries** (see p143) and **Good Stuff Eatery** (see p111), while **Pizzeria Paradiso** and **2 Amys** (see p168) are good for pizza. **Ben's Chili Bowl** (see p122) is famous for its hot dogs, and **Old Glory** serves southern barbecue. **Johnny Rockets** and **American City Diner** offer retro-diner decor, while the **Hard Rock Cafe** (see p142) is a hit with teens for its music memorabilia.

The better eateries may offer a kids' menu. Some good choices that cater to children are **Legal Sea

*Below left* The modest but legendary Ben's Chili Bowl
*Below center* Mouth-watering cupcakes on offer at Hello Cupcake

## The Lowdown

### Breakfast

**Bread & Chocolate** 2301 M St NW, 20037; 202 833 8360; www.breadandchocolate.net

### Local and ethnic fare

**Lebanese Taverna** 2641 Connecticut Ave NW, 20008; 202 265 8681; www.lebanesetaverna.com

**Meskerem** 2434 18th St NW, 20009; 202 462 4100; www. meskeremethiopianrestaurantdc.com

### Children's favorites

**American City Diner** 5532 Connecticut Ave NW, 20015; 202 244 1949; www.americancitydiner.com

**Austin Grill** 750 E St NW, 20004; 202 393 3776; www.austingrill.com

**Johnny Rockets** 3131 M St NW, 20007; 202 333 7994; www.johnnyrockets.com

**Legal Sea Foods** 704 7th St NW, 20001; 202 347 0007; www.legalseafoods.com

**Old Glory** 3139 M St NW, 20007; 202 337 3406; www.oldglorybbq.com

**Pizzeria Paradiso** 2003 P St NW, 20036; 202 223 1245; www.eatyourpizza.com

### Sweet treats

**Cocova** 1904 18th St NW, 20009; 202 903 0346; www.cocova.com

**Dickey's Frozen Custard** 1710 I St NW, 20006; 202 293 7100

**Firehook** 1909 Q St NW, 20009; 202 429 2253; www.firehook.com

**Hello Cupcake** 1361 Connecticut Ave NW, 20036; 202 861 2253; www.hellocupcakeonline.com

**Sticky Fingers Sweets & Eats** 1370 Park Rd NW, 20010; 202 299 9700; www.stickyfingersbakery.com

**Thomas Sweet Ice Cream** 3214 P St NW, 20007; 202 337 0616; www.thomassweet.com

Foods, serving great cod fish sticks among other seafood dishes, **Austin Grill** for Tex-Mex, and the atmospheric **Old Ebbitt Grill** (see p69).

### Sweet treats

**Firehook** specializes in butterscotch blondies and fudge chocolate brownies. **Dickey's Frozen Custard** (see p125) excels with its creamy French vanilla, and **Thomas Sweet Ice Cream** gets rave reviews for its bittersweet chocolate. **Sticky Fingers Sweets & Eats**, a vegan café, is known for cinnamon sticky buns. Savor cupcakes at **Hello Cupcake** or **Georgetown Cupcake** (see p159). **Cocova** has a selection of chocolates from around the world.

*Below center The popular food court at Union Station*
*Below right Delicious burgers at Five Guys Burgers and Fries*

# Shopping

Washington, DC is filled with shopping temptations for the whole family, from souvenirs of the city's iconic sights and unique gifts to fashionable and funky clothing for every taste. The many shops offering toys, books, and chocolates should please the younger members of the family. As a bonus, a shopping expedition can be a good chance to explore some of the most appealing neighborhoods in and around the city.

## Opening hours

Shops usually open from 10am to 5pm Monday to Saturday, but larger stores and boutiques may keep longer hours. Sunday hours are generally noon to 5pm, but can vary. It might be a good idea to call and check in advance. A 6 per cent sales tax is added to all purchases.

## Where to shop

Georgetown is home to boutiques that have long made it a shopper's mecca. Capitol Hill has the city's liveliest arts and crafts market, while **Dupont Circle** (see p174) boasts bookstores, shops, and a farmers' market. U Street Corridor, at the intersection of 14th Street NW and U Street NW, is the place for the hip and funky, and you can find upscale department stores in Friendship Heights on Wisconsin Avenue.

**Union Station** (see p115) draws as many shoppers as travelers for its cache of some 75 stores, including LittleMissMatched and Fantom Comics. **The Shops at Georgetown Park** (see p157) includes H&M and J.Crew, while the **Fashion Centre at Pentagon City** is home to names like Gymboree and babyGap. Sales take place in January, July, after Thanksgiving, and before Christmas.

**Eastern Market** (see p113) is a mix of farmers', flea, and crafts markets. Seasonal **FRESHFARM Markets** see local farmers sell fresh produce, meat, breads, cheeses, potted plants, and herbal products.

## Books and music

**Politics and Prose Bookstore** (see p37) can suggest a gift bag of books and also sells children's bookends, while **Kramerbooks & Afterwords** (see p174) is as popular for its café and live music as for its selections. **Fairy Godmother** is for kids, while **Barnes & Noble** (see p37) sells both books and music. **Red Onion Records & Books** has a fine selection of books, and there is a wide range of music and movies at **FYE**.

## Toys and games

**Sullivan's Toy Store** offers toys and art supplies, and pleases parents with jars filled with 99-cent offerings. **Barston's Child's Play** has a baby section and is stocked with favorites for all ages. **Labyrinth Games & Puzzles** has enough to keep little ones occupied.

## Children's clothing

**Proper Topper** offers clothes, stuffed toys, and educational

*Below left* The Young Artists' Collection in the National Gallery of Art's bookstore
*Below center* Exterior of the Torpedo Factory in Alexandria

## Size Chart

Size numbers in the UK, the US, and Europe are different. Clothes sizes for children go by age in the US.

| Women's Clothes | | | Women's Shoes | | | Men's Clothes | | | Men's Shoes | | | Children's Shoes | | |
|---|---|---|---|---|---|---|---|---|---|---|---|---|---|---|
| UK | Europe | US | UK | Europe | US | UK | Europe | US | UK | Europe | US | UK | Europe | US |
| 4 | 32 | 2 | 3 | 35½ | 5½ | 34 | 44 | 34 | 6 | 39 | 7 | 7 | 24 | 8 |
| 6 | 34 | 4 | 4 | 37 | 6½ | 36 | 46 | 36 | 7 | 40½ | 8 | 8 | 25 | 9 |
| 8 | 36 | 6 | 5 | 38 | 7½ | 38 | 48 | 38 | 8 | 42 | 9 | 9 | 27 | 10 |
| 10 | 38 | 8 | 6 | 39 | 8½ | 40 | 50 | 40 | 9 | 43 | 10 | 10 | 28 | 11 |
| 12 | 40 | 10 | 7 | 40½ | 9½ | 42 | 52 | 42 | 10 | 44½ | 11 | 11 | 29 | 12 |
| 14 | 42 | 12 | 8 | 41 | 10½ | 44 | 54 | 44 | 11 | 46 | 12 | 12 | 31 | 13 |
| 16 | 44 | 14 | 8½ | 42½ | 11 | 46 | 56 | 46 | 12 | 47 | 13 | 13 | 32 | 1 |
| 18 | 46 | 16 | | | | 48 | 58 | 48 | 14 | 49½ | 15 | 1 | 33 | 2 |
| 20 | 48 | 18 | | | | | | | 15 | 51 | 16 | 2 | 34½ | 3 |

games. **Tugooh Toys** (see p161) carries environmentally responsible toys, while **Yiro** (see p161) has organic clothing for young children.

## Gifts and souvenirs

**Groovy dc** is a gift shop with unusual cards, stationery, and home accessories. **Chocolate Moose** also offers the offbeat, from snow globes to earrings. Every one of the city's multiple museum shops offers fun stuff, geared to the museum's theme. Shops at popular stops like the **Kennedy Center** (see p129) and the **Smithsonian's National Zoological Park** (see pp168–9) offer souvenirs. **America!** is a place to pick up political memorabilia, and **Souvenir City** has every kind of souvenir imaginable. Inexpensive T-shirts can be picked up from sidewalk vendors.

## Crafts

Contemporary American handicrafts can be found at **Appalachian Spring** (see p161), while the finest Native American crafts are available at the **Indian Craft Shop** (photo ID needed for admission). Make your own bead jewelry or buy it ready-made at **Beadazzled** (see p174). Watch artisans at work in over 80 studios and buy some of their distinctive work at the **Torpedo Factory** (see p188) in Alexandria.

*Below center* Fresh produce for sale at Eastern Market
*Below right* Glass and ceramics on display at a gift shop in Mount Vernon

## The Lowdown

### Where to shop
**Fashion Centre at Pentagon City** 1100 South Hayes St, VA 22202; 703 415 2401

**FRESHFARM Markets** www.freshfarmmarkets.org

### Books and music
**Fairy Godmother** 319 7th St SE, 20003; 202 547 5474

**FYE** Union Station, see p115; 202 289 1405; www.fye.com

**Red Onion Records & Books** 1901 18th St NW, 20009; 202 986 2718; www.redonionrecordsandbooks.com

### Toys and games
**Barston's Child's Play** 5536 Connecticut Ave NW, 20015; 202 444 3602; www.barstonschildsplay.com

**Labyrinth Games & Puzzles** 645 Pennsylvania Ave SE, 20003; 202 544 1059; www.labyrinthgameshop.com

**Sullivan's Toy Store** 4200 Wisconsin Ave NW, 20016; 202 362 1343

### Children's clothing
**Proper Topper** 1350 Connecticut Ave NW, 20036; 202 842 3055; www.propertopper.com

### Gifts and souvenirs
**America!** First floor, Union Station, see p115; 202 289 4223

**Chocolate Moose** 1743 L St NW, 20036; 202 463 0992; www.chocolatemoosedc.com

**Groovy dc** 323 7th St SE, 20003; 202 544 6633; www.groovydc.com

**Souvenir City** 1001 K St NW, 20001; 202 638 1836

### Crafts
**Indian Craft Shop** 1849 C St NW, 20240; 202 208 4056; www.indiancraftshop.com

# Entertainment

Washington, DC has more theater and entertainment venues than any other East Coast city outside of New York. Many of its larger live theater and music venues have special programs for kids of all ages, and since DC is often considered a warm-up for NYC and Broadway, even smaller stages and acting companies offer highly professional and entertaining performances. Visitors should check individual websites for upcoming events and schedules.

## Theater, music, and dance

### KENNEDY CENTER

The granddaddy of entertainment venues in DC, the Kennedy Center (see p129) features five theaters that often present multiple forms of entertainment at the same time, from stage plays to jazz, opera, and ballet. Families can always find quality kid-oriented theater productions here.

The Family Theater presents a wide range of fun-for-kids plays such as The Amazing Adventures of Dr. Wonderful and Her Dog. Theater Lab offers plays for ages 9 and over like Snow White, Rose Red (and Fred). Tweens and teens may enjoy some of the center's mainstream theatrical performances, such as the musical Wicked, a different look at the Wizard of Oz, geared for kids 10 and above.

The National Symphony Orchestra's Teddy Bear Concerts are aimed at children between 3 and 5 years, who are encouraged to sing along and move to the music. Kinderkonzerts are for kids from 4 to 12 years, and shows have included Musical Opposites and Follow the Fiddle. The Family Concert Series offers performances designed for the whole family including The Mozart Experience with Magic Circle Mime. Regular adult programs often include excellent family performances of ballet, dance, opera, and popular music.

### WOLF TRAP NATIONAL PARK FOR THE PERFORMING ARTS

An outdoor venue dedicated to the performing arts, Wolf Trap (see p197) offers entertainment for the entire family. On summer evenings, crowds carry blankets and picnics to the large, open-walled Filene Center and its surrounding lawn as they come to enjoy music, dance, and stage performances. Much of the mainstream entertainment at the center is also suitable for families and kids, and in the past has included an evening of comedy with Bill Cosby and shows such as the Gilbert and Sullivan musical HMS Pinafore. The Filene Center also regularly hosts family-friendly music entertainment, ranging from the Mormon Tabernacle Choir to Aretha Franklin and Peter Frampton.

Smaller shows use the stage at the Barns at Wolf Trap, and during summer, the open-air Theatre-in-the-Woods presents about 70 children's theater, comedy, and music shows. These have included The Dreaming Tree by CityDance and The Ant and the Grasshopper by the Golden Rod Puppets.

**Below left** Families with blankets and picnics enjoying a performance at the Wolf Trap National Park for the Performing Arts
**Below center** The entrance of Arena Stage at the Mead Center

Workshops for art and theater for kids are often held prior to the performances. Younger kids can enjoy a regular schedule of music and dance events held at the theater during evenings in July and August. Past shows have featured the kid's rock band Milkshake playing jump-up-and-dance rock music.

## FORD'S THEATRE

In addition to being the site where President Lincoln was assassinated, Ford's Theatre (see pp142–3) stays true to its roots by presenting a wide range of family-oriented plays such as 1776, a witty take on the founding of America. The theater's production of Charles Dickens' A Christmas Carol is a highlight of Washington's Christmas season. The modern Center for Education and Leadership (www.fords.org/home/plan-your-visit/daytime-visits-fords-theatre/center-education-and-leadership) across the street gives children a comprehensive view of Lincoln's life and legacy, and includes a 34-ft (10.4-m) tower of books about the President.

## IMAGINATION STAGE

This 700-seat venue is all about children's theater – from the professionally produced plays for young adults and kids to the classes and theater camps that take place throughout the year. Expect fun productions with color, excitement, and laughs along the way. Past productions have included P. Nokio, a hip hop musical, Wind in the Willows, and Dr. Dolittle.

## DISCOVERY THEATER

The little domed kiosk near the Freer Gallery of Art (see p66) is actually a stairway to a real find. The Discovery Theater at the Ripley Center offers a regular schedule of family-oriented cultural movies and performances through the year. Shows here have included Tigers, Demons and other Wise "Tails" (Asian folk stories) and Tepua Hio Hio: A Celebration of Polynesian Dance and Culture.

## FOLGER SHAKESPEARE LIBRARY

Older kids will enjoy the Shakespeare plays at the Elizabethan theater here, modeled on the theaters of the Bard's day. Lighter fare like The Comedy of Errors is often a good choice for younger audiences.

## ADVENTURE THEATRE MTC

Beginning in 1881 as a Chautauqua community dedicated to adult education, Glen Echo became a famous amusement park in the early 1900s. Today, it is run by the National Park Service and offers many programs and events for children.

Located in a historic building, the Adventure Theatre MTC presents a wide range of classic and new children's plays aimed at kids between 4 and 12 years. Performances here have included Mirandy and Brother Wind and A Year With Frog and Toad. Before or after a show, kids can ride the historic Denzel carousel, or play in the playground.

## ARENA STAGE

Featuring three stages in a stunning building with dramatic walls of curved glass, the Arena Stage at the Mead Center is the largest theater building in Washington after the Kennedy Center.

Arena Stage has long had a reputation as one of the most renowned "Broadway warm-up" theaters. The list of famous performers that have trodden the boards here includes American actor James Earl Jones. The Arena stages some all-ages family fare such as Rogers and Hammerstein's Oklahoma!, while older kids may enjoy its more serious dramas.

**Below right** A colorful musical production geared for kids and young adults at Imagination Stage in Bethesda, Maryland

### WOOLLY MAMMOTH THEATER

This cutting-edge theater is renowned for producing the work of new and unknown playwrights. While some shows may not be appropriate for kids, there are plenty that will inspire young theater fans.

### VERIZON CENTER

If Miley Cyrus, Justin Bieber, or the Rolling Stones come to Washington, DC, they will most likely play at this 20,000-seat sports and entertainment arena that hosts over 220 events every year.

### JIFFY LUBE LIVE

This 25,000-seat stadium in northern Virginia hosts a constant stream of big-name acts including Sheryl Crow, Kid Rock, and Jimmy Buffett.

### BLUES ALLEY

Teens may enjoy listening to some of the great names in jazz perform at one of the nation's legendary jazz hot spots. Past shows have included trumpet legend Jon Faddis and keyboard virtuoso Marcus Johnson.

### SUNSET PARADE

Every Tuesday at 7pm, the Marine Drum and Bugle Corps present a program of military music and precision drill by the impressive Iwo Jima Memorial. Show up early and watch them practice. Shuttle buses run before and after the program from **Arlington National Cemetery** (see pp192–3). This is a great spot to watch the evening lights of Washington come on, and provides one of the best views of the National Mall to be had anywhere in the city.

### NETHERLANDS CARILLON CONCERTS

Between Iwo Jima Memorial and the Arlington National Cemetery is the 50-bell Netherlands Carillon. Bring a blanket and a picnic, enjoy great views of the Mall from across the Potomac, and listen to a guest artist play on this incredible instrument.

## Film

### ALBERT EINSTEIN PLANETARIUM

Head to this planetarium at the National Air and Space Museum (see pp56–9) for a 20-minute show that rockets viewers to the outer reaches of the universe. Explore black holes, travel through time, and see what happens when planets collide. Shows like One World, One Sky: Big Bird's Adventure appeal to a younger audience.

### LOCKHEED MARTIN IMAX

Join astronauts in the cockpit of the Space Shuttle for an adventure in space, or see the universe through the "eye" of the Hubble Space Telescope. This IMAX at the National Air and Space Museum features movies on air and space flight, from the story of the Wright Brothers to the space voyages of tomorrow.

### THE SAMUEL C. JOHNSON IMAX

This IMAX at the National Museum of Natural History (see pp72–5) features films about the natural world. Get up close to dinosaurs in 3-D, swing with chimpanzees through a tropical jungle, and dive into the depths of the Grand Canyon.

### SCREEN ON THE GREEN

This large outdoor screen on the Mall shows classic movies (Jul & Aug: Mon nights). Films shown here have included Bonnie and Clyde (1967), Close Encounters of the Third Kind (1977), and Goldfinger (1964). Many families show up early, along with a blanket, a picnic basket, and perhaps a kite, and pass the evening watching the lights of the United States Capitol (see pp104–105) come on as they wait for the movie to start.

## Literature

The delightfully independent **Politics and Prose Bookstore** offers free author readings for children

*Below left* Entrance to the Millennium Stage at the Kennedy Center
*Below center* The 400-seat Lerner Family Theater at Imagination Stage

between one and six times a month. The **Barnes & Noble** bookstore in Washington offers weekly story times for kids. It also holds author readings and other literary events, some of which are appropriate for kids.

## Fabulous freebies

### MILLENNIUM STAGE

At 6pm every day, the Millennium Stage at the Kennedy Center presents top-notch family-oriented shows that vary widely and include dance, theater, music, puppets, mimes, magicians, and comedians.

### LIVE! AT THE WOODROW WILSON PLAZA

Great bands play on the Woodrow Wilson Plaza outside the Ronald Reagan Building & International Trade Center. The outdoor seating of the area's restaurants is great for enjoying a meal while watching jazz, blues, and popular music shows.

### THE STARS TONIGHT AT THE ALBERT EINSTEIN PLANETARIUM

This show at the National Air and Space Museum's Albert Einstein Planetarium features the remarkable Zeiss Planetarium Projector, which re-creates the stars of the current night sky. Planetarium guides describe the highlights of what you can see.

# The Lowdown

## Theater, music, and dance

**Adventure Theatre MTC** 7300 MacArthur Blvd, Glen Echo, MD 20812; 301 634 2270; *www.adventuretheatre-mtc.org*

**Arena Stage** 1101 6th St SW, 20024; 202 488 3300; *www.arenastage.org*

**Blues Alley** 1073 Wisconsin Ave NW, 20007; 202 337 4141; *www.bluesalley. com*; 8pm & 10pm daily

**Discovery Theater** 1100 Jefferson Dr SW, 20024; 202 633 8700; *www.discoverytheater.org*

**Folger Shakespeare Library** 201 East Capitol St SE, 20003; 202 544 4600; *www.folger.edu*

**Ford's Theatre** 511 10th St NW, 20004; 202 347 4833; *www.fords.org*

**Imagination Stage** 4908 Auburn Rd, Bethesda, MD 20814; 301 280 1660; *www.imaginationstage.org*

**Jiffy Lube Live** 7800 Cellar Door Dr, Bristow, VA 20136; 703 754 6400; *www.livenation.com/venues/14407/ jiffy-lube-live*

**Kennedy Center** 2700 F St NW, 20566; 800 444 1324, 202 467 4600; *www.kennedy-center.org*

**Netherlands Carillon Concerts** near the US Marine Corps War Memorial, Arlington; 202 433 2927; *www.nps. gov/gwmp/planyourvisit/carillon_ concerts.htm*; May–Aug: Sat & alternative weekdays

**Sunset Parade** Iwo Jima Memorial, US Marine Memorial Circle, Arlington; 202 433 6060; *www.barracks.marines. mil/Parades/SunsetParade.aspx*; early Jun–mid-Aug: 7pm Tue

**Verizon Center** 601 F St NW, 20004; 202 628 3200; *www.verizoncenter.com*

**Wolf Trap National Park for the Performing Arts** 1645 Trap Rd, Vienna, VA 22182; 703 2551900; *www.wolftrap.org*

**Woolly Mammoth Theater** 641 D St NW, 2004; 202 393 3939; *www.woollymammoth.net*

## Film

**Albert Einstein Planetarium** National Air and Space Museum; 202 633 4629; *www.airandspace.si.edu/planetarium*

**Lockheed Martin IMAX** National Air and Space Museum; 202 633 4629; *www.si.edu/Imax/Theater/ lockheed-martin-imax-theater*

**The Samuel C. Johnson IMAX** National Museum of Natural History; 202 633 4629; *www.si.edu/ theater/samuel-c-johnson-imax-theater*

**Screen on the Green** Near the Washington Monument, *see pp84–5*; *www.friendsofscreenonthegreen.org*

## Literature

**Politics and Prose Bookstore** 5015 Connecticut Ave NW, 20008; 202 364 1919; *www.politics-prose.com*

**Story time at Barnes & Noble** 555 12th St NW, 20004; 202 347 0176; *www. barnesandnoble.com*; 10:30am Tue

## Fabulous freebies

**Live! at the Woodrow Wilson Plaza** Ronald Reagan Building & International Trade Center, 13th St & Pennsylvania Ave; 202 312 1300; *www.itcdc.com*

**Millennium Stage** Kennedy Center *www.kennedy-center.org/programs/ millennium/schedule.html*

**Below right** *People watching a movie on the gigantic movie screen at Screen on the Green on the National Mall*

# Parks and Gardens

It is extremely easy for families to find a place to get outside, walk a forest trail, fly a kite, ride a bike, or have a picnic in Washington. The city offers some spectacular gardens filled with color, and paths that beg to be followed and explored. While several parks and green spaces were part of Washington's original plan, others, like the C&O Canal and Georgetown Waterfront Park, are the results of later efforts at development.

## Rock Creek Park

Spread across 1,750 acres (708 ha), Rock Creek Park is often called Washington's best-kept green secret. Visitors can see live turtles at its nature center or enjoy different programs at the planetarium. The park is also home to the **Smithsonian's National Zoological Park** (see pp168–9) and the 19th-century **Peirce Mill** (see p170). It offers a network of biking and hiking trails, a picnic site, an 18-hole golf course, and tennis courts.

## Georgetown Waterfront Park

Following the edge of the Potomac for several blocks, this park offers comfortable benches with splendid river views, a labyrinth that is a favorite with kids, and a riverfront walkway popular with walkers, joggers, and cyclists.

## C&O Canal

The towpath that follows the C&O Canal (see pp156–7) for 1 mile (1.5 km) along the Potomac is one of the most popular walking and biking trails in Washington. It passes through pastoral landscapes and woodland, offering glimpses of the river. Bikes, kayaks, and canoes can be rented at **Thompson Boat Center** at the east end of the trail, or at **Fletcher's Boat House** (see p156), about 1 mile (1.5 km) west of Georgetown. Families may also enjoy taking a ride on a re-created mule-drawn canal boat, staffed by period-costumed guides, in the Great Falls part of the canal.

## Theodore Roosevelt Island

An 88-acre (36-ha) wooded park, Theodore Roosevelt Island (see

*Below left* Kayaking on the stunning Chesapeake & Ohio Canal  *Below right* An artist painting the Capitol Columns and a blossoming cherry tree at the National Arboretum

## Bishop's Garden

Designed to look and feel like a medieval European garden, the small and charming Bishop's Garden, next to the **Washington National Cathedral** *(see pp172–3),* offers small fountains and several quiet, contemplative nooks. Kids are welcome to play and run around in some of the open places here.

## US National Arboretum

Covering over 400 acres (161 ha), the arboretum *(see pp178–9)* is part park, part study facility. This space has plenty of open places to play in, paths to follow, and lovely hidden spots kids can claim as their own. Tram tours give a good overview of the facility ($4 adults, $2 kids). Feed the voracious and colorful koi in the pond surrounding the visitor center, and check out the tiny trees – some of which are 400 years old – at the National Bonsai Collection.

*p191)* is a simple and effective tribute to the conservationist and 26th president. It is a fun family destination, offering trails that circle and cross the island. At the center, a large plaza is dominated by a bronze statue of "Teddy" himself. It has been estimated that in his lifetime, Roosevelt was responsible for preserving over 200 million acres (80 million ha) of US wilderness.

## East Potomac Park and Tidal Basin

A long, comma-shaped spear of land, East Potomac Park *(see p95)* is built entirely on land that was reclaimed from the tidal waters of

*Top Blooming azaleas and neatly trimmed hedges lining the paths of Morrison Garden at the US National Arboretum* **Left** *Lush foliage in the US Botanic Garden* **Below** *The orangery at Dumbarton Oaks, Georgetown*

the Potomac. It is ringed by a concrete path that traces the water's edge, creating a lovely waterfront walk around the peninsula. Just inland, roadways provide a scenic route for cyclists. The park also has a public golf course, tennis courts, and waterfront picnic areas.

At the north end of the park, Tidal Basin offers more waterfront walkways and access to the **Martin Luther King, Jr. Memorial** *(see pp94–5),* **Thomas Jefferson Memorial** *(see pp96–7),* and **Franklin Delano Roosevelt Memorial** *(see pp92–3).* At its north end there is paddleboat rental dock, picnic tables, and a snack stand.

## US Botanic Garden

Centered around an elegant conservatory, US Botanic Garden *(see pp106–107)* is the oldest continually operating public garden in the US. Its conservatory, with a Hawaiian landscape, a tropical jungle, and desert, medicinal, and prehistoric plant collections, is a great place to explore. Outside, the National Garden showcases plants from the US gardens and landscapes.

## Dumbarton Oaks

Every corner of Dumbarton Oaks *(see pp160–61),* from the walled rose garden to the fountain terrace and the ornate pebble garden, offers delight and discovery. Older kids can tour the collection of Byzantine and pre-Columbian arts in the house.

# Spectator Sports

Washington, DC has a strong history of sports and an avid fan base that fervently cheers on the home teams. Visiting families can also enjoy the thrill of watching some of the big names of the sports world in action. Whether your favorite sport is baseball, soccer, hockey, football, or men's or women's basketball, going to see a game is as easy as going on the Internet, choosing a team, selecting a game, and buying tickets.

## Baseball

### WASHINGTON NATIONALS

The former Montreal Expos play from their own Nationals Park (see p41), located just south of the National Mall. Kids can join the Jr. Nationals Kids' Club to receive souvenirs and ticket discounts. The team also offers $1 kids' ticket days; see website for schedule.

### BALTIMORE ORIOLES

One of the most historic ball clubs in Major League Baseball, the Baltimore Orioles have passionate fans, not just in Baltimore, but in Washington, DC as well. Catch a game at the excellent Oriole Park at Camden Yards (see p41). Part of the thrill for fans is taking part in the Orioles traditions, such as singing along with John Denver's Thank God I'm a Country Boy, which is always played in the 7th inning stretch of Orioles games. The Jr. Orioles Dugout Club for kids entitles them to souvenirs and discount tickets.

## Football

### WASHINGTON REDSKINS

Washington's oldest professional sports team plays at the FedEx Field (see p41) in Maryland. They have played over 1,000 games since 1932, and won five NFL Championships, including three Super Bowls. While the FedEx Field is the largest stadium in the NFL, individual game-day tickets are hard to come by if the team is having a strong season. Check the official website for schedules and tickets.

### MARYLAND TERRAPINS

People go nuts rooting for this football team, which seems to represent all of Maryland and DC, or even all of the mid-Atlantic at the college level. The Terrapins never fail to create pandemonium in the bleachers when they play at the University of Maryland College Park.

## Basketball

### WASHINGTON WIZARDS

Basketball fans can watch Michael Jordan's fabulous former team play at the Verizon Center (see p41).

### WASHINGTON MYSTICS

A professional women's basketball team, the Mystics draw audiences of 10,000 or more for their home games, usually at the Verizon Center.

### GEORGETOWN HOYAS

This college basketball team delivers games that are long on strategy and never short of daring. Home games are held at the Verizon Center.

**Below left** The Washington Nationals against the St. Louis Cardinals on their home ground, the Nationals Park
**Below center** Exterior of the hub of Washington's sports world, the Verizon Center

National Football League. The largest stadium in DC, it fills to capacity for some Redskins games.

### NATIONALS PARK
The 41,000-seat Nationals Park is a high-tech facility, with upscale luxury seating and a 102-ft (31-m)-long digital scoreboard that dominates the left field.

### ORIOLE PARK AT CAMDEN YARDS
This retro-modern baseball stadium evokes the feel of a 20th-century ballpark while offering the latest in high-tech facilities, such as the huge digital display over the right field and a state-of-the-art sound system. Nearby is the birthplace of baseball legend Babe Ruth, the restored 1899 B&O Railway Warehouse from where you can pick up Orioles souvenirs, and the **Sports Legends Museum** (see pp220–21), dedicated to the history of the Orioles.

## Hockey
### WASHINGTON CAPITALS
Hockey fans can watch Washington's great National Hockey League team in action at the Verizon Center.

## Soccer
### DC UNITED
One of the hottest teams in Major League Soccer, DC United plays at the 45,000-seat RFK Stadium on East Capitol Street SE. DC United has won the US Open Cup twice and the MLS cup four times. This is a fast-moving, winning team, and a delight for families who are soccer fans. The team also has special kids' days, where there are giveaways, meet the mascot, or a chance to play on the field with the team.

*Top Crowds cheering on the DC United team **Above** Washington Wizards' star Michael Jordan against the Minnesota Timberwolves in 2002*

## Sports venues
### VERIZON CENTER
This 20,000-seat center is the site of home games for the Wizards (men's basketball), Washington Capitals (hockey), and Mystics (women's basketball). There are many eateries in and around the center, and several sights are a short walk away.

### FEDEX FIELD
A 91,000-seat football stadium on the far east side of the city is the home of the Washington Redskins

## The Lowdown

### Teams
**Baltimore Orioles**
http://baltimore.orioles.mlb.com
**DC United** www.dcunited.com
**Georgetown Hoyas**
www.guhoyas.com
**Maryland Terrapins**
www.umterps.com
**Washington Capitals**
http://capitals.nhl.com
**Washington Mystics**
www.wnba.com/mystics
**Washington Nationals** http://
washington.nationals.mlb.com
**Washington Redskins**
www.redskins.com
**Washington Wizards**
www.nba.com/wizards

### Tickets
**StubHub** www.stubhub.com

### Venues
**FedEx Field** 1600 FedEx Way, MD 20785; www.redskins.com/fedexfield
**Nationals Park** 1500 South Capitol St SE, 20003; http://washington.nationals.mlb.com/was/ballpark
**Oriole Park at Camden Yards** 333 West Camden St, Baltimore, MD 21201; http://baltimore.orioles.mlb.com/bal/ballpark/index.jsp
**Verizon Center** 601 F St NW, 20004; www.verizoncenter.com

# The History of Washington, DC

In many ways, the history of Washington mirrors the development of America itself. Before the Revolutionary War, there was no Washington, only the ports of Georgetown and Alexandria. Grand plans for a capital city that would be distinct from the other states were drawn up in 1791, but it was only in the 20th century that the city began to take shape and slowly symbolize the still-young United States, which was taking an evermore prominent role in world affairs.

## Native Americans

The first people to settle in the Washington, DC area were Archaic Indians about 4,000 years ago. By the time English explorer John Smith arrived in 1607, the Powhatan were the dominant tribe, with about 14,000 members occupying Virginia's coastal plain, south of what is today the border with North Carolina. Settlers arriving in the 1700s found a small band of Algonquins, who called themselves the Nacotchtank, living on the shores of Anacostia.

## Colonial Virginia

When John Smith and other men from the Virginia Company founded a colony in Jamestown, they were not ready to survive the wilderness, and had to be helped by the Powhatan. The winter of 1609–10 saw "The Starving Time," when all but 60 settlers died from starvation and disease. A year later, one of the settlers, John Rolfe, planted tobacco, then shipped and sold it to England, kick-starting a rush to claim land and plant tobacco.

*Powhatan giving baskets of food to English settlers*

In 1619, two ships brought the first indentured servants to this young colony. Within 40 years slavery was fully established, and by 1750, Virginia was home to more than 100,000 slaves, who made up nearly 40 per cent of the population. The second ship contained a number of women, who married many of the Jamestown men, giving them reason to remain in the New World, rather than return to England.

The relationship between the colonists and the Powhatan was always fragile. In 1622, the latter massacred 400 settlers, starting a war that was not resolved until the Powhatan were soundly defeated in 1644. In 1699, the capital of Virginia moved from the marshy grounds of Jamestown to the higher, drier ground of Williamsburg.

## The road to revolution

As Virginia, Maryland, and the rest of the 13 colonies became more prosperous, particularly after the French and Indian War (1754–63), the demands of a cash-strapped England increased and the colonists began to chafe under the yoke of raising taxes and laws imposed by a distant king. The colonies evicted their British representatives and elected a local government. The British reacted by sending armed troops in 1775 to re-establish order. On April 19 that year, the famous "shot heard round the world" was fired at Lexington, Massachusetts as the colonies fought for independence. This was the start of nine years of war between Britain and the fledgling United States of America. The Declaration of

## Timeline

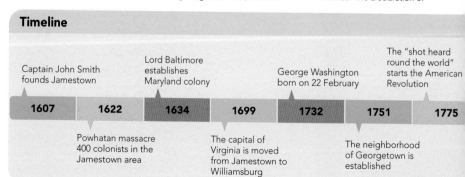

Captain John Smith founds Jamestown

Lord Baltimore establishes Maryland colony

George Washington born on 22 February

The "shot heard round the world" starts the American Revolution

| 1607 | 1622 | 1634 | 1699 | 1732 | 1751 | 1775 |

Powhatan massacre 400 colonists in the Jamestown area

The capital of Virginia is moved from Jamestown to Williamsburg

The neighborhood of Georgetown is established

*The British surrender at The Siege of Yorktown (1781)*

Independence was issued on July 4, 1776 and was followed by a few victories for the colonists interspersed with periods when the better equipped and trained British forces had the upper hand.

In 1780, British General Cornwallis suffered a series of defeats that forced him to retreat to his stronghold at Yorktown in Chesapeake Bay. Fortunately for General Washington, leader of the Continental army, the French had arrived in force to help the American cause. As Washington's Continental army and a large French force marched south to pin Cornwallis and his men against the sea, a large French naval force arrived at the mouth of Chesapeake Bay just in time to keep British ships from evacuating him. Trapped, Cornwallis surrendered in 1781, ending hostilities, but peace was only negotiated two years later with the Treaty of Paris.

## Birth of a country and a capital

In 1787, the Constitutional Convention met to draft a Constitution for the newly created United States. A model for the Constitution, proposed by James Madison, laid the foundation for the three branches of government – executive, legislative, and judicial.

A substantial effort was made on the part of many states to include the abolition of slavery in the Constitution. The southern states, however, refused to sign the Constitution if slavery was abolished. More than one signatory to the Constitution expressed misgivings, predicting that leaving the issue unresolved would lead to deep divisions among the states, but the Constitution was written to control slavery, not to make it illegal.

The Constitution also allowed for the creation of a new capital, where the federal government would be housed. George Washington was in charge of locating the site and he chose a square of land that lay on either side of the Potomac River. The idea was to create a capital that was not part of any state, so as to avoid any state having undue influence on the government.

*George Washington, first president of the US (1789–1797)*

| | | | | |
|---|---|---|---|---|
| | Cornwallis surrenders to Washington at Yorktown | | US Constitution adopted on 17 September | |
| '6 | **1781** | **1783** | **1787** | **1789** |
| Declaration of Independence | | The British sign the Treaty of Paris, surrendering their claim on America as a colony | | George Washington becomes president |

Washington asked French civic planner Pierre L'Enfant to design the city, which he did with a European flair, creating broad avenues, a symmetrical street system, lots of parks and circles, and a large central open area that would become the National Mall. In 1792, work began on the "President's House," which would later be called the White House. The following year, George Washington laid the cornerstone for the US Capitol.

## The 19th century

In 1800, the government officially transferred from Philadelphia to Washington, but the city was barely more than a plan at that point. The US and England went to war in 1812, and in 1814 the British attacked Washington and burnt many of the buildings, including the White House and the US Capitol. A few years later, construction began

*The British army burning the White House in 1814 during the War of 1812*

*President Arthur places the capstone to complete the Washington Monument*

on the Washington Monument, but the project, like so many in 19th-century Washington, ran out of money. By 1860, with the Civil War looming, virtually all construction in the city had come to a halt.

## The Civil War

The mid-1800s witnessed an increasing tension between pro-slavery and anti-slavery groups, which culminated in the Civil War (1861–5). Washington became a huge military camp surrounded by forts. Public buildings were requisitioned as hospitals and thousands of freed slaves sought refuge in the city. When the war ended, Washington resembled little more than a rough frontier town – cattle and horses roamed the Capitol Grounds, Constitution Avenue was a canal filled with sewage, and tanneries, slaughterhouses, and industrial factories stood just a short distance from the White House.

## Rebuilding the capital

From the 1870s to 1929, the American economy grew at a rapid rate, the population of Washington soared, and the city that L'Enfant had planned on paper a century before began to take shape. This period of prosperity was perhaps best symbolized by the opening of the Washington Monument to visitors in 1888. In 1901 the city took part in the City Beautiful movement, laying out the plan for the National Mall.

## Turbulent times

Even though slavery had been abolished in 1865, African Americans were denied the right to vote, and faced discrimination in education and housing. Racial riots tore at the civic fabric of the city in the hot summer of 1919, and civil rights issues thrust Washington onto the national stage. The 1920s were a boom time, but the stock market crash of 1929 heralded the Great Depression. In 1933, Franklin D. Roosevelt was elected president and ushered in the New Deal, a bold set of programs aimed at getting Americans back to work. His wife, Eleanor Roosevelt, was a supporter of civil rights and in 1939, when African-American singer Marian Anderson was banned from performing at DAR Constitution Hall, she arranged for her to sing on the steps of the Lincoln Memorial, which drew a crowd of 75,000.

## Timeline

| 1814 | 1846 | 1884 | 1929 | 1933 | 1963 | 1974 |
|---|---|---|---|---|---|---|
| The White House, US Capitol, and other buildings burnt by British troops | | Washington Monument completed | | Roosevelt takes office and starts the New Deal | President John F. Kennedy is assassinated | |
| | Congress creates the Smithsonian Institution using Smithson's bequest | | US stock market crashes | | Civil rights March on Washington | Presi Richard N is force re |

# World War II and protests

During World War II, the US government grew rapidly. The construction of the world's largest office building, the Pentagon, commenced in 1941 and was finished just 16 months later, in January 1943. Women from all over America flocked to the capital to take office jobs vacated by men who had joined the military. Housing was in short supply, and war rationing and waiting in line for food and gasoline became a way of life.

*Preacher and civil rights activist Martin Luther King, Jr. addressing a crowd*

After the war, the US took a more central role in world affairs. The 1950s ushered in the Cold War – a period of military tension, political hostility, and economic rivalry between the US and the Soviet Union. However, America continued to experience an unparalleled period of prosperity.

The 1960s were a time of great social change and upheaval in the US. In 1963, Martin Luther King, Jr. led the March on Washington, which culminated in his "I Have a Dream" speech, demanding equal rights for

African Americans. The city soon became the place for all types of social movements to stage marches and demonstrations. In 1969, a quarter of a million anti-Vietnam War protestors descended on the National Mall. 1995 saw the Million Man March, in which social activists and civil rights organizations came together to advocate unity and brotherhood. This was followed by the Million Mom March in 2000, which asked for restrictions to keep firearms out of kids' reach.

# The 21st century

On September 11, 2001, terrorist attacks on the World Trade Center in New York and the Pentagon changed life in Washington forever. Security became an integral part of everyday life, with airport-style security checks at the entrances to all major government buildings, museums, and attractions. However, the residents of Washington tend to take difficulties in their stride, and the city continues to grow. The World War II Memorial was built in 2004 and the Capitol Visitor Center in 2008. Also in 2008, the US elected its first African-American president, Barack Obama. He was re-elected for a second term in 2012.

In 2011, the Martin Luther King, Jr. Memorial was opened on the banks of the Tidal Basin, and in 2016, the Smithsonian plans to inaugurate the National Museum of African American History and Culture near the Washington Monument.

| Million Man March gathers on the Mall | Barack Obama becomes first African-American US president | | Muriel Bowser becomes the city's second female mayor |
|---|---|---|---|
| **2001** | **2008** | **2012** | **2014** |
| 9/11 attack on the Pentagon kills 184 people | | Barack Obama is re-elected for a second term as US president | |

# Quirky Events in Washington's History

Politics often attracts strange and sometimes downright whacky individuals. Since Washington has more power and politics per square mile than most places, it should come as no surprise that over the years "Powertown USA" has had more than its share of odd people, from hot-headed civic planners and blundering presidents to arrogant diplomats and agitated discontent groups, resulting in some unusual events and stories.

## America's first federal employee gets fired

In 1791, George Washington hired French planner Pierre L'Enfant to design the new capital city of Washington. L'Enfant created a brilliant city plan that featured wide boulevards, lush parks, an elegant President's House, the great National Mall, and the domed US Capitol.

The new government had no money to build such a fancy city though, and the plan needed to be financed by sales of building lots. However, L'Enfant didn't understand politics and he refused to show his plan to anyone, fearing that speculators would buy up the best lots and drive prices up. As a result, nobody knew where the lots were and they could not be sold.

When construction finally started, a powerful commissioner began building a tall house where it disrupted a view in L'Enfant's plan. When the commissioner was away from town, L'Enfant had his house torn down! Pressure mounted on Washington, and he finally fired L'Enfant in 1792. However, 100 years later, most of his planned city had been built.

## Eat a free dinner and burn the city

In 1814, President James Madison left the White House to supervise the city's defense against the British troops led by Admiral Cockburn. After he left, his capable wife, Dolley, had her staff prepare a

*Aaron Burr killing Alexander Hamilton in a duel*

sumptuous feast for her husband and his officers who would surely return victorious.

When Dolley was warned that the British were approaching the White House, she quickly had servants fill a wagon with valuables, and was off moments before the troops arrived. When the men entered, they found tables set with lavish fare, and enjoyed a hearty meal before setting fire to the White House, the US Capitol, and other prominent buildings in the city.

## The vice president who wanted to be emperor

In 1801, when Thomas Jefferson was running for president, he was forced to accept Aaron Burr, a man he mistrusted, as his vice-presidential running mate. Jefferson and Burr won, but Jefferson cut Burr out of most of the decision-making processes. In 1804, Burr challenged former secretary of the treasury

Alexander Hamilton (the face on the $10 bill) to a duel. Burr killed Hamilton and returned to the city to resume his duties.

Jefferson did not invite Aaron Burr to run with him for a second term, so Burr headed to the wild western frontier, where he tried to raise men and weapons for an army. Many historians believe that his goal was to take over the central part of what is now the US and part of Mexico, create his own country, and declare himself emperor. Jefferson came to know of his plan; Burr was arrested but eventually acquitted.

## The President meets the King

In December 1970, rock 'n' roll legend Elvis Presley checked into a Washington, DC hotel under an assumed name. He then sent a long letter to the White House asking to meet President Nixon and saying he wanted to become a "Federal

*Elvis Presley meeting President Nixon at the White House*

Agent at Large" to combat drug use among the young, as well as "communist brainwashing techniques" and anti-establishment behavior. He also wrote that he had a gift for Nixon.

Feeling it would be a boost for his sagging popularity, the president agreed to meet with Presley. During the meeting, they discussed the negative effect hippie drug culture was having on America's youth. Nixon, for his part, urged Presley to work with young people to promote drug-free living.

Presley presented Nixon with a World War II-era Colt 45 and pictures of his family. Elvis didn't get the federal badge he wanted, however, and eventually, both men met ignominious ends. In 1974, tainted by the Watergate scandal, Nixon was forced to resign the presidency. In 1977, Elvis Presley, "The King of Rock 'n' Roll" died from a heart attack aged 42.

## The stolen stone

Most visitors take the elevator ride to the top of the Washington Monument, but there are also tours that walk up the 897 – gasp, wheeze – steps, where people can see stones in the walls that are engraved with commemorative messages. In the mid-1800s many states and countries donated stones to the monument's construction. One of these stones, marked *A Romea Americae* (from Rome to America), was sent by the pope in 1854. At the same time, a vehemently anti-Catholic party called the

"Know-Nothings" was gaining power in Washington. One of their beliefs was that the pope wanted to take over the US. When they learnt of the stone the pope had donated to the monument, they armed themselves and broke into the construction site, stole the stone, and destroyed it. They then went on to take over the committee in charge of building the monument. During their tenure they managed to add 13 courses of stone to the monument, but the work was so shoddy it later had to be replaced.

## Why Washington isn't square

The Founding Fathers originally envisioned that Washington would be inhabited by people who had permanent homes elsewhere, and there would be few, if any, full-time residents. Therefore, they made no allowances for voting rights for residents of the city. However, there have been full-time residents in DC virtually from the beginning, and today the population stands at about 600,000.

In 1847, Virginia, incensed that the residents of the land it had donated to create the capital no longer had voting rights, took back the land on the west side of the Potomac – and that is why Washington is no longer a square city. DC residents have only been able to vote for the president since 1964; they have one non-voting member of the House of Representatives and no representation in the Senate.

*DC residents voting for the US president for the first time in 1964*

Gleaming aircraft on display at the
Steven F. Udvar-Hazy Center

# Exploring
# WASHINGTON, DC

# The National Mall

Hard to beat for its sheer wow-factor, the National Mall is a 2-mile (3-km) stretch peppered with famous monuments, memorials, and exciting museums. From the priceless artworks at the National Gallery of Art and the moving simplicity of the Lincoln Memorial, to prehistoric delights at the National Museum of Natural History, this tree-lined expanse has enough to keep the entire family entertained for days.

Georgetown

The White House and Foggy Bottom

Penn Quarter

Capitol Hill

**The National Mall**

## Highlights

**National Air and Space Museum**
See the Wright Brothers' first aircraft, a plane piloted by Amelia Earhart, and the Apollo 11 Command Module that traveled to the Moon *(see pp56–9)*.

**National Museum of Natural History**
Check out a huge, stuffed African elephant, hundreds of live butterflies, and a forensically accurate face of a Neanderthal man *(see pp72–5)*.

**National Gallery of Art**
Gaze at works by Degas, da Vinci, Monet, Cézanne, and hundreds of other well-known

artists, in a building almost as spectacular as its contents *(see pp76–80)*.

**Washington Monument**
Zip to the top of the tallest building in Washington, DC, a fitting memorial to America's first president *(see pp84–5)*.

**Lincoln Memorial**
Visit the statue of a seated and pensive Lincoln looking out over the Reflecting Pool *(see pp90–91)*.

**Thomas Jefferson Memorial**
Take in Jefferson's most famous words, engraved on this monument's inner stone walls *(see pp96–7)*.

**Left** *Thomas Jefferson Memorial on the Tidal Basin*
**Above left** *Illuminated Lincoln Memorial overlooking the Reflecting Pool*

# The Best of
# The National Mall

A vast expanse of lush lawns and gardens in the center of the city, the National Mall is surrounded by some of the best museums, art galleries, and monuments in America. In addition, there are wonderful experiences to be had, from renting a paddleboat for a tour of the Tidal Basin to riding the Smithsonian carousel. Kids will have fun flying a kite and playing to their hearts' content in the open spaces on the Mall.

## World-class museums

The **National Museum of Natural History** *(see pp72–5)* is just one of the fantastic museums on the National Mall. In the Rotunda, an African bush elephant takes center stage, its fearsome tusks and majestic trunk raised as though in triumphant trumpet. Elsewhere, some of the world's largest diamonds compete with fluttering butterflies and a chance to go face-to-face with a Neanderthal.

Look at one-of-a-kind aircraft like the "Spirit of St. Louis," the first plane to break the sound barrier, and the Lunar Lander at the **National Air and Space Museum** *(see pp56–9)*. Next door, the **National Museum of the American Indian** *(see pp60–61)* opens up the world of Native life in America and serves as a stage for Native dances, ceremonies, and opportunities for kids to meet with Native Americans. Across the Mall, the **National Museum of American History** *(see pp70–71)* holds a collection that reflects special moments in the story of America, and includes exhibits such as the original Star-Spangled Banner and an antique locomotive.

**Left** *The obelisk of the Washington Monument, surrounded by US flags*
**Below** *The fountain at the World War II Memorial with the Lincoln Memorial in the background*

**Above** *View of the Thomas Jefferson Memorial across the Tidal Basin* **Right** *Admiring The Adoration of the Magi by Fra Angelico and Fra Filippo Lippi, National Gallery of Art*

## Memorable memorials

Few people who climb the steps of the **Lincoln Memorial** *(see pp90–91)* are unmoved by the experience. In addition to being a memorial to a beloved president, it is a monument to the price America paid for unity, and the belief in the equality of all people. The **Martin Luther King, Jr. Memorial** *(see pp94–5)* is a tribute to the champion of African-American civil rights. The **Thomas Jefferson Memorial** *(see pp96–7)* is both beautiful and inspiring, and the exhibit area on the lower level offers an overview of the former president's life. The plazas and fountains of the **Franklin Delano Roosevelt Memorial** *(see pp92–3)* illustrate how FDR led America through the grim period of the Great Depression and World War II. The simple black wall of the **Vietnam Veterans Memorial** *(see pp88–9)* conveys a powerful message on the human cost of war, as does the **World War II Memorial** *(see pp86–7)*. Of course, no trip to the capital of the United States would be complete without a visit to the **Washington Monument** *(see pp84–5)*.

## Capital art

Some of the world's finest art can be found in the museums that surround the National Mall. The **National Gallery of Art** *(see pp76–80)* has more than 100 rooms filled with remarkable paintings, sculptures, and other artworks from the medieval period to the modern day. The donut-shaped **Hirshhorn Museum** *(see p62)* holds a remarkable collection of modern art, including works by Pablo Picasso, Willem de Kooning, and Alexander Calder. Outside the museum, the sunken **Hirshhorn Sculpture Garden** *(see p62)* is a quiet retreat dotted with sculptures by Henri Matisse and Auguste Rodin. Enjoy the color and drama of the masks, sculptures, and other fascinating artifacts at the **National Museum of African Art** *(see p64)*, and for remarkable artworks from across Asia, visit the **Arthur M. Sackler Gallery** *(see p65)* and the **Freer Gallery of Art** *(see p66)*.

## Mall moments

Take a walk around the beautiful lake in the **Constitution Gardens** *(see p88)* or paddle a boat around the **Tidal Basin** *(see p94)*, which is at its best at cherry blossom time. Relax beside the quiet Rainbow Pool at the **World War II Memorial** or have a whirl on the historic Smithsonian carousel. Enjoy sunset views of the **Lincoln Memorial** and **Washington Monument** from the east end of the **Reflecting Pool**. Or dream of becoming a millionaire as sheets of 100-dollar bills fly off the presses at the **Bureau of Engraving and Printing** *(see p67)*.

# National Mall East

Most of the museums and sights on the east end of the Mall are part of the Smithsonian Institution. Not surprisingly, then, the main metro stop is called Smithsonian and is located just southwest of the Smithsonian Castle. Walk from one museum to another, as most are close together, take a cab or pedicab (summer only), or get a ticket for one of the step-on, step-off tour systems that have several stops around the museums. All the major museums have cafés and there are snack stands placed around the Mall, and along Independence Avenue and Constitution Avenue.

The National Mall

## The Lowdown

🚗 **Metro** Smithsonian, L'Enfant Plaza, Federal Triangle, Judiciary Square & Archives/ Navy Memorial. **Bus** DC Circulator Purple line (weekends) and Red line (weekdays). **Trolley** ANC Tours by Martz Gray Line (202 488 1012) and Old Town Trolley (888 910 8687) offer step-on, step-off sightseeing tours that stop at all the museums. **Bike** Bicycles can be rented at Union Station. Cycle racks are near all museum entrances.

ℹ️ **Visitor information** Smithsonian Information Center, 1000 Jefferson Dr SW, 20560; 202 633 1000; www.si.edu/visit. Destination DC, 901 7th NW, 4th Floor, 20001-3719; 202 789 7000; www.washington.org. Ronald Reagan Building & International Trade Center, 1300 Pennsylvania Ave NW, 20004; 202 312 1300; www.itcdc.com

🎊 **Festivals** Living Earth Festival, Museum of the American Indian (late Jul); 202 633 1000. National Book Festival (late Sep); 888 714 4696; www.loc.gov/bookfest. National Capitol Barbecue Battle (late Jun); 202 828 3099; www.bbqdc.com

➕ **Pharmacy** CVS Pharmacy, 400 Massachusetts Ave NW, 20001; 202 289 2236; 24 hours daily

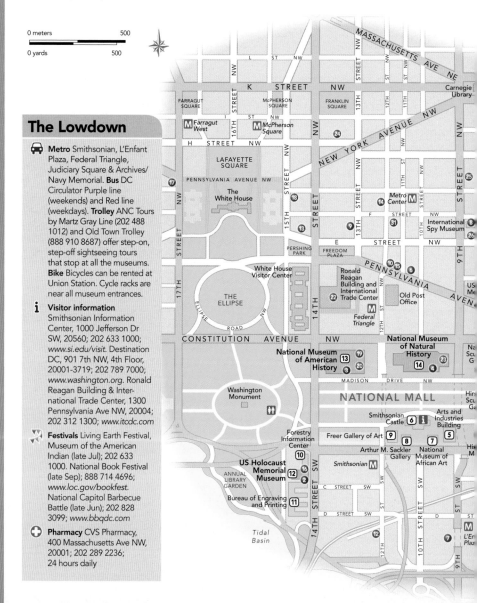

# Places of interest

## SIGHTS

1. National Air and Space Museum
2. National Museum of the American Indian
3. Hirshhorn Museum
4. Hirshhorn Sculpture Garden
5. Arts and Industries Building
6. Smithsonian Castle
7. National Museum of African Art
8. Arthur M. Sackler Gallery
9. Freer Gallery of Art
10. Forestry Information Center
11. Bureau of Engraving and Printing
12. US Holocaust Memorial Museum
13. National Museum of American History
14. National Museum of Natural History
15. National Gallery of Art West Building
16. National Gallery of Art East Building
17. National Sculpture Garden

## ● EAT AND DRINK

1. Wright Place Food Court
2. Mitsitam Cafe
3. Charlie Palmer Steak
4. McDonald's
5. The Source
6. Central Michel Richard
7. L'Enfant Plaza Food Court
8. NoPa
9. Chef Geoff's Downtown
10. West Wing Café
11. Sei
12. Café Twelve
13. Occidental Grill and Seafood
14. Chop't Creative Salad Company
15. Fogo de Chão
16. Holocaust Museum Café
17. Cosi
18. Old Ebbitt Grill
19. Constitution Café
20. Stars and Stripes Café
21. Jaleo
22. Ronald Reagan Building & International Trade Center Food Court
23. Fossil Café
24. Cafe Mozart German Deli
25. Zaytinya
26. Bruegger's Bagels Baked Fresh
27. Cascade Café
28. Carmine's
29. Garden Café
30. Art and Soul
31. Tosca

See also National Air and Space Museum (p59), Hirshhorn Museum (p62), Smithsonian Castle (p64), US Holocaust Memorial Museum (p69), National Gallery of Art East Building (p80), and National Sculpture Garden (p81).

## ● SHOPPING

1. National Air and Space Museum store
2. US Holocaust Memorial Museum store
3. National Museum of American History stores
4. National Museum of Natural History store

See also National Museum of the American Indian (p60) and National Gallery of Art West Building (p77).

## ● WHERE TO STAY

1. Holiday Inn Capitol
2. Residence Inn Marriott

Our Universes exhibit at the National Museum of the American Indian

An African elephant displayed at the Rotunda of the National Museum of Natural History

# ① National Air and Space Museum
## Bringing the science of flying down to Earth

With an awesome array of history-making airplanes and spacecraft that tell the story of man's pursuit of flight, this is perhaps the most popular museum in the city. The exhibits span hundreds of years, from the balloons used in the first flights in the 18th century to the 1969 Apollo mission spacecraft and beyond. Look out for once-in-a-lifetime experiences such as the chance to take the controls of a fighter jet in a flight simulator or to touch a real Moon rock.

*One of the displays in the Early Flight gallery*

## Key Features

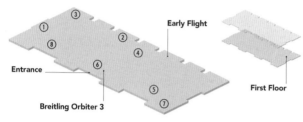

Early Flight

First Floor

Entrance

Breitling Orbiter 3

■ **First Floor** Milestones of Flight, America by Air, Flight Simulators, Early Flight, How Things Fly, IMAX Theater, Explore the Universe, Lunar Exploration Vehicles, Space Race, and Welcome Center

① **Lunar Lander** One of two test landers built early in the Apollo missions is displayed in the Lunar Exploration Vehicles gallery. Its bottom landing stage was designed to be left behind on the Moon's surface, and the upper stage was built to take the astronauts back to their orbiting Command Module.

② **How Things Fly** Learn how flight works and experience the forces that make space travel possible with an extraordinary collection of hands-on, interactive exhibits. Children can sit in the cockpit of a Cessna 150 or float a ball on a column of air.

③ **Explore the Universe** The exhibits here present the story of man's search for an understanding of the universe, from an AD 1090 Islamic astrolabe to the Hubble Space Telescope and modern computer and digital systems made to explore the cosmos.

④ **Columbia** This Apollo 11 Command Module carried well-known astronauts Neil Armstrong, Edwin "Buzz" Aldrin, and Michael Collins to the Moon in 1969.

Prices given are for a family of four

(5) **America by Air** Walk through the history of air transportation in the US. Check out the historic Boeing 747, the sturdy little Pitcairn PA-5 Mailwing, which pioneered airmail in the US, and the Boeing Model 247D, the first modern airliner.

(6) **Moon rock** At the Milestones of Flight gallery, kids line up to touch a triangular sliver of Moon rock from the 1972 Apollo 17 Mission. Collected from the Valley of Taurus-Littrow, it is a volcanic rock called basalt that is almost 4 billion years old.

(7) **Flight Simulators** Here, space age-looking pods offer families multimedia experiences such as taking a walk in space or flying a supersonic fighter in combat.

(8) **Space Race** Look way up to see the top of a World War II V-2 rocket or a Tomahawk cruise missile. Other exhibits include the Skylab Orbital Workshop and the Apollo-Soyuz Test Project, which led the way to a space link-up between an American and a Soviet spacecraft.

## KIDS' CORNER

### Find out more...

**1** How many Moon rocks did the Apollo missions come back with? Stop by the Milestones of Flight gallery for clues.

**2** The Apollo 11 Command Module "Columbia" carried astronaut Neil Armstrong and others to the Moon. What is Armstrong famous for?

**3** Which planet did Viking 1, at the Milestones of Flight gallery, explore?

**4** Where can you pretend to be the pilot of a Cessna 150?

Answers at the bottom of the page.

### AROUND THE WORLD IN LESS THAN 80 DAYS

The Breitling Orbiter 3 was the first balloon to fly nonstop around the world. The 180-ft (55-m)-tall hot air balloon took off from Switzerland on March 1, 1999 and landed in the Egyptian desert 19 days, 21 hours, and 55 minutes later.

*Floating illusions*
*The reason spacecraft can seem to float in space is that they fall toward the Earth and move away from the Earth at the same speed.*

Answers: **1** Over 2,200. **2** Being the first man to walk on the moon. **3** Viking 1 was the first spacecraft to operate on Mars. **4** At the How Things Fly exhibit.

## The Lowdown

🌐 **Map reference** 7 C4
**Address** 6th St & Independence Ave SW, 20560; 202 633 1000; www.airandspace.si.edu

🚗 **Metro** Smithsonian & L'Enfant Plaza. **Bus** DC Circulator Purple line to Independence Ave SW & 6th St SW

🕐 **Open** 10am–5:30pm daily, closed Dec 25. Check website for summer hours

💲 **Price** Free

**Cutting the line** The museum gets crowded on weekends by noon. It is best to visit on a weekday morning.

**Guided tours** Free docent-led tours 10:30am & 1pm daily;

depart from the Welcome Center on the first floor

**Age range** 5 plus

**Activities** Lots of interactive exhibits

**Allow** 2–4 hours

♿ **Wheelchair access** Yes

☕ **Café** Wright Place Food Court on the first floor (see p59)

🛍 **Shop** National Air and Space Museum store on the first floor (see p59)

🚻 **Restrooms** On both floors

### Good family value?
The museum is free and very entertaining for the whole family.

(1) National Air and Space Museum continued ▶

# National Air and Space Museum continued...

## Key Features

Second Floor

Bell X-1

Second Floor Apollo to the Moon, Wright Brothers, World War II Aviation, Pioneers of Flight, Time and Navigation, Albert Einstein Planetarium, and Great War in the Air

① **Douglas DC-3** This twin-engine plane, exhibited in the America by Air gallery, was so fast and reliable that it became a worldwide success and one of the most popular passenger planes in history.

③ **Ford Tri Motor** Nicknamed the Tin Goose, this three-engined transport plane, displayed in the America by Air gallery, started commercial passenger and freight service in 1926. The Ford name and a good safety record helped passengers overcome their fear of flying.

④ **Ryan NYP "Spirit of St. Louis"** In 1927, Charles Lindbergh became the first person to fly nonstop solo across the Atlantic. He started his flight from New York in this plane, now displayed in the Milestones of Flight gallery, and landed 33 hours and 30 minutes later in Paris, France.

⑤ **1903 Wright Flyer** On December 17, 1903, in North Carolina, this plane, shown in the Wright Brothers gallery, was piloted by Orville Wright in the first recorded powered flight. The flight lasted 12 seconds and covered a distance of 120 ft (39 m). Orville's brother Wilbur piloted the plane later that day for a flight that lasted 59 seconds and covered a distance of 852 ft (256 m).

② **Lockheed 5B Vega** In 1932, Amelia Earhart became the first woman to fly nonstop solo across the Atlantic in this plane, displayed in the Barron Hilton Pioneers of Flight gallery. With its streamlined fuselage and lack of wing struts, this monoplane became a favorite for setting speed or distance records.

Prices given are for a family of four

⑥ **World War II Aviation** Get up close to the planes seen in a thousand World War II movies. Check out a British Spitfire, a Japanese Zero Fighter, and the German Messerschmitt Bf. 109G-6 – one of the fastest and deadliest fighter planes of the war.

⑦ **Apollo to the Moon** In 1962, President John F. Kennedy proposed putting a man on the Moon within 10 years, and the result was the Apollo Space Program. In this gallery kids can examine a Lunar Roving Vehicle and the Command capsule used to link with Skylab, the first space station launched by the US.

⑧ **Albert Einstein Planetarium** Travel to the stars, explore the planets, and zoom into space to discover the mind-bending world of black holes at this cutting-edge multimedia entertainment, with its dual digital projection and six-channel digital surround-sound system. There are two to four shows, which rotate every half hour.

⑨ **Time and Navigation** See how innovations in timekeeping over three centuries have influenced how people find their way. Don't miss Stanley, a robotic car that can drive itself, and the Lockheed 5C Vega "Winnie Mae", which flew around the world twice in the 1930s.

Walking Man by Auguste Rodin in the Hirshhorn Sculpture Garden

## Letting off steam

Head to the sunken **Hirshhorn Sculpture Garden** (see p62). This green, art-filled oasis offers a sheltered getaway from the hubbub of the Mall, and is a great place to let kids run, bring a picnic, or to just wander among the sculptures.

## Eat and drink

Picnic: under $30; Snacks: $30–40; Real meal: $40–75; Family treat: over $75 (based on a family of four)

**PICNIC** The **Outdoor Kiosk and Cart** (west side of the National Air and Space Museum) is a good place to buy hamburgers, fries, hot dogs, chips, ice cream, and beverages, and relax on the Mall grounds.

Stall selling smoothies at the Wright Place Food Court

**SNACKS Wright Place Food Court** (east side of the first floor, National Air and Space Museum) has several eateries. Families can enjoy rotisserie chicken and salads from Boston Market, hamburgers, fries and chicken from McDonald's, and pizza from Donatos Pizzeria.
**REAL MEAL** Mitsitam Cafe (first floor, National Museum of the American Indian) specializes in seasonal, Native American cuisine. The dishes are prepared using indigenous ingredients and cooking techniques.

**FAMILY TREAT** Charlie Palmer Steak (101 Constitution Ave NW, 20001; 202 547 8100; www. charliepalmer.com; closed Sun) serves American steaks and seafood, with good wine and stellar service.

## Shopping

The National Air and Space Museum store is filled to the brim with toys, games, clothing, and gifts with space and aviation themes. Star Trek fans will love the 11-ft (3-m)-tall model of the starship Enterprise, which was used in the original 1960s TV show.

## Find out more

**DIGITAL** Fly across America and participate in flight activities at www.airandspace.si.edu/exhibitions/america-by-air/online/flyacross/index.cfm. Experience the first Moon mission with Apollo 11 at www.smithsonianeducation.org/students/idealabs/walking_on_the_moon.html.

**FILM** Some scenes in the movie Night at the Museum: Battle of the Smithsonian (2009) were filmed in the National Air and Space Museum. The Spirit of St. Louis (1957) depicts Charles Lindbergh's historic trans-Atlantic flight, while Amelia (2009) is the story of pioneering pilot Amelia Earhart. Kitty Hawk: The Wright Brothers' Journey of Invention (2003) tells the story of brothers Orville and Wilbur and mankind's first powered flight.

## Next stop...

**NATIONAL MUSEUM OF THE AMERICAN INDIAN** Explore the history and culture of Native Americans, as well as their lives today, at the fascinating National Museum of the American Indian (see pp60–61).

Photographs at the Our Lives exhibit, National Museum of the American Indian

# KIDS' CORNER

### Find out more...
**1** The Ford Tri Motor plane was popularly known by another name. Do you know what it was?
**2** Find one of Charles Lindbergh's favorite planes, the Tingmissartoq. This name was given to it by a young Inuit boy in Greenland. What does it mean?
**3** How much money did Charles Lindbergh win by flying solo across the Atlantic?

Answers at the bottom of the page.

### SUPERSONIC SPEED
The Bell X-1 was the first airplane to break the sound barrier. It was piloted by US Air Force Captain Chuck Yeager, whose exploits were made famous by the movie *The Right Stuff* (1983).

### Blown away
On the day the Wright Brothers made their historic first flights, a sudden powerful gust of wind rolled the parked Wright Flyer down the beach, severely damaging it. The plane never flew again. Many years later it was restored and shipped to the London Science Museum, and then finally moved to the National Air and Space Museum in 1976.

**Answers: 1** Tin Goose. **2** "One who flies like a big bird." **3** $25,000 (about $332,000 today).

# ② National Museum of the American Indian
## From feather headdresses to totem poles

With some artifacts that date back 10,000 years, the collection at this remarkable museum showcases the history and culture of Native American peoples. It also offers an insight into the daily lives, spirituality, and contributions of the present-day Native Americans. One of the most spectacular exhibits is the building itself – surrounded by lush natural landscapes and waterfalls, its dramatic curved-stone facade resembles wind-carved cliffs. Inside, kids can meet Native storytellers, artists, and educators.

A Tsimshian Alaskan totem pole carved from red cedar wood

## Key Features

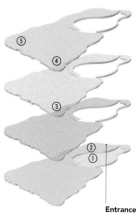

**Entrance**

■ **Fourth Floor** Our Universes, Our Peoples, Lelawi Theater, and Window on Collections: peace medals, animal figures, and projectile points

■ **Third Floor** Our Lives, Window on Collections: bead work, dolls, and containers, imagiNATIONS Activity Center

■ **Second Floor** Roanoke Museum Store and temporary exhibitions

■ **First Floor** Mitsitam Cafe and Tribal News Stand

① **Potomac Atrium** Borrowing architectural styles from Native American traditions, this space welcomes visitors and is used for dances and other ceremonies.

② **Totem Pole** (2012) Artist David Boxley has recreated a traditional Tsimshian Alaskan totem pole depicting the legend of the eagle and the young chief.

③ **Our Lives** Videos and exhibits highlight the challenges that Native Americans face today as they balance the demands of modern life with their traditional beliefs and spirituality.

④ **Our Universes** Unusual objects here include the elaborate Yup'ik feather headdress (1880) made with eagle feathers, wool, glass beads, horsehair, and fur.

⑤ **Wall of Gold** This massive and impressive display case in the Our Peoples gallery holds more than 400 gold figurines and objects dating from before 1491.

## The Lowdown

🌐 **Map reference** 7 D4
**Address** 4th St & Independence Ave SW, 20560; 202 633 1000; www.nmai.si.edu

🚗 **Metro** L'Enfant Plaza. **Bus** DC Circulator Purple line to Independence Ave SW & 2nd St SW (weekends only)

🕐 **Open** 10am–5:30pm daily

💲 **Price** Free

👫 **Cutting the line** The museum does not get very crowded.

🚩 **Guided tours** Available daily. See website for details.

👫 **Age range** 4 plus

👫 **Activities** Hands-on cultural activities for families and free film screenings available daily; check website for details.

⏱ **Allow** 1 hour

♿ **Wheelchair access** Yes

☕ **Café** Mitsitam Cafe on the first floor (see p61)

🛍 **Shops** Chesapeake Museum Store on the first floor and Roanoke Museum Store on the second floor

👫 **Restrooms** On each floor

**Good family value?**
Admission is free and the content is well thought out, with artifacts to hold the attention of all ages.

## Letting off steam

There is plenty of room for kids to run around, and lots to explore in the 5-acre (2-ha) grounds around the museum. These are designed with wetlands, waterfalls, and wildflowers that reflect the landscapes of Native American settlements from the mid-Atlantic region. The grounds are perfect for picnics. For more space, head to **National Garden** (see p106) or **Bartholdi Park** (see p109).

*The curved exterior of the National Museum of the American Indian*

## Eat and drink

*Picnic: under $30; Snacks: $30–40; Real meal: $40–75; Family treat: over $75 (based on a family of four)*

**PICNIC National Park Service Refreshment Stand** (in front of the National Air and Space Museum, see pp56–9) is a good place to pick up food for a picnic in the museum's landscaped grounds or near the elegant fountain in Bartholdi Park.
**SNACKS McDonald's** (National Air and Space Museum, see pp56–9) offers standard fast food in an airy and lively ambience.
**REAL MEAL Mitsitam Cafe** (first floor, National Museum of the American Indian) is one of the top-rated eateries in National Mall. It offers exceptional meals based on the rich culinary heritage of Native peoples from around the Americas.

*The Mitsitam Cafe, National Museum of the American Indian*

The menu changes seasonally, but generally features items such as quinoa salad, yucca stew, yellow corn tortillas, buffalo burgers, and chicken tamales, as well as a large selection of desserts.
**FAMILY TREAT The Source** (Newseum, 575 Pennsylvania Ave NW, 20001; 202 637 6100; www.wolfgangpuck.com), Wolfgang Puck's elegant restaurant, is spread over two levels. Enjoy the delicious Asian-fusion cuisine in the informal bistro downstairs or the more formal seating upstairs (see p139).

## Find out more

**DIGITAL** Check out www.nmai.si.edu/exhibitions/all_roads_are_good for a virtual tour of two of the museum's exhibitions. www.nationsonline.org/oneworld/native_americans.htm gives an insight into Native American tribes throughout North America. For Native American legends, arts and crafts, and an interactive map, visit www.kidinfo.com/american_history/native_americans.html.
**FILM** Reel Injun (2009) is an award-winning documentary, which looks at the portrayal of North American natives through cinema. Smoke Signals (1998) is a story set in a reservation of contemporary native Coeur d'Alene people in Idaho.

*One of the exhibits in the conservatory of the US Botanic Garden*

## Next stop...

**US BOTANIC GARDEN** The towering glass conservatory of the US Botanic Garden (see pp106–107) shelters a remarkable collection of plants from around the world. Popular glassed-in worlds here include a jungle, an orchid collection, desert environments, and a garden for kids.

# ③ Hirshhorn Museum

### A giant donut filled with art

"Art is fun" could easily be the motto of this contemporary art museum, named for the Latvian entrepreneur and philanthropist Joseph Hirshhorn, who presented his superb art and sculpture collection to the US in 1966. The circular form of the huge building is fun in itself, and most kids will enjoy the bright, colorful, and casual nature of the abstract art on display. An exceptional collection of international modern art, from the late 19th century to the present day,

Fountain at the center of the plaza, Hirshhorn Museum

it includes works by artists such as Pablo Picasso, Alberto Giacometti, and Andy Warhol. The permanent collection contains about 11,500 works of art in an eclectic variety of media, including painting, sculpture, mixed media, works on paper, photography, film, and video.

### Letting off steam

The expansive museum grounds offer plenty of space for kids to run, play, and explore. The large plaza that extends underneath the museum has a large fountain in the center and is surrounded by green spaces dotted with huge sculptures.

# ④ Hirshhorn Sculpture Garden

### The Mall's secret garden

Offering an *Alice in Wonderland* vibe, this exceptional sculpture garden has a surprise in store on

Auguste Rodin's The Burghers of Calais at the Hirshhorn Sculpture Garden

every corner. Sunken below street level, this lush garden is an oasis of tranquility hidden away from the hustle and bustle of the Mall. It is filled with fine sculptures and divided into room-like spaces that allow different pieces to come into view as visitors walk through them. Look for masterpieces by artists such as French sculptor Auguste Rodin, French artist Henri Matisse, and American artists Jeff Koons and Alexander Calder.

## The Lowdown

- 🌐 **Map reference** 7 C4
  **Address** Independence Ave at 7th St SW, 20024; 202 633 1000; www.hirshhorn.si.edu
- 🚗 **Metro** L'Enfant Plaza & Smithsonian. **Bus** DC Circulator Purple line to Independence Ave SW & 6th St SW (weekends only) & Red line to 7th St SW & Independence Ave SW (daily)
- 🕐 **Open** 10am–5:30pm daily, closed Dec 25. Plaza: 7:30am–5:30pm daily
- 💲 **Price** Free
- 👫 **Cutting the line** The museum is usually not crowded.
- 🚩 **Guided tours** Impromptu 30-minute free tours leave from the information desk noon–4pm. Free 30-minute gallery talks 12:30pm Mon–Fri; docents are available in the galleries.
- 👫 **Age range** All ages
- 👫 **Activities** Tours, talks, lectures, films, workshops, and family events; check calendar or pick up the free family guide at the information desk.
- 🕐 **Allow** 1–2 hours
- ♿ **Wheelchair access** Yes
- 🍴 **Eat and drink** *Snacks* Hirshhorn Café (*in the museum plaza*) has sandwiches and salads and offers lovely views. *Family treat* Central Michel Richard (*1001 Pennsylvania Ave NW, 20004; 202 626 0015; www.central michelrichard.com; lunch Mon–Fri & dinner daily*) is a casual but stylish restaurant serving traditional American comfort food with a French twist. Burgers, sandwiches, and full meals on the menu.
- 👫 **Restrooms** On the first floor

## The Lowdown

- 🌐 **Map reference** 7 C3
  **Address** Across Jefferson Dr SW from the Hirshhorn Museum, 20024; 202 633 1000; www.hirshhorn.si.edu
- 🚗 **Metro** L'Enfant Plaza & Smithsonian. **Bus** DC Circulator Purple line to Independence Ave SW & 6th St SW (weekends only) & Red line to 7th St SW & Independence Ave SW (daily)
- 🕐 **Open** 7:30am–dusk daily
- 💲 **Price** Free
- 👫 **Age range** All ages
- 🕐 **Allow** 30 minutes
- ♿ **Wheelchair access** Yes
- 🍴 **Eat and drink** *Snacks* L'Enfant Plaza Food Court (*9th St SW & D St SW, 20024; 240 333 3600*) has eateries such as Au Bon Pain, Roti Mediterranean, and Mamma Ilardo's. *Real meal* Mitsitam Cafe (*National Museum of the American Indian, see pp60–61*), offers Native American cuisine.
- 👫 **Restrooms** In the Hirshhorn Museum

## Take cover

The nearby **Smithsonian Castle** (see p64) offers displays and exhibits that give an overview of all the Smithsonian museums.

## ⑤ Arts and Industries Building

### Of another day and age

Looking like an exotic building out of *The Arabian Nights*, this Victorian red brick and sandstone edifice was created as the original Smithsonian National Museum. It opened in 1881, just in time to host the inaugural ball of President James A. Garfield. The collection at the National Museum used to include many of the exhibits from the 1876 Philadelphia Centennial Exposition.

Despite $200 million being poured into it for renovation, the building is to remain closed for

the foreseeable future, as it awaits additional funds to complete the extensive renovation. The fanciful exterior is still fun to see, as well as the surrounding gardens.

### Letting off steam

The **Mary Livingston Ripley Gardens** (located between the Hirshhorn Museum and the Arts and Industries Building) is a great place to let children run. This delightful space is full of hundreds of varieties of perennial and annual plants. Splash hands in the 19th-century cast-iron fountain and have a rest on the antique and reproduction benches surrounded by a profusion of flowers.

### The Lowdown

- 🌐 **Map reference** 7 C4
  **Address** 900 Jefferson Dr SW, 20560; 202 633 1000; www.si.edu/Museums/arts-and-industries-building
- 🚗 **Metro** L'Enfant Plaza & Smithsonian. **Bus** DC Circulator Purple line to Independence Ave SW & 6th St SW (weekends only) & Red line to 7th St SW & Independence Ave SW (daily)
- 🕐 **Open** Check website for timings and details of exhibitions
- 👪 **Age range** All ages
- ⏱ **Allow** A few minutes
- 🍴 **Eat and drink** *Snacks* Castle Café (Smithsonian Castle, see p64; open daily) serves soups, salads, and drinks. *Family treat* NoPa (International Spy Museum, see pp144–5; 202 347 4667; www.nopadc.com), an American brasserie, offers market vegetables and housemade charcuterie.
- 🚻 **Restrooms** At Smithsonian Castle

**Above** *Antique-looking fountain and bench, Mary Livingston Ripley Garden*
**Below** *The Victorian facade of the Arts and Industries Building*

Smithsonian Castle overlooking the manicured Enid A. Haupt Garden

# ⑥ Smithsonian Castle

## Is Dumbledore home?

Looking like it was just lifted from the grounds of Hogwarts School of Witchcraft and Wizardry, this striking red-sandstone Norman-style castle was the Smithsonian's first building. Completed in 1855, it originally housed all aspects of the institution, including an exhibit hall, research facility, and the home of the first secretary of the Smithsonian, Joseph Henry, and his family.

Today, the Castle's visitor center is a great first stop when visiting the Mall as it offers a quick overview of the Smithsonian's 10 museums on the Mall, seven more beyond the Mall, and the Smithsonian's National Zoological Park (see pp168–9). Watch the Smithsonian orientation video and check out the electronic monitors and exhibits calendar for an up-to-the-minute view of events across the Smithsonian museum system. Also check for the schedule of children's theater productions at Discovery Theater (see p37) next to the Castle.

### Letting off steam

Kids of all ages enjoy riding the horses, dragons, and other fanciful creatures on the historic **Smithsonian carousel**, located just outside the Castle ($2.50).

## The Lowdown

- 🌐 **Map reference** 7 B3
  **Address** 1000 Jefferson Dr SW, 20560; 202 633 1000; www.si.edu/Museums/smithsonian-institution-building
- 🚇 **Metro** Smithsonian. **Bus** DC Circulator Purple line to Independence Ave SW & 10th St SW (weekends only)
- 🕐 **Open** 8:30am–5:30pm daily, closed Dec 25
- 💲 **Price** Free
- 🚶 **Cutting the line** There is rarely a line to get in.
- 🚩 **Guided tours** Free tours 9:30am Mon & Fri, 9:30am & 10:30am Sat, 10:30am Sun
- 👫 **Age range** All ages
- 🧒 **Activities** Interactive monitors in the visitor center
- ⏱ **Allow** 30 minutes
- ♿ **Wheelchair access** Yes
- 🍴 **Eat and drink** Picnic Purchase food from a street vendor or the National Park Service Refreshment Stand (in front of the Castle) and enjoy a picnic on the Mall lawns. Snacks Castle Café (Smithsonian Castle) has an espresso/cappuccino bar, ice cream, sandwiches, organic salads, and pastries.
- 🚻 **Restrooms** In the visitor center

# ⑦ National Museum of African Art

## A trip to another continent

The artworks at this underground museum come from almost every region of Africa. The collection,

A mask on display in the National Museum of African Art

which spans the ancient world to the present, focuses on art and culture and includes religious and everyday objects. Artifacts include wooden masks, furniture, musical instruments, paintings, jewelry, and pottery. Kids enjoy the bright colors and materials used, which include beads, fabrics, raffia, shells, and clay. Exhibits also focus on the cultural aspects of African societies, highlighting buildings, customs, clothing, and crafts.

### Letting off steam

The Victorian **Enid A. Haupt Garden** (between Smithsonian Castle & Independence Ave) with broad paths and secret courtyard hideaways, is a fun place for kids to explore and burn off their excess energy. The centerpiece is the formal parterre garden, whose colorful geometric patterns change seasonally. Check out the Moongate Garden, which is

## The Lowdown

- 🌐 **Map reference** 7 C4
  **Address** 950 Independence Ave SW, 20560; 202 633 1000; www.africa.si.edu
- 🚇 **Metro** Smithsonian & L'Enfant Plaza. **Bus** DC Circulator Purple line to Independence Ave SW & 10th St SW (weekends only)
- 🕐 **Open** 10am–5:30pm daily, closed Dec 25
- 💲 **Price** Free
- 🚶 **Cutting the line** There is rarely a line to get in
- 🚩 **Guided tours** 1-hour tours when docents available: 10:30am & 11:30am Tue–Fri, 11am, 1pm & 3pm Sat & Sun
- 👫 **Age range** 4 plus
- 🧒 **Activities** Check the calendar for special programs for kids.
- ⏱ **Allow** 1 hour
- ♿ **Wheelchair access** Yes
- 🍴 **Eat and drink** Snacks Castle Café (Smithsonian Castle, see bottom left; open daily) is a handy on-site refueling station, with coffees, sandwiches, salads and an assortment of freshly baked pastries on offer. Beer and wine are also available. Chef Geoff's Downtown (1301 Pennsylvania Ave NW, 20004; 202 464 4461; www.chefgeoff.com) offers salads, pizzas, steak, and seafood entrées. It also does weekend brunches.
- 🚻 **Restrooms** No, at the Smithsonian Castle's visitor center

*Entrance to the National Museum of African Art*

entered through a round moon gate – in China, the circle is a symbol of heaven.

## ⑧ Arthur M. Sackler Gallery

### An Indiana Jones hangout

This Asian art museum is associated with the Freer Gallery of Art (see p66), but maintains its own extensive collection of almost 9,000 art objects. The Sackler Gallery opened in 1987, to house physician Arthur Sackler's donation of 1,000 Asian artworks to the Smithsonian. The underground museum is entered through a small pavilion in the Enid A. Haupt Garden.

Kids may have their inner Indiana Jones awakened by cases filled with beautiful 4,000 year old jades, ornate Bronze-Age axes, ancient ceramics and gold ornaments, and fierce Asian lions made of vibrantly glazed pottery. Also of interest are Japanese prints, modern porcelain, paintings from

India, Japan, China, Korea, and South Asia, as well as sculpture and ceramics from Japan and Southeast Asia.

### Letting off steam

Head to the **Enid A. Haupt Garden** (see pp64–5), which fills the space between the Castle, Sackler Gallery, and National Museum of African Art.

### The Lowdown

- 🌐 **Map reference** 7 B4
  **Address** 1050 Independence Ave SW, 20013; 202 633 4880; *www.asia.si.edu*
- 🚇 **Metro** Smithsonian & L'Enfant Plaza. **Bus** DC Circulator Purple line to Independence Ave SW & 10th St SW (weekends only)
- 🕐 **Open** 10am–5:30pm daily, closed Dec 25
- 💲 **Price** Free
- 🧍 **Cutting the line** There is rarely a line to get in.
- 🚩 **Guided tours** Docent-led tours noon Thu–Sun, except on Federal holidays. Ask for the guide at the information desk for a self-guided experience; check the events calendar for family programs, performances, and festivals.
- 👫 **Age range** 6 plus
- 👫 **Activities** Family programs and events; check the calendar
- ⏱ **Allow** 1 hour
- ♿ **Wheelchair access** Yes, partial
- ☕ **Eat and drink** *Picnic* The National Park Service Refreshment Stand (in front of Smithsonian Castle) and street vendors offer food which can be had on the lawns of the National Mall. *Snacks* Castle Café (see Smithsonian Castle) offers a range of quick eats.
- 🚻 **Restrooms** On the first and second floors

*Timeless artworks from China on display in the Arthur M. Sackler Gallery*

# ⑨ Freer Gallery of Art

## Big and angry Asian demons

Charles Lang Freer, a railroad magnate, was passionate about Asian art, and in 1923 the Freer Gallery of Art opened to display some of his collection of 7,500 pieces. Today, this is a good museum for families, as even younger children may enjoy – or be frightened by – the two huge, fearsome statues of the demon Kongorikishi, or Ni-O, that stand at opposite ends of a long hallway in the gallery. Freer was also friends with, and collected the works of, American artist James McNeill

An angry Ni-O guarding the collection at the Freer Gallery of Art

Whistler (1834–1903). Most kids will appreciate the resplendent "Peacock Room," an opulent dining room created and decorated by Whistler for a townhouse in London in 1876–7. It was taken apart and brought to the US in 1904 by Freer, and eventually reinstalled in the Freer Gallery in 1919.

Today, the gallery's collection comprises over 24,000 pieces including bronze ritual vessels from ancient China, calligraphy from Japan, ceramics from Korea, and paintings and sculptures from India, Pakistan, Turkey, and Central Asia.

### Letting off steam

On the east side of the Freer Gallery of Art is the **Enid A. Haupt Garden** (see pp64–5). Parents can relax on one of the cast-iron benches while the kids explore the grounds.

# ⑩ Forestry Information Center

## Smokey the Bear's office

For younger kids, the highlight of this small museum is meeting Smokey, a large animatronic bear who moves his head from side to side and greets children with the US Forest Service message, "Only you can prevent wildfires." Smokey the Bear is a mascot of the US Forest Service, and has been educating the public about the dangers of forest fires since 1944. In The Lodge, modeled after a

Smokey the Bear reading his mail at the Forestry Information Center

## The Lowdown

- 🌐 **Map reference** 7 A4
  **Address** 14th St SW & Independence Ave SW, 20024; 800 832 1355; www.fs.fed.us/info
- 🚗 **Metro** Smithsonian. **Bus** DC Circulator Purple line to Independence Ave SW & 14th St SW (weekends only)
- 🕐 **Open** Currently closed for renovation; check the website for the latest information
- 💲 **Price** Free
- 🧍 **Cutting the line** Usually not a long line to get in.
- 👫 **Age range** 2 plus
- ⏱ **Allow** 30 minutes
- ♿ **Wheelchair access** No
- 🍴 **Eat and drink** Snacks Café Twelve (409 12th St SW, 20024) offers hand-carved meats and veggies on a choice of bread. Come early or late to get a table for lunch. Family treat Occidental Grill and Seafood (1475 Pennsylvania Ave, 20004; 202 783 1475; www.occidentaldc.com) serves seafood in a traditional American style.
- 🚻 **Restrooms** Near the entrance

1920s rustic forest lodge, there are displays of original Forest Service artifacts from the early 20th century, and a series of videos about the service's history. The building is presently being renovated; check the website before visiting.

### Letting off steam

Walk west across Raoul Wallenberg Place to the **Tidal Basin** (see p94), where the kids can run and play.

## The Lowdown

- 🌐 **Map reference** 7 B4
  **Address** Jefferson Dr at 12th St SW, 20013; 202 633 1000; www.asia.si.edu
- 🚗 **Metro** Smithsonian & L'Enfant Plaza. **Bus** DC Circulator Purple line to Independence Ave SW & 10th St SW (weekends only)
- 🕐 **Open** 10am–5:30pm daily, closed Dec 25
- 💲 **Price** Free
- 🧍 **Cutting the line** Usually not a long line to get in.
- 📍 **Guided tours** Docent-led tours 1pm Thu–Sun, except on Federal holidays. Ask at the information desk for a guide at the self-guided experience; check the events calendar for family programs, performances, and festivals.
- 👫 **Age range** 6 plus
- 🧍 **Activities** Family programs and events; check the calendar
- ⏱ **Allow** 1 hour
- ♿ **Wheelchair access** Yes
- 🍴 **Eat and drink** Snacks West Wing Café (1111 Pennsylvania Ave, 20004; 202 628 2233) offers sandwiches and bagels for breakfast, and smoothies, salads, soups, and deli sandwiches for lunch. Family treat Sei (444 7th St NW, 20004; 202 783 7007; www.seirestaurant.com) serves Asian fusion cuisine such as wasabi guacamole (spicy avocado dip) appetizers, sashimi pizza, and fish-and-chip rolls.
- 🚻 **Restrooms** On the lower level near the north and south entrances

# ⑪ Bureau of Engraving and Printing

## The buck starts here

Seeing pallets of money piled high and presses printing thousands of bills per minute, is an eye-popping experience. This 40-minute tour of the Money Factory is fun for the whole family, and kids are often amazed to see how money is actually made. After watching a short movie and exploring exhibits on the history of money making, the guided tour follows the process of printing US currency. Pallets of special paper arrive at the bureau for printing on presses with quality control and security features. The paper flows through several presses, with each one applying a specific color or the serial number. Sheets of currency are scanned electronically for imperfections before being cut into separate bills and stacked, bundled, shrink-wrapped, and loaded onto pallets. The gift shop has interesting souvenirs, including bags of shredded money.

### Letting off steam

Check out the **Annual Library Garden** (*Maine Ave SW & Independence Ave SW*) near the Tidal Basin. It is best known for the display of nearly 100 types of tulips each spring. Over 10,000 bulbs are planted every November, and bloom from early April through early May, followed by other dazzling varieties in summer.

Entrance to the Bureau of Engraving and Printing, where American money is made

*Colorful flowers in bloom at the Annual Library Garden*

## The Lowdown

🗺 **Map reference** 7 A4
**Address** 14th St SW & C St SW, 20228; 202 874 2330; www.moneyfactory.gov

🚇 **Metro** Smithsonian. **Bus** DC Circulator Purple line to Independence Ave SW & 14th St SW (weekends only)

🕐 **Open** Apr–Aug: 8:30am–7:30pm (last entry at 7pm) Mon–Fri; Sep–Mar: 8:30am–3:30pm Mon–Fri; closed Sat, Sun & Federal holidays

💲 **Price** Free. Mar–Aug: timed entry tickets available at the booth on Raoul Wallenberg Place from 8am until the day's tickets have been distributed; lines form early and tickets are often gone by 8:30am.

👫 **Cutting the line** Contact a congressman's office months in advance to request a tour reservation.

🚩 **Guided tours** Mar–Aug: every 15 minutes from 9am until 7pm; Sep–Feb: every 15 minutes from 9 until 10:45am & 12:30 until 2pm

👫 **Age range** 6 plus

⏱ **Allow** 2 hours

♿ **Wheelchair access** Yes

🍴 **Eat and drink** *Snacks* Chop't Creative Salad Company (*618 12th St NW, 20050; 202 783 0007; www.choptsalad.com*) has interesting salads, plus meat and vegetarian sandwich options. *Family treat* Fogo de Chão (*1101 Pennsylvania Ave NW, 20004; 202 347 4668; www.fogodechao.com; closed for lunch on weekends*) offers a huge salad bar, sizzling Brazilian fire-roasted meats, cheese bread, and caramelized bananas.

👫 **Restrooms** No, but nearby in the Smithsonian Castle (*see p64*)

# ⑫ US Holocaust Memorial Museum
## Ghosts from the past

Creating the most moving experience in Washington, this museum leads visitors through a horrifying chapter in world history. Beginning with the story of the rise of Hitler and the Nazis, the museum ends on a hopeful note at the Wexner Learning Center, where visitors are invited to support the fight against genocide around the world. The graphic nature of the displays in the permanent exhibitions makes it suitable for kids 11 years or older.

Tiles at Children's Tile Wall in US Holocaust Museum

## Key Features

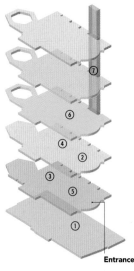

Entrance

**Tower of Faces** Across the third, fourth, and fifth floors

**Fifth Floor** Museum offices and library

**Fourth Floor** Permanent exhibition: The Nazi Assault 1933–39

**Third Floor** Permanent exhibition: The "Final Solution" 1940–45

① **Children's Tile Wall** More than 3,000 tiles, painted by US schoolchildren in remembrance of the families that died in the Holocaust, can be seen here.

② **Danish Liberation Boat** During World War II, Danish people smuggled as many as 7,000 Danish Jews to Sweden in boats like the one exhibited here.

**Second Floor** Permanent exhibition: Last Chapter and Wexner Learning Center

**First Floor** Museum shop, elevator to library, archives and the photo archives

**Lower Level** Meyerhoff Theater, Rubinstein Auditorium, Kimmel-Rowan Gallery, and Gonda Education Center

③ **Daniel's Story** This exhibit follows 11-year-old Daniel as his peaceful existence is shattered when his family is forced into a concentration camp.

④ **From Memory to Action: Meeting the Challenge of Genocide** An interactive exhibit, which answers the question of what can be done to prevent acts of genocide.

⑤ **Hall of Witness** The names of Jewish towns that vanished during the Holocaust are etched on the glass panels here.

⑥ **Rail car** Tens of thousands of Jews from all over Europe were transported to concentration camps in rail cars like the one displayed in The "Final Solution" gallery.

⑦ **Tower of Faces** Here, the walls are lined with pictures of men, women, and children who died during the Holocaust.

## The Lowdown

🌐 **Map reference** 7 A4
**Address** 1100 Raoul Wallenberg Place SW, 20024; 202 488 0400; www.ushmm.org

🚗 **Metro** Smithsonian. **Bus** DC Circulator Purple line to Independence Ave SW & 14th St SW (weekends only)

🕐 **Open** 10am–5:20pm daily, closed Yom Kippur & Dec 25

💲 **Price** Free, timed same-day passes required in Mar–Aug for permanent exhibitions, available on first-come first-served basis.

👫 **Cutting the line** Mar–Aug: limited passes available for purchase online or by phone; check website for details.

🚩 **Guided tours** For the visually and hearing impaired; reserve 2 weeks in advance. Brochures available for self-guided tours.

👫 **Age range** 11 plus; Daniel's Story suitable for 8 plus.

🏃 **Activities** At the Wexner Learning Center, explore genocide threats and the ways in which it can be prevented.

⏱ **Allow** 2–3 hours

♿ **Wheelchair access** Yes

☕ **Café** Holocaust Museum Café (see p69)

🛍 **Shop** On the first floor (see p69)

👫 **Restrooms** On the lower level, near the permanent exhibitions, and in the café

**Good family value?**
Admission is free and while this is not a "fun" museum, it provides a powerful experience and may be the DC museum that people will remember the longest.

Paddleboats for rent at the dock on the Tidal Basin

## Letting off steam

A boat ride on the **Tidal Basin** (see p94) offers a great counterpoint to the intensity of the museum. Rent a paddleboat and head out to enjoy the sparkle of the water and the beauty of the surrounding parkland and memorials.

## Eat and drink

*Picnic: under $30; Snacks: $30–40; Real meal: $40–75; Family treat: over $75 (based on a family of four)*

**PICNIC** The **National Park Service Refreshment Stand** (*Paddleboat dock on the Tidal Basin*) offers a selection of fast food. Buy lunch from here and enjoy an outdoor meal with a view.

**SNACKS Holocaust Museum Café** *(located off the west entrance plaza; 202 488 6151; www.ushmm.org/visit/cafe; open 8:30am–4:30pm daily)* has standard vegetarian or kosher options, including bagels, soups, salads, pizzas, panini, sandwiches, desserts, and beverages.

**REAL MEAL Cosi** *(1700 Pennsylvania Ave NW, 20004; 202 638 7101; www.getcosi.com; breakfast & lunch only)* serves an assortment of sandwiches (including delicious breakfast sandwiches), soups, salads, and flat-bread pizzas. Adventurous diners can try the Pho Ga soup or tandoori chicken. The house favorite is turkey and brie sandwich with spicy mustard.

**FAMILY TREAT Old Ebbitt Grill** *(675 15th St NW, 20005; 202 347 4800; www.ebbitt.com)*, is a popular oyster bar near the White House. Seafood is the specialty here, but there are also plenty of pasta, chicken, and meat dishes, plus a kids' menu, to keep even the fussiest eaters happy. The Victorian interior decked out with antique artifacts exudes classical charm.

## Shopping

The well-stocked museum shop specializes in books and gifts with connections to its theme. Also on offer are remembrance items, posters, and artworks.

## Find out more

**DIGITAL** The museum's website has interactive information at *www. ushmm.org/education/forstudents*.
**FILM** *The Diary of Anne Frank* (1959) is based on the diary of a Jewish girl, Anne Frank, who lived in hiding with her family in Amsterdam during World War II. *Daring to Resist* (1999) tells the stories of three Jewish women who were teenagers during the Holocaust at *www.pbs. org/daringtoresist/synopsis.htm*.

The main entrance of the National Museum of Natural History

## Next stop...

**NATIONAL MUSEUM OF NATURAL HISTORY** From the huge African elephant in the Rotunda to the dazzling Hall of Geology, Gems and Minerals, the National Museum of Natural History (see pp72–5) offers stimulating visual and tactile experiences at every turn.

# ⑬ National Museum of American History
## From George Washington's sword to Kermit the Frog

What makes this museum so much fun is its mixture and range of exhibits – there is a feeling of never knowing what lies around the next corner. The eclectic, and sometimes downright odd, collection includes Lincoln's top hat, TV chef Julia Child's kitchen, massive steam locomotives, and even Dorothy's ruby slippers from the 1939 movie *The Wizard of Oz*. Everything here has been beautifully preserved. The west exhibition wing is currently undergoing renovation, although the core area remains open.

## Key Features

**Third Floor** First Ladies, Price of Freedom, Gunboat Philadelphia, American Presidency, and museum shop

**Second Floor** American Stories, Artifact Walls, Star-Spangled Banner, Welcome Center, and museum shop

**First Floor** Food, On the Water, America on the Move, Stories on Money, Lighting a Revolution, and museum shop

Entrance

④ **The First Ladies** Check out the 24 formal dresses, including 11 inaugural gowns, worn by first ladies from Martha Washington to Michelle Obama.

## The Lowdown

🌐 **Map reference** 7 B3
**Address** 14th St & Constitution Ave NW, 20004; 202 633 1000; www.americanhistory.si.edu

🚗 **Metro** Federal Triangle. **Bus** Smithsonian DC Circulator Purple line to Constitution Ave NW & 14th St NW (weekends only)

🕐 **Open** 10am–5:30pm daily, closed Dec 25

💲 **Price** Free

🚶 **Cutting the line** There is rarely a line to get in.

🚩 **Guided tours** Brochures for self-guided tours available in the Welcome Center.

👫 **Age range** 6 plus

👫 **Activities** Check the Welcome Center for the day's special activities. Interactive carts with historical paraphernalia are located throughout the museum.

⏱ **Allow** 2–4 hours

♿ **Wheelchair access** Yes

☕ **Cafés** Stars and Stripes Café and Constitution Café (see p71)

🛍 **Shops** In the museum, on every floor (see p71)

🚻 **Restrooms** On every floor

**Good family value?**
Offers a fun and informative day out for the entire family.

① **The American Presidency** This exhibit explores the impact of the 43 former US presidents on the course of history. A key exhibit is Thomas Jefferson's lap desk.

② **American Stories** More than 100 objects showcase the people, inventions, issues, and events that have shaped American history over the ages.

③ **Gunboat Philadelphia** This is one of the gunboats that were manned by a small unit of continental soldiers as they fought the British on Lake Champlain in 1776.

⑤ **The Price of Freedom: Americans at War** Hundreds of artifacts relate the history of the US military from the French and Indian Wars to today.

⑥ **Stories on Money** This exhibition explores the development of American coinage and currency from Colonial times to the present day.

⑦ **The Star-Spangled Banner** The flag that flew over Baltimore's Fort McHenry during the War of 1812, and later inspired the National Anthem, is on display here.

⑧ **America on the Move** This incredible collection of antique cars, steam trains, and motorcycles includes the 1401 Southern Railway steam locomotive.

## Letting off steam

The **Constitution Gardens** (see p88) are a great place for kids to run, hike, or ride a rented bike. There are lovely, tree-shaded paths that wind past grassy expanses perfect for a picnic.

## Eat and drink

Picnic: under $30; Snacks: $30–40; Real meal: $40–75; Family treat: over $75 (based on a family of four)

**PICNIC Food trucks**, a convenient on-the-go option, can be found lining the Mall near the National Museum of American History.
**SNACKS Constitution Café** (first floor, National Museum of American History) is a great place for a snack or light meal.

People at the counter of the Stars and Stripes Café

**REAL MEAL Stars and Stripes Café** (lower level, National Museum of American History) serves American barbecue dishes, salads, hamburgers, pizzas, and desserts.
**FAMILY TREAT Jaleo** (480 7th St NW, 20004; 202 628 7949; www.jaleo.com), the flagship restaurant of chef José Andrés, serves up delicious Spanish tapas, small dishes of edible sharables like calamari, ham, and oysters, plus vegetables and salads. It sounds exotic, but there's plenty here to keep the kids happy, too.

## Shopping

The museum has three stores. The main museum store on the first floor offers toys, gifts, games, artworks, and collectibles with a variety of American history themes. The shop on the second floor has goods that feature icons of American culture, from I Love Lucy to Elvis. On the third floor, the Price of Freedom shop has military-themed merchandise.

Broad walkway around the lake in Constitution Gardens

## Find out more

**DIGITAL** Play and download interactive crossword puzzles on American history from www.earlyamerica.com/crossword.
**FILM** Night at the Museum: Battle of the Smithsonian (2009) was filmed at the museum. Watch Julie and Julia (2009), a comedy drama about the life of chef Julia Child and a young woman who tries to cook all of her recipes within one year. Lincoln (2012) is about the 16th US President, Abraham Lincoln, and Selma (2014) chronicles the campaign by Dr Martin Luther King Jr. to secure equal voting rights.

## Next stop...

**WASHINGTON MONUMENT** It is a pleasant stroll from the museum to the Washington Monument (see pp84–5). Built in memory of George Washington, it is the tallest freestanding obelisk in the world.

The Egyptian-style obelisk of Washington Monument

# ⑭ National Museum of Natural History
## Dinosaurs, diamonds, and Neanderthals

For over a century, Smithsonian scientists have roamed the globe, returning with specimens of every imaginable type of animal, plant, and mineral, and making this museum a compelling place to visit. Favorites include the Hall of Mammals, with mounted animals from around the world; the Sant Ocean Hall, where young minds meet the mysteries of the deep; and the Hall of Human Origins, where kids can come face-to-face with our distant ancestors.

*Facade of the National Museum of Natural History*

## Key Features

**Second Floor** IMAX Theater Lobby, Special Exhibit Gallery, Hall of Human Origins, Sant Ocean Hall, Discovery Room, African Cultures, Rotunda, Life in the Ancient Seas, and Fossil Café

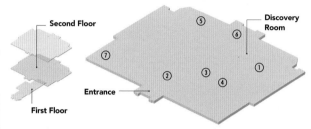

Second Floor

Discovery Room

First Floor

Entrance

① **African Voices** The diversity, dynamism, and global influence of Africa's peoples and cultures over time are explored in this exhibition through historical artifacts, contemporary objects, sculptures, textiles, and pottery. Multimedia components add vibrant sounds and visuals throughout.

② **African Elephant** Dominating the Rotunda, this massive African Bush Elephant was the largest land animal to be on display in any museum when it was unveiled in 1959. Since then, it has become a symbol of the museum itself.

## The Lowdown

🌐 **Map reference** 7 B3
**Address** 10th St & Constitution Ave NW, 20560; 202 633 1000; *www.mnh.si.edu*

🚍 **Metro** Smithsonian. **Bus** DC Circulator Purple line to Constitution Ave NW & 10th St NW (weekends only)

🕐 **Open** Sep–Mar: 10am–5:30pm daily; Apr–Aug:10am–7:30pm daily; closed Dec 25

💲 **Price** Free

👫 **Cutting the line** The museum gets crowded on weekends and in the afternoons. Arrive before 10am on weekdays.

👫 **Age range** All ages

👫 **Activities** Kids can learn and touch bones and minerals, and try on costumes from around the world for free in the Discovery Room; noon–2:30pm Tue–Thu, 10:30am–2:30pm Fri, 10:30am–3:30pm Sat & Sun. The IMAX Theater Lobby offers movies; check website for tickets.

⏱ **Allow** 2–4 hours

♿ **Wheelchair access** Yes

☕ **Cafés** Fossil Café on the second floor *(see p75)*. Atrium Café on the first floor serves burgers, pizzas, and sandwiches. The Ice

Cream and Espresso Bar on the first floor has ice cream, coffee, and desserts.

🛍 **Shops** Six shops spread across different floors offer goods that support the museum's main themes. The Family Store on the first floor offers educational toys, dinosaurs, and mementos.

👫 **Restrooms** On every floor

**Good family value?**
This free museum offers hours of fascinating exhibits and something for everyone in the family.

*Prices given are for a family of four*

③ **Life in the Ancient Seas** The exhibits in this gallery re-create the sights and sounds of prehistoric oceans, which teemed with giant fish, swimming reptiles such as the Ichthyosaur, and huge sharks like the megalodon that grew up to 52 ft (16 m) in length.

④ **FossiLab** Visitors can watch as the museum's scientists work on fossilized bones, extracting them from rock and making casts for research.

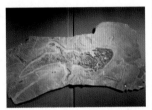

⑤ **Hall of Human Origins** What makes this exhibit so captivating are the forensic re-creations that put flesh to bone to produce life-like faces of Neanderthal, Homo erectus, Australopithicus afarensis, and other early humans. The Hall of Human Origins shows how different humans evolved over time, why they failed or succeeded, and how modern man came to dominate the species pyramid so quickly.

⑥ **Sant Ocean Hall** From the largest ocean-going mammals to the smallest microorganisms, this hall explores the ocean realms in all their diversity. Look up at the suspended life-size right whale, discover a living coral reef, and learn little-known facts about the giant squid.

⑦ **Hall of Mammals** This visually impressive hall features mounted animals from all major continents. Lions roam and giraffes graze leisurely in the Africa section. Kangaroos and koalas represent the Australia section, and a towering grizzly rearing on his hind legs hosts the North America section.

# KIDS' CORNER

### Look out for...

**1** Can you name the largest mammal found on land? Its model can be seen in the Rotunda.

**2** Do you know why the whale found in the Sant Ocean Hall is known as the right whale?

**3** Colorful butterflies evolved from which related, if less eye-catching, insect?

**4** Where in the museum are you likely to find a Cape Buffalo?

........................................................

Answers at the bottom of the page.

*Follow Iggy the Iguana*
*Look for Iggy the Iguana throughout the museum. You will find him in exhibits where you can learn something special about evolution.*

### CLEVER CREATURE

Elephants can walk underwater, using their trunks as a snorkel, and can hear through their feet, sensing subsonic vibrations from great distances. When an elephant's stomach rumbles, it can be heard 600 ft (183 m) away. They can live up to 70 years.

### Fishy fact

The largest fish in the world is the whale shark; the biggest ever caught weighed 47,300 lbs (21,454 kg).

........................................................

**Answers: 1** The African elephant. **2** It is so named because whalers knew that they were rich in whale oil, and also that they swim slowly and float after they die, therefore the "right" whales to kill. **3** Moths. **4** In the Africa section of the Hall of Mammals.

⑭ National Museum of Natural History continued ▶

# National Museum of Natural History continued...

## Key Features

**Third Floor** Insect Zoo, Eternal Life in Ancient Egypt, Written in Bone, Hall of Geology, Gems, and Minerals, Butterflies + Plants, Hall of Bones, and The Moon, Meteorites, and Solar System

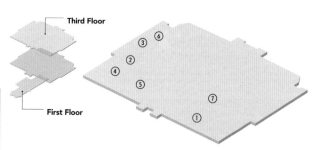

Third Floor

First Floor

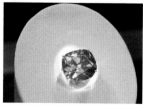

**① Hall of Geology, Gems, and Minerals** Admire the Hope Diamond, which once belonged to two kings and was stolen during the French Revolution. A mysterious curse is said to fall on all who own this 45.52-carat blue diamond. The other gems and jewelry in this gallery include the 75-carat Hooker Emerald, the Victoria-Transvaal Diamond, the spectacular Carmen Lúcia ruby, Marie Antoinette's diamond earrings, and the Dom Pedro, the world's largest cut-gem aquamarine in the world.

**② Hall of Bones** This dramatic swordfish skeleton in the Hall of Bones is just one example that highlights the variety and diversity that exists among even related species on our unique planet.

**④ Insect Zoo** Not only can kids see living examples of creepy crawlies from around the world, but they can, under the supervision of trained volunteers, also touch and hold several types of bugs. Tarantula feeding is another popular attraction here.

**⑥ Written in Bone** This exhibition shows how forensic anthropology can help scientists, particularly archaeologists, to discover how people lived and died long ago. A hands-on forensic lab lets kids use professional tools to solve problems that forensic investigators face in real life.

**⑦ The Moon, Meteorites, and Solar System** Explore the birth and evolution of the solar system through films, interactive computer displays, specimens of Moon rocks, a touchable Mars rock, meteorites, and stardust.

**③ Eternal Life in Ancient Egypt** The most popular item in this exhibition is a mummy from the Ptolemaic Period (332–330 BC). Given to the Smithsonian in 1886, the mummy is of a 40-year-old male.

**Prices given are for a family of four**

**⑤ Butterflies + Plants** This rainforest-filled pavilion dances with hundreds of brightly colored live butterflies. There are Orange-Barred Sulphurs, Gulf Fritillaries, Madagascar Moon Moths, and many more. Children who can stand still for a few moments are often rewarded with a butterfly landing on a shoulder, hand, or even a nose.

*Riding around the scenic National Mall area*

## Letting off steam

Take a leisurely stroll along the Mall and past some of the famous sights of the city. A good route goes past the Washington Monument (see pp84–5) and along the winding paths of Constitution Gardens (see p88), then taking in the Lincoln Memorial (see pp90–91) and heading back east along the Reflecting Pool (see p88).

## Eat and drink

*Picnic: under $30; Snacks: $30–40; Real meal: $40–75; Family treat: over $75 (based on a family of four)*

**PICNIC Ronald Reagan Building & International Trade Center Food Court** (1300 Pennsylvania Ave NW, 20004; 202 312 1300; www.itcdc. com) offers 18 different food services, and the food can be ordered to go. Choose from wraps, hamburgers, or salads, and then head to the Mall for a picnic on the lawns.

**SNACKS Fossil Café** (second floor, National Museum of Natural History) is a great place for specialty coffee, salads, sandwiches, fresh fruit, and desserts.

**REAL MEAL Cafe Mozart German Deli** (1331 H St NW, 20005; 202 347 5732; www.cafemozart germandeli.com) is a sit-down restaurant serving authentic German entrées, Viennese beef stew, and grilled trout. Kids like the burgers and sausages, and there are salads and vegetarian options too.

**FAMILY TREAT Zaytinya** (701 9th St NW, 20001; 202 638 0800; www.zaytinya.com), a trendy and popular restaurant, serves small plates of eastern Mediterranean fare. Try the zucchini fritters, baba ghanoush (mashed eggplant), and falafel (ground chickpea patties).

## Shopping

There are six shops in the museum. The first-floor Gallery Shop sells art and books with natural history themes. The floor's other shop is chock-full of games, puzzles, and more. The Mammal Shop on the second floor is a dream come true for those who love stuffed toys. On the third floor is the Gem and Mineral Shop offering glittering mineral specimens, crystals, and jewelry made from Earth's treasures.

## Find out more

**DIGITAL** Check out the museum's website www.mnh.si.edu for interactive links, and be sure to visit the Ocean portal www.ocean. si.edu to listen and learn about ocean science.

**FILM** *Night at the Museum: Battle of the Smithsonian* (2009) was filmed at the Smithsonian museums. In the 2008 film *Get Smart*, the headquarters of fictional spy organization CONTROL is located underneath the National Museum of Natural History. Disneynature has produced several spectacular family nature movies, including *Oceans* (2010), *Nature* (2009), and *African Cats* (2011).

*Paintings on display at the National Gallery of Art West Building*

## Next stop...

**NATIONAL GALLERY OF ART WEST BUILDING** One of the world's top art collections can be seen at the National Gallery of Art West Building (see pp76–9). Spanning seven centuries, the collection features works by da Vinci, Rembrandt, and Rubens, as well as galleries of French Impressionist masterpieces.

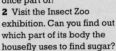

## KIDS' CORNER

### Find out more...
1 Go to the Hall of Geology, Gems and Minerals and look out for the Hooker Emerald. Can you guess which type of accessory the 75-carat emerald was once part of?
2 Visit the Insect Zoo exhibition. Can you find out which part of its body the housefly uses to find sugar?
3 The Hope Diamond is one of the largest and most valuable blue diamonds in the world. Do you know how it arrived at the Smithsonian?

Answers at the bottom of the page.

### Fluttering fact
There are 24,000 species of butterfly. The smallest butterfly, the Western Pygmy Blue, has a wingspan of less than 3/8 inch (1 cm) and the largest, the Queen Alexandra's Birdwing, has a wingspan of up to 12 inches (30 cm).

### THE MAKING OF A MUMMY
It took ancient Egyptian priests 70 days to turn a dead human body into a mummy. They removed the vital organs, dried the body with special salts, and wrapped it with hundreds of yards of linen cloth. They also mummified bulls, cats, and even baboons.

**Don't judge a bug by its size**
The strongest creature in the world (by size) is the Hercules beetle, which can lift 850 times its body weight.

**Answers: 1** A sultan's belt buckle. **2** Its feet. **3** Famous jeweler Harry Winston donated the diamond; he put it in a box and mailed it.

# ⑮ National Gallery of Art West Building
## Show me the Monet!

This spectacular building is filled from end to end with one of the finest collections of art in North America. The French Impressionist works alone would make this a world-class museum. Add to that seven centuries of masterworks from Dutch, German, Flemish, Italian, British, and American artists, and here is a one-of-a-kind gallery. Most major exhibits are on the main floor. There are plenty of programs to engage kids, but the building itself is equally fascinating, with the circular staircases, the jungle-like courtyards, and a cool, moving walkway through a dark tunnel of twinkling lights that connects the West Building with the East Building *(see p80)*.

*The front entrance of the National Gallery of Art West Building*

## Key Features – Modern Art

**Main Floor** European Painting and Sculpture, 13th–16th-Century Painting and Sculpture, American Art, Temporary Exhibitions

**Ground Floor** Sculpture Gallery, Decorative Arts, Prints and Drawings, Temporary Exhibitions, Garden Café, Shop, Lecture Hall

**East Building** Modern and Contemporary Art, Special Exhibitions, Film and Lecture Auditoria

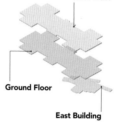

Main Floor

Ground Floor

East Building

Entrance

② *Girl with a Watering Can* (1876) This image of a young blonde girl wearing a fancy dress and holding a watering can is one of Renoir's most popular paintings, and a big hit with the kids.

① *Rouen Cathedral* (1894) Encourage kids to spot the difference between the two versions of this painting by French Impressionist Claude Monet. One depicts Rouen Cathedral in bright sunlight and the other in the cool shade of evening.

③ *The Dance Lesson* (1878) Impressionist Edgar Degas was famous for his portrayals of dancers. This painting depicts ballet dancers exhausted after an intense practice session.

Prices given are for a family of four

④ **Family of Saltimbanques** (1905) For over a year, from late 1904 to early 1906, Pablo Picasso focused on painting circus acrobats known as *saltimbanques*. Seen as outsiders by polite society, *saltimbanques* were a symbol of the rejection that Picasso felt as an artist. He often visited the circus, sketching the performers, creating and re-creating images in which they were together as a group, while appearing lonely as individuals.

⑤ **The Peppermint Bottle** (1893–5) One of Post-Impressionist painter Paul Cézanne's favorite subjects was the French countryside, and this still life, with the swirls in the fabric, looks a little like a landscape. The angular fruits and glassware seem to lean towards the viewer. Also notice the misshapen bottle – Cézanne purposefully distorted objects and perspectives in order to create a balanced composition.

⑥ **Girl Arranging Her Hair** (1886) Impressionist painter Mary Cassatt was noted for capturing everyday scenes of home life without romanticizing her subjects. She often asked local French women to pose for her.

⑦ **The Olive Orchard** (1889) Vincent van Gogh's vivid, powerful brushstrokes bring to life the gnarled olive trees found in the south of France that were the focus of the artist's paintings in the last few months of his life. In the way in which he depicts a harvest scene, showing women picking olives, Van Gogh was trying to express an emotional bond between humans and the nature that sustained them.

## KIDS' CORNER

### Find out more...
**1** Which town in France inspired Van Gogh to use bright colours in his paintings?
**2** Find the painting of the Indian Chief White Cloud by George Catlin in the National Gallery of Art West Building. What is the pattern painted on his face?
**3** Which fruits can you see in Cézanne's still life *The Peppermint Bottle*?
**4** Ballerinas wear short skirts made of a stiff material. Do you know what their skirts are called?

..................................................

Answers at the bottom of the page.

### Frightening fact
Before the National Gallery of Art was built, this was the site of the 6th Street railway station, most famous as the place where President James Garfield was assassinated in 1881.

### IT'S ALL IN A NAME
Pablo Picasso signed his paintings just "Picasso." It would have been hard to sign his full name, which was Pablo Diego José Francisco de Paula Juan Nepomuceno María de los Remedios Cipriano de la Santísima Trinidad Ruiz y Picasso.

..............................................

**Answers: 1** Aries. **2** A human hand, representing his strength in hand-to-hand combat. **3** Apples, a pear, and a lemon. **4** Tutu.

## The Lowdown

🌐 **Map reference** 7 D3
**Address** Between 4th St NW & 7th St NW at Constitution Ave NW, 20565; 202 737 4215; *www.nga.gov*

🚗 **Metro** Judiciary Square, Archives/Navy Memorial & Smithsonian. **Bus** DC Circulator Purple line to Constitution Ave NW & 7th St NW (weekends only)

🕐 **Open** 10am–5pm Mon–Sat, 11am–6pm Sun, closed Jan 1 & Dec 25

💲 **Price** Free

👫 **Cutting the line** As weekend afternoons can be busy, visit on mornings or on weekdays.

🚩 **Guided tours** Free tours on a variety of subjects, audio tours (including a version for children 7–12 years), and foreign language tours are available; check website for details.

👫 **Age range** 4 plus

🤸 **Activities** Stories In Art, for children from 4 to 7 years, uses storytelling to introduce them to art; Artful Conversations (ages 8 to 11) focuses on one work of art. Check the website for all workshops and schedules.

🕐 **Allow** 1 hour

♿ **Wheelchair access** Yes

☕ **Cafés** Garden Café (*see p79*) and Cascade Café (*see p79*)

🛍 **Shops** The museum shop sells art reproductions, special exhibition items, jewelry, and gifts. The concourse shops have books, games, puzzles, and toys, and there is also a large bookstore with museum catalogs and art books.

👫 **Restrooms** On every floor

### Good family value?
The museum has some great artworks, plus quality shops and restaurants, which makes it a memorable family experience.

# National Gallery of Art continued...

## Key Features – 13th–19th-Century Painting and Sculpture

Main Floor

Entrance

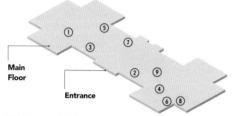

⑤ *Ginevra de' Benci* (1474–8) This is the only portrait by da Vinci that exists in the US. It is mounted in such a way that the secret message the artist painted on the back of the artwork can be read.

⑥ *Robert Gould Shaw and the Massachusetts Fifty-fourth Regiment* (1883–93) This magnificent relief sculpture by Augustus Saint-Gaudens pays tribute to the first African-American regiment to fight in the Civil War. Robert Shaw and 281 men of the regiment died in an assault on Fort Wagner in Charleston.

① *Daniel in the Lions' Den* (1614–16) Kids will delight in Peter Paul Rubens' vibrant and powerful rendition of the classic Bible story. In it, Daniel has been hurled into a den full of hungry lions, but is saved by Providence.

⑦ *Enthroned Madonna and Child* (13th century) Spend some time with the Byzantine *Enthroned Madonna and Child*, and note Mary's elaborate throne. In the 13th and 14th centuries, religious themes were the primary subjects for artists.

② *Rotterdam Ferry-Boat* (1833) Enjoy the beauty and drama of this painting by the British artist J.M.W. Turner. He was known for his dramatic portrayal of ships at sea, English landscapes, and scenes of the city of Venice.

③ *Girl with the Red Hat* (1665–6) Sense the intimacy, warmth, and expectancy in the eyes of the girl as she looks at the viewer. This small painting by Dutch painter Johannes Vermeer was one of his most beloved.

④ *The Voyage of Life: Youth* (1842) A favorite with kids, this colorful painting is one of four fantasy works by American painter Thomas Cole, each depicting childhood, youth, adulthood, and old age.

Prices given are for a family of four

⑧ *Wapping* (1860–64) This unusual painting by famed American artist James McNeill Whistler contrasts a somber meeting of three people at an inn with the lively river traffic of London's docklands behind them.

⑨ *Green River Cliffs, Wyoming* (1881) Admire this stunning painting by landscape artist Thomas Moran. His paintings of western landscapes like Yellowstone and the Grand Canyon helped create momentum for early conservation efforts in the US.

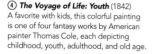
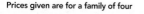

## Letting off steam

Head to the **National Sculpture Garden** (see pp80–81) to enjoy fresh air and art. Seventeen major outdoor sculptures dot this beautiful park-like space, some decidedly kid-oriented, like the whimsical and very large Typewriter Eraser, Scale X. A large fountain forms the centerpiece of the garden and the elegant Art Nouveau Pavilion Café is a good place to grab a bite to eat.

## Eat and drink

Picnic: under $30; Snacks: $30–40; Real meal: $40–75; Family treat: over $75 (based on a family of four)

**PICNIC Bruegger's Bagels Baked Fresh** (505 9th St NW, 20004; 202 393 1663; www.brueggers.com) serves bagels, muffins, sandwiches, and salads. Kids can have grilled cheese or peanut butter and jelly sandwiches. Take food from here and head to the National Mall, a great place to have a picnic.

Cascade Café in the National Gallery of Art East Building

**SNACKS Cascade Café** (concourse level, National Gallery of Art East Building, see p80) offers delicious gelato, sorbet, pastries, hot dogs, and burgers, all at reasonable prices. **REAL MEAL Carmine's** (425 7th St NW, 20004; 202 737 7770; www. carminesnyc.com) is a spacious restaurant serving Italian American entrées such as spaghetti and meatballs, lasagna, and chicken parmigiana, as well as chicken wings, salads, and desserts. The portions are very generous (see p147). **FAMILY TREAT Garden Café** (lower level, National Gallery of Art West Building) is a serene sit-down restaurant with a seasonally changing menu. The buffet and à la carte menu are related to the museum's special exhibits.

## Find out more

**DIGITAL** Make interactive art in The Art Zone, use Brushster to create abstract art, explore all the rooms in a Dutch house, and play with many cool art tools at www.nga.gov/content/ngaweb/education/kids.html. **FILM** The Film Program for Children and Teens offers free innovative programming to further visitors' understanding of the gallery's collections. Visit www.nga.gov/content/ngaweb/education/families/film.html for details. Mystery of Picasso (1956) shows Pablo Picasso through a transparent canvas as he creates 20 works of art. The artworks were destroyed after filming, leading the French government to declare the film itself a national treasure. Girl With a Pearl Earring (2003), based on the novel by Tracy Chevalier, imagines the life of a 17th-century servant girl in the household of painter Johannes Vermeer. Mr Turner (2014) explores the last 25 years of eccentric British painter J.M.W. Turner.

## Next stop...

**NATIONAL MUSEUM OF AMERICAN HISTORY** Check out the National Museum of American History (see pp70–71), which has a wondrous and offbeat collection of items that offer an insightful look at American culture. Items on display include a giant steam locomotive, an actual section of Route 66, and Abraham Lincoln's top hat.

Model of a ship at the National Museum of American History

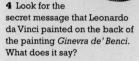
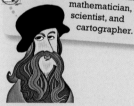

*Walkway through Leo Villareal's* Multiverse *at the National Gallery of Art*

## ⑯ National Gallery of Art East Building

**An art and crafts session**

The East Building of the National Gallery of Art, dedicated to the best modern art from around the world, is a masterpiece in itself. Designed by renowned architect I.M. Pei, the building's two interconnected triangles and open spaces create an expansive feel. Kids are enthralled by the fun and colorful contemporary art on display here. Older kids may enjoy the mobile sculpture (1977), designed by Alexander Calder. Suspended in the atrium, its black and red metal shapes are in constant motion, powered only by the faintest air currents. On the north side is Andy Goldsworthy's *Roof* (2004–2005), which consists of nine stacked-slate hollow domes, each about 5.5 ft (1.7 m) high and 27 ft (8.3 m) in diameter. It is inspired by the origin of Washington's building stones.

In the underground concourse that connects the East Building with the West (see pp76–9), children can

*The statue of Columbus in front of the Union Station building*

**Prices given are for a family of four**

ride through Leo Villareal's dazzling *Multiverse* (2008), a motorized walkway that hums through a curved tunnel lit with tiny twinkling

### The Lowdown

🌐 **Map reference** 7 D3
**Address** Between 3rd St NW & 4th St NW at Constitution Ave NW, 20565; 202 737 4215; www.nga.gov

🚇 **Metro** Judiciary Square, Archives/Navy Memorial & Smithsonian. **Bus** DC Circulator Purple line to Constitution Ave NW & 7th St NW (weekends only)

🕙 **Open** 10am–5pm Mon–Sat, 11am–6pm Sun, closed Dec 25 & Jan 1

💲 **Price** Free

🚻 **Cutting the line** There is rarely a line to get in.

🚩 **Guided tours** Free tours on a variety of subjects, audio tours (including a children's version), and foreign-language tours are available; check website for details.

👫 **Age range** 4 plus

🎨 **Activities** Stories In Art, a program series for children aged 4–7, uses storytelling to introduce kids to art. Check the website for detailed information about family workshops and schedules.

⏱ **Allow** 1–2 hours

♿ **Wheelchair access** Yes

☕ **Eat and drink** *Snacks* Espresso & Gelato Bar *(concourse level, National Gallery of Art East Building)* is an espresso bar offering ice cream, desserts, and sandwiches. *Family treat* Art and Soul *(415 New Jersey Ave NW, 20001; 202 393 7777; www. artandsouldc.com)* is a trendy hot spot serving New American Southern cuisine.

🚻 **Restrooms** On every floor

LED lights. Barring the concourse, the atrium, and the shops, the East Building is due to reopen after an extensive renovation. Check the website before planning a visit.

**Letting off steam**
No one in Washington knows where **Union Station Plaza** ends and **Lower Senate Park** *(C St NW & New Jersey Ave NW)* begins, but it makes no difference. Taken together, they offer a great place for kids to play. Across Massachusetts Avenue, just beyond the statue of Columbus, there are several acres of parkland with open lawns, wide walkways, shady spaces, and great views of the US Capitol (see pp104–105).

*Fountain in the National Sculpture Garden in front of the National Archives*

## ⑰ National Sculpture Garden

**Ice rink on a fountain**

Take a stroll, enjoy art, or dine in a Pavilion Café, a classy Art Nouveau restaurant in one of the prettiest spaces on the National Mall. With open green lawns that beg to be run across or flopped on for a rest, this is a great place for children to have fun. Colorful flower gardens, and meandering walkways wind past giant sculptures. A thin rabbit sits on a rock, borrowing a pose from the famous Auguste Rodin statue *The Thinker*. A large, creepy spider in bronze, created by Louise Joséphine Bourgeois, stands on legs tall enough for a family to have a picnic on the grass underneath. Alexander Calder's vibrant *Cheval Rouge*, or Red Horse (1974), is a favorite with children. The work is an imaginative representation of a graceful, galloping horse.

The centerpiece of the park is a huge, round fountain whose jets send streams of water up to 40 ft (12 m) in the air. From November through March, the fountain area transforms into an enormous ice rink, and is known to locals simply as "the skating rink". Music plays as laughing revelers of all ages glide (with more or less grace) in a great dance-like circle before a backdrop that includes the epic architecture of the National Archives (see pp140–41) and the National Museum of Natural History (see pp72–5).

## Take cover

If inclement weather threatens, take shelter next door at the **National Gallery of Art West Building** (see pp76–9) and explore some of the world's finest works of art.

The popular Pavilion Café in the National Sculpture Garden

## The Lowdown

- 🌐 **Map reference** 7 C3
- **Address** 7th St NW at Constitution Ave NW, 20565; 202 289 3360; www.nga.gov/content/ngaweb/exhibitions/permanent/sculpture_garden.html
- 🚗 **Metro** Judiciary Square, Archives/Navy Memorial & Smithsonian. **Bus** DC Circulator Purple line to Constitution Ave NW & 7th St NW (weekends only)
- 🕐 **Open** Sculpture Garden: 10am–5pm Mon–Sat, 11am–6pm Sun, closed Jan 1 & Dec 25. Skating rink: mid-Nov–mid-Mar: 10am–9pm Mon–Thu, 10am–11pm Fri–Sat, 11am–9pm Sun, closes at 5pm on Thanksgiving Day & Dec 24, closed Dec 25 & Jan 1
- 💲 **Price** Sculpture Garden: free; Skating rink: 2-hour sessions every hour for $26–30; skate rental $3 (ID required), locker rental $.50 ($5 deposit required)
- 🚶 **Cutting the line** In winter, ice rink limited to 200 skaters at a time; weekends and evenings are the busiest times.
- 🚩 **Guided tours** Information guides with descriptions and locations of each sculpture are available at the main 7th St NW entrance and at all art information desks.
- 👫 **Age range** 4 plus
- 🤸 **Activities** Free jazz performances at Jazz in the Garden; late May–early Sep: 5–8:30pm every Fri. Ice-skating in winter.
- ⏱ **Allow** 30 minutes–1 hour
- ♿ **Wheelchair access** Yes
- 🍴 **Eat and drink** Snacks Pavilion Café (National Sculpture Garden; www.pavilioncafe.com), the Art Nouveau-style café, sells soups, sandwiches, and pizzas. Hot chocolate offered in winter. Family treat Tosca (1112 F St NW, 20004; 202 367 1990; www.toscadc.com) serves seafood entrées and pasta.
- 🚻 **Restrooms** At Pavilion Café

The Copley Family by John Singleton Copley in the National Gallery of Art West Building

**Picnic** under $30; **Snacks** $30–40; **Real meal** $40–75; **Family treat** over $75 (based on a family of four)

# National Mall West

From the Washington Monument to the Thomas Jefferson Memorial, this end of the Mall is a tribute to America's Founding Fathers. It also has great open-air venues, such as Constitution Gardens and the nearby East Potomac Park, which offer miles of scenic paths and exceptional views. Wear comfortable shoes and be prepared to walk a lot as the attractions here are all farther apart than in Mall East. An excellent alternative is to explore the area by bicycle. It is also a good idea to take one of the step-on, step-off tours that visit all the major monuments and memorials.

**The National Mall**

Pretty flower beds in the Annual Library Garden, with the Washington Monument in the distance

## Places of interest

**SIGHTS**

1. Washington Monument
2. World War II Memorial
3. Reflecting Pool
4. Constitution Gardens
5. Vietnam Veterans Memorial
6. Korean War Veterans Memorial
7. Lincoln Memorial
8. Franklin Delano Roosevelt Memorial
9. Tidal Basin
10. Martin Luther King, Jr. Memorial
11. East Potomac Park
12. Thomas Jefferson Memorial

**EAT AND DRINK**

1. Fossil Café
2. Chef Geoff's
3. Central Michel Richard
4. Ronald Reagan Building & International Trade Center Food Court
5. Founding Farmers
6. Jaleo
7. The F Street Bistro
8. Breadline
9. The Prime Rib
10. Holocaust Museum Café
11. Cantina Marina
12. Phillips Flagship
13. Potomac Grille
14. US Department of Agriculture Cafeteria
15. Sou'Wester

See also Washington Monument (p85), World War II Memorial (p87), Reflecting Pool (p88), Lincoln Memorial (p91), Franklin Delano Roosevelt Memorial (p93), Tidal Basin (p94), East Potomac Park (p95), and Thomas Jefferson Memorial (p97)

**SHOPPING**

1. Washington Monument Lodge
2. Maine Avenue Fish Market

**WHERE TO STAY**

1. L'Enfant Plaza Hotel
2. Mandarin Oriental, Washington DC

### Map labels

WASHINGTON CIRCLE
PENNSYLVANIA AVENUE
K STREET NW
Farra
Foggy Bottom
M Foggy Bottom
STREET NW
STREET NW
H STREET NW
STREE
FOGGY BOTTOM
AVENUE NW
H STREET NW
George Washington University
STREET NW
G STREET NW
F STREET NW
STREET NW
E STREET NW
RAWLING PARK
VIRGINIA AVENUE NW
Oc
Cor Gallery
C STREET NW
National Academy of Sciences
Albert Einstein Memorial
Federal Reserve Building
Daughters of the American Revolution Museum
CONSTITU
23RD STREET
HENRY BACON DR NW
5 Vietnam Veterans Memorial
4 Constitution Gardens
World Mer
Lincoln Memorial 7
Reflecting Pool 3
WEST POTOMAC PARK
DANIEL FRENCH DR SW
6 Korean War Veterans Memorial
INDEPENDENCE AVENUE SW
Martin Luther King, Jr. Memorial Bookstore
10 Martin Luther K Jr. Memorial
OHIO DRIVE SW
W BASIN DRIVE SW
Franklin De Roosve Memoria 8
Potomac River
George M

0 meters 500
0 yards 500

*A view of the Jefferson Memorial across the cherry tree-lined Tidal Basin*

## The Lowdown

🚗 **Metro** Smithsonian & Foggy Bottom. **Bus** DC Circulator Purple line. **Trolley** Tourmobile (202 554 7950) and Old Town Trolley (888 910 8687) offer step-on, step-off sightseeing tours. **Bike** Bicycles can be rented at Union Station (202 842 2453; www.bikethe sites.com)

ℹ **Visitor information** Destination DC, 901 7th NW, 4th Floor, 20001-3719; 202 789 7000; www.washington. org. Smithsonian Information Center, 1000 Jefferson Dr SW, 20560; 202 633 1000; www. si.edu/visit

🎊 **Festivals** National Cherry Blossom Festival, Constitution Avenue NW (late Mar–early Apr); 877 442 5666; www. nationalcherryblossomfestival. org. Independence Day, Constitution Avenue (Jul 4); 202 789 7000; www. washington.org.

➕ **Pharmacies** CVS Pharmacy, 433 L'Enfant Plaza Center SW, 20024; 202 554 5270; 7am–7pm Mon–Fri, 9am–3pm Sat. CVS Pharmacy, 2000 Pennsylvania Ave NW, 20006; 202 296 0329; 7–12am Mon–Fri, 8am–midnight Sat & Sun

*The Social Programs artwork depicting FDR's New Deal programs, Franklin Delano Roosevelt Memorial*

# ① Washington Monument
## An obelisk in the US capital

This imposing spire, at a height of 555 ft (169 m), is the tallest freestanding stone obelisk in the world and the most prominent building in the US capital. Officially opened to the public in 1888, the monument is a fitting tribute to George Washington, a revolutionary leader and the first president of the US. A 2011 earthquake damaged the monument, forcing its closure for lengthy renovation works. It was reopened to the public in 2014.

Washington Monument towering above the cherry tree-lined Tidal Basin

## The Lowdown

🌐 **Map reference** 6 H3
**Address** 15th St near Constitution Ave NW, 20007; 202 426 6841; www.nps.gov/wamo

🚗 **Metro** Smithsonian. **Bus** DC Circulator Purple line to Constitution Ave NW & 17th St NW

🕐 **Open** 9am–5pm daily, to 10pm Memorial Day–Labor Day

💲 **Price** Free same-day tickets on a first-come first-served basis; advance tickets $8–10

👫 **Cutting the line** In spring and summer, lines for free tickets form at 7am. For advance tickets, visit www.recreation.gov or call 877 444 6777.

👫 **Age range** 4 plus

👫 **Activities** Ask any ranger for a Junior Ranger activity booklet or download one at www.nps.gov/wamo/forkids and solve fun puzzles to find out more about the monument.

⏱ **Allow** 30 minutes or 1 hour if taking a tour to the top of the monument

♿ **Wheelchair access** Yes

☕ **Café** Food carts along the National Mall (see p85)

🛍 **Shop** In the Washington Monument Lodge (see p85)

🚻 **Restrooms** In the Washington Monument Lodge

**Good family value?**
The free entry to this famous landmark and space for kite flying make it very good value for the family.

## Key Features

**Flagpoles** Forming a circle around the monument's plaza are 50 flagpoles flying the national flag, one for each US state.

**Viewing windows** Enjoy splendid views of the city from the observation level near the top of the monument.

**Elevator** Zip 500 ft (152 m) up to the viewing platform in 70 seconds. Some commemorative stones are visible through the elevator's window during the descent.

**Commemorative stones** These 193 stones were donated by organizations, civic groups, US states, and nations.

**Two-tone stonework** Marble from a different quarry was used when construction resumed in 1880 after having stopped in 1856 when funds ran low.

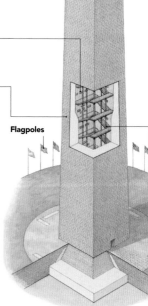

**Flagpoles**

**Obelisk** The monument's shape, designed by architect Robert Mills, is modeled on ancient Egyptian obelisks.

**Stairwell** Eight hundred and ninety-six steps pass by the commemorative stones that are set into the interior walls.

## Letting off steam

Kids can try their hand at kiteflying in the area around the monument. On breezy days, the sky is filled with colorful kites of all sizes and shapes, available at many of the food vendors and the nearby Smithsonian gift shops. Every March, the National Cherry Blossom Kite Festival holds a kiteflying competition.

*Flying kites in the grounds of the Washington Monument*

## Eat and drink

*Picnic: under $30; Snacks: $30–40; Real meal: $40–75; Family treat: over $75 (based on a family of four)*

**SNACKS** From street vendors selling hot dogs and burgers to green carts serving selections from local restaurants, there is a wide range of good snack options along the Mall.
**REAL MEAL Fossil Café** *(National Museum of Natural History, see pp72–5)* offers sandwiches, salads, fruit, coffee, beer, and soft drinks.
**Chef Geoff's** *(1301 Pennsylvania Ave NW, 20004; 202 464 4461; www.chefgeoff.com)* is a great all-American bistro with simple, well-prepared food such as steak frites, shrimp and grits, burgers, and seared scallops. The menu includes gluten-free offerings as well.
**FAMILY TREAT Central Michel Richard** *(1001 Pennsylvania Ave NW, 20004; 202 626 0015; www.centralmichelrichard.com; closed Sun)*, a fun and casual bistro, offers Franco-American cuisine, cocktails, and champagne.

*The fountain at the Memorial Plaza, World War II Memorial*

## Shopping

The Washington Monument Lodge, located at the base of the monument along 15th Street, has a smattering of monument-related gifts, books and other educational materials. For more shopping, head to the Smithsonian Institution shops along the National Mall.

## Find out more

**DIGITAL** Learn about George Washington while solving a mystery at *www.georgewashington.si.edu/kids/portrait.html*. At *www.socialstudiesforkids.com/subjects/georgewashington.htm*, discover his role in the American Revolutionary War (1775–83) and as the first president of the US. Visit *www.apples4theteacher.com/holidays/presidents-day/george-washington* for activities and interactive games.
**FILM** *The Crossing* (2000), on DVD, tells the story of General George Washington in the early days of the American Revolutionary War.

*An antique train on display in the National Museum of American History*

## Take cover

Visit the nearby **National Museum of American History** *(see pp70–71)* and see the Star-Spangled Banner exhibit, which displays the flag that inspired the US national anthem. The exhibits and activities here will appeal to every member of the family.

## Next stop...

**WORLD WAR II MEMORIAL** Head west to the World War II Memorial *(see pp86–7)* and contemplate the heroic efforts of more than 16 million Americans who served in the armed forces during the war – over 400,000 of whom died – and countless others who supported the war effort.

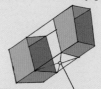

# ② World War II Memorial
## Parents and kids reflect, veterans remember

The words "Here we mark the price of freedom" are engraved in stone in front of the memorial's Freedom Wall to honor the service and sacrifice of the more than 400,000 US military personnel who died in World War II, the 16 million Americans who served in the armed forces, and the countless more who supported the war effort from home. The two arched pavilions at the north and south ends of the plaza celebrate the victory that was achieved in the Atlantic and Pacific theaters. The memorial is bright and open, with the feeling of an old-world plaza.

State pillar at the memorial

## Key Features

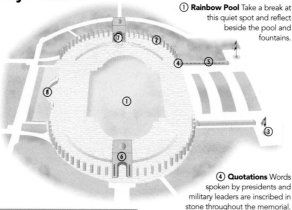

① **Rainbow Pool** Take a break at this quiet spot and reflect beside the pool and fountains.

② **Granite pillars** The 56 pillars represent the 48 states of America in 1945, the District of Columbia, and the territories of Alaska, Hawaii, the Philippines, Puerto Rico, Guam, American Samoa, and the US Virgin Islands.

③ **Military service seals** The bases of the granite and bronze flagpoles feature seals from all of the nation's military forces.

④ **Quotations** Words spoken by presidents and military leaders are inscribed in stone throughout the memorial.

⑤ **12 bronze bas-reliefs** Each side of the memorial's ceremonial entrance on 17th St displays scenes of America at war.

⑥ **Pavilions** The two 43-ft (13-m)-high pavilions commemorate the heroic efforts of military personnel on both the Atlantic and Pacific war fronts who helped achieve the Allied victory.

⑦ **World War II victory medals** Used to commemorate military service during World War II, these oversized medals are set into the floor of the pavilions.

⑧ **Freedom Wall** Mounted on the wall are 4,048 gold stars. Each star represents 100 military personnel who died in the war.

## The Lowdown

**Map reference** 6 G3
**Address** 17th St NW, 20037; 202 426 6841; www.nps.gov/nwwm

**Metro** Smithsonian. **Bus** DC Circulator Purple line to Constitution Ave NW & 17th St NW

**Open** Daily; rangers available 9am–11:30pm; last tour at 10pm

**Price** Free

**Guided tours** Scheduled programs are presented on the hour 10am–10pm daily.

**Age range** 8 plus

**Activities** Ranger-led tours hourly, from 10am–11pm daily. Ask a park ranger for the Junior Ranger activity booklet or download one at www.nps.gov/nwwm/forkids for fun activities that help children discover more about the memorial.

**Allow** 1 hour

**Café** No, but street vendors nearby

**Restrooms** Southwest of the memorial

**Good family value?**
Admission is free, and the fountain is a great place for children to relax while adults and older kids explore the memorial.

*Taking a photograph at the Reflecting Pool*

## Letting off steam

The **Reflecting Pool** (see p88) stretches over 2,000 ft (610 m) between the World War II Memorial and Lincoln Memorial (see pp90–91). Walk on the outer path that wends its way through tree-lined borders and enjoy great views of the memorials and the Washington Monument (see pp84–5). There are plenty of grassy areas perfect for picnics, as well as shady benches where parents can rest while kids explore the open expanses along the pool's edge.

## Eat and Drink

*Picnic: under $30; Snacks: $30–40; Real meal: $40–75; Family treat: over $75 (based on a family of four)*

**PICNIC** Ronald Reagan Building & International Trade Center Food Court (1300 Pennsylvania Ave NW, 20004; 202 312 1300; www.itcdc. com) offers hamburgers, wraps, and sandwiches that can be enjoyed in the grounds around the Reflecting Pool. There are plenty of street vendors around as well.

**SNACKS** The National Park Service Refreshment Stand (northwest of the World War II Memorial) serves chicken fingers, hot dogs, and cold drinks.

**REAL MEAL** Founding Farmers (IMF Building, 1924 Pennsylvania Ave NW, 20006; 202 822 8783; www.wearefoundingfarmers.com) offers American comfort food with a Southern twist in a modern, casual setting. Fresh seafood, steak, chicken, and sandwiches are on offer here, along with wine and cocktails.

**FAMILY TREAT** Jaleo (480 7th St NW, 20004; 202 628 7949; www. jaleo.com) dishes up a delectable range of Spanish tapas, along with meat and seafood offerings such as calamari, scallops, Iberian ham, and sausage.

## Find out more

**DIGITAL** Visit www.teacher. scholastic.com/activities/wwii/index. htm for World War II stories. Personal accounts of American war veterans can also be found at www. loc.gov/vets as part of the Veterans History Project. There is a short description of the memorial for kids at http://bensguide.gpo.gov/3-5/symbols/ww2memorial.html.

**FILM** Empire of the Sun (1987) depicts the horrors of war and how a 12-year-old boy overcomes the hardships of a prison camp. The Book Thief (2007) is about a young girl whose foster parents shelter a Jewish refugee.

## Take cover

Walk north along 17th Street NW, across Constitution Avenue, to the **Corcoran Gallery of Art** (see p126). The art displayed here ranges from historic American to contemporary, with additional galleries devoted to the decorative arts, European art, and photography.

*The Beaux-Arts style Corcoran Gallery of Art building*

## Next stop...

**LINCOLN MEMORIAL** Stroll west along the path beside the Reflecting Pool to the Lincoln Memorial. Look for the words from the "Gettysburg Address" that have been inscribed on the walls. The statue of Lincoln was designed by Daniel French and took four years to complete.

# ③ Reflecting Pool

## Trees, serenity, and an amazing view

The largest of the many reflecting pools in Washington, DC stretches over 2,000 ft (610 m) from the base of the Lincoln Memorial (see pp90–91) to the World War II Memorial (see pp86–7). True to its name, it offers splendid reflections of both the Washington Monument (see pp84–5) and the Lincoln Memorial. The pool is ringed with broad lawns and tree-shaded benches that are open invitations for families looking for a place to picnic or just relax on a sunny day. It is also lined with pathways that are popular places to jog and cycle.

Historic events drawing huge crowds have taken place in the open spaces around the pool. In August 1963, people gathered here to hear Martin Luther King, Jr. give his "I Have a Dream" speech during a civil rights rally. It was also here, in January 2009, that an estimated 400,000 people assembled for the Barack Obama pre-inaugural celebration.

## Take cover

Head to the **Lincoln Memorial** that gives an overview of Lincoln's life and presidency, and the sheltered porticos offer panoramic city views.

### The Lowdown

- 🌐 **Map reference** 6 G3
  **Address** Between Lincoln Memorial & World War II Memorial
- 🚗 **Metro** Smithsonian & Foggy Bottom
- 🕐 **Open** 24 hours daily
- 💲 **Price** Free
- 👪 **Age range** All ages
- 🤸 **Activities** Children can play beside the shallow pool.
- ⏱ **Allow** 15 minutes–1 hour
- ♿ **Wheelchair access** Yes
- 🍽 **Eat and drink** Picnic Take food from the nearby street vendors or the National Park Service Refreshment Stand (north and south sides of the Lincoln Memorial) and have it beside the pool. Snacks The Ronald Reagan Building & International Trade Center Food Court (1300 Pennsylvania Ave NW, 20004; 202 312 1300; www.itcdc.com) has a selection of snacks.
- 🚻 **Restrooms** No, but nearby in the Lincoln Memorial

The Lincoln Memorial mirrored in the Reflecting Pool

# ④ Constitution Gardens

## Ponds, pathways, and patriots

The best place on the Mall for walking, biking, or picnicking, this gently rolling woodland was set aside as a living tribute to the United States Constitution and its framers (see pp42–3). The 52-acre (21-ha) park area features meandering paths and a lake where ducks, fish, and turtles swim about. Walk across the footbridge, near the north end of the lake, to reach the memorial island, where a semicircle of granite blocks record the names of the 56 brave men who signed the Declaration of Independence.

## Take cover

Visit the **Daughters of the American Revolution Museum** (see p125) and tour the 31 rooms decorated with period furniture. Children can play with antique toys in the tucked-under-the-eaves New Hampshire Room.

The artificial lake and winding paths in Constitution Gardens

### The Lowdown

- 🌐 **Map reference** 6 G3
  **Address** South of Constitution Ave NW, and between Vietnam Veterans Memorial & World War II Memorial; www.nps.gov/coga
- 🚗 **Metro** Smithsonian & Foggy Bottom. **Bus** DC Circulator Purple line to Constitution Ave NW & 17th St NW
- 🕐 **Open** 24 hours daily
- 💲 **Price** Free
- 👪 **Age range** All ages
- 🤸 **Activities** Look for ducks, fish, and turtles in the lake.
- ⏱ **Allow** 15 minutes–1 hour
- ♿ **Wheelchair access** Yes
- 🍽 **Eat and drink** Picnic National Park Service Refreshment Stand (see Reflecting Pool). Snacks The Ronald Reagan Building & International Trade Center Food Court (see Reflecting Pool)
- 🚻 **Restrooms** No, but nearby in the Lincoln Memorial and SW of the World War II Memorial

# ⑤ Vietnam Veterans Memorial

## The human cost of war

Deceptively simple and remarkably moving, the memorial designed by 21-year-old Maya Ying Lin is inscribed with the names of more than 58,000 Americans who died or remained unaccounted for in the Vietnam War (1955–75). Symbolizing a wound in the Earth, the memorial comprises two long, polished black granite walls that start a few inches high and get taller as they descend into the ground, forming a broad V. The names, which start with the first listed casualty in 1959, each have a symbol designating status next to them; a diamond indicates

## The Lowdown

- 🌐 **Map reference** 6 F3
  **Address** 21st St NW & Constitution Ave NW, 20037; 202 426 6841; www.nps.gov/vive
- 🚇 **Metro** Smithsonian
- 🕐 **Open** 24 hours daily; rangers available 9:30am–11:30pm
- 💲 **Price** Free
- **Guided tours** Ranger-led free tours hourly, from 10am to 11pm
- **Age range** 10 plus
- **Activities** Look up the name of a war veteran at the kiosk and then try to locate it on the wall.
- ⏱ **Allow** 1 hour
- ♿ **Wheelchair access** Yes
- ☕ **Eat and drink** *Picnic* National Park Service Refreshment Stand (see Reflecting Pool). *Snacks* The Ronald Reagan Building & International Trade Center Food Court (see Reflecting Pool)
- 🚻 **Restrooms** No, but nearby in the Lincoln Memorial

killed or presumed deceased and a cross means unaccounted for. Around the memorial are flowers, letters, and personal objects left by visitors.

## Take cover

Visit the **Lincoln Memorial** (see pp90–91) to learn more about Abraham Lincoln's life.

## ⑥ Korean War Veterans Memorial

### Remembering a forgotten war

In the center of this memorial are 19 larger-than-life sculptures of

*Granite wall with names of soldiers who died in the war, Vietnam Veterans Memorial*

soldiers on patrol in some unknown Korean battlefield, dressed in full combat gear and moving through a field toward the American flag. The expressions on the soldiers' faces capture the essence of war in an unfamiliar country, in rugged terrain, and under difficult weather conditions. A black granite wall displays photographic images, sandblasted into the wall, of 2,400 members of the armed forces. An inscription above the Pool of Remembrance honors those who served in the three-year war (June 25, 1950–July 27, 1953).

### Take cover

Visit the nearby **Lincoln Memorial** (see pp90–91) to take shelter from inclement weather and learn about the legacy of the 16th US president.

## The Lowdown

- 🌐 **Map reference** 6 F4
  **Address** 21st St NW & Constitution Ave NW, 20037; 202 426 6841; www.nps.gov/kowa
- 🚇 **Metro** Smithsonian & Foggy Bottom
- 🕐 **Open** 24 hours daily; rangers available 9:30am–11:30pm
- 💲 **Price** Free
- **Guided tours** Ranger-led free tours hourly, from 10am to 11pm
- **Age range** All ages
- ⏱ **Allow** 15 minutes–1 hour
- ♿ **Wheelchair access** Yes
- ☕ **Eat and drink** *Picnic* National Park Service Refreshment Stand (see Reflecting Pool). *Real meal* The F Street Bistro (2117 E St NW, 20037; 202 861 8200; www.stateplaza.com/dining) offers American-fusion cuisine.
- 🚻 **Restrooms** No, but nearby in the Lincoln Memorial

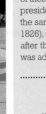

# ⑦ Lincoln Memorial
## Symbol of freedom, equality, and democracy

This memorial celebrates Abraham Lincoln (1809–65), who guided the divided nation through the Civil War, and was the architect of the Emancipation Proclamation which freed many slaves. The memorial's simple, yet beautiful style borrows from the temples of ancient Greece and Rome. It has been the site of important public gatherings such as the civil rights march in 1963 where Martin Luther King, Jr. gave his famous "I Have a Dream" speech.

*The grounds in front of the Lincoln Memorial*

## Key Highlights

■ **First Floor** The Speeches, The Murals, The Statue

■ **Lower Level** Exhibit area

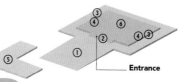

Entrance

## The Lowdown

🌐 **Map reference** 6 F3
**Address** 23rd St NW, between French Dr SW & Bacon Dr NW, 20037; 202 426 6841; www.nps.gov/linc

🚇 **Metro** Foggy Bottom.
**Bus** DC Circulator Purple line to Constitution Ave NW & 17th St NW

🕐 **Open** 24 hours daily; staffed 9:30am–11:30pm

💲 **Price** Free

🪧 **Guided tours** Scheduled programs are presented daily, on the hour, usually from 10am–11pm, or call 202 747 3420 to listen to interpretive programs on the memorial.

👫 **Age range** 4 plus

👫 **Activities** Read the "Gettysburg Address" aloud. Ask a ranger for the Junior Ranger activity booklet or download one at www.nps.gov/linc/forkids to discover more about the memorial.

⏱ **Allow** 1 hour

♿ **Wheelchair access** Yes

☕ **Café** No, but there are National Park Service Refreshment Stands at the north and south sides of the memorial (see p91).

👫 **Restrooms** In the Exhibit Area

### Good family value?
One of the most moving memorials in Washington, the Lincoln Memorial is free to visit.

① **Steps** Many famous speeches have been given from the top of the steps, including the "I Have a Dream" speech by Martin Luther King, Jr. on August 28, 1963.

② **State names** The names of the 36 states of the Union at the time of Lincoln's death are inscribed above the columns, along with the date when they entered the Union. Above it, the attic frieze is inscribed with the names of the 48 Union states at the time of the memorial's dedication on May 30, 1922.

③ **Murals** Painted by Jules Guérin, these illustrate the principles important to Lincoln. *Unification*, which represents Fraternity, Unity, and Charity, is on the north wall and *Emancipation*, which represents Freedom, Immortality, Justice, Law, and Liberty, is on the south wall.

④ **Speeches** Two of Lincoln's best-known speeches are carved on the inner walls of the memorial: the "Gettysburg Address" and the "Second Inaugural Address."

⑤ **Exhibit Area** Thought up by school kids, who helped fund it by collecting pennies, this area has panels with information on Lincoln's life, and stone tablets etched with famous words by the former president.

⑥ **Lincoln statue** Sculptor Daniel Chester French carved this 19-ft (5-m)-high statue of the seated President Lincoln from 28 pieces of Georgian marble.

## Letting off steam

Walk to the grove of elm and holly trees at the southwest corner of the National Academy of Sciences (*2101 Constitution Ave NW*), which is home to the **Albert Einstein Memorial**. Kids of all ages enjoy sitting with the larger-than-life Einstein statue as he seemingly studies a paper with three of his famous mathematical equations written on it.

*The huge bronze statue of Einstein at the Albert Einstein Memorial*

## Eat and drink

*Picnic: under $30; Snacks: $30–40; Real meal: $40–75; Family treat: over $75 (based on a family of four)*

**PICNIC Ronald Reagan Building & International Trade Center Food Court** (*1300 Pennsylvania Ave NW, 20004; 202 312 1300; www.itcdc. com*) offers fries, burgers, salads, wraps, sandwiches, and pizzas that can be enjoyed on the Mall lawns.

*One of the many cafés on the National Mall*

**SNACKS National Park Service Refreshment Stands** (*north and south of the Lincoln Memorial*) offers outdoor seating and a selection of fast food, including hot dogs, burgers, and cold drinks.
**REAL MEAL Breadline** (*1751 Pennsylvania Ave NW, 20006; 202 822 8900; www.breadline.com*), a popular breakfast and lunch place, serves made-from-scratch fresh bread, creative sandwiches,

irresistible salads, and home-made soups. The daily menu offers specials from around the globe.
**FAMILY TREAT The Prime Rib** (*2020 K St NW, 20006; 202 466 8811; www.theprimerib.com; dress code*) evokes the posh supper clubs of 1940s Manhattan, with elegant black leather chairs and live piano music. The restaurant offers steaks and seafood along with a good wine list; specialties include roasted prime rib and crab cakes.

## Find out more

**DIGITAL** For interesting information about the 16th president, check out *www.socialstudiesforkids.com/ subjects/abrahamlincoln.htm* or *www.2020site.org/fun-facts/Fun-Facts-About-Abraham-Lincoln.html.* Go to *http://video.national geographic.com/video/kids/history-kids/abraham-lincoln-kids* for a video on Abraham Lincoln's life.
**FILM** The comedy-drama *Forrest Gump* (1994) has a scene filmed at the Lincoln Memorial, where Forrest Gump gives a speech from the base of the steps while war protestors are gathered around the Reflecting Pool (*see p88*). For more on Abraham Lincoln, watch movies such as *Young Mr. Lincoln* (1939), *Abe Lincoln in Illinois* (1940), and *Lincoln* (2012).

## Next stop...

**VIETNAM VETERANS MEMORIAL** Walk a short distance northeast of the Reflecting Pool to one of the most visited sites in Washington, DC: the Vietnam Veterans Memorial (*see pp88–9*). The two black granite walls are inscribed with the names of more than 58,000 American men and women who died in the war.

*The black granite wall in the Vietnam Veterans Memorial*

*see p88*

*see pp88–9*

## KIDS' CORNER

### Look out for...
**1** Count the number of columns in the Lincoln Memorial. Why are there that many?
**2** Can you spot the place from where Martin Luther King, Jr. gave his famous "I Have a Dream" speech on August 28, 1963?
**3** Look closely at the statue of Lincoln. What is he sitting against?

Answers at the bottom of the page.

### PRESIDENTIAL FACTS
At 6'4" (1.9 m), Lincoln was the tallest president to date. He was famous for wearing tall stovepipe hats. He liked them because he could store letters and other small items in them.

**Abe of many trades**
Abraham Lincoln liked to tinker and was also an amateur inventor. In 1849, he received a patent for a device to lift boats over shoals.

### "Gettysburg Address"
One of the best-known speeches in US history, the "Gettysburg Address" was delivered by Abraham Lincoln during the Civil War on November 19, 1863. This two-minute speech includes Lincoln's famous words describing democracy as the "government of the people, by the people, for the people."

**Answers: 1** 36, one for each state in the United States at the time of Lincoln's death, plus two more beside the entrance behind the colonnade for a total of 38. **2** The spot is marked 18 steps down from Lincoln's statue. **3** He is sitting against the American flag, symbolizing eternal protection of the United States.

# ⑧ Franklin Delano Roosevelt Memorial

## Evocative sculptures and the famous "First Dog"

Built on land reclaimed from the Potomac River, this memorial is dedicated to Franklin Delano Roosevelt (FDR), the 32nd US president and visionary leader of America during the dark days of the Great Depression and World War II. A place for kids to learn and explore, with plenty of greenery and ample space, this mammoth, open, and inviting site has four plaza-like outdoor "rooms," one for each of Roosevelt's terms in office. The rooms are filled with tumbling waterfalls, sculptures, and other artworks, as well as some of FDR's most famous quotes etched into the stone of the walls.

## Key Features

**The Breadline** (1991) The hard times of the Great Depression are depicted in this moving sculpture by George Segal.

**Contact station** This includes an information area and a bookstore. A reproduction of the wheelchair that FDR used after he contracted polio is displayed here.

**Statue of Eleanor Roosevelt** This Neil Estern sculpture honors Eleanor Roosevelt's role as first lady and her later work as a delegate to the United Nations.

**Waterfalls**

**Statue of Eleanor Roosevelt**

**Sculpture of Roosevelt**

**The Fireside Chat** (1991) This sculpture by George Segal portrays a man listening to one of FDR's radio speeches.

**Social Programs** (1996) This artwork illustrates FDR's New Deal programs, aimed at ending the Great Depression and improving the quality of life in America.

**Waterfalls** Cascading into a series of pools, the five waterfalls symbolize the different events that took place during Roosevelt's presidency.

**Sculpture of Roosevelt** This statue of FDR with his Scottish Terrier Fala is a favorite with kids. FDR's wheelchair is hidden under his cape, as the president took care never to be seen with it while he was in office.

## The Lowdown

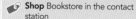
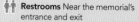

**Map reference** 6 G5
**Address** West Basin Dr SW, 20024; 202 426 6841; www.nps.gov/frde

**Metro** Smithsonian and Foggy Bottom. **Bus** DC Circulator Purple line to Independence Ave SW & 14th St SW

**Open** 24 hours daily; rangers available from 9:30am–11:30pm

**Price** Free

**Guided tours** Ranger-led free tours hourly, from 10am to 11pm

**Age range** 4 plus

**Activities** Ask any ranger for the Junior Ranger activity booklet or download one at www.nps.gov/frde/forkids.

**Allow** 30 minutes

**Café** No, but there is a National Park Service Refreshment Stand close by (see p93).

**Shop** Bookstore in the contact station

**Restrooms** Near the memorial's entrance and exit

### Good family value?
The bright, open spaces make this a great place for children to burn off some energy. Young children enjoy petting the statue of Fala.

Cherry trees in bloom along the Tidal Basin

## Letting off steam

One of the prettiest walks in the city, and a great place for kids to run free, the broad paved path that encircles the **Tidal Basin** *(see p94)* is lined with cherry trees. To the north side of the basin's parking lot is the lovely Annual Library Garden, where gardens planted with beautiful annual flowers offer a colorful respite from the bustle of Washington, DC.

## Eat and drink

*Picnic: under $30; Snacks: $30–40; Real meal: $40–75; Family treat: over $75 (based on a family of four)*

**PICNIC Ronald Reagan Building & International Trade Center Food Court** *(1300 Pennsylvania Ave NW, 20004; 202 312 1300; www.itcdc. com)* serves burgers, wraps, and delectable sandwiches to go.
**SNACKS The National Park Service Refreshment Stand** *(south of Thomas Jefferson Memorial)* has a large selection that includes hot dogs, fries, and cold drinks.
**Holocaust Museum Café** *(US Holocaust Memorial Museum, see pp68–9)* is a pleasant eatery that offers soups, salads, kosher meals, *knishes* (stuffed dumplings), and desserts.
**REAL MEAL Cantina Marina** *(600 Water St SW, 20024; 202 554 8396; www.cantinamarina.com)* is a

waterfront restaurant with an outdoor patio. Gulf Coast and Cajun specialties such as BBQ shrimp and fish tacos are available here.
**FAMILY TREAT Phillips Flagship** *(900 Water St SW, 20024; 202 488 8515; www.phillipsseafood.com)* is a family-friendly restaurant on the waterfront known for its all-you-can-eat seafood buffet. An à la carte menu is also available.

## Find out more

**DIGITAL** Find games and coloring sheets, and learn facts and trivia about FDR at *www.apples4the teacher.com/holidays/presidents-day/franklin-roosevelt.* Visit *www. tvakids.com/whatistva/history_whoandwhy.htm* to find out about FDR's role in creating the Tennessee Valley Authority, a New Deal project.
**FILM** The film *Sunrise at Campobello* (1960) tells the story of FDR from the time he became paralyzed until his return to politics.

## Take cover

Head to the **Freer Gallery of Art** *(see p66)*, which specializes in Asian art. Ask for the family guide and see the "Peacock Room," a blue-and-gold dining room designed by James McNeill Whistler and moved here from London in 1904.

## Next stop...
**UNITED STATES CAPITOL**
Learn how the country is run, see impressive works of art, and gaze up into the dome, high above the Rotunda, at the United States Capitol *(see pp104–105)*. All visits begin in the Capitol Visitor Center.

Asian artworks on display at the Freer Gallery of Art

*Cherry trees in full bloom lining the path around the Tidal Basin*

## ⑨ Tidal Basin

**Cherry trees and paddleboats**

Located in West Potomac Park, this 107-acre (43-ha) man-made reservoir was designed to be a visual centerpiece as well as to flush the Washington Channel – the basin handles 250 million gallons (94 million liters) of water from the Potomac River twice a day.

Much of this land was originally marshy riverfront, and had to be filled with soil and sculpted over the years. In 1912, Yukio Ozaki, the mayor of Tokyo, presented Washington, DC

with over 3,000 cherry trees, many of which were planted around the basin. Now, every spring, white and pink cherry trees bloom in profusion here. At the height of the cherry blossom season, visitors can stroll along the winding pathways and hear the plaintive sound of Japanese music. One small breeze at the right time can cause a cascade of pink and white petals to shower passersby, creating a memorable experience.

In good weather, rent a paddleboat and take a pedal-powered ride around the Tidal Basin for great views of the Thomas Jefferson Memorial (see pp96–7), Franklin Delano Roosevelt Memorial (see pp92–3), and the Martin Luther King, Jr. Memorial, all located along the shores of the basin. Or just relax on the park benches or enjoy a picnic on the grassy expanses.

### Take cover

In case of inclement weather, walk two blocks east to the oldest Smithsonian art museum, the **Freer Gallery of Art** (see p66), and admire its fine collection of Asian artworks.

### The Lowdown

- 🌐 **Map reference** 6 H4
  **Address** South of Independence Ave SW, between Washington Monument and Lincoln Memorial
- 🚇 **Metro** Smithsonian
- 🕐 **Open** 24 hours daily
- 💲 **Price** Free
- 🚻 **Age range** All ages
- 🧗 **Activities** Walking and paddleboating. Boathouse: 1501 Main Ave SW, 20024; 202 479 2426; www.tidalbasinpaddle boats.com; open mid-Mar–Oct: 10am–6pm
- ⏱ **Allow** 1–2 hours
- 🍽 **Eat and drink** *Picnic* The National Park Service Refreshment Stand (beside the Tidal Basin) offers fast food that can be enjoyed at the paddleboats dock. *Real meal* Fossil Café (National Museum of Natural History, see p75) serves salads, sandwiches, fruit, coffee, beer, and soft drinks.
- 🚻 **Restrooms** At Thomas Jefferson, Franklin Delano Roosevelt, and Martin Luther King, Jr. memorials

## ⑩ Martin Luther King, Jr. Memorial

**Peace, hope, democracy, and one really big statue**

This open, airy plaza filled with cherry trees is a great place for kids to frolic while learning about one of the great champions of civil rights. The memorial is composed of natural elements that represent major themes from Martin Luther King, Jr.'s life and speeches. The centerpiece, carved by Lei Yixin, features a sculpture of King emerging from a huge boulder. A long, curved wall is inscribed with many of his best-known quotations. The memorial's location, between the Thomas Jefferson Memorial and the Lincoln Memorial (see pp90–91), is also symbolic. Thomas Jefferson wrote the Declaration of Independence, which formed the foundation of Martin Luther King, Jr.'s civil rights work and King delivered his famous "I Have a Dream" speech from the steps of the Lincoln Memorial.

*Paddleboats and picnic area at the Tidal Basin*

### The Lowdown

- 🌐 **Map reference** 6 G4
  **Address** West Basin Drive SW, 20024; 202 426 6841; www.nps.gov/mlkm
- 🚇 **Metro** Smithsonian & Foggy Bottom. **Bus** DC Circulator Purple line to Independence Ave SW & 14th St SW
- 💲 **Price** Free
- 🕐 **Open** 24 hours daily; rangers available from 9:30am–11:30pm
- 🚩 **Guided tours** Ranger-led free tours hourly, from 10am to 11pm
- 🚻 **Age range** All ages
- ⏱ **Allow** 1 hour
- 🍽 **Eat and drink** *Picnic* The National Park Service Refreshment Stands (south of Lincoln and Thomas Jefferson memorials) offer fast food that can be enjoyed along the Tidal Basin. *Snacks* Holocaust Museum Café (see p69) offers salads, sandwiches, and desserts.
- 🛍 **Shop** Bookstore in the contact station
- 🚻 **Restrooms** In the contact station

## Take cover

If it rains, head across the street to the Martin Luther King, Jr. Memorial Bookstore. Offering the only nearby shelter, it also has a collection of books and items connected to the life and works of Martin Luther King, Jr.

## ⑪ East Potomac Park

### Waterfront walkway and a miniature golf course

This popular 300-acre (121-ha) park is within walking distance of the Thomas Jefferson Memorial. The key attraction is the riverfront walkway, which traces both the east and west sides of the park. A favorite with hikers, walkers, bikers, and skaters, the path offers ever-changing views of the water and the monuments. It is also a popular spot for fishermen to cast a line.

This park is very family-friendly, with lots of open spaces to play around in, as well as an aquatic center with a public swimming pool, tennis courts, and the oldest miniature golf course in the US. Throughout the month of April, thousands of cherry trees that thickly line the roadways burst into pink and white blooms, making it one of the city's most scenic stretches.

## Take cover

If the weather turns, head to the nearby **Thomas Jefferson Memorial** (see pp96–7). The exhibit area in the lower level has exhibits on the life and works of the third US president and principal drafter of the Declaration of Independence.

Cycling on the tree-lined path in East Potomac Park

## The Lowdown

- 🌐 **Map reference** 7 B6
  **Address** Ohio Dr SW, Hains Point, south of the Thomas Jefferson Memorial and the 14th St Bridge SW, 20024; 202 554 7660
- 🚇 **Metro** Smithsonian
- 🕐 **Open** 24 hours daily
- 💲 **Price** Free
- 🚻 **Age range** All ages
- 🏃 **Activities** Walking, jogging, golf, tennis, and swimming
- ⏱ **Allow** 1–2 hours
- ♿ **Wheelchair access** Yes
- 🍴 **Eat and drink** Snacks The National Park Service Refreshment Stand (south of the Jefferson Memorial) offers a selection of fast food. Family treat Potomac Grille (972 Ohio Dr SW, 20024; 202 554 7660; www.golfdc.com) is open for breakfast, lunch, and dinner and serves salads, sandwiches, and omelets.
- 🚻 **Restrooms** At the Potomac Grille restaurant and stations throughout the park

# KIDS' CORNER

### Things to do...

**1** Find the Japanese lantern. A gift from Japan in 1954, it was carved to commemorate a famous shogun (chief military commander) around 1650 and stood for 300 years in the grounds of the Toeizan Kan'eiji Temple. Hint: It is on the northern end of the Tidal Basin, east of the Martin Luther King, Jr. Memorial.

**2** Visit the Japanese pagoda. A gift from the mayor of Yokohama, Japan, in 1957, this pagoda is really old. It was probably carved in the 12th century. Hint: It is not too far from the Japanese lantern.

**3** Rent a paddleboat and head out on the Tidal Basin. See if you can spot the Thomas Jefferson Memorial, Franklin Delano Roosevelt Memorial, Martin Luther King, Jr. Memorial, and Washington Monument.

## FLOWERING FACTS

The Japanese lantern by the Tidal Basin is lit each year at the beginning of the Cherry Blossom Festival by a woman chosen by the Japanese embassy as the Cherry Blossom Princess.

## Freedom fact

In 1964, Martin Luther King, Jr. won the Nobel Peace Prize for his non-violent leadership of the civil rights movement.

Thomas Jefferson Memorial on the shore of the Tidal Basin

**Picnic** under $30; **Snacks** $30–40; **Real meal** $40–75; **Family treat** over $75 (based on a family of four)

# ⑫ Thomas Jefferson Memorial
## Classical memorial to a founding father

With its tall columns and gently curved dome, this memorial is regarded as one of the most beautiful sites in Washington. Thomas Jefferson loved Classical architecture, so when J.R. Pope was selected to design the memorial in 1936, he wanted to create a building that the third US president would have approved of. A flight of steps leads to the Rotunda, where Jefferson's statue is surrounded by walls engraved with his words. The view from the portico takes in the Tidal Basin, the White House, and beyond.

The facade of the Neo-Classical memorial

## Key Features

■ **Main Floor** Dome, Frieze, Columns, Statue, Quotations, Excerpt from the Declaration of Independence.

■ **Lower Level** Exhibit Area, gift shop, bookstore.

① **Dome** The circular dome is based on the Pantheon in Rome. Jefferson used a similar design at the University of Virginia and his home, Monticello (see pp204–205).

② **Frieze** Inscribed on the inner dome are Jefferson's words: "I have sworn upon the altar of God eternal hostility against every form of tyranny over the mind of man."

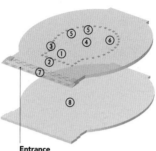

**Entrance**

③ **Circular columns** The open building features a colonnade of marble columns. The curly-topped Ionic columns support the large, shallow dome.

④ **Statue** Sculpted by Rudulph Evans, the 19-ft (6-m)-tall bronze statue of Jefferson as a senior statesman stands on top of a 6-ft (2-m)-high granite pedestal and looks out toward the White House.

⑤ **Quotations** Four panels on the interior walls display inscriptions drawn from Jefferson's writings, illustrating his thoughts about religious freedom, education, and government.

⑥ **Declaration of Independence** Some of Jefferson's famous words from the Declaration of Independence appear on the southwest interior panel.

⑦ **Stairway** A sweep of marble steps leads to the interior. The view of the White House from these steps is one of the very best.

⑧ **Exhibit Area** Located in the lower level, this area is a great place for kids and adults to learn more about Jefferson's life, his many interests and accomplishments, and his role as one of the Founding Fathers of the United States of America.

## The Lowdown

🌐 **Map reference** 6 H5
**Address** South bank of the Tidal Basin, 20037; 202 426 6841; www.nps.gov/thje

🚇 **Metro** Smithsonian.
**Bus** DC Circulator Purple line to Constitution Ave NW & 17th St NW

🕐 **Open** 24 hours daily; rangers available from 9:30am–11:30pm

💲 **Price** Free

**Guided tours** Ranger-led free tours hourly from 10am–11pm

👫 **Age range** 4 plus

**Activities** Ask any ranger for a Junior Ranger activity booklet

or download one at www.nps.gov/thje/forkids and find out more about the memorial.

⏱ **Allow** 1 hour–90 minutes

☕ **Café** No, but there is a National Park Service Refreshment Stand just south of the memorial

🛍 **Shops** Bookstore and gift shop on the lower level

🚻 **Restrooms** On the lower level

### Good family value?
Free to visit, the memorial affords one of the best views of the White House. The museum provides insights into the broad-ranging interests of the third president.

*Taking photographs at the George Mason Memorial*

## Letting off steam

The **George Mason Memorial** (*900 Ohio Dr SW, 20024*) is a pretty, circular plaza surrounded by flower gardens with a fountain in the center. Honoring a nearly forgotten Founding Father, it has a larger than life bronze statue of Mason relaxing on a bench with his walking stick and books, sculpted by Wendy M. Ross. Mason was the author of the Virginia Declaration of Rights.

## Eat and Drink

*Picnic: under $30; Snacks: $30–40; Real meal: $40–75; Family treat: over $75 (based on a family of four)*

**PICNIC** Ronald Reagan Building & International Trade Center Food Court (*1300 Pennsylvania Ave NW, 20004; 202 312 1300; www.itcdc.com*) offers order-to-go food. Take goodies from here and enjoy a picnic on the Mall grounds.
**SNACKS** The **National Park Service Refreshment Stand** (*south of the Jefferson Memorial or near the Tidal Basin paddleboat dock*) serves a selection of fast food such as hot dogs, fries, and cold drinks.
**REAL MEAL** The **US Department of Agriculture Cafeteria** (*South Building, 12th St SW & C St SW, 20250; 202 488 7279; www.usda.gov/oo/cafemenu.htm; ask for a visitor's lunch pass; closed Sat & Sun*) is open to the public and offers a large selection of food, including hot meals, soups, and sandwiches.
**FAMILY TREAT** Sou'Wester (*Mandarin Oriental, 1330 Maryland Ave SW, 20024; 202 554 8588; www.mandarinoriental.com/washington/fine-dining/sou-wester*) serves regional American cuisine.

The menu includes Southern classics such as skillet-fried chicken, sautéed red snapper, and Old Bay chowder. The restaurant has a good wine selection, as well as American draft beers and cocktails.

## Shopping

Head to the open-air **Maine Avenue Fish Market** (*1100 Maine Ave SW, 20024*), where stands sell fish and clam chowder, fried shrimp, and freshly cooked fish.

## Find out more

**DIGITAL** Learn about Jefferson's inventions at *www.socialstudiesforkids.com/subjects/thomasjefferson.htm*. Visit *www.let.rug.nl/usa/biographies/thomas-jefferson* to discover more about his life.
**FILM** Watch *Thomas Jefferson* (1996) by Ken Burns, an excellent documentary on the life of the Founding Father.

## Take cover

In case of rain, head to the **Forestry Information Center** (*see p66*), where kids are greeted by an animatronic Smokey the Bear at the entrance. Exhibits include a reproduction of a 1920s rustic pine-log lodge with Forest Service artifacts from the early 1900s. Rotating displays present topics related to the activities of the Forest Service.

## Next stop...

**FRANKLIN DELANO ROOSEVELT MEMORIAL** Walk west along the Tidal Basin to the Franklin Delano Roosevelt Memorial (*see pp92–3*). The memorial has four rooms with water features and sculptures that convey the essence of FDR's four terms in office.

*Statue of Franklin Delano Roosevelt and his dog Fala*

# Capitol Hill

With its magnificent dome, the US Capitol is a stunning building, blending superb architecture with art and history. Beyond it, the landscaped Capitol Grounds offer a shady retreat from the city's hustle and bustle. Nearby, tropical jungles festooned with orchids thrive beside cacti-filled deserts in the US Botanic Garden, and a few blocks away, the remarkable Library of Congress never ceases to impress.

A MIDSUMMER NIGHTS DREAM

Georgetown

The White House and Foggy Bottom

Penn Quarter

The National Mall

**Capitol Hill**

## Highlights

**United States Capitol**
Admire the splendid architecture and historic spaces of one of the world's best-known symbols of democracy (see pp104–105).

**US Botanic Garden**
Walk through a huge conservatory that houses plants from the world's tropical, subtropical, and desert regions. Outside, the National Garden offers acres of floral plantings, paths, and sculpted lawns (see pp106–107).

**Capitol Grounds**
Head to this lushly landscaped space, full of nooks and crannies, to escape the busy pace of Washington (see p108).

**Library of Congress**
Visit the biggest library on the planet, with millions of books and other publications, including the world's largest collection of comic books (see pp110–11).

**Eastern Market**
Check out this historic market, where vegetable vendors vie with butchers and bakers for the shoppers' attention. Don't miss the cafés, restaurants, and crafts stalls outside the market (see p113).

**Union Station**
Take in the grand architecture of a bygone age while shopping in a boutique or dining in the fine food court here (see p115).

**Left** The Capitol Grounds with cherry blossom trees in full bloom
**Above left** Bas-relief on the exterior of the Folger Shakespeare Library depicting a scene from the Bard's play, A Midsummer Night's Dream

# The Best of
# Capitol Hill

A remarkable repository of history, the US Capitol is where the day-to-day "government of, by, and for the people" takes place. Beyond this architectural gem, there is plenty to do and see here. Explore the hidden corners of the US Botanic Garden, look at the rare books in the Library of Congress, shop and dine at the stunningly restored Union Station, or just stroll along a side street to admire the gracious 19th-century row houses.

## Hidden history

Lots of historic stories are tucked in and around Capitol Hill, from Thomas Jefferson offering his own collection to restart the **Library of Congress** (see pp110–11) after a fire, to the unique acoustics of a chamber in the **United States Capitol** (see pp104–105) that may have allowed John Quincy Adams to eavesdrop on his rivals.

Some of the things to see here are older than Washington, DC itself, like the rare first folio of Shakespeare's plays at the **Folger Shakespeare Library** (see p112), while others have been around since the city's early days, like **Eastern Market** (see p113), which has been drawing shoppers since 1873, and **Union Station** (see p115), which sees commuters hurrying to catch their trains, just as it did when it was built in 1907.

## Great gardens

The **Capitol Grounds** (see p108) offer over 274 acres (110 ha) of magnificently landscaped lawns, and shady, park-like areas with winding paths and inviting benches. This is a great place to stroll, or sit and watch the world walk by, especially in spring when azaleas, tulips, cherry trees, and hundreds of other shrubs and flowers turn every walkway into an artist's palette.

The conservatory of the **US Botanic Garden** (see pp106–107) – featuring a jungle, a suspended second-floor walkway, and thematic collections ranging from Hawaii to Jurassic Park – is a kids' favorite. Just across Independence Avenue is **Bartholdi Park** (see p109), with flower gardens spreading around the marine-themed, cast-iron Bartholdi Fountain.

**Below** Outsized models of flowers on display at the US Botanic Garden

## Architectural wonders

Some of most beautiful buildings in the US can be found on Capitol Hill, including the **United States Capitol** itself. Its great Rotunda, the intricately painted Brumidi corridors, and the basement crypt, which was supposed to – but doesn't – hold George Washington's body, dazzle adults and children alike.

Other architectural delights include the stunning Italianate entrance of the **Library of Congress**, the clean lines of the splendid, Neo-Classical **US Supreme Court** (see pp112–13), and the oak-paneled, Tudor-style Great Hall of the **Folger Shakespeare Library**, whose exterior is one of the finest expressions of Art Deco in Washington.

## A perfect Capitol Hill day

Start with a delicious brunch at **Bistro Bis** (see p111) then head to the Capitol Visitor Center to get a timed ticket for the 1-hour tour of the **United States Capitol**. Afterward, step across 1st Street for a tour of the **Library of Congress**, which is as renowned for its Italianate architecture as it is for its collection of historic books and documents.

For lunch, walk north through the **Capitol Grounds** to **Union Station**, where families can choose from a wide selection of goodies in the food court. After lunch, stroll back across the Capitol Grounds to the **US Botanic Gardens**, where kids can run around in the National Garden or get their hands dirty in the Children's Garden.

# Capitol Hill

Rising from the center of Capitol Hill, the US Capitol is one of the most impressive Neo-Classical buildings in America. The Capitol Visitor Center offers information on the Capitol as well as timed tickets, though on busy days there can be quite a wait for these. Many attractions surround the Capitol, ranging from major sites such as the Library of Congress, to lesser known places like Sewall-Belmont House and Museum. This area is relatively compact, and walking is by far the easiest way to get around, though the metro, with several stops nearby, is also handy. There are plenty of restaurants in this area, around Eastern Market and particularly east of the Capitol on Pennsylvania Avenue.

**Capitol Hill**

US Capitol
*p104*

US Botanic
Garden
*p106*

Library of
Congress
*p110*

*Imposing marble fountain in front of the grand US Capitol*

## Places of interest

**SIGHTS**

1. United States Capitol
2. US Botanic Garden
3. Capitol Grounds
4. Capitol Reflecting Pool and Monuments
5. Bartholdi Park
6. Library of Congress
7. Folger Shakespeare Library
8. US Supreme Court
9. Eastern Market
10. Sewall-Belmont House and Museum
11. National Postal Museum
12. Union Station

● **EAT AND DRINK**

1. Dubliner Restaurant
2. Cava
3. Jimmy T's Place
4. Mitsitam Cafe
5. Montmartre
6. Tortilla Cafe
7. Good Stuff Eatery
8. Pete's Diner
9. Hawk 'n' Dove
10. Bistro Bis
11. We, The Pizza
12. Le Pain Quotidien
13. Talay Thai Restaurant
14. Johnny's Half Shell

*See also Capitol Grounds (p108), Library of Congress (pp110-11), US Supreme Court (p112), Eastern Market (p113), and Union Station (p115)*

● **SHOPPING**

*See United States Capitol (p104) & Library of Congress (p110)*

● **WHERE TO STAY**

1. Capitol Hill Suites
2. Hotel George
3. Hyatt Regency Washington on Capitol Hill
4. The Liaison
5. Phoenix Park Hotel
6. Washington Court Hotel

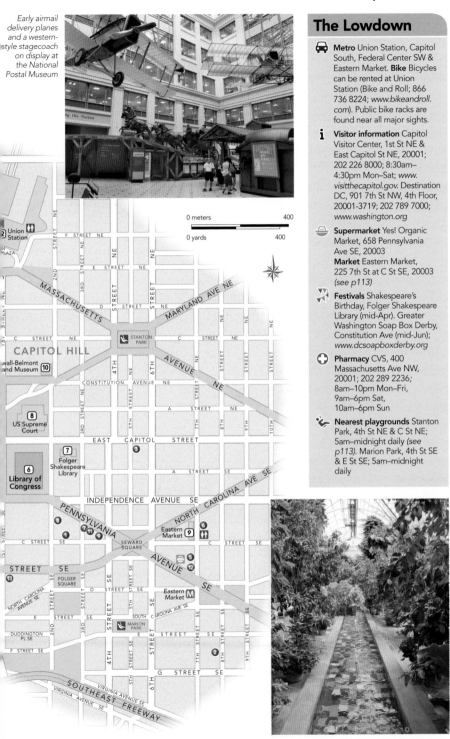

*Early airmail delivery planes and a western-style stagecoach on display at the National Postal Museum*

# The Lowdown

🚗 **Metro** Union Station, Capitol South, Federal Center SW & Eastern Market. **Bike** Bicycles can be rented at Union Station (Bike and Roll; 866 736 8224; *www.bikeandroll.com*). Public bike racks are found near all major sights.

ℹ️ **Visitor information** Capitol Visitor Center, 1st St NE & East Capitol St NE, 20001; 202 226 8000; 8:30am–4:30pm Mon–Sat; *www.visitthecapitol.gov*. Destination DC, 901 7th St NW, 4th Floor, 20001-3719; 202 789 7000; *www.washington.org*

🛒 **Supermarket** Yes! Organic Market, 658 Pennsylvania Ave SE, 20003
**Market** Eastern Market, 225 7th St at C St SE, 20003 *(see p113)*

🎌 **Festivals** Shakespeare's Birthday, Folger Shakespeare Library (mid-Apr). Greater Washington Soap Box Derby, Constitution Ave (mid-Jun); *www.dcsoapboxderby.org*

➕ **Pharmacy** CVS, 400 Massachusetts Ave NW, 20001; 202 289 2236; 8am–10pm Mon–Fri, 9am–6pm Sat, 10am–6pm Sun

🧸 **Nearest playgrounds** Stanton Park, 4th St NE & C St NE; 5am–midnight daily *(see p113)*. Marion Park, 4th St SE & E St SE; 5am–midnight daily

*Lush and serene Garden Court in the conservatory of the US Botanic Garden*

# ① United States Capitol
## Home of power, glory, and great debates

Home to the US government, the Capitol offers families the chance to explore 400 years of American history and the remarkable art and architecture that make it one of the most beautiful buildings in the US. The cornerstone for the original Capitol was laid by George Washington in 1793, and although this building was partly burnt by the British in 1814, the Capitol has undergone renovation and expansion ever since.

## Key Features

**Rotunda** The 180-ft (55-m) dome features Constantino Brumidi's fresco *The Apotheosis of Washington* (1865). Statues of former presidents and scenes from US history circle the Rotunda.

**Statue of Freedom** This female figure looks toward the east, facing people who approach the building's principal entrance.

**Dome** Originally made of wood and later covered with copper, the present cast-iron dome has windows and ornate columns.

**Crypt** This circular room with 40 Doric columns was built to display a memorial to George Washington above his planned tomb on the floor below, but he was buried in Mount Vernon instead.

**National Statuary Hall**

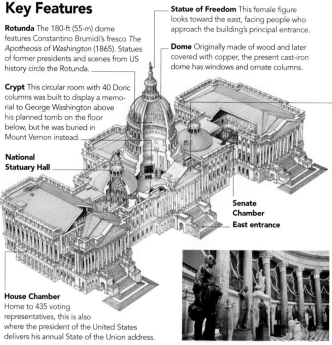

**Senate Chamber**

**East entrance**

**House Chamber** Home to 435 voting representatives, this is also where the president of the United States delivers his annual State of the Union address.

**Capitol Visitor Center** Opened in 2008, the center is set on three underground levels. Its entrance is on the Capitol's east side.

**Old Senate Chamber** Used by the Senate until 1859, the chamber has been restored to its mid-19th-century appearance.

**Senate Chamber** The desks of the 100 senators are arranged in an arc, Republicans on the left of the central aisle, and Democrats on the right.

**National Statuary Hall** Two statues from each of the 50 states in the US are displayed in this hall, once the chamber of the House of Representatives. The guides can help children spot statues from any state they choose.

## The Lowdown

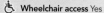

🌐 **Map reference** 8 E3
**Address** 1st St NE & East Capitol St NE, 20001; 202 226 8000; www.visitthecapitol.gov

🚗 **Metro** Capitol South. **Bus** DC Circulator Purple line to 1st St NE & Maryland Ave NE

🕐 **Open** 8:30am–4:30pm Mon–Sat, closed major holidays

💲 **Price** Free

👪 **Cutting the line** Tour arrangements can be made in advance at www.visitthecapitol.gov or by contacting the office of a representative or senator. Arrive at least 30 minutes ahead of time to go through the security check.

🏳 **Guided tours** Free 1-hour tours between 8:50am and 3:20pm for pre-arranged tour passes; for same-day passes visit the information desk.

👫 **Age range** 6 plus

👫 **Activities** Watch the Senate or House in session, enacting and passing laws. For advance gallery passes contact the office of a senator or house representative; foreign visitors can also request passes at the House and Senate appointment desk near the visitor center entrance.

⏱ **Allow** 2 hours

♿ **Wheelchair access** Yes

🍴 **Café** The Capitol Visitor Center Restaurant on the lower level serves salads, sandwiches, desserts, and beverages (see p108).

🛍 **Shops** In the visitor center

👫 **Restrooms** In the visitor center

**Good family value?**
Young children can enjoy the Capitol Visitor Center, but may become restless on the tour. Older children are often fascinated to learn about the Congress and see the grandeur of the building.

Colorful flowers and meandering paths in the National Garden, US Botanic Garden

## Letting off steam

Walk toward the southwest corner of the Capitol Grounds to the outdoor **National Garden** (see p106), which is part of the US Botanic Garden. Follow paths to explore mid-Atlantic native plants in the Regional Garden, see the US's national flower in the Rose Garden, and spot colorful butterflies in the fascinating Butterfly Garden.

## Eat and drink

Picnic: under $30; Snacks: $30–40; Real meal: $40–75; Family treat: over $75 (based on a family of four)

**PICNIC Eastern Market** (see p113) is a great place to pick up fresh fruit and vegetables, deli meats, and sweets before walking back to the Capitol for an alfresco lunch near the Bartholdi Fountain (see p109) or to Folger Park (D St SE) for a picnic on a bench by the fountain.
**SNACKS Union Station** (see p115) has a huge food court with more than two dozen choices for snacks or meals, as well as sit-down restaurants.
**REAL MEAL Dubliner Restaurant** (Number 4, F St NW, 20001; 202 737 3773; www.dublinerdc.com) is

The Capitol Visitor Center Restaurant on the center's lower level

a friendly Irish pub offering fresh salads and comfort food, including fish and chips, hearty sandwiches, burgers, and Irish stew.
**FAMILY TREAT Cava** (527 8th St SE, 20003; 202 543 9090; www.cavamezze.com) is a restaurant serving Greek mezze-style dishes – small, shareable plates of authentic yet modern food. It has a welcoming environment and a friendly vibe.

## Find out more

**DIGITAL** See www.congressforkids.net/index.htm for fun interactive learning activities about Congress. Go to http://kids.clerk.house.gov/young-learners to learn about the role of the House of Representatives and the legislative process. At www.kids.dc.gov/kids_main_content.html there are interactive games and puzzles for young children. Older children interested in history, construction, and preservation should check out the Architect of the Capitol at www.aoc.gov.
**FILM** Well-known movies about Congress include Mr. Smith Goes to Washington, a 1939 classic starring James Stewart as a new US senator. For some laughs, watch Congress get zapped by aliens in the 1996 sci-fi spoof starring Jack Nicholson, Mars Attacks.

## Next stop…

**US BOTANIC GARDEN** Take a leisurely stroll through the lovely Capitol Grounds to the domed conservatory in the US Botanic Garden (see pp106–107). Check out thousands of exotic and native plants displayed under glass.

## KIDS' CORNER

### Do you know...

**1** There is an empty crypt below the Rotunda. Who was supposed to be buried there?
**2** Toward the end of the War of 1812 (which lasted well over two years), the Capitol was set on fire. Do you know by whom?
**3** What does it mean when a flag flies over the House or Senate wing of the Capitol building?
**4** Visit the Senate and House chambers. Can you guess which has more members?

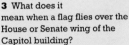

Answers at the bottom of the page.

*Quest for the perfect blueprint*
*In order to get a design for the Capitol, Thomas Jefferson held a design competition with a $500 first prize. Unfortunately, all the proposed designs were pretty bad, until self-taught architect William Thornton submitted his late entry, which won the prize.*

### DOME WITHIN A DOME

The Capitol dome is actually two domes, an "inner" and an "outer" one. Between the two, there is a secret staircase that leads to a balcony that can be seen if you look up from the Rotunda floor.

### Wandering whispers

The National Statuary Hall's acoustics are so good that a whisper on one side of the room can be heard on the other. It is said that the sixth president, John Quincy Adams, located his desk at an ideal spot to eavesdrop on the other party, helping him prepare winning arguments.

**Answers: 1** George Washington, but he requested to be buried instead on his beloved farm, Mount Vernon (see pp186–7). **2** The British, who attacked Washington, DC in 1814 **3** That the Senate, north side, or the House of Representatives, south side, are in session. **4** The House has 435 voting members, while the Senate has 100.

# ② US Botanic Garden

## A kids' garden, a wild jungle, and fabulous flowers

A lush, green oasis, the US Botanic Garden is a great place for families to escape to from the busy Mall. Its central feature is a 29,000-sq-ft (2,600-sq-m) glass-and-stone conservatory that displays 4,000 plants from around the world. Here, kids can enjoy the steamy Jungle and learn the basics of gardening in the Children's Garden. Surrounding the conservatory, the National Garden is a delight to explore in the warmer months.

## Key Features

① **Children's Garden** Kids can smell and touch the plants in this informal learning garden. Seasonal activities include watering plants and digging soil.

② **Hawaiian Collection** Discover native plants from the volcanic Hawaiian Islands.

③ **Garden Primeval** With ferns and other plant species that have survived and thrived for 150 million years, this reconstructed Jurassic landscape could have been a place where dinosaurs roamed long ago.

④ **Jungle** This tropical rainforest, complete with a waterfall and stream, has a second-story walkway offering bird's-eye views onto the treetop canopy.

**Conservatory** First constructed in 1933, and renovated in 2001, the conservatory is a striking structure topped by a dome that rises 93 ft (28 m) above the garden.

**Entrance to conservatory**

⑤ **Orchid Collection** There are around 5,000 orchids in the garden's collection, with some 200 vibrantly colored ones in bloom on display.

⑥ **Medicinal Plants** Many medicines are made from plants. This display shows plants used both historically and currently to treat everything from headaches to cancer.

⑦ **National Garden** Outdoors, different gardens are devoted to butterflies and roses, while a granite fountain in the First Ladies Water Garden takes its design from a Colonial quilt pattern known as Martha Washington.

## Letting off steam

**Bartholdi Park** (see p109) enables kids to run and explore the garden paths in a space where it is easy for parents to keep an eye on them. Winding paths lead through lovely gardens that showcase emerging trends in gardening, and there are some grassy areas perfect for a picnic with a great view of the United States Capitol (see pp104–105).

*Prices given are for a family of four*

## Eat and drink

*Picnic: under $30; Snacks: $30–40; Real meal: $40–75; Family treat: over $75 (based on a family of four)*

**PICNIC Eastern Market** (see p113) is the ideal place to shop for picnic goodies that can be enjoyed in Bartholdi Park.

**SNACKS Jimmy T's Place** (501 East Capitol St SE, 20003; 202 546 3646; www.jimmytsplace.com) serves lunch and breakfast all day.

*Fresh fruit for sale at the open-air stalls, Eastern Market*

## The Lowdown

🌐 **Map reference** 8 E4
**Address** 1st St SW & Independence Ave SW, 20024 (main entrance at 100 Maryland Ave SW); 202 225 8333; www.usbg.gov

🚗 **Metro** Federal Center SW.
**Bus** DC Circulator Purple line to 1st St NE & Maryland Ave NE

🕐 **Open** 10am–5pm daily

💲 **Price** Free

👬 **Cutting the line** There is rarely a line to get in.

🔫 **Guided tours** Call 202 730 9303 for cell phone tours. Occasional free 45-minute highlight tours; check at the visitor information desk.

👫 **Age range** All ages

🤸 **Activities** The free family guide to the conservatory is fun and educational, and the free Junior Botanist backpack provides kids aged 9 and above with tools to help them explore the garden (adult ID required); check at the visitor information desk.

🕐 **Allow** 1 hour

♿ **Wheelchair access** Yes

☕ **Café** No, but the conservatory terrace or Bartholdi Park (see p109) are great for a picnic.

🚻 **Restrooms** In the conservatory

**Good family value?**
The conservatory and outdoor National Garden provide a welcome change of pace from other Mall offerings.

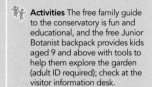

*Mitsitam Cafe at the National Museum of the American Indian*

**REAL MEAL Mitsitam Cafe** (National Museum of the American Indian, see pp60–61) has an excellent selection of Native American dishes such as plantain empanadas, yellow corn tortillas, buffalo chili, fry bread with honey, and quinoa pudding, with light meals to full dinners available.
**FAMILY TREAT Montmartre** (327 7th St SE, 20003; 202 544 1244; www.montmartredc.com; closed Mon) is a top-notch French bistro offering hearty provincial cuisine in a small, charming space with additional sidewalk seating. The menu offers a fine selection of entrées and wine.

## Find out more

**DIGITAL** Visit www.usbg.gov to learn about the Junior Botanist Program, and for fun interactive activities and puzzles. Watch amazing video clips of seeds germinating and flowers unfurling at http://plantsinmotion.bio.indiana.edu/plantmotion/starthere.html. www.sciencekids.co.nz/gamesactivities/plantsgrow.html has an interactive game about how plants grow. Older children interested in plants and biology can check out www.biology4kids.com/files/plants_main.html.
**FILM** Sci-fi movie Jurassic Park (1993) pairs well with the Garden Primeval, while Medicine Man (1992) is about plant collectors searching for a cure for cancer.

## Next stop...

**LIBRARY OF CONGRESS** Enjoy a relaxing stroll east to the entrance of the Library of Congress (see pp110–11) in the Jefferson Building. Before going in, take a look at the riveting Court of Neptune Fountain with its dramatic portrayal of sea monsters, sea horses, and turtles.

*Court of Neptune Fountain outside the Jefferson Building*

# ③ Capitol Grounds

## Capitol views and park-like spaces

In 1873, Congress decided to beautify the grounds surrounding the United States Capitol (*see pp104–105*). It had all the pigs, chickens, and cattle that were wandering loose rounded up, and called in famed landscape architect Frederick Law Olmsted, who designed and supervised the construction of this magnificent area over the next 20 years.

Today, the Capitol Grounds comprise 274 acres (110 ha) of lush spaces and gardens that are a delight for parents and kids to explore together. More than 100 varieties of trees and shrubs are displayed, and thousands of flowers can be seen blooming in season. Olmsted's design provides grand views of the Capitol, often framed by some of the 900 trees from four continents. Curved walkways lined with flower beds and benches lead to the Capitol, the monuments (*see right*), and to the shady, cool fountain of the

*A bubbling fountain pool in the Capitol Grounds*

red-brick, hexagon-shaped Summer House. This building was created for visitors to get a cooling drink. Today, kids love the mossy, cool interior and enjoy drinking from its fountain.

### Take cover

Head to the **Capitol Visitor Center Restaurant** for a break. Enjoy ice cream, a light snack or meal, or select a hearty dinner in the spacious cafeteria.

# ④ Capitol Reflecting Pool and Monuments

## Civil War drama and an invisible highway

Looking at the peaceful and lovely Capitol Reflecting Pool created in 1976 by Skidmore, Owings, and Merrill, it is hard to believe that there is a river of cars and trucks

*The US Capitol forming a backdrop to the Ulysses S. Grant Memorial*

## The Lowdown

- 🌐 **Map reference** 8 E3
  **Address** 1st St NW & East Capitol St NW, 20001; 202 226 8000; www.aoc.gov
- 🚇 **Metro** Capitol South. **Bus** DC Circulator Purple line to 1st St NE & Maryland Ave NE
- 🕐 **Open** 24 hours daily
- 💲 **Price** Free
- 👫 **Age range** All ages
- 🧍 **Activities** There is enough room for kids to walk, run, and play.
- ⏱ **Allow** 1–2 hours
- ♿ **Wheelchair access** No
- 🍴 **Eat and drink** *Picnic* Shop for fresh fruits and vegetables, deli meats, candy, and grocery items at the Eastern Market (*see p113*) and enjoy a picnic on the Capitol Grounds. *Real meal* Capitol Visitor Center Restaurant (*East Capitol St NE & 1st St NE, 20515; 202 593 1785; www.visitthecapitol.gov; 8:30am–4pm Mon–Sat; closed Sun*) offers full meals, grilled burgers, hot dogs, sandwiches, and desserts.
- 🚻 **Restrooms** Inside the Capitol Visitor Center

*Prices given are for a family of four*

## The Lowdown

- 🌐 **Map reference** 8 E3
  **Address** 1st St NE & East Capitol St NE, 20001; 202 226 8000; www.aoc.gov
- 🚇 **Metro** Capitol South. **Bus** DC Circulator Purple line to 1st St NE & Maryland Ave NE
- 🕐 **Open** 24 hours daily
- 💲 **Price** Free
- 👫 **Age range** All ages
- 🧍 **Activities** Kids can run around in the park-like grounds.
- ⏱ **Allow** 30 minutes
- ♿ **Wheelchair access** No
- 🍴 **Eat and drink** *Snacks* The Union Station Food Court (*see p115*) has a selection of snacks and meals from eateries such as Corner Bakery, Cookie Café, Ben & Jerry's Ice Cream, and Primo Cappuccino. *Real meal* Center Café (*Union Station Main Hall, see p115; 202 682 0143; www.arkrestaurants.com/center_cafe.html*) offers plenty of options, from chicken wings to pizzas, to go with a good view of the busy station.
- 🚻 **Restrooms** Inside the Capitol Visitor Center

rushing just a few yards underneath it. The pool is built on top of a tunnel through which flows the busy Interstate Highway 395. Above ground, however, all is tranquil.

There are three monuments between the pool and the west terrace entrance to the Capitol. The central monument is the three-part Ulysses S. Grant Memorial. A calm President Grant sits astride his famous war horse, Cincinnati. During the Civil War (1861–5), the then General Grant rode Cincinnati when he negotiated Robert E. Lee's surrender at Appomattox Court House, effectively ending the war. This statue is flanked on both sides by remarkable sculptures of the fighting Union Army. Toward the south, a caisson (two-wheeled cart) with three artillerymen is pulled by three horses. To the north, seven cavalrymen can be seen charging into battle.

On the southern edge of the Reflecting Pool, the Garfield Monument honors President James A. Garfield, who was assassinated in 1881 after being in office for just four months. The Peace Monument just north of the Reflecting Pool was

*Our Universes exhibit at the National Museum of the American Indian*

erected in memory of the officers and marines of the US Navy who died while defending the Union during the Civil War.

## Letting off steam

Kids can cool off at the Summer House fountain, or play and explore the garden-like hillside surrounding the house, while parents keep an eye on them from tree-shaded benches.

## ⑤ Bartholdi Park

**A garden within a garden**

Flower-lined footpaths and tiny themed gardens make Bartholdi Park a favorite Capitol Hill picnic spot for families. The centerpiece of this park is the 30-ft (9-m)-tall Bartholdi Fountain, decorated with carved sea nymphs, turtles, fish, and seashells. Created for the 1876 International Centennial Exhibition in Philadelphia by Frédéric August Bartholdi (sculptor of the Statue of Liberty), it was purchased by the US government and then moved here at the suggestion of landscape architect Frederick Law Olmsted. The model gardens of the park

change seasonally and showcase innovative plant combinations using a variety of styles and designs.

## Take cover

In case of cold or rainy weather, walk across Independence Avenue to the **National Museum of the American Indian** *(see pp60–61)* on the National Mall. Artifacts and interactive exhibits offer a glimpse into the past and present lives of Native Americans.

### The Lowdown

🌐 **Map reference** 8 E4
**Address** Independence Ave SW & 1st St SW, 20024; 202 225 8333; www.usbg.gov/gardens

🚗 **Metro** Federal Center SW. **Bus** DC Circulator Purple line to Independence Ave SW & 4th St SW

🕑 **Open** Daylight hours

💲 **Price** Free

👫 **Age range** All ages

🤸 **Activities** Kids enjoy playing around the fountain.

⏱ **Allow** 30 minutes–1 hour

♿ **Wheelchair access** Yes

🍴 **Eat and drink** *Snacks* Tortilla Cafe *(210 7th St SE, 20003; 202 547 5700)* is a popular eatery serving Mexican and Salvadorian favorites, and is great for a snack or a full meal at reasonable prices. *Real meal* Mitsitam Cafe *(National Museum of the American Indian, see pp60–61)* features Native foods from five different regions of the Americas. Menu items include buffalo burgers, traditional fry bread, and a great selection of desserts.

🚻 **Restrooms** Inside the Capitol Visitor Center

*Jets of water spouting from the Bartholdi Fountain in Bartholdi Park*

**Picnic** under $30; **Snacks** $30–40; **Real meal** $40–75; **Family treat** over $75 (based on a family of four)

# ⑥ Library of Congress
## The largest comic book collection on the planet

Founded by the US Congress in 1800, the Library of Congress was originally housed in the US Capitol. The world's biggest library, it contains just about everything in print, from presidential papers and books to music, as well as motion pictures. Of special interest to kids is the fact that the collection has more than 100,000 comics, from *Archie* to *Wonder Woman*. The library occupies three buildings on Capitol Hill, but it is the Jefferson Building *(below)* that is best known for its stunning architecture and interior design.

**Court of Neptune Fountain** This 19th-century fountain in front of the Jefferson Building shows the Roman god of the sea, Neptune, surrounded by mythical sea creatures.

## Key Features

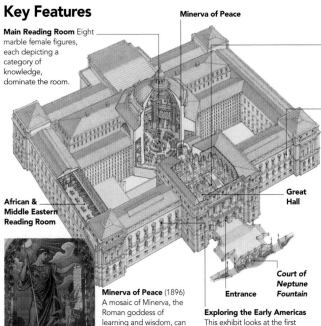

**Main Reading Room** Eight marble female figures, each depicting a category of knowledge, dominate the room.

**Minerva of Peace**

**African & Middle Eastern Reading Room**

**Great Hall**

**Entrance**

**Court of Neptune Fountain**

**Gutenberg Bible** This was the first book to be printed using movable metal type; the library has one of only three perfect and whole vellum copies.

**Jefferson Collection** This recreates Thomas Jefferson's vast 6,000-volume library, damaged in a fire in 1857, and contains many of his original books.

**Minerva of Peace** (1896) A mosaic of Minerva, the Roman goddess of learning and wisdom, can be seen on the staircase landing near the Main Reading Room.

**Exploring the Early Americas** This exhibit looks at the first European explorations of the New World through documents, maps, and artworks.

**Great Hall** Just beyond the entrance, this grand space is decorated with arches, columns, and balconies, and rises 75 ft (23 m) from the marble floor to a ceiling with stained-glass skylights.

## The Lowdown

🌐 **Map reference** 8 F3
**Address** 101 Independence Ave SE, 20540; 202 707 5000/8000; *www.loc.gov*

🚗 **Metro** Capitol South. **Bus** DC Circulator Purple line to 1st St NE & Maryland Ave NE

🕐 **Open** Jefferson Building: 8:30am–4:30pm Mon–Sat. Madison Building: 8:30am–9:30pm Mon–Fri. Adams Building: 8:30am–9:30pm Mon, Wed & Fri, 8:30am–5pm Tue, Fri & Sat

💲 **Price** Free

👪 **Cutting the line** It is best to visit in the mornings to avoid crowds.

🚩 **Guided tours** Free hour-long tours of the Jefferson Building: 10:30am–3:30pm Mon–Sat. No 3:30pm tour on Sat; first tour at 9:30am on Federal holidays

👫 **Age range** All ages

👬 **Activities** Interactive exhibits; Kids can also meet their favorite authors at the Young Readers Center (*www.read.gov/yrc*).

⏱ **Allow** 2 hours, as there may be a line to enter

♿ **Wheelchair access** Yes

☕ **Café** On the sixth floor of the Madison Building; 9am–3pm weekdays, closed to the public between 10:30am–12:30pm

🛍 **Shop** On the ground floor of the Jefferson Building

👫 **Restrooms** On the first floor of the Jefferson Building

**Good family value?**
This is a good outing for children who are interested in books.

*Alfresco seating at the popular Good Stuff Eatery*

## Letting off steam

Walk north on 1st Street NE, and turn left on Constitution Avenue to the huge **Union Station Plaza** *(1st St NW & Constitution Ave NW)*. This large park has fountains, trees, and lots of space for children to run and play around in.

## Eat and drink

*Picnic: under $30; Snacks: $30–40; Real meal: $40–75; Family treat: over $75 (based on a family of four)*

**SNACKS Good Stuff Eatery** *(303 Pennsylvania Ave SE, 20003; 202 543 8222; www.goodstuff eatery.com; closed Sun)*, a trendy and casual burger joint, offers innovative toppings, hand-cut fries, and excellent milkshakes. It is usually busy so be prepared to wait in line.

**REAL MEAL Pete's Diner** *(212 2nd St SE, 20003; 202 544 7335; credit cards not accepted)*, a local favorite for breakfast and lunch, has a good variety of American, vegetarian, and sushi choices with daily specials, all at affordable prices.

**Hawk 'n' Dove** *(329 Pennsylvania Ave, 20003; 202 547 0030; www. hawkndovedc.com)* is an Irish pub popular with politicians and sports fans. The menu offers light meals such as home-made soups and chili, burgers, sandwiches, salads, and cheesecakes at lunchtime, while

*Scene from The Tragedy of Julius Caesar at the Folger Shakespeare Library*

dinner dishes include steak and chicken, pasta dishes, and crab cakes.

**FAMILY TREAT Bistro Bis** *(Hotel George, 15 E St NW, 20001; 202 661 2700; www.hotelgeorge.com)* attracts power brokers and gourmands alike to its upscale French bistro setting. The modern French cuisine has unique American twists, the Zinc Bar is excellent, and the waiters skilled.

*Poster for National Treasure 2: Book of Secrets, starring Nicolas Cage*

## Find out more

**DIGITAL** Download the free Discovery Guide for Kids and Families from *www. loc.gov*. Visit *www.myloc.gov* for activities, a knowledge quest game, and to learn about the library's exhibits. For fun interactive learning activities on US history, go to *www. americaslibrary.gov*. Older children can learn about American history, music, and culture, as well as science and geography at *www.loc.gov/ families/*. Check out *www.read.gov/ kids/* for reading lists on a variety of topics, games, and audio recordings.

**FILM** Watch Nicolas Cage hunt for a hidden book at the Library of Congress in *National Treasure 2: Book of Secrets* (2007).

## Next stop...

**FOLGER SHAKESPEARE LIBRARY**
Cross 2nd Street SE behind the Jefferson Building to step into an Elizabethan world. A tour of the Folger Shakespeare Library *(see p112)* includes a look inside the intimate 250-seat theater where the Bard's plays are performed. Check out the Folger gift shop, which sells Shakespeare's works adapted for kids and offers children's events – see the calendar on the website.

# KIDS' CORNER

## Look out for...

**1** Try to spot the sun decoration on the floor of the Great Hall. What does it represent?
**2** How many buildings are used to hold the library's collections?
**3** Which former US president sold his personal library so the Library of Congress could have his books?

Answers at the bottom of the page.

*Treasures from the past*
*One of the oldest children's books in the collection is* The Children's New Plaything, *which was printed in Philadelphia in 1763.*

## MATTERS OF SIZE

The tiniest book in the library, *Old King Cole*, is the size of a full stop, and a needle is needed to turn its pages. The largest book here, on the other hand, features color images of Bhutan and is a whopping 5 ft by 7 ft (1.5 m by 2 m).

## Ever-expanding collection

The Library of Congress contains 145 million items in 470 languages. The collection fills around 745 miles (1,199 km) of shelves, and grows by more than 20,000 items every day. However, the library does not lend books – they must be read there.

# 7 Folger Shakespeare Library

### The play's the thing!

Behind the facade of this Art Deco building is one of the world's most important collections of material relating to William Shakespeare. The library contains over 300,000 items, including rare books and manuscripts, and 82 First Folios – the first collection of Shakespeare's works printed in 1632.

Around the building's exterior, on a viewing-friendly level, exquisite carved marble panels depict Shakespeare's best-known plays, and there is a small but charming Elizabethan knot garden to explore. Step inside the oak-paneled Great Hall and take a look at a First Folio – kept in a climate-controlled glass case. A display next to it allows kids to digitally flip through the book's pages. For a more lively experience, take in a Shakespeare play in the 250-seat Elizabethan theater, which also hosts cultural events including talks, poetry readings, and concerts.

The grand Elizabethan theater at the Folger Shakespeare Library

## The Lowdown

- 🌐 **Map reference** 8 G3
  **Address** 201 East Capitol St SE, 20003; 202 544 4600; www.folger.edu
- 🚇 **Metro** Capitol South
- 🕐 **Open** 10am–5pm Mon–Sat, noon–5pm Sun & Federal hols
- 💲 **Price** Free for library; varies for ticketed performances held on Sun & some evenings
- 👫 **Cutting the line** There is rarely a line to get in.
- 🚩 **Guided tours** 11am & 3pm Mon–Fri, 11am & 1pm Sat
- 👫 **Age range** 10 plus
- 🤸 **Activities** Attend a play or event in the theater.
- 🕐 **Allow** 1 hour (longer for plays)
- ♿ **Wheelchair access** Yes
- 🍽 **Eat and drink** *Snacks* We, The Pizza (305 Pennsylvania Ave SE, 20003; 202 544 4008; www. wethepizza.com) offers salads, pasta, ice cream, sodas, and beers. *Real meal* Le Pain Quotidien (660 Pennsylvania Ave SE, 20003; 202 459 9148; www.lepainquotidien.us) has bread, pastries, farm-fresh meals like omelets made with organic eggs, wines, juices, and coffee.
- 👫 **Restrooms** On the main floor

### Letting off steam

The lovely **Capitol Grounds** (see p108), with broad walkways lined with benches and flower beds, is a great place to let the children loose.

# 8 US Supreme Court

### Watch America's highest tribunal in action

Looking like a stunning Greek temple, the Supreme Court building opened in 1935, 148 years after the highest judicial body in the US was founded. The most compelling thing for families to do here is to visit the courtroom when in session and watch the highest court in the land shape the laws that are the foundation of American society. Above the main entrance, the court's motto, "Equal Justice Under Law," is inscribed. Take a look at the bronze entrance doors,

Corinthian-columned facade of the US Supreme Court

## The Lowdown

- 🌐 **Map reference** 8 F3
  **Address** 1st St NE between East Capitol St SE & Maryland Ave NE, 20543; 202 479 3000; www.supremecourt.gov
- 🚇 **Metro** Capitol South. **Bus** DC Circulator Purple line to 1st St NE & Maryland Ave NE
- 🕐 **Open** 9am–4:30pm Mon–Fri, closed Sat, Sun & Federal hols
- 💲 **Price** Free
- 👫 **Cutting the line** Entrance to watch the court proceedings is on a first-come first-served basis; best to arrive before 9am. There are two lines, one for short-term visitors (a few minutes) and one for those who want to watch a whole argument (1 hour or more).
- 🚩 **Guided tours** Docent-led 30-minute courtroom lectures every hour 9:30am–3:30pm when the court is not in session. When the court is in session, lectures are available after it adjourns for the day.
- 👫 **Age range** 10 plus
- 🤸 **Activities** Watch the 25-minute movie on the Supreme Court and the judicial process.
- 🕐 **Allow** 1–2 hours
- ♿ **Wheelchair access** Yes
- 🍽 **Eat and drink** *Snacks* US Supreme Court Cafeteria serves a variety of sandwiches, soups, salads, and beverages, but service may be interrupted from noon–1pm while employees are served. *Real meal* Talay Thai Restaurant (406 1st St SE, 20003; 202 546 5100; www.talaythaidc. com; closed for lunch on Sun) offers a broad selection of Thai appetizers, soups, salads, and entrées for lunch and dinner.
- 👫 **Restrooms** On the main floor

which are richly decorated with scenes depicting the development of law from ancient Greek to modern times. Then look up for a dizzying view of the five-story, self-supporting marble and bronze spiral staircases – among the few of this kind that exist in the world.

An exhibit room on the first floor provides a wealth of information on the Supreme Court, the Justices who have served on it, and the building itself. Outside, the plaza around the building is dotted with lovely fountains and statuary.

## Letting off steam

Head to **Stanton Park** (4th St NE & C St NE). This pretty 4-acre (1.6-ha) park has green spaces and a playground. Check out the statue of Revolutionary War hero General Nathanael Greene, said to be George Washington's most gifted and dependable officer.

## ⑨ Eastern Market
### Old market in a new building

Washington's oldest continually operating public market is a thriving center of activity. Built in 1873, the market building has been completely refurbished following a fire in 2007. Historic markets such as this offer a rare chance to experience firsthand how city dwellers shopped for groceries a few decades, or even a century ago.

Rows of booths are home to butchers, sausage makers, fresh fruit and vegetable merchants, and bakers, all vying for the attention of shoppers. This is an excellent place for lunch or to pick up the makings of a picnic. The streets surrounding

the market are home to numerous restaurants in all price ranges, some of them quite good.

Weekends are exceptionally lively as the outdoor spaces surrounding the market fill with dozens of vendors offering farm-fresh produce, fine crafts, and flea market-type items, and the indoor shops do a brisk business.

### Letting off steam
Walk south on 7th Street to the pretty park surrounding the Eastern Market metro stop. With broad pathways and benches, the park is a pleasant place for the kids to explore, and ideal for a picnic lunch.

Fresh produce for sale in the indoor shops at Eastern Market

## The Lowdown

🌐 **Map reference** 8 H4
**Address** 225 7th St at C St SE, 20003; 202 543 7470; www.easternmarket-dc.org

🚇 **Metro** Eastern Market

🕐 **Open** 7am–7pm Tue–Fri, 7am–6pm Sat & 9am–5pm Sun

💲 **Price** Free

👫 **Age range** All ages

🏃 **Activities** Shopping and dining

⏱ **Allow** 1–2 hours

♿ **Wheelchair access** Yes

☕ **Eat and drink** Picnic Eastern Market vendors offer fresh fruits and vegetables and deli meats that can be eaten in the park around the metro station. Snacks Market Lunch (202 547 8444; www.easternmarket-dc.org) is a popular diner-style sit-down eatery serving breakfast and lunch. Charbroiled burgers and softshell crabs are popular items.

👫 **Restrooms** Indoors

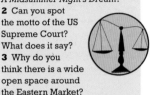

# KIDS' CORNER

## Look out for...
**1** The panels on the facade of the library show Shakespeare's most famous plays. Can you spot the one representing A Midsummer Night's Dream?
**2** Can you spot the motto of the US Supreme Court? What does it say?
**3** Why do you think there is a wide open space around the Eastern Market?

••••••••••••••••••••••••••••••
Answers at the bottom of the page.

## Fighting for equality
The famous case Brown v Board of Education, which ruled that separate state schools for black and white children was against the Constitution, was settled in the US Supreme Court in 1954.

## AN OBSCURE FAMOUS MAN
Nobody knows when Shakespeare was born, or for that matter, much at all about him, since little of his life was recorded. April 23rd is generally celebrated as his birthday since it is known he was baptized three days after this on April 26, 1564.

## Role reversal
It was considered shameful for a woman to be an actor in Shakespeare's time: the female roles in his plays were played by boys and young men.

••••••••••••••••••••••••••••••
**Answers: 1** The first one from the left as you face the building. Here Bottom is in his donkey head. **2** "Equal Justice Under the Law" is engraved under the main entrance. **3** In the 1800s, the space was needed for horse-drawn delivery wagons.

## ⑩ Sewall-Belmont House and Museum

### Changing role of women

Headquarters of the National Woman's Party since 1929, the historic Sewall-Belmont House and Museum celebrates the evolving role of American women and their contributions to society. It presents the story of the suffragettes' fight for the right to vote from the mid-19th century until the constitutional amendment granting it was approved in 1920.

Browse through rooms filled with photographs, political banners, and cartoons. Kids can also hear the docents tell stories about the history of women's progress toward equality.

The interior is decorated with period furnishings, paintings, and a desk used by Susan B. Anthony, a prominent member of the suffrage movement. The upstairs room of activist Alice Paul, founder of the National Woman's Party, still contains her four-poster bed and desk.

### The Lowdown

- 🌐 **Map reference** 8 F3
  **Address** 144 Constitution Ave NE, 20002; 202 546 1210; www.sewallbelmont.org
- 🚇 **Metro** Union Station. **Bus** DC Circulator to Union Station: Blue line (weekdays) & Yellow line (daily)
- 🕐 **Open** Only for group tours (check website for details), closed Jan 1, Thanksgiving Day & Dec 25
- 🚩 **Guided tours** Mail grouptours@ sewallbelmont.org or fill a request form on the website to schedule tours; check website for details.
- 👫 **Age range** 10 plus
- 🕐 **Allow** 1 hour
- ♿ **Wheelchair access** Yes
- 🍴 **Eat and drink** *Snacks* Good Stuff Eatery (303 Pennsylvania Ave SE, 20003; 202 543 8222; www.good stuffeatery.com) is a popular place for burgers, fries, and milkshakes. *Real meal* Capitol Visitor Center Restaurant (E Capitol St NE & 1st St NE, 20515; 202 593 1785; www.visitthecapitol.gov; closed Sun) serves vegetarian options, burgers, sandwiches, BBQ meats, soups, fruit, and desserts.
- 👫 **Restrooms** On the first floor

*A stagecoach on display at the National Postal Museum*

### Letting off steam

The pretty **Stanton Park** (4th St NE & C St NE, 20002) is a popular playground among the younger kids. The park has walkways and benches that are ideal for a family picnic lunch, and plenty of grassy areas for children to run around and play in.

## ⑪ National Postal Museum

### You've got mail

This charming, little-known museum often comes as a pleasant surprise to families, due to its wealth of exhibits that bring to life the history of mail delivery in the US. In the huge atrium are antique airmail delivery planes, early mail delivery trucks, a horse-drawn mail coach, and even a dogsled used in Alaska. Young kids can hop into and pretend to drive a real mail truck, and the whole family can enjoy the computer games and interactive programs.

*Statue of the French martyr Joan of Arc, at the Sewall-Belmont House and Museum*

### The Lowdown

- 🌐 **Map reference** 8 F1
  **Address** 2 Massachusetts Ave NE, 20002; 202 633 5555; www.postalmuseum.si.edu
- 🚇 **Metro** Union Station. **Bus** DC Circulator to Union Station: Blue line (weekdays) & Yellow line (daily)
- 🕐 **Open** 10am–5:30pm daily, closed Dec 25
- 💲 **Price** Free
- 👫 **Cutting the line** There is rarely a line to get in.
- 🚩 **Guided tours** 30-minute docent-led tours at 11am & 1pm
- 👫 **Age range** All
- 👫 **Activities** Interactive exhibits
- 🕐 **Allow** 1 hour
- ♿ **Wheelchair access** Yes
- 🍴 **Eat and drink** *Snacks* Walk across the street to Union Station Food Court (see Union Station), which offers snacks and full meals from King BBQ, Paradise Smoothies, and Subway, among many others. *Family treat* Johnny's Half Shell (400 North Capitol St NW, 20001; 202 737 0400; www.johnnyshalf shell.net; closed Sun) has Chesapeake and Gulf Coast New American seafood specialties, crab cakes, and shrimp po'boys (submarine sandwiches), served on an outdoor terrace.
- 👫 **Restrooms** Near the museum entrance

A computerized exhibit with maps and sound shows how a piece of mail is delivered to its destination. In the Binding the Nation exhibit, visitors can walk through a 1673 forest on a path used by mail carriers between Boston and New York, following notches in the trees to find the way. The Customers and Communities exhibit showcases modern mail delivery in the city and also in rural areas. Also a must-see is the museum's vast stamp collection, which includes every stamp issued in the US since the mid-19th century.

## Letting off steam
Visit the **Robert A. Taft Memorial** *(Union Station Plaza, Constitution Ave NW & 1st St NW)* dedicated to Senator Robert Taft, a staunch opponent of FDR's 1930s New Deal. The memorial has a 100-ft (30-m) high carillon that overlooks a beautiful park of stately trees and grassy areas, a favorite place to let the kids loose. The carillon's 27 Roosevelt's bells were cast in France and ring on the quarter hour.

## ⑫ Union Station
### Not just another terminal
Designed as the grand entrance to Washington, DC, Union Station opened in 1907 as the largest train station in the world. This magnificent Beaux Arts marble building, with a grand interior, was superbly restored in the 1980s and re-imagined as a dining and shopping center. Take in

the high, gilded ceilings, elegant arched windows, open spaces, and beautiful statuary. Enjoy the fine dining, casual restaurants, huge food court, and dozens of boutique shops that fill this remarkable space. The building still serves its original purpose and is the second busiest Amtrak train station with over 4 million riders every year. Union Station sustained significant earthquake damage in 2011 and restoration works are ongoing, but it remains open for business. In addition, it is currently being renovated to streamline the access and egress of trains into the station.

## Letting off steam
Cross Massachusetts Avenue to explore **Senate Park** *(10 C St NE, 20002)*. The park is on two levels, both of which offer tree-shaded paths, comfortable benches, and plenty of space for children to expend their excess energy among flower beds and a striking fountain. A great place to photograph the kids is by the fountain on the upper level, which has an unobstructed view of the US Capitol as a backdrop.

One of the many eating places in the Main Hall of Union Station

## The Lowdown

🌐 **Map reference** 8 F1
**Address** 50 Massachusetts Ave NE, 20002; 202 289 1908; www.unionstationdc.com

🚇 **Metro** Union Station. **Bus** DC Circulator to Union Station: Blue line (weekdays) and Yellow line (daily). **Train** Amtrak

🕐 **Open** Daily. Food court: 6am–9pm, to 6pm on Sun. Shops: 10am–9pm Mon–Sat, noon–6pm Sun

💲 **Price** Free

👫 **Age range** All ages

🎭 **Activities** Shopping and dining

⏱ **Allow** 1 hour

♿ **Wheelchair access** Yes

🍽 **Eat and drink** *Snacks* Union Station Food Court *(on lower level)* offers a huge selection of snacks and meals from restaurants that include Au Bon Pain and Flamers Charburgers. *Real meal* Center Café *(Union Station Main Hall; 202 682 0143; www.arkrestaurants.com/center_cafe.html)* has a varied menu that offers quick bites, full meals, and elegant candlelit dinners.

🚻 **Restrooms** On the first floor

### KIDS' CORNER

**Look out for...**
1 Find the statues of Roman legionnaires holding shields on the balcony ledge in the Main Hall of Union Station. How many are there?
2 The Sewall-Belmont House became the headquarters of the National Woman's Party in 1929. What great victory did this party win 9 years earlier?
3 The huge clock in the station's Main Hall, over the entrance to the East Hall, has IIII for 4 o'clock. What do most clocks have?

Answers at the bottom of the page.

**Mail express**
At its height, the Pony Express employed about 120 riders and had 184 stations located about 10 miles (16 km) apart. Riders had to weigh less than 125 lb (57 kg), would get a fresh horse at each station, and would travel about 100 miles (160 km) before a fresh rider took over. Along with the mail, they carried a pistol, water, and a Bible.

### FROM RAIL TO REEL
Union Station is a popular movie location. The best-known film to be filmed here was the James Stewart classic, *Mr. Smith Goes to Washington* (1939).

# The White House
## and Foggy Bottom

The White House is one of the most instantly recognizable buildings in the world, and seeing it in person is an experience like no other. The area beyond the White House is easy to explore with a mix of historic buildings and interesting attractions, including the Corcoran Gallery of Art, Decatur House, and Freedom Plaza. Foggy Bottom, to the west of the White House, contains the renowned Kennedy Center.

Georgetown

**The White House and Foggy Bottom**

Penn Quarter

The National Mall

Capitol Hill

## Highlights

**The White House**
Tour America's most famous residence if you have a ticket, or stroll around the block surrounding the building and enjoy views of its north and south porticos (see pp122–3).

**White House Visitor Center**
Get a sneak peek of the interiors in the modern-day White House. Paintings by Peter Waddell show various rooms in the White House at key points in history, complete with historic figures including presidents, first ladies, and prominent White House guests (see p124).

**Corcoran Gallery of Art**
Take a leisurely stroll around this charming gallery that houses world-renowned artworks. The Beaux-Arts building is one of Washington's finest (see p126).

**Daughters of the American Revolution Museum**
Walk around this magnificent Neo-Classical building and marvel at the antiques in the 31 museum rooms (see p125).

**Lafayette Square**
Sit and enjoy the wonderful view of the White House and the comings and goings of visitors and White House staff (see p128).

**Left** The lavishly decorated library at the White House
**Above left** Detail of the Renwick Gallery facade

# The Best of
# The White House and Foggy Bottom

While visitors cannot simply stroll into the White House and watch the president at work, they can walk the block that surrounds it and enjoy the world-famous views of its porticos and beautiful grounds. The art galleries, parks, and historic sites around the White House add interest to this area. West of the White House, Foggy Bottom is home to an array of restaurants and the world-class Kennedy Center.

## Presidential perambulations

The residence of the president of the United States, **The White House** *(see pp122–3)* has been home to every president but George Washington, who approved the location for the building, but was not in office long enough to see it completed. The area surrounding the White House exudes presidential history. North of the White House, Puerto Rican nationalists attempted to assasinate President Harry S. Truman in 1950 at the **Blair House** *(see p127)*. Close by, **St. John's Church** *(see pp128–9)*, designed by Benjamin Latrobe, is where every president since James Madison has attended services.

## Great galleries and perfect parks

The White House area features two great art museums – the **Renwick Gallery** *(see pp126–7)* and the **Corcoran Gallery of Art**

*Right Exterior of the DAR Museum **Below** The equestrian statue of Civil War General William Tecumseh Sherman*

**Above** *Taking photographs of the south portico of the White House* **Right** *The pleasant pond and waterfall at Pershing Park*

*(see p126).* Although both the museums are currently closed for renovation, the splendid facades of these buildings are worth admiring. The Renwick Gallery has an impressive Second Empire-style building built in 1874, while the Corcoran's historic Beaux-Arts structure, designed by Ernest Flagg and completed in 1897, has a distinct charm of its own, especially the atrium with its symmetrical stairway.

For a break from art, head to one of the excellent parks in the area, starting with the beautiful **Lafayette Square** *(see p128)*, which affords splendid views of the White House. **Pershing Park** *(see p124)* is an oasis – a sunken fountain and pool in the midst of the bustle of Pennsylvania Avenue, and **The Ellipse** *(see p125)* offers quiet, tree-shaded nooks, winding paths, and landscaped lawns.

## Hidden adventures

There are some lesser-known attractions tucked away around the White House. At the **Daughters of the American Revolution (DAR) Museum** *(see p125)*, there are 30-odd period furnished rooms, but the real treat is on the third floor, where an attic room has been filled with historic toys, reproductions of which the kids are encouraged to play with. **Decatur House** *(see p128)*, once home of the famous naval hero Stephen Decatur Jr., has interesting displays accompanied by stories of his daring deeds as he battled Barbary pirates.

## A presidential day out

Pre-arranged, timed tickets for the White House tour let visitors get a glimpse of America's most famous residence. Tour or not, the **White House Visitor Center** *(see p124)* is a good place to learn about US history, presidents and first ladies, and the White House itself. Take a stroll around the block formed by E Street and 17th Street, Pennsylvania Avenue and 15th Street, to admire the north and south porticos of the White House, stopping at the **Corcoran Gallery of Art**, a treasure trove of fine art. Enjoy a presidential-style lunch at **Café du Parc** *(see p124)*, and afterward head to the **Freedom Plaza** *(see p124)* to look at a giant inlaid stone map of the District of Columbia. Time permitting, visit **Pershing Park** to feed the ducks in the beautiful fountain pool.

# The White House and Foggy Bottom

The official residence of the US president, the White House sits in the middle of a manicured, city block-sized lawn. Stroll around this fenced block and admire both the north and south porticos of the house. Other attractions, including the Corcoran Gallery of Art and Decatur House, are situated within two blocks of the White House. The pedestrian-only Pennsylvania Avenue, along with the green spaces of Lafayette Square, are popular places to dally and watch the bustle around the White House. Getting to the White House area is easiest by metro, with Farragut North and McPherson Square stations located near the main sights.

The White House and Foggy Bottom

The White House
p122

## The Lowdown

🚗 **Metro** Farragut West, Farragut North, McPherson Square, Metro Center, Federal Triangle, Smithsonian & Foggy Bottom. **Bus** DC Circulator Purple line to 14 St NW & Constitution Ave NW

ℹ️ **Visitor information** White House Visitor Center, 1450 Pennsylvania Ave, NW; 202 208 1631. Destination DC, 901 7th NW, 4th Floor, 20001-3719; 202 789 7000; www.washington.org

🛒 **Supermarket** Whole Foods, 1440 P St NW, 20005; 202 332 4300
**Market** City Market, 1150 17th St NW, 20036; 202 822 0009

🎉 **Festival** Easter Egg Roll, White House (mid-Apr); www.whitehouse.gov

➕ **Pharmacies** CVS Pharmacy, 6 Dupont Circle NW, 20036; 202 785 1466; 24 hours daily. Walgreens Pharmacy, 1217 22nd St NW, 20037; 202 776 9084; 8am–10pm Mon–Fri, 9am–6pm Sat, 10am–6pm Sun

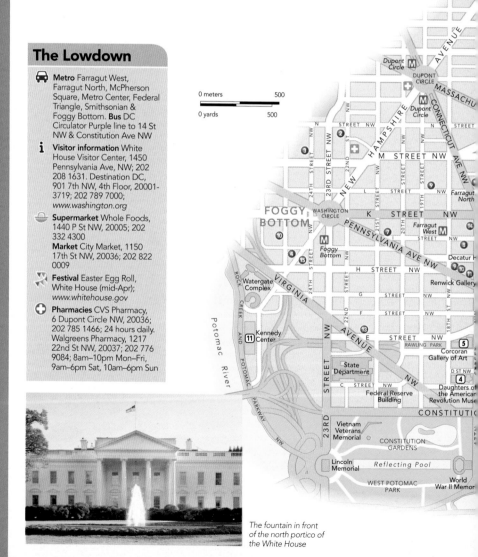

The fountain in front of the north portico of the White House

## Places of interest

**SIGHTS**

1. The White House
2. White House Visitor Center
3. Freedom Plaza
4. Daughters of the American Revolution Museum
5. Corcoran Gallery of Art
6. Renwick Gallery
7. Blair House
8. Decatur House
9. Lafayette Square
10. St. John's Church
11. Kennedy Center

**EAT AND DRINK**

1. Ben's Chili Bowl
2. Elephant & Castle
3. Equinox
4. Cosi
5. Café du Parc
6. Potbelly Sandwich Shop
7. Old Ebbitt Grill
8. Dickey's Frozen Custard
9. Breadline
10. Roti Mediterranean Grill
11. Potbelly Sandwich Shop
12. Courtyard Café
13. The Daily Market
14. Firehook Bakery and Coffeehouse
15. Red Velvet Cupcakery

16. Cafe Phillips
17. Pedro and Vinny's Food Stand
18. Juice Joint Café

See also Corcoran Gallery of Art (p126) and Kennedy Center (p129)

**WHERE TO STAY**

1. Capital Hilton
2. Embassy Suites Washington DC
3. Fairmont Washington
4. The George Washington University Inn
5. Hilton Garden Inn Washington DC Downtown
6. Hotel Helix Dupont
7. Hotel Lombardy
8. The Mayflower Renaissance Washington, DC
9. The Quincy
10. The River Inn
11. Sofitel Washington DC Lafayette Square
12. St. Regis Hotel
13. State Plaza Hotel
14. W Washington DC
15. Washington Guest Suites
16. Washington Plaza
17. Willard Intercontinental

A period-furnished room at the Daughters of the American Revolution Museum

# ① The White House
## The world's most famous home

For many families, a tour of the White House is one of the biggest highlights of a visit to Washington. Once inside, a self-guided tour serves up a mélange of US history and insights into the everyday workings of this famous symbol of America. A number of rooms are open to view – among the most popular are the elegant State Dining Room, the Vermeil Room, and the Green Room, which Thomas Jefferson used as a dining room.

The north portico of the White House

## Key Features

**State Dining Room** Seating up to 140 people, this grand room is where large state dinners are held. When Thomas Jefferson was president, he used this room as his office.

**East Room** The largest room in the house, this is the only one that spans the whole building from north to south. Seven presidents, including Lincoln and Kennedy, have lain in state here.

**Vermeil Room** This houses the largest vermeil (silver coated with gold) collection in the world.

**Green Room** Visit this small, elegant room used as a cocktail and reception room before state dinners. This is also where the first Declaration of War against the British was signed in 1812.

Red Room

Diplomatic Room

**Red Room** Legendary First Lady Dolley Madison used this room for the gatherings that brought opposing political parties together during the lead up to the War of 1812. The Madisons, the Lincolns, and the Kennedys used it as a music room.

**Blue Room** One of the three oval rooms in the White House, the Blue Room offers a spectacular view of the south lawn, making it ideal for formally receiving diplomatic guests. It was here that President Grover Cleveland got married in 1886.

**Diplomatic Room** It was from here that Franklin D. Roosevelt broadcast his fireside chats to the American people during the Great Depression.

## Letting off steam

Located north of the White House is **Lafayette Square** (see p128), a good place to let kids run around and have fun. The park also has ringside seats to watch the comings and goings of the White House.

## Eat and drink

Picnic: under $30; Snacks: $30–40; Real meal: $40–75; Family treat: over $75 (based on a family of four)

**PICNIC** Bring picnic supplies – as there is nowhere to purchase these closeby – and then head to Lafayette

Square to eat them. With its splendid view, the park is a good place for adults to relax and kids to play.

The equestrian statue of Andrew Jackson at the center of Lafayette Square

**SNACKS** Ben's Chili Bowl (1213 U St NW, 20009; 202 667 0909; www. benschilibowl.com; credit cards not accepted) is a landmark restaurant famous for its chili dogs, "half-smokes," and milk shakes. Comedian Bill Cosby, rocker Bono, and Barack Obama, all call it a DC favorite.
**REAL MEAL** Elephant & Castle (1201 Pennsylvania Ave NW, 20004; 202 347 7707; www.elephantcastle. com/dc_penn) is a family-friendly British pub serving classics such as shepherd's pie and American favorites including chicken pot pie, salads, burgers, and sandwiches.

Prices given are for a family of four

## The Lowdown

🌐 **Map reference** 6 H1
**Address** 1600 Pennsylvania Ave NW, 20500; 202 456 7041; www.whitehouse.gov

🚗 **Metro** Federal Triangle, Metro Center & McPherson Square.
**Bus** DC Circulator Purple line to 14th St & Constitution Ave NW (weekends only)

🕐 **Open** Only to those with pre-arranged tickets. Contact your congressman by calling 202 224 3121 up to six months in advance. Foreign visitors should contact their embassy in DC.

💲 **Price** Free

👫 **Cutting the line** When visiting in summer or during the Cherry Blossom festival, book a tour six months in advance.

🚩 **Guided tours** Self-guided tours of 30 minutes available from 7:30–11am Tue–Thu, 7:30am–noon Fri, 7:30am–1pm Sat (excluding Federal holidays or unless otherwise noted); arrive 15 minutes early. Call 202 456 7041 the morning of the tour for any last-minute changes, check www.nps.gov/whho/planyourvisit/white-house-tours.htm for information on required identification and prohibited items. Visit the visitor center before or after the tour to get the most from the experience.

👫 **Age range** 10 plus

⏱ **Allow** 1 hour

♿ **Wheelchair access** Yes

🚻 **Restrooms** No, at the Ellipse Pavilion, south of White House and visitor center (see p124)

**Good family value?**
A visit to the White House is a once-in-a-lifetime opportunity. That said, security is tight and lines can be long, making it a better choice for older kids.

## KIDS' CORNER

### Find out more...
**1** As you step outside the White House after a tour, turn around and look for a windowsill on the right side of the door that is not painted. Do you know why?
**2** Only one president has got married in the White House. He married a socialite who, at 21, was less than half his age and became the youngest first lady in history. Which president was this?
**3** Which first lady insisted that the rooms that are on the White House tour be given "museum status" so that they could not be changed and would tell the story of the White House to visitors?

Answers at the bottom of the page.

### FIRST HOUSE FACTS
The White House encompasses 55,000 sq ft (5,110 sq m) of living space on six floors that contain 132 rooms and 35 bathrooms. For recreation, the White House has a jogging track, swimming pool, movie theater, a tennis court, and even a bowling alley.

### The new groundskeeper
During World War I, the White House groundskeepers were conscripted into the military. President Woodrow Wilson had sheep brought in to keep the lawn trimmed.

**Answers: 1** It is left bare to show the charring from the historic fire of 1814. **2** Grover Cleveland. **3** Jacqueline Kennedy, in 1961.

---

*The colorful exterior of Ben's Chili Bowl, a Washington institution*

**FAMILY TREAT Equinox** (818 Connecticut Ave NW, 20006; 202 331 8118; www.equinoxrestaurant.com; closed for lunch on Sat & Sun) offers New American cuisine, with Italian influences. The seasonal menu features locally grown organic food from small farms.

## Find out more

**DIGITAL** The White House website www.whitehouse.gov/about has interactive tours and facts, and photos and videos of the president and his staff at work.

**FILM** The opening scene in The Day the Earth Stood Still (2008), a science fiction film, shows a flying saucer landing on the Ellipse in front of the White House. The West Wing (1999–2006) details the life of the president and his staffers, giving unique insight into the White House and its workings.

## Next stop...
### CORCORAN GALLERY OF ART
A great cross-section of old and new art can be seen at the Corcoran Gallery of Art (see p126). The museum's world-renowned collection includes works by Frederic Church and John Singer Sargent, and classic ceramics and jewelry alongside colorful contemporary works. The museum is going through renovation. Check website for further information.

*Facade of the Corcoran Gallery of Art*

## ② White House Visitor Center

### Everything you ever wanted to know about the White House

Why is the Oval Office oval? Which famous people have met with the president in the library? Where in the White House does the president actually live? The exhibits at the White House Visitor Center answer these questions and more, preparing visitors to get the most out of a tour of the White House.

For those who did not reserve ahead for a tour, the center offers a 30-minute video about the White House that is the next best thing to actually being there. Also, ask a ranger for a copy of the National Park Service brochure, which offers a brief overview of each room seen during a White House tour, and check if any ranger talks or special events are available. The center's exhibits highlight the architecture, furnishings, and decor of the White House, present funny, real-life stories about the first families, and offer a glimpse of the social events

*Entrance to the informative White House Visitor Center*

and international relations as seen by the press, political cartoonists, artists, and photographers.

### Letting off steam

Walk across to **Pershing Park** *(14th St & Pennsylvania Ave NW)*, where grassy banks, flower beds, and a sunken pond with a waterfall make a great place for kids to explore. In summer ducks often swim on the pond. After working up an appetite, head to a restaurant across the street.

## ③ Freedom Plaza

### Politics and people-watching

Freedom Plaza, a raised open plaza adjacent to Pershing Park, is a popular place for political protests, but is also interesting for its giant inlaid stone map of the District of Columbia, designed by Pierre L'Enfant. Visitors can see that modern Washington has remained largely unchanged from L'Enfant's original grid. The large fountain at one end, between the White House and the Mall, is a good place to stop and admire the scene.

The plaza was constructed in 1980 and originally known as

### The Lowdown

- 🌐 **Map reference** 7 A2
  **Address** 1450 Pennsylvania Ave NW, 20230; 202 208 1631; *www.nps.gov/whho*
- 🚇 **Metro** Federal Triangle.
  **Bus** DC Circulator Purple line to Constitution Ave NW & 14th St NW (weekends only)
- 🕐 **Open** 7:30am–4pm daily
- 💲 **Price** Free
- 🚻 **Age range** 9 plus
- ⏱ **Allow** 45 minutes
- ♿ **Wheelchair access** Yes
- 🍽 **Eat and drink** *Real meal* Cosi *(1001 Pennsylvania Ave NW, 20004; 202 628 0602; www. getcosi.com)* is a popular lunch place with fresh made-to-order salads, soups, sandwiches, and its own distinctive sauces. *Family treat* Café du Parc *(1401 Pennsylvania Ave NW, 20004; 202 942 7000; www. cafeduparc.com),* a French bistro with indoor and terrace seating, offers pastries, and entrées including roast chicken, fish and chips, and crab cakes, and has a kids' menu.
- 🚹 **Restrooms** Within the visitor center

### The Lowdown

- 🌐 **Map reference** 7 B2
  **Address** Pennsylvania Ave NW, between 13th St & 14th St, 20004
- 🚇 **Metro** Metro Center & Federal Triangle.
  **Bus** DC Circulator Purple line to Constitution Ave NW & 14th St NW (weekends only)
- 🕐 **Open** 24 hours
- 💲 **Price** Free
- 🚻 **Age range** 6 plus
- ⏱ **Allow** 15–30 minutes
- ♿ **Wheelchair access** Yes
- 🍽 **Eat and drink** *Snacks* Potbelly Sandwich Shop *(718 14th St NW, 20005; 202 628 9500; www. potbelly.com)* is a convenient place to pick up sandwiches, soups, and salads, along with shakes and fresh baked cookies. *Real meal* Elephant & Castle *(1201 Pennsylvania Ave NW, 20004; 202 347 7707; www. elephantcastle.com)* is a good place to find typical English pub grub, including such perennial kiddie favorites as fish and chips, "bangers and mash," and nachos.
- 🚻 **Restrooms** In Elephant & Castle, or the Ronald Reagan Building & International Trade Center

Western Plaza. It was renamed Freedom Plaza in honor of Martin Luther King, who worked on his "I Have a Dream" speech in the nearby Willard Hotel.

### Letting off steam

Head south along 14th Street NW and cross Constitution Avenue to the shady paths and beautiful landscapes of the **Constitution Gardens** *(see p88).* Kids can run around to their hearts' content, and enjoy a picnic beside the pond.

*The fountain at the western end of Freedom Plaza*

# ④ Daughters of the American Revolution Museum

### Antique toys in the attic

The Daughters of the American Revolution (DAR) was founded in 1890, and to be a member, a woman must be able to prove that she has an ancestor who was part of the struggle for American freedom during the Revolutionary War (1775–83). The headquarters of DAR is housed in what is considered to be one of the most beautiful Neo-Classical structures in the city, and while it is worthwhile to walk around the building and admire its various design features, there is enough inside to interest adults and children as well.

The museum's 31 rooms have been furnished with antiques, and each represents a key period for a particular state. A room on the third floor displays antique toys, including tea sets, stuffed animals, dolls and dollhouses, and cast-iron toys, and kids can actually play with some of these. The museum also features first-rate temporary exhibits.

Also in the museum is the DAR Constitution Hall, which has been hosting famous performers, from Russian composer Sergei Rachmaninoff (1873–1943) to the popular American rock band, Aerosmith, for almost a century. One of the finest orchestras in the world, the National Symphony, got its start at DAR Constitution Hall and called it home for 40 years.

### Letting off steam

Across 17th Street is the park-like northwest corner of **The Ellipse** (south of the White House), which is a great place for kids to burn off excess energy in the shadow of the spectacular column of the First Division Monument.

*Illustration at the Taking Care of Business section, DAR Museum*

## The Lowdown

- 🌐 **Map reference** 6 G2
  **Address** 1776 D St NW, 20006; 202 628 1776; *www.dar.org/museum*
- 🚇 **Metro** Federal Triangle
- 🕐 **Open** 9:30am–4pm Mon–Fri, 9am–5pm Sat, closed Sun, Federal holidays & 1 week in Jun or Jul during the DAR congress
- 💲 **Price** Free
- 🧍 **Cutting the line** There is rarely a line to get in
- 🎫 **Guided tours** 9am–4:30pm Mon–Sat
- 👫 **Age range** 4 plus
- 🤸 **Activities** Young children can play with antique toys in the attic; ask at the information desk for details.
- ⏱ **Allow** 1 hour
- ♿ **Wheelchair access** Yes
- 🍴 **Eat and drink** *Snacks* Dickey's Frozen Custard (1710 I St NW, 20006; 202 293 7100; Mon–Fri) is a small, popular neighborhood custard shop. Along with frozen custard, it also serves sandwiches, including the Panini Amore with roast turkey and avocado. *Real meal* Breadline (1751 Pennsylvania Ave NW, 20006; 202 822 8900; *www.breadline.com*) serves fresh sandwiches made with its exceptional bread, and daily specials popular at lunch time.
- 🚻 **Restrooms** On the first floor

*The First Division Monument honoring US soldiers who fought in World War I*

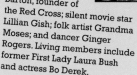

# ⑤ Corcoran Gallery of Art

## A galloping buffalo and Washington's false teeth

The city's oldest and largest privately funded art museum has over 16,000 historic, decorative, contemporary, and multimedia artworks from America and Europe. In 2014 the Corcoran Gallery was sold to George Washington University and the collection was given to the National Gallery of Art. The museum is closed for an extensive renovation. Upon completion, it will feature a Legacy

### The Lowdown

🌐 **Map reference** 6 G2
**Address** 500 17th St NW, 20006; 202 639 1700

🚇 **Metro** Farragut West & Farragut North. **Bus** DC Circulator Purple line to Constitution Ave NW & 17th St NW (weekends only)

🕐 **Open** 10am–5pm Mon–Sat, 11am–6pm Sun; closed Jan 1 & Dec 25

💲 **Price** Free

👫 **Cutting the line** Members of other US museums may be eligible for free admission.

🚩 **Guided tours** Free tours daily, plus gallery maps, self-guided tour routes, audio tours and a mobile phone app

👫 **Age range** 6 plus

👫 **Activities** The children's brochure highlights artworks of interest to 6–12-years-olds. 90-minute family programs for 8- to 12-year-olds and their adult companions include an interactive gallery tour and artist-led activity in the studio (select Sat; reservations required). Check details before visiting.

🕐 **Allow** 1 hour

♿ **Wheelchair access** Yes

🍽 **Eat and drink** *Snacks* Roti Mediterranean Grill *(1747 Pennsylvania Ave NW, 20006; 202 466 7684; www.roti.com)* serves Mediterranean dishes such as *pita* (flat bread), fire-roasted meats, *falafel* (chickpea patties), and *baba ghanoush* (eggplant dip). *Real meal* Cosi *(1700 Pennsylvania Ave NW, 20004; 202 638 7101; www.getcosi. com; breakfast & lunch only)* is a good choice for a quick and delicious sandwich or flat-bread pizza. The restaurant offers soups, salads and more.

👫 **Restrooms** On the first floor

One of the two bronze lions guarding the Corcoran Gallery of Art

Gallery to display some of the museum's most famous holdings. The other galleries will exhibit collections from National Gallery of Art, especially exhibits from the now-closed East Building.

### Letting off steam

Walk across 17th Street and into a pretty section of **The Ellipse** *(see p125)*, also known as President's Park. Located just south of the White House fence, it is a quiet corner, with broad curved walks and sunny expanses of lawn perfect for running.

# ⑥ Renwick Gallery

## A fish encrusted with toys

A part of the Smithsonian American Art Museum *(see p146–7)*, the Renwick Gallery features American contemporary crafts and decorative arts. It is housed in a Second Empire-style building which, in itself, is a spectacular work of art. Designed

### The Lowdown

🌐 **Map reference** 6 H1
**Address** 1661 Pennsylvania Ave NW, 20006; 202 633 1000; *www.americanart.si.edu*

🚇 **Metro** Farragut West & Farragut North. **Bus** DC Circulator Purple line to Constitution Ave NW & 17th St NW (weekends only)

🕐 **Open** 10am–5:30pm daily, closed Dec 25; check website for summer opening times

💲 **Price** Free

👫 **Cutting the line** Usually not very crowded

🚩 **Guided tours** noon Mon–Fri, 1pm Sat & Sun; start from the information desk

👫 **Age range** 6 plus

👫 **Activities** Scavenger hunts; check at the information desk

🕐 **Allow** 1 hour

♿ **Wheelchair access** Yes

🍽 **Eat and drink** *Snacks* Potbelly Sandwich Shop *(1701 Pennsylvania Ave NW, 20050; 202 775 1450; www.potbelly. com)* has pizzas, sandwiches, soups, spaghetti and meatballs, and the popular Oreo shake. *Real meal* Courtyard Café *(Smithsonian American Art Museum and National Portrait Gallery, see p147)* serves soups, salads, sandwiches, beverages, and seasonal dishes made from local or organic ingredients.

👫 **Restrooms** On each floor

by architect James Renwick, Jr., the structure was completed in 1874.

An impressive staircase leads up to the Grand Salon, the walls of which are hung floor to ceiling with fine artworks. Beyond it is room after room of crafts and art, much of it colorful and imaginative. Kids love Larry Fuente's *Game Fish* (1988), a large, fantasy sailfish decorated with

Blair House complex, a guesthouse for heads of state visiting the White House

*Facade of the Second Empire-style Renwick Gallery*

toys, coins, beads, buttons, plastic figures, pool balls, and other bright and colorful objects.

Another favorite with kids is Kim Schmahmann's *Bureau of Bureaucracy* (1993–9), a fancy 8-ft (2.5-m)-tall cabinet made of hardwood, mother-of-pearl, gold leaf, and brass. A labyrinth of cubbyholes, hidden compartments, shelves, drawers, and curved spaces, it is a metaphor for government complexity.

The gallery is currently closed due to major restoration work and will reopen in 2016.

### Letting off steam

Head to the pretty **Farragut Square** (912 17th St NW, 20006), where kids can build up an appetite on the lawns surrounding the statue of Union Navy Admiral David G. Farragut, who rallied his Civil War fleet with the battle cry "Damn the torpedos, full speed ahead!" This is also a popular place for summer picnics, and for listening to the free jazz and rock concerts held on Thursdays during June and July.

## ⑦ Blair House
### Botched assassination

There are no tours of this town-house near the White House, but it is worth stopping to look at, both for what it is now and for the famous incident that did not happen here: the assassination of President Harry S. Truman. In 1948, President Truman moved to Blair House while the White House was undergoing major renovations. In 1950, two Puerto Rican nationals seeking independence for their island home decided to gain attention for their cause by assassinating the president. With guns blazing, they rushed at Blair House from two directions. The

gunfire was returned by the White House and Capitol police and Secret Service agents, and while one White House policeman was killed and other officers injured, the president was unharmed. Read the plaques on the gate, which describe the history of the house and the attempted assassination.

### Letting off steam

**Lafayette Square** *(see p128)*, across the street, is a great place to let children have fun and run around.

*Equestrian statue of President Andrew Jackson in the center of Lafayette Square*

### The Lowdown

🌐 **Map reference** 6 H1
**Address** 1651–1653 Pennsylvania Ave NW, 20503; *www.blairhouse.org*

🚇 **Metro** Farragut West & Farragut North. **Bus** DC Circulator Purple line to Constitution Ave NW & 17th St NW (weekends only)

👫 **Age range** All ages

⏱ **Allow** A few minutes

♿ **Wheelchair access** No

☕ **Eat and drink** *Picnic* The Daily Market (1001 Connecticut Ave NW, 20036; 202 296 2727) is a good place to buy bagels, sandwiches, salads, and smoothies before heading to Farragut Square for a picnic. *Snacks* Firehook Bakery and Coffee House (912 17th St NW, 20006; 202 429 2253; www.firehook.com) is noted for its flavorful breads. The cookies, tarts, brownies, and muffins are popular with kids and adults alike.

👫 **Restrooms** No, but nearby in the Renwick Gallery and Decatur House

## ⑧ Decatur House

### The house of a naval hero

Commodore Stephen Decatur, Jr. was a naval hero who used the prize money from ships he captured in the War of 1812 to build the first private residence in the White House neighborhood in 1818. Just 14 months later, Decatur was mortally wounded in a duel and was taken to this house, where he died. Rumor has it that his ghost still wanders the halls. Decatur House, a museum now, exhibits historical documents, highlights the home's history, and provides educational programs on the history of the White House.

### Letting off steam

Head to the lovely **Lafayette Square** (see below), a great place for kids to play and examine the many statues.

### The Lowdown

- 🌐 **Map reference** 6 H1
  **Address** 1610 H St NW, 20006; 202 218 4338; www.white housenistory.org/decatur-house
- 🚇 **Metro** Farragut West & McPherson Square
- 🕐 **Open** Tours at 11am, 12:30pm, and 2pm Mon; groups of more than 20 call 202 737 8292
- 💲 **Price** Free
- 👥 **Cutting the line** There is rarely a line to get in.
- 🧍 **Age range** 10 plus
- 🏃 **Activities** A summer jazz concert series is held on the first Thu of each month from Jun–Sep.
- ⏱ **Allow** 60 minutes
- ♿ **Wheelchair access** Yes
- 🍴 **Eat and drink** Snacks Firehook Bakery and Coffee House (912 17th St NW, 20006; 202 429 2253; www.firehook.com) serves breads, cookies, soups, salads, and sandwiches. Real meal Old Ebbitt Grill (675 15th NW, 20005; 202 347 4800; www.ebbitt.com), has a raw bar (serving raw shellfish), and also offers pasta, chicken wings, and burgers.
- 🛍 **Shop** In the museum (Mon–Fri)
- 🚻 **Restrooms** On the first floor

## ⑨ Lafayette Square

### Park for presidents

This lovely park with wide paths, open green spaces, and a killer view of the White House was originally

### The Lowdown

- 🌐 **Map reference** 6 H1
  **Address** H St NW, between 15th St NW & 17th St NW, 20006; www.nps.gov/nr/travel/wash/dc30.htm
- 🚇 **Metro** Farragut West & McPherson Square
- 🕐 **Open** 24 hours daily
- 💲 **Price** Free
- 🧍 **Age range** All ages
- 🏃 **Activities** Cell-phone walking tours of neighborhood available; ask at entrance to Decatur House.
- ⏱ **Allow** 30 minutes–2 hours
- 🍴 **Eat and drink** Snacks Red Velvet Cupcakery (501 7th St NW, 20004; 202 347 7895; www.redvelvetcupcakery.com) makes cupcakes with ingredients from around the world. Flavors include red velvet, peanut butter cup, and carrot cake. Real meal Cafe Phillips (1401 H St NW, 20005; 202 408 4900; www.cafephillips.com) is a lunch spot serving fresh-carved meats with bread and beef, turkey, and pork sandwiches.
- 🚻 **Restrooms** No, but at Decatur House

known as President's Park. In 1804, the square became separated from the White House grounds when President Jefferson had Pennsylvania Avenue created. It officially became Lafayette Square in 1824, in honor of General Lafayette of France, who fought alongside George Washington during the Revolutionary War. In the center of the square stands the 1853 statue of President Andrew Jackson at the Battle of New Orleans. The park is a great place for families to take a break.

Decatur House, the first private residence in the White House neighborhood

### Take cover

Head to the Corcoran Gallery of Art (see p126) to see an extensive collection of some of the most significant American artists.

## ⑩ St. John's Church

### Where presidents come to pray

Designed by Benjamin Latrobe, America's first professional architect, this lovely yellow church on the north side of Lafayette Square held its first service in 1816. From James Madison to Barack Obama, every president of the US has attended at least one service at St. John's Church. The bell in the church's tower weighs 1,000 lb (455 kg) and was cast by American Revolution patriot Paul Revere's son, Joseph.

### Letting off steam

The pretty **Farragut Square** (see p127) offers broad green areas and walkways where kids can have fun. Buy sandwiches from Firehook

The statue of Rochambeau, a French Revolutionary War hero, in Lafayette Square

## The Lowdown

- 🌐 **Map reference** 6 H1
  **Address** 1525 H St NW, 20005; 202 347 8766; www.stjohns-dc.org
- 🚗 **Metro** Farragut West & McPherson Square
- 🕐 **Open** 9am–3pm daily
- 💲 **Price** Free; donations welcome
- 🚩 **Guided tours** Following the 11am service (10:30am summer) on most Sundays
- 👪 **Age range** All ages
- 🏃 **Activities** Attend services; check website for details
- 🕐 **Allow** 30 minutes–1 hour
- ♿ **Wheelchair access** Yes
- 🍴 **Eat and drink** *Picnic* Pedro and Vinny's Food Stand (*1500 K St NW, 20005; 571 237 1875; www.pedroandvinnys.com*) is a small burrito stand. Buy food from here and head over to McPherson Square for a picnic. *Real meal* Juice Joint Café (*1025 Vermont Ave, 20005; 202 347 6783; www.juicejointcafe.com*) serves fresh juices, wraps, and sandwiches.
- 🚻 **Restrooms** On the lower level of the parish house

Bakery and Coffee House, on the west side, and have a picnic on a bench or in a tree-shaded area.

## ⑪ Kennedy Center
### Teddy bears, clowns, and acrobats

Home to the National Symphony Orchestra, the Washington Ballet, and the Washington National Opera, the Kennedy Center opened in 1971, and was named after President John F. Kennedy, who was a strong supporter of the arts. For kids, attending a performance at the Kennedy Center is a great way to experience this legendary venue. The center houses six theaters – venues for a dazzling variety of top-notch performances.

There are more than 100 full stage performances for young audiences each year and kids are encouraged to sit up-front and move to the music. Children may also enjoy a tour of the center, particularly the Hall of Nations and the Hall of States, where flags from more than 140 countries and the 50 US states are on display.

### Letting off steam
Walk along the **Rock Creek Park Trail** (*north along the Potomac River to Washington Harbour and the Georgetown Waterfront Park*). Hire a bike or a boat from Thompson Boat Center (*see p156*), or set out on a sightseeing cruise from the harbor.

*Biking on a trail in the Georgetown Waterfront Park*

## The Lowdown

- 🌐 **Map reference** 6 E2
  **Address** 2700 F St NW, 20566; 202 467 4600; www.kennedy-center.org
- 🚗 **Metro** Foggy Bottom, then walk or take the free Kennedy Center Shuttle
- 🕐 **Open** 10am–9pm daily
- 💲 **Price** Free guided tours and 6pm Millennium Stage performance; prices for other performances vary
- 🎟 **Cutting the line** Purchase performance tickets ahead of time; check website or call for details
- 🚩 **Guided tours** Free tours 10am–5pm Mon–Fri & 10am–1pm Sat & Sun; check website for details
- 👪 **Age range** All ages
- 🏃 **Activities** Enjoy free performances held at 6pm on Millennium Stage.
- 🕐 **Allow** 1 hour; longer for performances
- ♿ **Wheelchair access** Yes
- 🍴 **Eat and drink** *Real meal* KC Café (*at the Kennedy Center*) offers casual dining with food served cafeteria-style from many food stations. *Family treat* Roof Terrace Restaurant (*at the Kennedy Center; dinner 5–8pm before concert hall & opera house performances & brunch 11am–2pm most Sun*) serves prime ribs, salads, and pasta.
- 🚻 **Restrooms** On main level near tour desk and terrace level

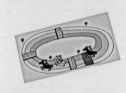

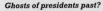

# Penn Quarter

Some of the city's most interesting and kid-friendly museums, such as the International Spy Museum and the informative Newseum, are located in Penn Quarter. This area is also an ideal place to get a good dose of history, particularly at Ford's Theatre, where President Lincoln was shot, and at the National Archives, where visitors can look closely at the original Declaration of Independence, Constitution, and Bill of Rights.

## Highlights

**Newseum**
Trace the history of news reporting from the Middle Ages to the present day at this museum filled with interactive displays and exhibits *(see pp136–9)*.

**National Archives**
Examine original and rare documents, such as Lincoln's wartime telegrams, as well as movies and sound clips from the archives' collection *(see pp140–41)*.

**Ford's Theatre**
Visit the scene of President Lincoln's assassination, and look at highlights from his life and political career at the excellent museum here *(see pp142–3)*.

**International Spy Museum**
Look out for James Bond's car, hidden cameras, and a replica of the secret tunnel that the US used to spy on East Germany *(see pp144–5)*.

**Smithsonian American Art Museum and National Portrait Gallery**
Identify sports legends and rock stars, and enjoy works depicting all things American at these two superb art museums *(see pp146–7)*.

**National Museum of Women in the Arts**
Check out this museum dedicated to women artists from the 16th century to the present day *(see p149)*.

**Left** The evocative Berlin Wall exhibit at Newseum
**Above left** Sculpture of civil rights activist Rosa Parks by Marshall D. Rumbaugh in the National Portrait Gallery

# The Best of
# Penn Quarter

The center of Washington's day-to-day business, Penn Quarter also delights with some offbeat attractions and superb museums. Get an insight into the world of secret agents at the International Spy Museum, admire evocative portraits at the National Portrait Gallery, and indulge in a range of dining experiences, from Asian street food to restaurants offering gastronomic delights.

## Journalists, crooks, and spies

The quartet of wonderful, and sometimes eccentric, museums in Penn Quarter offer tons of entertainment that will be appreciated by kids and adults alike. Stand in front of the pseudo-cadaver on a morgue table in the **National Museum of Crime and Punishment** (see p148) and imagine being on a *CSI* set. The interactive displays and fascinating themes, such as modern crime scene analysis, make this a kids' favorite. Take a photograph with a movie-, music-, or sports-star at **Madame Tussauds** (see p148), and don't forget to check out the clever and entertaining **International Spy Museum** (see pp144–5), where everyone can be a spy for a day. The unique **Newseum** (see pp136–9) offers a vast array of fascinating displays and interactive exhibits that highlight both the historical and the present-day world of journalism.

**Right** *Entrance of Madame Tussauds wax museum*
**Below** *Statue outside the Neo-Classical National Archives*

**Above** *Visitors admire works of art at the Smithsonian American Art Museum*

## Art and history in the Penn

For a heaped helping of history, head to the **National Archives** *(see pp140–41)* to see the original US Constitution or the Declaration of Independence, or to **Ford's Theatre** *(see pp 142–3)*, where Abraham Lincoln watched his last play. Walk past the elegant **Old Post Office** *(see p142)*, whose spectacularly ornate wrought-iron and glass atrium is home to an assortment of shops and food stalls.

A haven for art lovers, the **Smithsonian American Art Museum and National Portrait Gallery** *(see pp146–7)* showcases works by American artists as well as some superb portraiture, while the **National Museum of Women in the Arts** *(see p149)* presents four and a half centuries of artworks created by women.

## Dining adventures

Perhaps no other corner of Washington has so many fine dining possibilities in such a small area. Located in the Newseum building, Wolfgang Puck's **The Source** *(see p139)* has created a lot of buzz with its Asian fusion menu and a distinctive two-level layout, while, at the visually captivating **Poste Moderne Brasserie** *(see p147)*, chef Robert Weland serves up specialties with organic and farm-fresh ingredients.

On Pennsylvania Avenue, **Fogo de Chão** *(see p67)* is a superb Brazilian steakhouse serving large portions of perfectly seasoned and charred beef, lamb, and pork. An elegant steak and seafood spot with over 800 wines in its cellar, **Capitol Grill** *(601 Pennsylvania Ave)* is the place to rub elbows with recognizable politicians.

## A walk along Pennsylvania Avenue

Ambling along the main street that runs directly from the US Capitol to the White House can be a rewarding experience. Start near the Capitol at Pennsylvania and 1st Street NW and head west, stopping to look at the 74-ft (23-m)-tall First Amendment Tablet on the facade of the **Newseum** building or to admire the bronze statue of a young sailor in a foreign port at the **US Navy Memorial** *(see p142)*.

Continue along Pennsylvania Avenue, passing the FBI headquarters, **Old Post Office**, and Ronald Reagan Building & International Trade Center. Rest awhile at **Freedom Plaza** *(see p124)*, where the stones around the fountain are carved with quotes about the history of Washington.

**Right** *The installation* Electronic Superhighway: Continental U.S., Alaska, Hawaii *at the Smithsonian American Art Museum*

# Penn Quarter

Flanked by the US Capitol in the east and the White House in the west, this grand quarter is where much of the day-to-day business of the city gets done. Penn Quarter is also home to many of the city's best attractions, including the National Archives, Newseum, Smithsonian American Art Museum and National Portrait Gallery, and Madame Tussauds. Walking is a good way to get around here, but the metro has several stations, and it might be a better option if there are several destinations scattered across this area on the family's must-see list. The DC Circulator line also has two routes that serve the area, and the Old Town Trolley step-on, step-off tours stop at several attractions.

**Penn Quarter**

Spy Museum p144    Smithsonian p146

National Archives p140    Newseum p136

## Places of interest

### SIGHTS
1. Newseum
2. National Archives
3. Old Post Office
4. Ford's Theatre
5. The Petersen Boarding House
6. International Spy Museum
7. Smithsonian American Art Museum and National Portrait Gallery
8. National Museum of Crime and Punishment
9. Madame Tussauds
10. National Museum of Women in the Arts

### ● EAT AND DRINK
1. Express Bar
2. Teaism
3. Food Section
4. The Source
5. Au Bon Pain
6. Jaleo
7. Rasika
8. Elephant & Castle
9. Crepes On The Walk
10. Hard Rock Cafe
11. Five Guys Burgers and Fries
12. Matchbox Chinatown
13. Shake Shack
14. Ella's Wood Fired Pizza
15. Full Kee Restaurant
16. Courtyard Café
17. Carmine's
18. Poste Moderne Brasserie

19. Gordon Biersch Brewery Restaurant
20. Lincoln's Waffle Shop
21. Nando's Peri Peri
22. Siroc Restaurant

See also Old Post Office Pavillion (p142) and National Museum of Women in the Arts (p149)

### ● SHOPPING
1. Newseum Store
2. International Spy Museum Store
3. Smithsonian American Art Museum and National Portrait Gallery Store

### ● WHERE TO STAY
1. Embassy Suites Washington DC – Convention Center
2. Fairfield Inn & Suites Washington, DC/Downtown
3. Grand Hyatt Washington
4. Henley Park Hotel
5. Hilton Garden Inn
6. Hotel Harrington
7. Hotel Monaco Washington DC
8. JW Marriott on Pennsylvania
9. Marriott Courtyard Washington Convention Center
10. Morrison-Clark Historic Inn

MASSACHUSETTS AV

L STREET NW

K STREET NW

McPHERSON SQUARE

FRANKLIN SQUARE

STREET NW

McPherson Square

NEW YORK AVENUE NW

National Museum of Women in the Arts

H STREET

G STREET NW

Metro

Madame Tussauds 9

The Petersen Boarding House 5

Willard Hotel

National Theater

F STREET NW

E STREET NW

PERSHING PARK

FREEDOM PLAZA

PENNSYLVANIA

White House Visitor Center

Ronald Reagan Building and International Trade Center

Benjamin Franklin Statue

Federal Triangle

Old Post Office 3

CONSTITUTION AVENUE N

National Museum of American History

National Mus of Natura History

MADISON DRIVE NW

JEFFERSON DRIVE SW

Smithso Castl

The exhibit School for Spies in the International Spy Museum

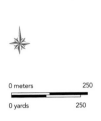

## The Lowdown

🚗 **Metro** Archives/Navy Memorial, Gallery Place-Chinatown, Federal Triangle, Metro Center. **Bus** DC Circulator Red and Orange lines. **Trolley** Old Town Trolley Green and Orange routes have step-on, step-off sightseeing tours that stop at several sights (888 910 8687)

ℹ️ **Visitor information** Destination DC, 901 7th NW, 4th Floor, 20001-3719; 202 789 7000; www.washington.org. Ronald Reagan Building & International Trade Center, 1300 Pennsylvania Ave NW, 20004; 202 312 1300; www. itcdc.com

🛍️ **Market** Chinatown Market, 521 H St NW, 20001; 202 842 0130; 9am–9pm daily

🎪 **Festival** Penn Quarter Arts on Foot Festival, Donald W. Reynolds Center for American Art and Portraiture (late Sep); 202 638 3232; www.artsonfoot.org

➕ **Pharmacy** CVS Pharmacy, 435 8th St NW, 20004; 202 783 4293; 6am–midnight Mon–Fri & 7am–midnight Sat & Sun

The front entrance of the National Archives

# ① Newseum

## Become a real TV reporter

The only museum of its kind in the world, the Newseum offers an insight into the workings of the media world and the challenges faced by journalists worldwide. This is a great museum for kids, with lots of interactive activities, from learning to put together a news story on deadline to actually creating a TV news broadcast. Visit the moving 9/11 Gallery and the Knight Studios, which have hosted segments of popular shows such as *Good Morning America* and an NBC interview with President Obama.

*The entrance of the popular Newseum*

## Key Features

Journalists Memorial
Third Floor
Second Floor
First Floor
Concourse Level
Entrance

④ ⑥ ⑦ ⑧ ③ ⑤ ② ①

▨ **Third Floor** Digital News, Journalists Memorial, Edward R. Murrow Story, Newseum TV Studio, Knight Studio, and World News Gallery

▨ **Second Floor** Ethics Center, Interactive Newsroom, and Newseum Store

▨ **First Floor** Annenberg Theater, Great Hall of News, Newseum Store, Information Desk, and Pulitzer Prize Photographs

▨ **Concourse Level** Berlin Wall, Changing Exhibits, Comics, Documentary Theater, Learning Center, Orientation Theaters, and Sports Theater

① **Berlin Wall** This exhibit focuses on the role of journalists and the free press in helping topple the Berlin Wall in 1989 and opening East Germany to the West after 28 years of Communism.

② **The New York Times–Ochs-Sulzberger Family Great Hall of News** Watch breaking news from around the world on a massive screen that dominates the museum's soaring 90-ft (27-m) high atrium on the first floor.

③ **Pulitzer Prize Photographs Gallery** Look at some of the most iconic images of the 20th and 21st centuries, including that of a firefighter cradling an injured child during the Oklahoma City bombing (1995) and the reunion of a returning prisoner of war with his family after the Vietnam War.

④ **Knight Studio on Pennsylvania Avenue** This working broadcast studio is a popular venue for national news anchors and news shows. It is possible to watch a live broadcast when the studio is in use. Shows recorded here include *This Week*, ABC's Sunday morning news program.

⑤ **I-Witness: A 4-D Time Travel Adventure** Screened at the Annenberg Theater, this 13-minute 3-D movie with 4-D special effects immerses viewers in the world of journalism as it covers moments in history, from the American Revolution to World War II.

**Prices given are for a family of four**

⑥ **Time Warner World News Gallery** This exhibit looks at the challenges faced by journalists, and the state of journalism and press freedom around the world, from the perils of reporting from war zones to the dangers of being a journalist in a repressive society. A shrapnel-riddled truck is a stark reminder of the hazards of reporting, while the world map of journalistic freedoms represents the relative freedom of the press in countries around the globe.

⑦ **NBC News Interactive Newsroom** Interactive stations let visitors play the role of a reporter or photographer, and offer games and programs for all ages. Kids and adults can prepare stories, pick up a microphone, stand before a real TV camera, and read a breaking news story from a teleprompter. The resulting broadcast can later be downloaded from the Newseum website.

⑧ **Bancroft Family Ethics Center** The attractions here are well thought out interactive games that challenge participants with the questions that journalists face daily: When is it acceptable to alter a photograph? When is protecting a source appropriate? Can an event be re-created and presented as the real thing? The games are entertaining while offering a look at today's complex media world.

# KIDS' CORNER

### Find out more...
**1** Where in the Newseum can you play the role of a reporter?
**2** In a famous 1994 journalism ethics case, *Time* magazine darkened O.J. Simpson's complexion when they used his police mugshot on the cover, to make him look more "menacing" – was this wrong?
**3** Which device displays the words that reporters must say as they look into a TV camera?

..............................

Answers at the bottom of the page.

### A measure of freedom
Finland, Norway, and Sweden all tied at first place as countries with the greatest freedom of the press in 2012; the US was ranked 24th.

# The Lowdown

🌐 **Map reference** 7 D2
**Address** 555 Pennsylvania Ave NW, 20001; 888 639 7386; *www.newseum.org*

🚗 **Metro** Archives/Navy Memorial. **Bus** DC Circulator Blue line (weekdays only) & Purple line (weekends only)

🕐 **Open** 9am–5pm daily, closed Jan 1, Thanksgiving Day & Dec 25

💲 **Price** Family four pack $59.95 plus tax; general admission ticket is good for two days.

👫 **Cutting the line** Reserve tickets online and save 10 per cent.

🚩 **Guided tours** Ask for the 2-hour highlights tour brochure or download from the website.

👫 **Age range** 6 plus

🏃 **Activities** Lots of interactive exhibits designed with kids in mind.

⏱ **Allow** 2–6 hours

♿ **Wheelchair access** Yes

☕ **Cafés** Express Bar and Food Section *(see p139)*

🛍 **Shop** Newseum shop *(see p139)*

🚻 **Restrooms** On every floor

### Good family value?
While pricey, this is an exciting museum with exhibits that will interest kids. However, exhibits dealing with tragedy and death may be unsuitable for younger children.

## OF ANOTHER TIME
The oldest publication on display in the Newseum is a letter written in 1416 that relays news of the Battle of Agincourt, during the Hundred Years' War.

This battle ended with a British victory over the French.

..............................

**Answers: 1** The Interactive Newsroom. **2** Yes, and *Time* magazine publicly apologized. **3** A teleprompter.

# Newseum continued...

## Key Features

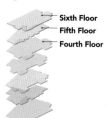

- Sixth Floor
- Fifth Floor
- Fourth Floor

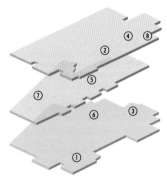

▓ **Sixth Floor** Early News, Greenspun Terrace, and Today's Front Pages

▓ **Fifth Floor** Big Screen Theater, Great Books, News History, and News Satellite

▓ **Fourth Floor** First Amendment Gallery, Five Freedoms Walkway, 9/11 Gallery, New Media Gallery, and Big Screen Theater

④ **ATS 1 Satellite** Suspended high above the sixth-floor atrium floor is a replica of the Applied Technology Science Satellite (ATS 1), launched in 1966. The ATS 1 was part of a group of satellites that made the first global television broadcast possible.

① **First Amendment Tablet** Impossible to miss, this 74-ft (23-m)-high tablet on the facade of the building has the 45 words of freedom promised to the citizens of the US. Inside, the First Amendment Gallery explores the importance of a free press in protecting these five freedoms.

② **Today's Front Pages** This gallery displays the daily front pages of newspapers from around the world. Many of these pages can also be seen outdoors – along the sidewalk for the entire length of the Newseum on the Pennsylvania Avenue side.

⑤ **News History Gallery** See newspaper front pages that record great moments in history such as the start of the Civil War, the death of outlaw Jesse James, the bombing of Pearl Harbor, or the day man first landed on the Moon. Ten interactive stations offer games and a close-up look at any of the hundreds of historic newspapers and magazines on display.

⑥ **The HP New Media Gallery** Visit this interactive gallery and see how cutting-edge media technology is transforming the way people around the world are accessing news and information.

⑦ **Great Books Gallery** This gallery exhibits the books and documents that have formed the foundations for freedom in society. Interactive kiosks and displays here allow visitors to get a close look at the Magna Carta and the US Constitution.

③ **9/11 Gallery** The centerpiece of this gallery is the dented World Trade Center communications antenna that once stood atop the complex's North Tower. The exhibits are a sobering reminder of the new challenges, including terrorism, facing our governments today.

⑧ **Hank Greenspun Terrace** Head to the top floor of the Newseum building for unmatched views of the US Capitol (*see pp104–105*) and Pennsylvania Avenue.

**Prices given are for a family of four**

*Taking a break by the fountain at the National Sculpture Garden*

## Letting off steam

Located across Pennsylvania Avenue, the **National Sculpture Garden** (see pp80–81) is filled with large sculptures, tree-shaded paths, gardens, and a magnificent central fountain that doubles as a skating rink in winter.

## Eat and drink

*Picnic: under $30; Snacks: $30–40; Real meal: $40–75; Family treat: over $75 (based on a family of four)*

**PICNIC** The **Express Bar** (concourse level, Newseum; 11am–4pm daily) is a great place to pick up sandwiches, soups, salads, or baked goods before heading to the National Mall or to John Marshall Park (4th St & Pennsylvania Ave) for a picnic.

*A range of salads, dips, and chips on display at the Food Section*

**SNACKS** Teaism (400 8th St NW, 20004; 202 638 6010; www.teaism. com), a casual Asian café and tea house, serves a selection of snacks and meals, along with tea, beer, wine, and sake. The Bento boxes, udon noodles, and salty oat cookies are popular.
**REAL MEAL** Food Section (concourse level, Newseum; 11am–3pm Thu–Sun) offers soups, salads, snacks, kids' meals, and desserts created by chef Wolfgang Puck.

**FAMILY TREAT** The Source (Newseum; 202 637 6100; www. wolfgangpuck.com), by Wolfgang Puck, is the signature restaurant at the Newseum. The downstairs bistro features a lighter Japanese Izakaya-style menu that offers sushi, sashimi, and noodle dishes, while the upstairs dining room features a menu of Asian-fusion dishes (see p61).

## Shopping

The Newseum shop offers media-themed books, gifts, and clothing, and gives special emphasis to games and toys that have an educational component and a high fun factor.

## Find out more

**DIGITAL** http://learning.blogs. nytimes.com is a fun learning blog that uses the New York Times' hottest stories and headlines to challenge young thinkers. Kids can learn how to be wise media consumers while playing games at www.pbskids.org/dontbuyit. Time magazine offers a regular online news service for kids at www. timeforkids.com/kid-reporters.
**FILM** All the President's Men (1976) is a political thriller that tells the story of two journalists uncovering the Watergate scandal for The Washington Post.

## Next stop...

**NATIONAL ARCHIVES** Look at the original US Constitution, Declaration of Independence, and Bill of Rights at the National Archives (see pp140–41). Both kids and adults can listen to secret tapes of Oval Office conversations, sign their own copy of the Declaration of Independence, and enjoy a host of other interactive experiences.

*A sculpture by James Earle Fraser outside the National Archives*

(see p61). (see pp80–81) (see pp140–41)

# KIDS' CORNER

### Look out for...
**1** Stand on the sidewalk on Pennsylvania Avenue and count the number of words in the First Amendment Tablet on the front of the building. How many are there?
**2** What are the five freedoms guaranteed to Americans by the First Amendment?
**3** The oldest item in the Newseum's collection is a cuneiform clay tablet from Sumer dated to around 1250 BC. Do you know in which part of the present-day world the civilization of Sumer was located?

Answers at the bottom of the page.

### BLOOPERS!

In 1948, the Chicago Daily Tribune flashed the headline "Dewey defeats Truman," predicting the outcome of the presidential race. Truman actually won, and an image of him holding the erroneous headline over his head has become a reminder to newspapers to check their facts before going to press.

### Front page affair

The Newseum's collection contains over 35,000 newspaper front pages going back almost 500 years.

Answers: 1 45. 2 Freedom of speech; freedom of the press; freedom of religion; freedom to peaceably assemble; and freedom to petition the government for a redress of grievances. 3 In Iraq.

# ② National Archives
## Get up close to the Declaration of Independence

The main attraction of the National Archives is the thrill of standing close to the original Declaration of Independence, US Constitution, and the Bill of Rights. The Rotunda is surrounded by the Public Vaults – a permanent exhibition with numerous galleries and interactive exhibits that display over 1,100 of the most interesting documents, audio tapes, and videos in the collection, from presidential home movies to the patent for the first phonograph.

Neo-Classical facade of the National Archives

## Key Features

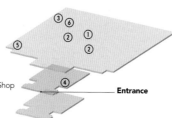

**Second Floor** Rotunda for the Charters of Freedom, Lawrence F. O'Brien Gallery, Public Vaults, and Boeing Learning Center

**First Floor** David M. Rubenstein Gallery, Visitor Services and Archives Shop

**Lower Level** William G. McGowan Theater and Charters Café

**Entrance**

① **Rotunda for the Charters of Freedom** Get a good look at the original Declaration of Independence, the Constitution of the United States, and the Bill of Rights, all of which are displayed in the Rotunda.

② **Faulkner Murals** Painted in 1936, these two long murals by Barry Faulkner illustrate fictional gatherings of the signatories of the Declaration of Independence and the US Constitution.

③ **Boeing Learning Center** Locate any National Archives document, including the Declaration of Independence. Kids will enjoy adding their signature to the famous deed and making a copy to take home.

④ **David M. Rubenstein Gallery** This interactive exhibit showcases the US's continuing efforts to advance liberty and democracy. Stories of the African Americans' struggle for rights are documented here. Also on view here is the 1297 Magna Carta, the only Magna Carta that resides in the US. State-of-the-art translation technology allows visitors to "read" the document written in Latin and explore the connections between the Magna Carta and American legal history.

⑥ **Public Vaults** Explore fascinating interactive exhibits, photos, and original records, including Abraham Lincoln's telegrams to his generals and audio recordings from the Oval Office.

⑤ **The Lawrence F. O'Brien Gallery** This 3,000-sq-ft (279-sq-m) gallery is reserved for special and traveling exhibitions that explore important themes, issues, and events in the history of the US.

**Prices given are for a family of four**

## The Lowdown

🌐 **Map reference** 7 C2
**Address** Constitution Ave at 9th St NW, 20408; 866 272 6272; www.archives.gov

🚗 **Metro** Archives/Navy Memorial. **Bus** DC Circulator Purple line to 7th St & Constitution Ave (weekends only)

🕐 **Open** Mar 15–Labor Day: 10am–7pm daily; day after Labor Day–Mar 14: 10am–5:30pm daily; last admission 30 minutes before closing; closed Thanksgiving Day & Dec 25

💲 **Price** Free

👫 **Cutting the line** Book advance tickets at www.archives.gov/nae/visit/reserved-visits.html or call 877 444 6777 to avoid waiting in line, especially Mar 15–Labor Day & major hols.

🚩 **Guided tours** Free docent-led tours at 9:45am Mon–Fri; advance reservation required

👫 **Age range** 6 plus

🧍 **Activities** Interactive exhibits at Public Vaults

⏱ **Allow** 1–2 hours

♿ **Wheelchair access** Yes

☕ **Café** Charters Café on the lower level

👫 **Restrooms** On all levels

**Good family value?**
The museum is free, and kids enjoy hands-on activities, and the Declaration of Independence.

## Letting off steam

The **National Sculpture Garden** (see pp80–81) has shady paths that lead past large sculptures, including Barry Flanagan's *Thinker on a Rock*, a favorite with kids. The huge central fountain is surrounded by inviting benches and the Pavilion Café is a great place for a relaxing lunch.

*The central fountain at the National Sculpture Garden*

## Eat and drink

*Picnic: under $30; Snacks: $30–40; Real meal: $40–75; Family treat: over $75 (based on a family of four)*

**PICNIC National Park Service Refreshment Stands** (on the National Mall) sell quick eats. Head for a picnic lunch at the National Sculpture Garden, which includes works from the National Gallery of Art.
**SNACKS Au Bon Pain** (1001 Pennsylvania Ave NW, 20004; 202 393 8809; www.aubonpain.com), a popular coffee house, bakery, and

*Various types of foods on display at Au Bon Pain in L'Enfant Plaza food court*

casual restaurant, is part of a chain that offers healthy soups, stews, sandwiches, and salads.
**REAL MEAL Jaleo** (480 7th St NW, 20004; 202 628 7949; www.jaleo. com) is a sleek and contemporary Spanish tapas bar, led by chef José Andrés. The choice of small plates is vast, ranging from cured meats and smoked cheeses, to garlic-sautéed shrimp and fried baby squid, to an extensive selection of vegetable dishes and tortillas.
**FAMILY TREAT Rasika** (633 D St NW, 20001; 202 637 1222; www.rasika restaurant.com/pennquarter; closed for lunch on Sat and Sun) serves modern Indian cuisine that gets good reviews. The appetizers and entrées can be shared, and food and wine pairings are available (see p145).

## Find out more

**DIGITAL** Go to www.constitution facts.com/us-constitution-kids for fun interactive activities and quizzes on the United States Constitution.
**FILM** Watch *National Treasure* (2004) in which Benjamin Gates (Nicolas Cage) plans to steal the Declaration of Independence. *John Adams* (2008) is a mini-series about the role of John and Abigail Adams in the founding of the USA.

*Display at the innovative International Spy Museum*

## Next stop...

**INTERNATIONAL SPY MUSEUM**
Kids love the intriguing International Spy Museum (see pp144–5), which is chock-full of spy gadgets. The hands-on and interactive exhibits let kids pretend to be code-breakers, create their own cover, and go behind the Iron Curtain.

*The historic Old Post Office building*

## ③ Old Post Office

**Look out from the clock tower**

Ticking away between the White House *(see pp122–3)* and Capitol Hill, the 315-ft (96-m)-high clock tower of the Old Post Office has kept the city and all its politicians on time for almost a century. Kids and parents alike will enjoy the National Park Service ranger-led tour to the observation deck high in the clock tower, which offers a spectacular panoromic view of the city, second only to the one on offer from the Washington Monument *(see pp84–5)*. Also located in the tower are the Bells

of Congress, which were donated by the British and are replicas of those in London's Westminster Abbey. The building has been bought by Donald Trump with plans to transform it into a high-end hotel. It is currently closed for renovation. Upon completion (set for 2016), Trump has said the public will once again have access to the observation deck in the clock tower.

### Letting off steam

The **US Navy Memorial** *(701 Pennsylvania Ave NW, 20004; www.navymemorial.org; 9:30am–5pm daily)* is an open-air plaza with fountains, waterfalls, and a statue of a young sailor arriving in his first foreign port. Adjacent to the plaza is the Naval Heritage Center with interactive displays on the history of the US Navy.

### The Lowdown

- 🌐 **Map reference** 7 B2
  **Address** Pennsylvania Ave NW, 20004
- 🚗 **Metro** Federal Triangle.
  **Bus** DC Circulator Purple line to Constitution Ave NW & 14th St (weekends only)
- 🕐 **Open** Currently closed for renovation, though its impressive exterior can still be admired.
- 💲 **Price** Free
- 👫 **Age range** All ages
- 🕐 **Allow** 30 minutes–1 hour
- ♿ **Wheelchair access** Yes
- 🍴 **Eat and drink** *Snacks* The Ronald Reagan Building & International Trade Center Food Court *(1300 Pennsylvania Ave NW, 20004; 202 312 1300; www.itcdc.com)* serves a range of snacks. *Real meal* Elephant & Castle *(1201 Pennsylvania Ave NW, 20004; 202 347 7707)* serves English-style satisfying pub food.
- 👫 **Restrooms** In the Elephant & Castle

*The Lone Sailor statue by Stanley Bleifeld at the US Navy Memorial*

## ④ Ford's Theatre

**Where Lincoln was shot**

On April 14, 1865, President Abraham Lincoln was shot and fatally wounded while attending a stage performance at Ford's Theatre. His assassin was an actor and Confederate sympathizer named John Wilkes Booth. Union soldiers finally cornered Booth and killed him on April 26. Today, Ford's Theatre is both a working theater and a museum dedicated to Lincoln's life and achievements. The museum fills the theater's lower level with excellent exhibits that document Lincoln's political rise and presidency, the Civil War, and the aftermath of his assassination. Among the many artifacts on display is the Derringer pistol that Booth used in the shooting. Upstairs, the theater looks virtually the same now as it did the

### The Lowdown

- 🌐 **Map reference** 7 C2
  **Address** 511 10th St NW, 20004; 202 347 4833; www.fordstheatre. org, www.nps.gov/foth
- 🚗 **Metro** Metro Center, Gallery Place-Chinatown & Archives/Navy Memorial. **Bus** DC Circulator Red line to 7th St NW & F St NW (daily)
- 🕐 **Open** 9am–4:30pm daily, closed Thanksgiving Day & Dec 25
- 💲 **Price** Free same-day tickets available on first-come first-served basis; advance online tickets for $3.50.
- 👫 **Cutting the line** Book tickets at www.ticketmaster.com.
- 👫 **Age range** 6 plus
- 🕐 **Activities** A talk by a National Park Service ranger or a performance by Ford's Theatre Society; prices vary for evening performances, with tickets available at the box office or www.ticketmaster.com.
- 🕐 **Allow** 1 hour
- ♿ **Wheelchair access** Yes
- 🍴 **Eat and drink** *Snacks* Crepes On The Walk *(701 7th St NW, 20001; 202 393 4910; www.crepes-a-gogo.com)* offers good-sized, filling savory and sweet crêpes. *Real meal* Hard Rock Cafe *(999 E St NW, 20004; 202 737 7625; www.hardrock.com)* offers starters, burgers, and full meals.
- 👫 **Restrooms** In the museum and in the theater

day Lincoln died. Visitors can get close to and look into the presidential box where the president was shot.

## Letting off steam

The delightful carousel in front of the **Smithsonian Castle** (see p64) is a perfect change-of-pace for children and adults. Kids can play on the lawn nearby and listen to the music, or hop on a horse and spin round and round.

## ⑤ The Petersen Boarding House
### Where Lincoln took his last breath

After President Abraham Lincoln was shot at Ford's Theatre, he was carried across the street to this house, where doctors cared for him. That night, some 90 or more people came to pay their respects. Soldiers had to guard the doors when large crowds began to gather in the streets as news of the shooting spread. At 7:22am on April 15, Abraham Lincoln died in a bedroom of this simple dwelling. Today, the house is operated by the National Park Service as a museum and is decorated with furnishings from the 1860s.

**Above** Entrance of the Five Guys Burgers and Fries restaurant
**Below** The presidential box where Abraham Lincoln was shot

## Letting off steam

Head to **Freedom Plaza** (1455 Pennsylvania Ave NW, 20004), where kids love to play on the inlaid stone map of L'Enfant's plan for the city. The White House, US Capitol, and parts of the Mall are shown on the map, which covers the plaza.

Children riding the carousel in front of the Smithsonian Castle

## The Lowdown

🌐 **Map reference** 7 B2
**Address** 516 10th St, 20004; 202 347 4833; www.fordstheatre.org, www.nps.gov/foth

🚇 **Metro** Metro Center, Gallery Place-Chinatown & Archives/Navy Memorial. **Bus** DC Circulator Red line to 7th St NW & F St NW (daily)

🕐 **Open** 9am–4:30pm daily, closed Thanksgiving Day & Dec 25

💲 **Price** Included with Ford's Theatre tickets

👫 **Cutting the line** There is rarely a line to get in.

🚺 **Age range** 6 plus

🕐 **Allow** 1 hour

♿ **Wheelchair access** Yes

🍴 **Eat and drink** Snacks Five Guys Burgers and Fries (808 H St NW, 20050; 202 393 2900; www.five guys.com) serves hearty American fare. **Real meal** Matchbox Chinatown (713 H St NW, 20001; 202 289 4441; www.matchbox chinatown.com) offers pizza, steak, salads, and sandwiches.

🚻 **Restrooms** In Ford's Theatre across the street

## The presidential box
Ford's Theatre stages many plays each year. While several presidents since Lincoln have attended performances here, none have sat in the presidential box where Lincoln was assassinated.

# ⑥ International Spy Museum
## Learn the tricks of the spy trade

Enormously popular with both adults and kids, this museum covers the history of spies and spying – from 13th-century Ninjas to the Cold War and the Internet age. Within its walls is the largest collection of international spy gadgets and artifacts on public display in the world, as well as interactive stations and exhibits where visitors can create a "cover identity," crack a code, and listen in on secret conversations.

*Living your Cover exhibit at the International Spy Museum*

## Key Features

▓ **Third Floor** Covers and Legends, School for Spies, Secret History of History, Spies Among Us, Code Breaking, and Cloak and Dagger Theater

▓ **Second Floor** Special Events Space

▓ **First Floor** Weapons of Mass Disruption, War of the Spies, Berlin Tunnel, Spy Games, Ground Truth Theater, and Museum Store

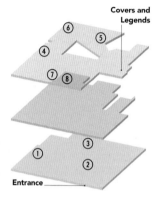

**Entrance**

① **Weapons of Mass Disruption** Hackers and viruses are the new WMD and this exhibit looks at the dangers posed by attacks on communications and how specialists are combating the threat.

② **Exquisitely Evil: 50 Years of Bond Villains** Meet James Bond's villains, uncover their evil schemes, and explore their exotic lairs and weapons. Make connections between fact and fiction and discover how the evildoers and their plots have changed to reflect their times.

③ **Atomic Countdown** Have your own "Bond Moment" as you attempt to beat the clock while trying to disarm a bomb.

④ **Secret History of History** Exhibits here explore the art of spying from biblical times to the present. Find out about real spies, including chef Julia Child and singer and actress Marlene Dietrich, and about spy tools such as carrier pigeons and hot-air balloons.

⑤ **School for Spies** Covering all the skills of spy craft, this exhibit has spy gadgets going back 50 years, from a KGB gun in a lipstick and hidden cameras to microdots, bugs, and surveillance equipment.

⑥ **James Bond's Aston Martin** Don't miss James Bond's silver Aston Martin DB5 from the 1964 movie *Goldfinger*. The car's gadgets include two hidden machine guns, an oil slick release, and tire hubs that extend to slash the bad guy's tires.

⑦ **Spies Among Us** Learn about spy rings and counter spies that operated in the US, or make an attempt at code breaking.

⑧ **The Enigma Machine** During World War II, these typewriter-like machines created coded messages that the Germans thought were indecipherable, but were eventually cracked by the Allies.

## The Lowdown

🌐 **Map reference** 7 C1
**Address** 800 F St NW, 20004; 202 398 7798; *www.spymuseum.org*

🚗 **Metro** Gallery Place–Chinatown & Metro Center. **Bus** DC Circulator Red line to 9th St NW & F St NW (daily)

🕐 **Open** Hours vary, check website or call for schedule; closed Jan 1, Thanksgiving Day & Dec 25

💲 **Price** $66–76. Extra charges for special exhibits and programs.

👥 **Cutting the line** Visit *www.spymuseum.org* for information on ticket sales

🚩 **Guided tours** Operation Spy for kids 12 and up; $14.95 per ticket. Spy in the City for 10 plus (start at $14.95). See website for more tours and details.

👫 **Age range** 10 plus

👪 **Activities** Decode messages, create a covert "cover," and listen to real recordings of intercepted messages; see website for details.

⏱ **Allow** 1–3 hours

♿ **Wheelchair access** Yes

☕ **Café** Shake Shack on the first floor (see p145)

🛍 **Shop** Museum store (see p145)

🚻 **Restrooms** On every floor

**Good family value?**
While pricey, this museum is a clever idea, well executed, and a favorite with kids. Lots of hands-on interactive exhibits keep them busy.

*Prices given are for a family of four*

## Letting off steam

A few blocks south of the museum, the **US Navy Memorial** (see p142) is a pretty, open plaza with two refreshing fountains that flank a large granite map of the world. Kids enjoy "running around the world" and around The Lone Sailor, a commemorative statue of a young sailor alone in a foreign port. The statue was forged in part with metal from eight historic ships.

The adventurous Cortez siblings in the 2001 movie Spy Kids

## Eat and drink

Picnic: under $30; Snacks: $30–40; Real meal: $40–75; Family treat: over $75 (based on a family of four)

**SNACKS Shake Shack** (first floor, International Spy Museum; 202 800 9930) is a modern-day "roadside" burger joint offering 100 per cent all-natural Angus beef hamburgers, flat-top dogs, crinkle-cut fries, fresh-made frozen custard, shakes, craft beer, wine, and much more.

Entrance of the popular Ella's Wood Fired Pizza

**REAL MEAL Ella's Wood Fired Pizza** (610 9th St NW, 20004; 202 638 3434; www.ellaspizza.com) is a family-friendly place serving thin-crust pizzas, appetizers, salads, calzones, pasta, and desserts. Beer, wine, and cocktails are also available.

**FAMILY TREAT Rasika** (633 D St NW, 20001; 202 637 1222; www.rasikarestaurant.com/pennquarter) is known for its rich curries, flavorful tandoori preparations, and spicy lamb, chicken, and seafood dishes. The menu has vegetarian options, and an extensive wine list. Service is gracious and efficient (see p141).

## Shopping

Everything a budding spy or spy fan could want can be found inside the unique museum store on the first floor. Choose from listening devices that capture conversations from 300 ft (91 m) away, video cameras in pens, camera sunglasses, wrist-watch cell phones, and a mind-boggling collection of spy-oriented books, posters, clothing, and art.

## Find out more

**DIGITAL** Visit www.scholastic.com/ispy/games/index.htm for spy puzzles, games, and challenges. Learn how to be a Geo Spy at www.kids.nationalgeographic.com/kids/games/geographygames/geospy. **FILM** Spy Kids (2001) is a family movie in which two children save their secret-agent parents from danger. Watch Agent Cody Banks (2003), a spy adventure story about a 15-year-old who goes undercover as a CIA agent to save the world.

Various exhibits on display at the Smithsonian American Art Museum

## Next stop...

**SMITHSONIAN AMERICAN ART MUSEUM** Housed in the beautifully restored Patent Office, the Smithsonian American Art Museum (see pp146–7) showcases American art from Colonial times to the present, including breathtaking landscapes by Thomas Moran and Albert Bierstadt.

# KIDS' CORNER

## Do you know...

**1** Who was the first spymaster in the United States?
**2** What was the name of the famous chef who was also a spy? Her kitchen is in the National Museum of American History (see pp70–71).
**3** Who drove the silver Aston Martin DB5 car in the movie Goldfinger, among others?
**4** Which medal was actress Marlene Dietrich awarded for her efforts during World War II?

Answers at the bottom of the page.

**I SPY**
A few years before the French Revolution (1789), Founding Father Benjamin Franklin lived in France as US ambassador and operated a network of intelligence agents.

## AGENT BUTTERSPY

Robert Baden-Powell, founder of the Boy Scouts, worked for British military intelligence during the Second Boer War (1899–1902). He traveled disguised as a butterfly collector, and added drawings of enemy military installations into his drawings of butterfly wings.

## Spy city

Washington, DC is home to more active spies than any other city in the world.

**Answers: 1** George Washington. He supervised a wide network of spies during the Revolutionary War. **2** Julia Child. **3** James Bond, played by Sean Connery. **4** Medal of Freedom, America's highest civilian honor.

# ⑦ Smithsonian American Art Museum and National Portrait Gallery
## Two great art museums in one building

A 19th-century American Greek Revival-style building is home to two fine museums. The Art Museum displays works that reflect American life from colonial times to the present day, and its contemporary art gallery has some fun and funky pieces by cutting-edge modern artists. The Portrait Gallery has portraits of 44 US presidents and of men and women who helped shape America from 1600 to 1900.

"Lansdowne" Portrait o George Washington

## Key Features

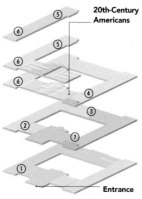

**20th-Century Americans**

**Fourth Floor** Luce Foundation Center and Lunder Conservation Center

**Third Floor Mezzanine** Luce Foundation Center, Lunder Conservation Center, Champions, and BRAVO!

**Third Floor** 20th-Century Americans, Contemporary Art, Great Hall, and Luce Foundation Center

**Second Floor** Early American Art, America's Presidents, and Graphic Arts

**First Floor** Folk Art, American Experience, and American Origins

**National Portrait Gallery**

Entrance

① **The Throne of the Third Heaven of the Nations' Millennium General Assembly** Night janitor James Hampton worked in a rented garage for 14 years to create this masterpiece from salvaged aluminum and other metal foils, plus other cast-off and reclaimed items.

② **George Washington "Lansdowne" Portrait** (1796) Painted from life by famed portrait artist Gilbert Stuart, this is one of the few paintings depicting Washington in civilian attire.

③ **The Grand Canyon of the Yellowstone** Landscapes of the American West, such as this one by Thomas Moran, fired the imaginations of easterners and were instrumental in the founding of the National Park Service system in 1916.

④ **Electronic Superhighway: Continental U.S., Alaska, Hawaii** This video-and-neon installation represents the way in which Korean artist Nam June Paik saw the new interstate highway system when he came to the US in 1964.

⑤ **Lunder Conservation Center** Watch conservators as they painstakingly restore fine artworks at this huge space shared by the two museums.

⑥ **Luce Foundation Center** Choose from over 3,300 sculptures, textiles, decorative arts, and paintings in rows of glass cases and pullout drawers.

⑦ **The Catlin Gallery** George Catlin traveled throughout the American West in the mid-19th century, painting rapidly disappearing Native American tribes.

## The Lowdown

**Map reference** 7 C1
**Address** 8th St & F St NW, 20004; Smithsonian American Art Museum: www.americanart.si.edu. National Portrait Gallery: www.npg.si.edu

**Metro** Gallery Place–Chinatown. **Bus** DC Circulator Red line to 7th St NW & G St NW

**Open** 11:30am–7:00 pm daily, closed Dec 25

**Price** Free

**Cutting the line** There is rarely a line to get in.

**Guided tours** Docent-led tours of both the museums are held daily (check the websites).

**Age range** 6 plus

**Activities** Monthly family day at the art museum; daily scavenger hunt in the Luce Foundation Center (www.americanart.si.edu/luce/downloads); weekend portrait discovery kits at the portrait gallery.

**Allow** 1–3 hours
**Wheelchair access** Yes
**Café** Courtyard Café on the first floor
**Shops** Store and bookshop on the first floor (see p147)
**Restrooms** On every floor

**Good family value?**
Great art for free, but there is little that is interactive and younger kids may get bored.

*Fountains and tree-shaded paths at Franklin Park*

## Letting off steam

**Franklin Park** *(14th St & I St NW, 20004)* offers a tranquil spot for kids to run around in. A central fountain adds to the cool atmosphere. The park's shaded benches are popular with office workers, who flock here at lunchtime during good weather.

## Eat and drink

*Picnic: under $30; Snacks: $30–40; Real meal: $40–75; Family treat: over $75 (based on a family of four)*

**PICNIC Full Kee Restaurant** *(509 H St NW, 20001; 202 371 2233; www. fullkeedc.com)* offers an extensive choice of Chinese dishes. Take food from here and enjoy it in Franklin Park.

**SNACKS Courtyard Café** *(Kogod Courtyard, Smithsonian American Art Museum and National Portrait Gallery)* serves seasonal treats in a relaxed atmosphere. Enjoy light lunch options, coffee, and desserts.

**REAL MEAL Carmine's** *(425 7th St NW, 20004; 202 737 7770; www. carminesnyc.com)* serves Italian and American entrées on large platters for sharing. Choose from antipasto, pasta, seafood, meat dishes, desserts, and a good wine list *(see p79)*.

**FAMILY TREAT Poste Moderne Brasserie** *(Hotel Monaco, 555 8th St NW, 20004; 202 783 6060; www. postebrasserie.com)* is an elegant restaurant with a fine wine list. The seasonal New American cuisine is garden fresh, with entrées that may include beef bourguignon, pastured chicken, and wild king salmon.

## Shopping

The museums' store is filled with fine art books, art-oriented clothing, and gifts. Custom prints of museum artworks can be made on request.

## Find out more

**DIGITAL** Meet Me at Midnight is an interactive mystery tour of the American Art Museum at *www. americanart.si.edu/education/ insights/midnight*. Women of our Time provides an interactive look at the 20th-century women who appear in the National Portrait Gallery at *www.npg.si.edu/cexh/woot/index. htm*. Learn about Native Americans through campfire stories and the art of George Catlin at *www.american art.si.edu/exhibitions/online/catlin classroom*. Many other online exhibitions and multimedia resources are available at *www.americanart. si.edu* and *www.npg.si.edu*.

**FILM** Night at the Museum: Battle of the Smithsonian (2009) features paintings from the National Portrait Gallery. Edison, the Man (1940) is a biographical film about the inventor of the electric light, while The Story of Alexander Graham Bell (1939) is a fictionalized biographical film about the inventor of the telephone.

*Row of buildings lining the popular M Street in Georgetown*

## Next stop...

**GEORGETOWN** Head to Georgetown, the city's first suburb. Here, rows of Federal-style townhouses line brick-paved, tree-shaded lanes, while shops and eateries crowd along M Street and Wisconsin Street. The riverfront park is a great spot for kids.

# 8 National Museum of Crime and Punishment

## Gangsters and morgues

This sensational look at crime, criminals, and punishment from medieval times to the present day is a big hit with children. Strong on interactive experiences aimed at a younger audience, the museum also has a modern, hi-tech studio where the popular TV show *America's Most Wanted* is filmed. In the History of Crime section, kids can step into a Colonial-era pillory, take part in a Wild West shootout, or try their hand at cracking a safe. There are also other exhibits, including a CSI crime lab where visitors can test their skill at solving a murder based on an examination of forensic evidence and a fake corpse in a morgue. Also popular with children

*The large fountain at the western end of Freedom Plaza*

is the bullet-riddled 1934 Ford Sedan used in the 1967 movie *Bonnie and Clyde*.

### Letting off steam

A good place to let kids run around, **Judiciary Square** *(450 F St NW, 20001)* is located two blocks east from the museum. The National Law Enforcement Officers Memorial stands in the center of the square.

# 9 Madame Tussauds

## Get snapped with a star

This is the place where dreams of having a picture taken with Barack Obama, Mick Jagger, or Oprah Winfrey come true. Children of all ages will enjoy walking among hundreds of life-like wax figures of sports stars such as Tiger Woods, entertainers like Rihanna, Beyoncé,

*Wax figures of Michelle and Barack Obama at Madame Tussauds*

## The Lowdown

- 🌐 **Map reference** 7 C1
  **Address** 575 7th St NW, 20004; 202 393 1099; www.crimemuseum.org
- 🚌 **Metro** Gallery Place–Chinatown. **Bus** DC Circulator Red line to 7th St SW & E St SW (daily)
- ⏱ **Open** Hours vary according to schedule; check website for details
- 💲 **Price** $70–80; under 5s free
- 🎫 **Cutting the line** Call or reserve online date- and time-specific tickets
- 🚩 **Guided tours** Self-guided audio tour $20. Behind-the-scenes tour $48; check availability
- 👫 **Age range** 8 plus
- 🤸 **Activities** Interactive exhibits
- ⏲ **Allow** 1–3 hours
- ♿ **Wheelchair access** Yes
- 🍽 **Eat and drink** *Snacks* Teaism *(400 8th St NW, 20004; 202 638 6010; www.teaism.com)* offers ginger limeade, salty oat cookies, and carrot cake scones. *Real meal* Gordon Biersch Brewery Restaurant *(900 F St NW, 20004; 202 783 5454; www.gordonbiersch.com)* has an extensive selection, a creative kids' menu, and family-friendly ambience.
- 👫 **Restrooms** On first and third floor

## The Lowdown

- 🌐 **Map reference** 7 B1
  **Address** 1001 F St NW, 20004; 202 942 7300; www.madame tussauds.com
- 🚌 **Metro** Metro Center, Gallery Place–Chinatown. **Bus** DC Circulator Red line to 9th St NW & F St NW (daily)
- ⏱ **Open** Daily, but timings vary. Check the website for specific timings through the year.
- 💲 **Price** $78–88; under 3s free; reserving tickets online saves 15 per cent.
- 🎫 **Cutting the line** There is rarely a line to get in.
- 👫 **Age range** 10 plus
- ⏲ **Allow** 1 hour
- ♿ **Wheelchair access** Yes
- 🍽 **Eat and drink** *Snacks* Lincoln's Waffle Shop *(504 10th St NW, 20004; 202 638 4008; closed for dinner Sat & Sun)* offers waffles, pancakes, fried steak, hot dogs, and chicken wings. *Real meal* Nando's Peri Peri *(819 7th St NW, 20001; 202 898 1225; www.nandosperiperi.com)* has chicken as its main entrée, with salads and vegetarian options too. Try their signature flame-grilled peri-peri chicken.
- 👫 **Restrooms** On lower level

and Madonna, and actors including Johnny Depp, Angelina Jolie, and Brad Pitt. And as this is Washington, expect lots of political figures, including all 44 US presidents in the Presidents Gallery.

### Letting off steam

**Freedom Plaza** *(see p143)* is a broad expanse of stone with a fountain and a statue of Revolutionary War hero General

Casimir Pulaski. Popular with kids and skateboarders, the park is dedicated to Martin Luther King, Jr. and has engraved quotes about Washington, DC and its place in the world.

## ⑩ National Museum of Women in the Arts

### Great women artists

This is the only major art museum in the world dedicated solely to works produced by women artists. Teens and tweens will enjoy the works of Impressionist Mary Cassat and animal painter Rosa Bonheur. Younger kids will like some of the modern and folk art, including Chakaia Booker's *Acid Rain* (2001), a funky statement constructed from used rubber tires. One of the earliest works in the collection is the richly ornate *Portrait of a Noblewoman*, painted around 1580 by Italian artist Lavinia Fontana. Moving three-and-a-half centuries forward in time, look for the 1937 self-portrait by famed Mexican artist Frida Kahlo, created for her one-time lover, the deposed Russian revolutionary, Leon Trotsky.

### Letting off steam

**Chinatown**, a small neighborhood along H Street and I Street, offers a chance to relax by strolling around, admiring the enormous Chinese Friendship Archway, and looking at Subway and Starbucks signs in both Chinese and English. Kids might also enjoy stopping at a Chinese grocery shop. If it is near lunchtime, then head to one of the several good Chinese restaurants here.

*The Chinese Friendship Archway painted in gold and red*

## The Lowdown

🌐 **Map reference** 7 B1
**Address** 1250 New York Ave NW, 20005; 202 783 5000; www.nmwa.org

🚇 **Metro** Metro Center

🕐 **Open** 10am–5pm Mon–Sat, noon–5pm Sun, closed Jan 1, Thanksgiving Day & Dec 25

💲 **Price** $20–30; under 18s free

🧍 **Cutting the line** There is rarely a line to get in

🚩 **Guided tours** Walk-in tours offered when docents available; $48; under 12s free; ask at the information desk.

👫 **Age range** 10 plus

👫 **Activities** Free family programs for kids 6–12, accompanied by an adult; first Sun of the month

🕐 **Allow** 1–3 hours

♿ **Wheelchair access** Yes

🍽 **Eat and drink** *Snacks* Mezzanine Café *(in the museum; lunch Mon–Fri; brunch first Sun each month)* is a relaxed spot to enjoy lunch surrounded by art from the museum. The seasonal menu offers soups, salads, sandwiches, a daily entrée, and desserts. *Family treat* Siroc Restaurant *(915 15th St NW, 20005; 202 628 2220; www.sirocrestaurant.com; closed for lunch on weekends)* serves creative contemporary Italian cuisine in a refined yet casual space. The menu includes home-made spaghetti with pancetta sauce, spinach fettuccini with smoked mozzarella and marjoram, chicken Milanese style, and entrée salads.

👫 **Restrooms** On every floor except the mezzanine

**Picnic** under $30; **Snacks** $30–40; **Real meal** $40–75; **Family treat** over $75 (based on a family of four)

# Georgetown

Historic and beautiful, Georgetown is part of, but much older than, Washington, DC. Renowned for its classy restaurants and boutiques, it is also home to a young, hip crowd that attends the nearby Georgetown University. For families, the fun here is in the history: walking the C&O Canal path, visiting the Old Stone House, and exploring the beautiful gardens and collections of Dumbarton Oaks.

## Highlights

**Chesapeake and Ohio Canal**
Visit this historic canal, which is one of the best outdoor venues for walking, jogging, paddling, kayaking, boating, and cycling in the city *(see pp156–7)*.

**Dumbarton Oaks**
Don't miss this elegant estate, whose museum collections are only outclassed by the magical acres of gardens *(see pp160–61)*.

**Georgetown Waterfront Park**
Explore labyrinths, paths, and gardens, or relax on a riverfront bench at one of the prettiest and most kid-friendly parks in the Washington area *(see p158)*.

**Old Stone House**
Tour the period-furnished rooms in what is reputed to be the oldest (and most haunted) house in Washington *(see p158)*.

**N Street**
Step back in time to a brick-and-ivy area that the rich and famous, as well as several past presidents, have visited and even called home *(see p159)*.

**M Street and Wisconsin Street**
Visit this premier dining and shopping district, full of colorful boutiques, and restaurants that waft delicious smells out into the street *(see p157 & p161)*.

**Left** Furniture, sculpture, and European tapestry on display in the historic Music Room at Dumbarton Oaks
**Above left** Biking on the towpath along the Chesapeake and Ohio Canal

# The Best of
# Georgetown

Washington, DC's most historic quarter, Georgetown, gives families a chance to experience the sights, activities, and sounds of what was a thriving seaport in the 19th century. Ramble through the historic and reportedly haunted Old Stone House or the elegant Dumbarton Oaks estate with its *Alice-in-Wonderland* gardens, before catching a glimpse of the city's earliest history at the scenic C&O Canal, once a bustling trade route.

## Boat rides and green spaces

Georgetown boasts some wonderful natural spaces. Among the most popular with families is the historic **C&O Canal** (see pp156–7). Here, a gravel towpath follows the tranquil waterway as it meanders through the area, past historic buildings. Boathouses along the way offer bicycles, canoes, and kayaks for rent.

**Georgetown Waterfront Park** (see p158) is a great place for kids to play while parents kick back on a waterfront bench and watch the boats glide by on the Potomac River. Offering a welcome respite from the busy hubbub of Washington, the lovely gardens of **Dumbarton Oaks** (see pp160–61) are an ideal place to spend a sunny afternoon.

*Left Fall colors in the gardens of Dumbarton Oaks*
*Below A mule-drawn canal tour boat on the C&O Canal*

**Above** *The pool and surrounding gardens at Dumbarton Oaks*

## Step back in time

Georgetown is home to historic sites such as the **Old Stone House** *(see p158)*, which, true to its name, is the oldest known home in the DC area. Another early home is **Dumbarton Oaks**, a Federal-style mansion whose rooms are filled with Byzantine art and pre-Columbian artifacts managed by Harvard University.

Admire **Tudor Place** *(see p157)*, built for Martha Washington's granddaughter with the money left to her by George Washington. The house is filled with family heirlooms, and furnished to reflect the styles of the 19th century.

The **C&O Canal** was a thriving commercial waterway from 1850 to 1924. Today, visitors can meander along it to escape the hustle and bustle of the busy main street.

## Shop till you drop, then stand up and eat

Shopping is a diverse and rewarding experience in Georgetown. Along with high-end chains like Ralph Lauren and Ugg, there are many one-of-a-kind boutiques and specialty shops offering fashion, gifts, and unique foods. Special shops for kids include **Tugooh Toys** and **Yiro** *(see p161)* on Wisconsin Avenue.

Places to eat in Georgetown range from the finest nouveau-fusion restaurants to fun and funky hole-in-the-wall eateries. Ethnic restaurants are particularly popular, with affordable offerings such as **Bistro Français** *(see p158)* and **Das Ethiopian Cuisine** *(see p157)*, or more expensive options like **Cafe Milano** *(see p161)*. And any kid's favorites list would have to include specialty shops like **Georgetown Cupcake**, on **M Street** *(see p159)*.

## Doing what locals do

Enjoy treats on the patio of **Dean & DeLuca** *(see p159)* and watch the world stroll by. Those looking to stretch their legs can walk the labyrinth in **Georgetown Waterfront Park** or amble along **N Street** *(see p159)* to see the house where President John F. Kennedy lived.

Rent a canoe at Thompson Boat Center and paddle on the Potomac River, or simply have a picnic by the river and watch the rowers and paddlers glide by. Climb to the top floor of the **Old Stone House** and search for its resident ghost, or look at Byzantine and pre-Columbian masks and sculptures at the excellent museum in **Dumbarton Oaks**.

**Right** *Row houses lining the popular M Street in Georgetown*

# Georgetown

Covering an area of less than 1 sq mile (3 sq km) and criss-crossed with inviting, tree-shaded lanes lined with 19th-century brick townhouses, Georgetown's historic district is the perfect place to explore on foot. The park and pedestrian walkway along the Potomac River are an ideal hangout for families, and the scenic towpath along the historic C&O Canal is a great place for walking or biking. The climb from the river up to busy M Street is steep, but the reward is the glittering myriad of shops and restaurants that line M Street and its major crossroad, Wisconsin Avenue.

Georgetown

Dumbarton Oaks p160

Chesapeake and Ohio Canal p156

## Places of interest

### SIGHTS
1. Chesapeake and Ohio Canal
2. Washington Harbour
3. Old Stone House
4. N Street
5. Dumbarton Oaks

### EAT AND DRINK
1. Thomas Sweet Ice Cream
2. Kafe Leopold
3. Das Ethiopian Cuisine
4. Farmers Fishers Bakers
5. Cafe Tu-O-Tu
6. Tony & Joe's Seafood Place
7. Booeymonger Restaurant
8. Bistro Français
9. Georgetown Cupcake
10. Moby Dick
11. Dean & DeLuca
12. Ching Ching CHA House
13. Clyde's of Georgetown
14. Cafe Milano

### SHOPPING
1. The Shops at Georgetown Park
2. Tugooh Toys
3. Yiro
4. The Magic Wardrobe
5. Focus
6. Appalachian Spring
7. The Phoenix

### WHERE TO STAY
1. Avenue Suites Georgetown
2. Capella Hotel
3. Four Seasons Hotel
4. The Georgetown Inn
5. Georgetown Suites
6. Holiday Inn Washington - Georgetown

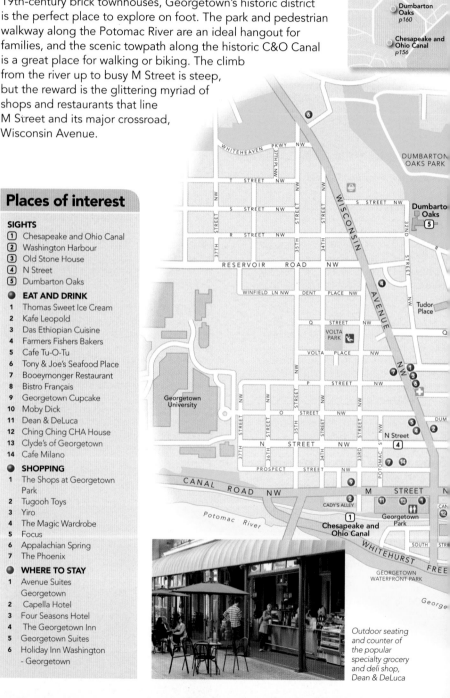

Outdoor seating and counter of the popular specialty grocery and deli shop, Dean & DeLuca

Biking along the Potomac River, Georgetown Waterfront Park

## The Lowdown

🚗 **Metro** Foggy Bottom & Dupont Circle. **Bus** Departs every 10 mins from Rosslyn and Dupont Circle. The DC Circulator Bus runs from Union Station and Dupont Circle to several locations in Georgetown (7am–9pm daily; www.dccirculator.com).

ℹ️ **Visitor information** Georgetown Visitor Center, 1057 Thomas Jefferson St NW, 20007; 202 653 5190; www.nps.gov/choh/ planyourvisit/georgetown visitorcenter.htm. Destination DC, 901 7th St NW, 4th Floor, 20001-3719; 202 789 7000; www.washington.org

🛒 **Supermarkets** Trader Joe's, 1101 25th St NW, 20037; 202 296 1921; www.traderjoes. com. Safeway, 1855 Wisconsin Ave, 20007; 202 333 3223; www.safeway.com **Market** Dean & DeLuca, 3276 M St NW, 20007; 202 342 2500; 8am–9pm Mon–Sat, 8am–8pm Sun

🚩 **Festivals** Taste of Georgetown, Wisconsin Ave (beginning of Jun). French Market, upper Wisconsin Ave (street fair, late Apr). Merriment in Georgetown, historic district (Christmas festival, early Dec)

➕ **Pharmacy** CVS 1403 Wisconsin Ave NW, 20007; 202 337 4848; 8am–10pm Mon–Fri, 9am–6pm Sat, 10am–6pm Sun

🤸 **Nearest playground** Volta Park, 34th St & Volta Place NW, 20007; 202 282 0381; 11:30am–8pm Mon–Fri

The beautifully landscaped Pebble Garden at Dumbarton Oaks

# ① Chesapeake and Ohio Canal
## Paddle a kayak through history

Stretching 184 miles (297 km) from Georgetown to Cumberland, Maryland, the Chesapeake and Ohio (C&O) Canal provides outdoor enthusiasts with a scenic place to walk, bike, or paddle. Rent a kayak or rowboat, or enjoy a leisurely stroll. From spring to early fall, mule-drawn canal-boat tours run from Great Falls Tavern in Potomac, Maryland.

*Ducks on the Chesapeake and Ohio Canal*

## Key Sights

① **Fletcher's Boat House** Rent rowboats, canoes, kayaks, and bicycles, or pick up fishing licenses, pole rentals, and bait for an afternoon of leisurely fishing.

③ **Hiking and Biking** The towpath along the pastoral canal makes an ideal hiking or cycling route. National Park Service campsites can be found all along the way.

④ **Paddling** An extensive stretch of the canal from Georgetown north has been restored to make a gentle and scenic paddling route for kayaks and canoes.

② **Abner Cloud House** Built in 1802, this was the home of miller Abner Cloud. The canal enabled his fine "Evermay" flour to reach Washington's market quickly.

⑤ **Alexandria Aqueduct** This busy waterway once floated boats across the often treacherous Potomac to Alexandria Canal. Only one pier remains, just upstream from the Virginia end of Key Bridge.

⑥ **Georgetown Waterfront Park** This park curves along 10 acres (4 ha) of the Potomac River, from Washington Harbour to Key Bridge. Cyclists and pedestrians can enjoy car-free pathways amidst beautiful nature.

⑦ **Georgetown Visitor Center** The center has displays on the history of the canal. Staff can answer questions and help plan activities, and park rangers offer guided walking, hiking, and bike tours.

⑧ **Locks** Seventy-four lift locks helped the canal lift boats up to 600 ft (182 m) above sea level. The locks were gates that raised or lowered the water level enabling the boats to move from one level to another.

## The Lowdown

🌐 **Map reference** 1 C5
**Address** 1057 Thomas Jefferson St NW, 20007; 202 653 5190; www.nps.gov/choh

🚇 **Metro** Foggy Bottom. **Bus** DC Circulator Georgetown–Union Station line to M St NW & Wisconsin Ave NW; Dupont–Georgetown–Rosslyn line to M St NW/30th St

🕐 **Open** Park: daylight hours. Georgetown Visitor Center: 9am–4:30pm Wed–Sun

💲 **Price** Free

🚩 **Guided tours** Canal-boat ride (Great Falls Tavern Visitor Center; 11710 MacArthur Bld, MD 20854; 301 767 3714); spring–summer; $25–30, under 3s free

👫 **Age range** All ages

👬 **Activities** Fletcher's Boat House (4940 Canal Rd NW, 20007; 202 244 0461; www.fletchersboat house.com), north side of Georgetown and Thompson Boat Center (2900 Virginia Ave NW, 20037; 202 333 9543; www.thompsonboatcenter.com), south side: canoe, kayak, rowboat, rowing shell, and bike rentals.

⏱ **Allow** Up to 4 hours

🛍 **Shops** On M Street (see p157)

🚻 **Restrooms** At the visitor center

**Good family value?**
Hours of free enjoyment for walkers, and moderately priced bike and boat rentals make this a fun place to visit.

*The sprawling garden in front of the 19th-century Tudor Place*

## Take cover

The elegant **Tudor Place** (*1644 31st St NW, 20007; 202 965 0400; www.tudorplace.org*) was built using the money that George Washington bequeathed to Martha Custis, his wife's granddaughter. Today, the period-furnished rooms of the house offer a time capsule of Georgetown's history. The collection includes over 100 objects that George and Martha Washington owned.

## Eat and drink

*Picnic: under $30; Snacks: $30–40; Real meal: $40–75; Family treat: over $75 (based on a family of four)*

**PICNIC Dean & Deluca** (*3276 M St NW, 20007*) is an upscale store that offers a selection of gourmet foods. Sample delicious sandwiches, pastries and other baked goods on-site, or fill your picnic basket with ingredients from the vast array of antipasti, bakery, and dessert items.

**SNACKS Kafe Leopold** (*3315 M St NW, 20007; 202 965 6005; www.kafeleopolds.com*) is a small, modern European-style café that serves excellent German pastries and desserts. It also offers breakfast, lunch, and dinner selections.

**REAL MEAL Das Ethiopian Cuisine** (*1201 28th St NW, 20007; 202 333 4710; www.dasethiopian.com*) serves dishes on large platters. Enjoy stews,

*The outdoor seating at the busy European-style Kafe Leopold*

salads, sauces, and dishes such as *zizil tibbs* (a beef dish), and *telba wot flax seed* (roasted in a spicy sauce).
**FAMILY TREAT Farmers Fishers Bakers** (*3000 K St NW, 20007; 202 298 8783; www.farmersfishersbakers.com*) has indoor or patio seating and water views. It offers an extensive selection of farm-sourced regional favorites from across the county. Kids can enjoy a burger or pizza while adults indulge in a dry-rubbed Cattleman rib-eye steak or market-priced fresh fish dinner.

## Find out more

**DIGITAL** Go to the National Park Service kids' page *www.nps.gov/choh/forkids/index.htm* to learn how a lock works and about the mules that pulled the boats. Print out the Junior Ranger activity booklet to take along when visiting the Chesapeake and Ohio Canal.

## Shopping

Just a short walk from the visitor center, there are lots of unique stores at **The Shops at Georgetown Park** (*3222 M St NW, 20007*). The mall is closed for refurbishment, but stores facing M Street are still open, including Anthropologie and J Crew.

*The beautiful fountain terrace on the Dumbarton Oaks estate*

## Next stop...

**DUMBARTON OAKS** The old-world graciousness of Dumbarton Oaks (*see pp160–61*) makes it a great place for kids to explore, especially the 10 acres (4 ha) of lush, beautiful gardens, which are considered among the finest in the US. Teens might enjoy the Harvard-curated collections of Byzantine and pre-Columbian art that are housed in the 1805 mansion.

# ② Washington Harbour

### Promenade along the Potomac River

The broad oval plaza and boardwalk along the banks of the Potomac River are a favorite place for local families to walk and bike. The boardwalk is lined with excellent restaurants and an architecturally stunning set of high-rise buildings. Enjoy great views of the boats docked along the riverfront as well as of the Kennedy Center *(see p129)*. In fair weather, a constant parade of kayakers, canoeists, and racing-shell rowers ply the river's sparkling waters. Riverboat tours depart frequently from the harbor and the walkway continues to the Georgetown Waterfront Park, creating an ideal stroll for families.

#### Take cover

A short walk up Jefferson Street leads to the **Georgetown Visitor Center** *(see p156)*, where displays highlight the history of the Chesapeake and Ohio Canal.

## The Lowdown

- 🌐 **Map reference** 1 D6
  **Address** 3000–3020 K St NW, 20007
- 🚇 **Metro** Foggy Bottom. **Bus** DC Circulator Georgetown–Union Station line to Pennsylvania Ave NW/28th St; Dupont–Georgetown–Rosslyn line to M St NW/30th St
- 💲 **Price** Free
- 👫 **Age range** All ages
- ⏱ **Allow** 30 minutes to an hour for shopping; longer for dining
- 🍴 **Eat and drink** *Snacks* Cafe Tu-O-Tu *(2816 Pennsylvania Ave NW, 20007; 202 298 7777; www.cafetuotu.com)* offers Mediterranean cuisine with a Turkish twist, including panini sandwiches, fresh veggie salads, soups, and wraps. *Family treat* Tony & Joe's Seafood Place *(3000 K St NW, 20007; 202 944 4545; www.tonyandjoes.com)* is a waterfront restaurant serving specialties that include crab bisque, seafood sandwiches, and fresh fish entrées.
- 🚻 **Restrooms** No, visit the Old Stone House or a restaurant

*The popular boardwalk with riverfront cafés at Washington Harbour*

# ③ Old Stone House

### That's pretty old!

The oldest standing building in Washington, DC, the Old Stone House offers families an interesting look at the time before America was a nation. The house was built in 1765 by a cabinetmaker, Christopher Layman, as his home and shop, in the days when Georgetown was a busy port that linked the western frontier to the sea. Today, it is maintained by the National Park Service. The rooms, from the kitchen to the children's and servant's bedchambers under the eaves, have been furnished in 18th-century style to reflect how the house looked in Layman's time. Behind the house, a lovely garden offers flower beds and benches shaded by a grand old willow.

*The leafy garden with tree-shaded benches behind the Old Stone House*

## The Lowdown

- 🌐 **Map reference** 1 D5
  **Address** 3051 M St NW, 20007; 202 895 6070; www.nps.gov/olst
- 🚇 **Metro** Foggy Bottom. **Bus** DC Circulator Georgetown–Union Station line to M St NW & Wisconsin Ave NW; Dupont–Georgetown–Rosslyn line to M St NW/30th St
- ⏱ **Open** Bookstore and park ranger: noon–5pm daily. Garden: daylight hours
- 💲 **Price** Free
- 👫 **Cutting the line** There is rarely a line to go in.
- 🚩 **Guided tours** Ask about ranger-led programs, or take an audio cell phone tour by calling 202 730 9307, option 12.
- 👫 **Age range** All ages
- ⏱ **Allow** 30 minutes
- ♿ **Wheelchair access** Yes, partial
- 🍴 **Eat and drink** *Snacks* Booeymonger Restaurant *(3265 Prospect St NW, 20007; 202 333 4810; www.booeymonger.com)* has hot, cold, and gourmet sandwiches, salads, and desserts. *Real meal* Bistro Français *(3124 M St NW, 20007; 202 338 3830; www.bistrofrancaisdc.com)* serves French country bistro cuisine in an old-world style dining room; special lunch prices.
- 🚻 **Restrooms** On the first floor

#### Letting off steam

**Georgetown Waterfront Park** *(www.georgetownwaterfrontpark. org)* is made for kids, with winding paths, a labyrinth, and a walking-jogging-bike trail along the water that offers splendid views of the river. Weary parents can relax on one of the riverfront benches.

# ④ N Street

## Following in famous footsteps

If there is a single street that sums up the heart and soul of Georgetown, it is the historic N Street. Families, especially those with history-loving kids, will enjoy following in the footsteps of the many famous people who have strolled along this pleasant, tree-shaded lane, including Thomas Jefferson, George Washington, and Alexander Graham Bell. The Beall Mansion at 3033 N Street dates from 1780 and is the oldest brick home in Georgetown. The elegant Federal-style row houses from 3255–63 N Street are known as Smith Row, and Cox Row, one of the city's best-preserved examples of Federal-era row houses, can be found at 3327–39 N Street. This street has also been home to several famous people. 3307 N Street is where John F. and Jacqueline Kennedy made their home before they moved to the White House, while 3017 N is where Jacqueline Kennedy lived after JFK's assassination. The street ends farther on at Georgetown University, the oldest Catholic university in the US.

## Take cover

The covered café-style seating of **Dean & DeLuca** (3276 M St NW, 20007) is a great place to seek shelter with a cup of coffee, or cocoa for the kids. Inside, row after row of delicious sausages, cheese, and candies from around the world will keep even impatient browsers entertained for at least half an hour.

### The Lowdown

🌐 **Map reference** 1 D5
**Address** N St NW, 20007; www.nps.gov/nr/travel/wash/dc15.htm

🚗 **Metro** Foggy Bottom. **Bus** DC Circulator Georgetown–Union Station line to M St NW & Wisconsin Ave NW; Dupont–Georgetown–Rosslyn line to M St NW/30th St

💲 **Price** Free

👫 **Age range** All ages

⏱ **Allow** 30 minutes; more with lunch

☕ **Eat and drink** *Snacks* Georgetown Cupcake (3301 M St NW, 20007; 202 333 8448; www.georgetowncupcake.com) is a gourmet cupcake shop run by two sisters who use Valrhona chocolate, Madagascar bourbon vanilla, and European sweet cream butter to create artful and tasty cupcakes. *Real meal* Moby Dick (1070 31st St NW, 20037; 202 333 4400; www.mobys online.com) serves Middle Eastern kebabs and appetizers. Order the family platters, lunch specials, or the specials for kids.

👫 **Restrooms** No, visit the Old Stone House or a restaurant

A typical Federal-style row house on historic N Street

The lush Georgetown Waterfront Park is perfect for playing ball, biking, or just relaxing

# ⑤ Dumbarton Oaks
## There have got to be elves in this garden

A legacy of Mildred and Robert Woods Bliss, Dumbarton Oaks was bought by the couple in 1920. Today, the big attraction here is the sprawling garden, which, at almost 90 years old, has developed an air of mystery and wonder. The best-loved corners include the elegant Rose Garden, the sparkling Fountain Terrace, and the beautiful swimming pool. Older kids may enjoy a tour of the house, which holds collections of Byzantine and pre-Columbian artworks.

A pre-Columbian golden hummingbird

## Key Sights

**Entrance**

### The Lowdown

🌐 **Map reference** 1 C3
**Address** www.doaks.org; Gardens: R St NW & 31st St NW, 20007; 202 339 6409. Museum: 1703 32nd St NW, 20007; 202 339 6401

🚗 **Metro** Dupont Circle. **Bus** DC Circulator Yellow line to Wisconsin Ave NW & 34 St NW

🕐 **Open** Gardens: Mar 15–Oct 31: 2–6pm Tue–Sun, closed Federal holidays and during inclement weather. Museum: 2–5pm Tue–Sun, closed Federal holidays

💲 **Price** Gardens: $26–32; students & kids 2–12 $5. Museum: free

👫 **Cutting the line** There is rarely a line to get in.

🔖 **Guided tours** Gardens: short tour 2:10pm Tue–Thu & Sat. Museum: 30-minute tour of private rooms 3pm most Sat

👫 **Age range** Gardens: all ages. Museum: 10 plus

⏱ **Allow** 1 hour to several hours

♿ **Wheelchair access** Yes, in the museum only

🛍 **Shop** The museum shop offers a large selection of gift items, textiles, and books.

👫 **Restrooms** In the lower level of the museum

**Good family value?**
Reasonable prices and impressive gardens and collections make this great value for money.

① **Fountain Terrace** A favorite with kids, this bright space is carpeted with thick grass and features two limestone pools with putto (cherub) fountains.

② **Orangery** Built in 1810, this still serves as a greenhouse sheltering gardenias, citrus trees, and oleanders through the winter. The Ficus pumila that covers the inside walls is a single, 150-year-old plant.

③ **Rose Garden** Over 900 rose bushes fill this terrace below the house. Blooms last from mid-spring through mid-fall.

④ **Pebble Garden** Redesigned in the 1930s, this garden was formed from Mexican stones and bordered with thyme and sedum beds. The sheaf-of-wheat pattern illustrates the Bliss family's motto: "As you sow, so shall you reap."

⑤ **Ellipse** Designed to be a place of quiet reflection, this gentle oval lawn features a ring of American Hornbeam trees that shade stone benches. In the center is a Provençal fountain.

⑥ **Byzantine Collection** Personal, church, and political artifacts and artworks from the Byzantine empire include outstanding mosaics, textiles, ceramics, coins, and sculptures.

⑦ **Music Room** Admire Flemish tapestries from the 1400s, a painting by El Greco, and a Steinway grand piano signed by the famous Polish composer Ignacy Paderewski.

⑧ **Pre-Columbian Collection** Aztec, Teotihuacan, Mayan, and other Meso-American artifacts on display include golden figures, masks, ritual items, and carved stone panels depicting Mayan kings.

*Displays in the Byzantine Collection at Dumbarton Oaks*

## Take cover

After frolicking amid the fountains and colorful flower beds, head inside the Dumbarton Oaks house and spend some time taking in the stunning collections. For a break, the shopping district of Wisconsin Avenue is not far away.

## Eat and drink

*Picnic: under $30; Snacks: $30–40; Real meal: $40–75; Family treat: over $75 (based on a family of four)*

**PICNIC Dean & DeLuca** *(3276 M St NW, 20007; 202 342 2500; www.deandeluca.com)* is a pricey but convenient place to pick up gourmet and deli items, or fresh fruits to take to eat in Montrose Park *(R St NW)*.

*Outdoor seating at the casual yet elegant Cafe Milano*

**SNACKS Ching Ching CHA House of Tea** *(1063 Wisconsin Ave NW, 20007; 202 333 8288; www.chingchingcha.com)* is a delightful Chinese teahouse offering over 70 iced, hot, or artisan teas with a varied selection of Chinese snacks, sweets, and full meals. The ambience is Oriental, serene, and peaceful.

**REAL MEAL Clyde's of Georgetown** *(3236 M St NW, 20007; 202 333 9180; www.clydes.com/georgetown)* is a family-friendly restaurant with a varied American menu to please all ages. Fish and chips, burgers, sandwiches, grilled cowboy steak, crab cakes, and warm apple pie are some of the most popular dishes.

**FAMILY TREAT Cafe Milano** *(3251 Prospect St NW, 20007; 202 333 6183; www.cafemilano.com)* is the place to spot diplomats, politicians, and celebrities while dining on high-priced Northern Italian cuisine.

## Shopping

It is just a hop, skip, and jump from Dumbarton to the upscale shopping zone of Wisconsin Avenue. Kids under 12 will find trendy fashions and clever games at **Tugooh Toys** *(1355 Wisconsin Ave NW, 20016)*. **Yiro** *(1419 Wisconsin Ave, 20007)* offers comfortable, organic clothing for kids under 10, while **The Magic Wardrobe** *(1663 Wisconsin Ave, 20007)* offers American and European designer wear for kids. **Focus** *(1330 Wisconsin Ave, 20007)* is the place for designer sunglasses. Fine handicrafts and vintage couture can be found at **Appalachian Spring** *(1415 Wisconsin Ave, 20007)* and **The Phoenix** *(1514 Wisconsin Ave, 20007)* respectively.

## Find out more

**DIGITAL** In 1944, as World War II raged, an international gathering of high-level diplomats held a series of talks at Dumbarton Oaks that led to the formation of the United Nations. See the UN website *www.un.org/en/aboutun/history/dumbarton_yalta.shtml* for more information.

## Next stop...

**SMITHSONIAN'S NATIONAL ZOOLOGICAL PARK** Visit great cats, elephants, pandas, and gorillas at the clean, park-like National Zoological Park *(see pp168–9)*. Look out for the meerkats and do not miss the antics of the prairie dogs.

*A cheetah resting in its enclosure, at the Smithsonian's National Zoological Park*

# Beyond
## Central Washington

Visitors are often delighted to discover that some of Washington's most captivating attractions are situated beyond the National Mall. Exceptional destinations like the Smithsonian's National Zoological Park and Oxon Hill Farm are designed to entertain kids. Families can also enjoy the beauty of the National Arboretum, admire the gargoyles at the Washington National Cathedral, and shop and dine at the boutiques and cafés at Dupont Circle.

Smithsonian's National Zoological Park
Washington National Cathedral
US National Arboretum
Central Washington, DC

## Highlights

**Smithsonian's National Zoological Park**
Meet playful pandas and orang-utans at this colorful, kid-oriented zoo, full of wonder and one-of-a-kind experiences (see pp168–9).

**Dupont Circle**
Explore the shops, bookstores, and restaurants in this historic neighborhood. A refreshing fountain stands at the center of the circle (see p174).

**Washington National Cathedral**
Admire one of the most magnificent buildings in the US. Built over 80 years, it combines a gracious Neo-Gothic style with modern touches (see pp172–3).

**The Phillips Collection**
Visit the oldest museum of modern art in the US. There are over 3,000 works on display, including some by Van Gogh, Monet, and Renoir (see p175).

**United States National Arboretum**
Explore the 446 acres (180 ha) of gardens and woodlands, and the miniature trees in the National Bonsai Collection (see pp178–9).

**Oxon Hill Farm**
Experience life on a farm as it was in the late-19th century at this living farm museum. Kids can learn how to milk cows, shear sheep, and feed chickens (see p181).

**Left** *Giraffes at the Smithsonian's National Zoological Park*
**Above left** *Looking at miniature trees displayed at the National Bonsai Collection in the United States National Arboretum*

# The Best of
# Beyond Central Washington

Away from the bustle of the National Mall, there are ample attractions to keep the whole family entertained. East of Washington, DC, the elegance of an earlier era can be seen in Kenilworth Park and Aquatic Gardens, the US National Arboretum, and Frederick Douglass's genteel home, while the northwest is home to the dazzling Washington National Cathedral and the ultimate kid zone – the Smithsonian's National Zoological Park.

## Elegant northwest

In the 19th century, northwest Washington was where the rich and influential built beautiful homes. Today, many of these buildings house the embassies and consulates of countries from every corner of the globe. Walk along **Embassy Row** (see p171), gawk at the fabulous architecture, and identify the countries represented by the flags flying outside.

Not far away, in the heart of the park-like **Dupont Circle** (see p174), a cascading, white-stone fountain is a gathering place in this trendy neighborhood of chic restaurants and funky shops. A short stroll northwest leads to **The Phillips Collection** (see p175), which displays a superb collection of modern art. Just a few blocks south, the **National Geographic Museum** (see p174) hosts displays of its famous photography as well as special exhibits that explore virtually every area of earth science.

**Right** Bishop's Garden at the Washington National Cathedral
**Below** Souvenirs for sale at the National Geographic Museum

*Above* Fountain pool and terracotta statue of Diana, Roman goddess of the hunt, in the French parterre garden, Hillwood Estate

## From gargoyles to wild animals

The northwest is also home to **Washington National Cathedral** *(see pp172–3)*, one of the most spectacular buildings in the US. The family tours here are guaranteed to get kids interested in the glories of Gothic architecture through the dozens of stories relayed in the intricate sculpture and artworks that fill the cathedral. Children can try and spot the Darth Vader gargoyle and the stained-glass window that highlights America's exploration of space and even includes a real Moon rock.

The **Smithsonian's National Zoological Park** *(see pp168–9)*, with winding paths and natural enclosures, is where visitors can get close to tigers, lions, African elephants, and pandas. Talks and demonstrations held throughout the day are geared at introducing kids to the zoo's residents.

## Rambling around Rock Creek Park

Head to **Rock Creek Park** *(see p170)*, which follows its namesake stream as it tumbles through northwest Washington down to the Potomac River in Georgetown. The park offers miles of walking, hiking, and equestrian trails. See displays on the park's flora and fauna in the nature center and explore the skies in the planetarium.

Standing in the green woodlands by sparkling Rock Creek, the historic **Peirce Mill** *(see p170)* shows how water power was used to grind wheat and corn into flour for the kitchens of 19th-century Washington. A short distance from the mill, **Hillwood Estate** *(see p170)* offers priceless art and treasures collected from around the world, as well as winding paths that lead through acres of gardens.

## Across the Anacostia

Anacostia began as a working class suburb around 1854, and today this largely African-American neighborhood is justifiably proud of its history. **Frederick Douglass House** *(see p180)* is a good place to get a feel for this history. The house is filled with the possessions and memorabilia of the famous orator and abolitionist, who lived here during the last years of his life. Across the river, the **United States National Arboretum** *(see pp178–9)* offers gardens, trails, and places for kids to explore. At **Kenilworth Park and Aquatic Gardens** *(see p180)*, see rare water lilies and lotuses in the cultivated ponds near the river.

*Left* The Corinthian-style Capitol Columns at the United States National Arboretum

# Smithsonian's National Zoological Park and around

Most of the land in the northwest quadrant of the city can be explored on foot. The zoo, however, is on a hillside, and walking around it can be mildly strenuous. Wear comfortable shoes, and on hot days look for the vapor cooling stations around the zoo. Dupont Circle is chock-full of good restaurants and interesting shops, and has its own metro station that links it to every part of the city. Washington National Cathedral is surrounded by a beautiful neighborhood that is seldom crowded. Take a pleasant stroll through the Embassy district, which is lined with grand old homes. Visit on a sunny day, but during summer come before 11am to avoid the heat.

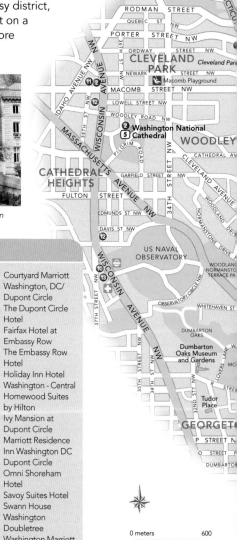

*Equestrian statue of Union general, Philip Sheridan at Sheridan Circle near Embassy Row*

## Places of interest

### SIGHTS
1. Smithsonian's National Zoological Park
2. Peirce Mill
3. Hillwood Estate
4. Embassy Row
5. Washington National Cathedral
6. Dupont Circle
7. National Geographic Museum
8. The Phillips Collection

### EAT AND DRINK
1. Panda Grill
2. 2 Amys
3. Zoo Bar Café
4. Indique
5. Vace Italian Deli
6. Siam House Thai Restaurant
7. Byblos Deli
8. Le Pain Quotidien
9. Bistrot Du Coin
10. Rocklands Barbeque and Grilling Company
11. Cactus Cantina
12. Cafe Deluxe
13. Heritage India
14. Kramerbooks & Afterwords Cafe & Grill
15. Marrakesh Palace
16. Julia's Empanadas
17. Tabard Inn Restaurant
18. Dupont Market
*See also Smithsonian's National Zoological Park (pp168–9), Hillwood Estate (p170) and The Phillips Collection (p175)*

### SHOPPING
1. Zoo stores
2. Cathedral store
*See also Dupont Circle (p174)*

### WHERE TO STAY
1. Beacon Hotel & Corporate Quarters
2. Carlyle Suites Hotel
3. Courtyard Marriott Washington, DC/ Dupont Circle
4. The Dupont Circle Hotel
5. Fairfax Hotel at Embassy Row
6. The Embassy Row Hotel
7. Holiday Inn Hotel Washington - Central
8. Homewood Suites by Hilton
9. Ivy Mansion at Dupont Circle
10. Marriott Residence Inn Washington DC Dupont Circle
11. Omni Shoreham Hotel
12. Savoy Suites Hotel
13. Swann House
14. Washington Doubletree
15. Washington Marriott Wardman Park

0 meters 600
0 yards 600

## The Lowdown

🚗 **Metro** Woodley Park-Zoo/ Adams Morgan, Cleveland Park, Van Ness-UDC, Dupont Circle, Farragut North & Farragut West. **Bus** DC Circulator Green line from Franklin Park north of the White House to Woodley Park-Zoo metro stop. From Tenleytown and Dupont Circle metro stations. **Trolley** Old Town Trolley offers a step-on step-off tour service (main ticket booth at Union Station; 202 832 9800; *www.trolleytours.com/ washington-dc*)

ℹ️ **Visitor information** Destination DC, 901 7th St NW, 4th Floor, 20001-3719; 202 789 7000; *www.washington.org*

🛒 **Supermarkets** Yes! Organic Market, 3425 Connecticut Ave NW, 20008; 202 363 1559. Giant in Van Ness, 4303 Connecticut Ave NW, 20008; 202 364 8250. Whole Foods, 2323 Wisconsin Ave NW, 20007; 202 333 5393.

**Markets** Manhattan Market, 2647 Connecticut Ave NW, 20008-2637; 202 986 4774. Glover Park Market, 2411 37th St NW, 20007; 202 333 4030; 8:30am–10pm daily

🎌 **Festivals** Boo at the Zoo, Smithsonian's National Zoological Park (Halloween festivities, late Oct); *www. nationalzoo.si.edu*. Christmas and Easter, National Cathedral. Walk Weekend, Dupont-Kalorama area museums (first weekend in Jun)

➕ **Pharmacies** CVS Pharmacy, 6 Dupont Circle NW, 20036; 202 785 1466; 24 hours daily. CVS Pharmacy, 2226 Wisconsin Ave NW, 20007; 202 944 8671; 24 hours daily

🛝 **Nearest playgrounds** Macomb Playground, 3409 Macomb St NW, 20016; 3:30–9pm Mon-Fri, 10am–4pm Sat. Montrose Park, 3099 R St, NW 20007-2923; daylight hours daily

*Banners and pretty flowers at the entrance of the Smithsonian's National Zoological Park*

# ① Smithsonian's National Zoological Park
## Lions, tigers, pandas, and more

Simply put, this is one of the world's greatest zoos. Designed from the ground up with children in mind, it is a great place for kids to run around, explore, and get close to animals from all over the world. The enclosures are large and as natural as possible, giving this 163-acre (66-ha) facility the feel of a large urban park. Interpretive programs give kids a chance to watch elephant training, octopus feeding, and scientists "talking" to orangutans.

*A cooling mist shower, National Zoological Park*

## Key Sights

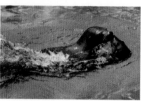

① **American Trail** Watch the playful gray seals, North American beavers, and North American river otters that live here along with California sea lions, ravens, gray wolves, bald eagles, and merganser ducks.

② **Great Ape House** Say hello to six western lowland gorillas, and observe orangutans as they use the "O-Line" rope system to travel from the Ape House to the Think Tank every day.

③ **Elephant Trails** This expansive enclosure for endangered Asian elephants allows them to trek through various habitats around the zoo.

④ **David M. Rubenstein Family Giant Panda Habitat** Two of the zoo's main attractions, Mei Xiang and Tian Tian can be seen snoozing, playing, or feeding on bamboo shoots.

⑤ **Think Tank** Watch daily presentations in this unique center where behavioral scientists study how primates think and communicate.

⑥ **Reptile Discovery Center** If it is deadly, slithery, or scaly, it can be found here along with first-rate exhibits that show how reptiles move, see, eat, and coexist with us on Earth.

⑦ **Great Cats** Spot the African lions Luke, Shera, Naba, and Lusaka, and watch Sumatran tigers enjoy a swim to cool off.

⑧ **Amazonia** Freshwater stingrays, titi monkeys, and Andean bears, as well as brilliantly colored birds and amphibians call this steamy, flooded forest home.

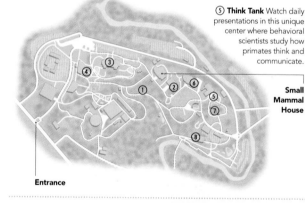

**Small Mammal House**

**Entrance**

## Take cover
In case of rain, head to the Think Tank, the Invertebrate Exhibit, or the Small Mammal House, which is home to black-footed ferrets, naked mole rats, and golden lion tamarins.

## Eat and drink
Picnic: under $30; Snacks: $30–40; Real meal: $40–75; Family treat: over $75 (based on a family of four)

**SNACKS Panda Grill** (near the bus stop and gift shop at Panda Market Square; www.nationalzoo.si.edu/

**Prices given are for a family of four**

*Visitors at the food counters of the popular Panda Grill*

Visit/food.cfm) offers pizza, pulled pork, and po' boys. Another specialty is the nachos with beef smoked on-site daily.

**SNACKS 2 Amys** (3715 Macomb St NW, 20016; 202 885 5700; www.2amyspizza.com; closed for lunch on Mon) specializes in Neapolitan wood-fired pizzas with a variety of toppings, and receives rave reviews as Washington, DC's best gourmet pizza place. Choose from cannoli, cookies, and home-made ice cream for dessert.

**REAL MEAL Zoo Bar Cafe** (3000 Connecticut Ave NW, 20008; 202 232 4225; www.zoobardc.com), located directly across the street from the main entrance to the zoo,

## The Lowdown

🌐 **Address** 3001 Connecticut Ave NW, 20008; 202 633 4888, www.nationalzoo.si.edu

🚗 **Metro** Woodley Park-Zoo/ Adams Morgan & Cleveland Park

🕐 **Open** Apr–Oct: 10am–6pm daily; Nov–Mar: 10am–4:30pm daily; closed Dec 25

💲 **Price** Free; parking for 3 hours $16, over 3 hours $22

👫 **Cutting the line** Arrive early in the day to avoid the crowds and to secure parking if driving.

👉 **Guided tours** Volunteers available for questions; check the calendar for daily programs.

👫 **Age range** 2 plus

👫 **Activities** Download the Guide for Visitors with Small Children and Family Activity Sheets from the website. Check the daily calendar for keeper talks, animal feedings, and other activities.

🕐 **Allow** 4 hours for highlights; all day to see more

♿ **Wheelchair access** Yes, to most areas. Some paths are steep.

☕ **Café** Mane Grill near Lion/Tiger Hill, Popstop near Small Mammal House, seasonal snack stands across the park, and Panda Grill (see p168)

🛍 **Shops** Stores located in Panda Plaza, Lion/Tiger Hill, and the visitor center

👫 **Restrooms** At several locations, including the visitor center and Mane Grill

**Good family value?**

Hours of fun and a chance to get close to endangered species makes it a great family activity.

is a casual restaurant with delicious kid-friendly food. Try the mac and cheese and burgers.
**FAMILY TREAT Indique** (3512 Connecticut Ave NW, 20008; 202 244 6600; www.indique.com) offers Indian cuisine including chicken *tikka makhani* (buttery sauce), *tandoori* (baked) king shrimp, and *samosas* (stuffed and fried savory pastry).

## Shopping

The zoo has three stores – at the visitor center, Panda Habitat, and Great Cats exhibit. Each shop is filled with animal-oriented toys, games, clothing, gifts, and books.

## Find out more

**DIGITAL** Take a virtual tour of the zoo on www.nationalzoo.si.edu, with almost two dozen live webcams featuring many of its popular residents. There are also photo galleries, e-cards to send, and animal photos to download.
**FILM** Available on DVD, *Kids Guides: Zoo* follows two young presenters as they visit the National Zoo and other zoos, learn to care for pandas and elephants, and handle venomous snakes.

## Next stop...

**WASHINGTON NATIONAL CATHEDRAL** The magnificent Washington National Cathedral (see pp172–3) was built with a large measure of imagination. There is a real Moon rock in one of the stained-glass windows dedicated to space exploration. *Star Wars* fans will be delighted to see a familiar-looking gargoyle high on the northwest tower – Darth Vader.

*The plush interior of Indique, an Indian restaurant on Connecticut Avenue*

# ② Peirce Mill
## The daily grind

This mill was built in the 1820s as part of a complex that included a residence, carriage house, nursery, and saw mill. Today, it is possible to tour the mill and watch as wheat is ground into flour using water-powered grindstones, just as it was done years ago.

Kids are encouraged to talk to the miller or the park ranger, who will describe the entire process of turning flowing water into the mill's driving power, and creating the flour and cornmeal that were the food staples of the early 19th century. In its day, the mill featured cutting-edge technology, with shafts that drove grain elevators, and sifters that lifted the raw grain to the attic for cleaning and separated the coarse- from the fine-ground flour.

*Trees, trails, and a stream at Rock Creek Park*

The original Peirce Barn still stands behind the mill and has displays that describe the place's history.

## Letting off steam

**Rock Creek Park** *(5200 Glover Rd NW, 20015; 202 895 6070; www.nps.gov/rocr; open daylight hours)* offers trails that beg to be explored on foot or by bike (available for hire in downtown Georgetown). Energetic kids can head 300 ft (91 m) upstream to spot the big round boulders that once formed the dam that powered the mill.

# ③ Hillwood Estate
## Post Toasties to great art

This is the estate of Marjorie Merriweather Post, heiress to the Post Cereal fortune; her father Charles William Post epitomized the American dream, making a fortune out of the invention of Post Toasties and Grape-Nuts breakfast cereals. For younger children the main attraction here is the 25-acre (11-ha) garden, which offers a delightful half-day of discovery, with dozens of nooks and crannies, flower-filled spaces, and hidden courtyards.

## Take cover

Head to the house, which is full of paintings, ceramics, and jewelry that Ms Post traveled the world collecting, and check out the eggs by legendary artist-jeweler Fabergé.

### The Lowdown

🌐 **Address** 4155 Linnean Ave NW, 20008; 202 686 5807; www.hillwoodmuseum.org

🚇 **Metro** Van Ness-UDC; then take cab or walk about half a mile (1 km) south on Connecticut Ave, east on Tilden St to Linnean Ave, north on Linnean to Hillwood

🕐 **Open** 10am–5pm Tue–Sat, 1–5pm select Sun, closed Mon, Federal holidays & Jan

💲 **Price** Suggested donation $40–50; under 6s free

👫 **Cutting the line** There is rarely a line to get in.

🚩 **Guided tours** Docent-led audio or printed tours of the house and garden available daily at the visitor center; call ahead or ask at the visitor center.

👫 **Age range** Garden: enjoyed by all ages. Museum: best for older children.

🏃 **Activities** A 15-minute film

⏱ **Allow** 1–2 hours

♿ **Wheelchair access** Yes

🍴 **Eat and drink** *Snacks* Byblos Deli *(3414 Connecticut Ave NW, 20008; 202 364 6549; www.byblosdc.com)* has a large variety of pitta, subs, and sandwiches. *Real meal* Hillwood Café *(Hillwood Estate; www.hillwoodmuseum.org/your-visit/hillwood-café)* is a bistro-style café with a kids' menu and more sophisticated fare. The changing menu might feature butternut squash bisque, roasted chicken with mushrooms, and crème brûlée for dessert.

👫 **Restrooms** In the visitor center

*The main entrance and garden of the Hillwood Estate*

### The Lowdown

🌐 **Address** Corner of Tilden St NW & Beach Dr, 20015; 202 282 0927; www.nps.gov/pimi

🚇 **Metro** Cleveland Park; from here take a cab or exit to Connecticut Ave. Walk two blocks east to the Melvin Hazen Trail. Follow the trail downhill into Rock Creek Park. The trail ends at Picnic Grove 1; turn left and the mill is one block ahead.

🕐 **Open** 10am–4pm Sat & Sun; group tours: 10am–4pm Wed–Fri (by reservation)

💲 **Price** Free

👫 **Cutting the line** There is rarely a line to get in.

👫 **Age range** 4 plus

🏃 **Activities** Ranger-led programs; call for schedule. See how flour is milled and talk to the miller.

⏱ **Allow** 30 minutes

🍴 **Eat and drink** *Picnic* Vace Italian Deli *(3315 Connecticut Ave NW, 20008; 202 363 1999)* is an ideal place to pick up pizza, Italian subs, or other picnic items that can be enjoyed in Rock Creek Park. *Real meal* Siam House Thai Restaurant *(3520 Connecticut Ave NW, 20008; 202 363 7802; www.siamhousedc.com; closed for lunch on Mon)* is a tiny family-owned restaurant offering lunch specials, and a large menu that includes drunken noodles, pad Thai, red curry, and more.

👫 **Restrooms** In the Peirce Barn

*The front entrance of the embassy of the Republic of Kenya*

# ④ Embassy Row

## Former abodes of the rich and famous

In the late 19th-century, this stretch of Massachusetts Avenue from Dupont Circle to the Naval Observatory was known as "Millionaires' Row" for the number of fine homes here. Today, many of these buildings house the embassies of countries from all over the world. Wide, tree-shaded sidewalks, grand architecture, and a chance for a geography lesson make this area great for a family stroll. Prominent buildings are the **Indonesian embassy** (*2020 Massachusetts Ave*), a splendid 1903 Beaux-Arts building built by Thomas Walsh, a miner who struck it rich in the Colorado gold fields and whose daughter Evalyn became the owner of the Hope Diamond (*see p74*). In front of the **Indian embassy** (*2107 Massachusetts Ave*) is an evocative sculpture of Mahatma Gandhi. Side trips off this avenue lead to the Phillips Collection (*see p175*) and

the **Woodrow Wilson House Museum** (*2340 S St*), which highlights the life and legacy of this US wartime president.

## Take cover

The **Phillips Collection** (*see p175*) is a modern art hidden gem. Galleries include the intimate Rothko Room, with Mark Rothko abstracts, and Laib Wax Room, with a fragrant beeswax artwork installed by Wolfgang Laib.

## The Lowdown

- 🌐 **Map reference** 2 E3
  **Address** Massachusetts Ave from Dupont Circle to the Naval Observatory, 20016–20036
- 🚗 **Metro** Dupont Circle
- 🕐 **Open** Woodrow Wilson House Museum: 10am–4pm Tue–Sun; closed Mon and major holidays
- 💲 **Price** Suggested donation of $8
- 🚻 **Age range** All ages
- ⏱ **Allow** 1–3 hours
- 🍴 **Eat and drink** *Snacks* Le Pain Quotidien (*2000 P St, Blaine Mansion, 20036; 202 459 9176; www.lepainquotidien.us*) offers freshly baked breads and pastries cooked to perfection by artisan bakers. An assortment of salads, sandwiches, and soups can be either taken away or eaten at the communal table. *Real meal* Bistrot Du Coin (*1738 Connecticut Ave NW, Dupont Circle, 20009; 202 234 6969; www.bistrotducoin.com*) serves classic French bistro cuisine in a casual, friendly setting. The menu includes French onion soup, *tartine* (focaccia-style bread with toppings), steak sandwich, and crème brûlée for dessert.
- 🚻 **Restrooms** In Woodrow Wilson House Museum

*Antique furniture on display in the Woodrow Wilson House Museum*

**Picnic** under $30; **Snacks** $30–40; **Real meal** $40–75; **Family treat** over $75 (based on a family of four)

# ⑤ Washington National Cathedral
## Darth Vader goes to church

It is hard not to love a cathedral that has a stained-glass window dedicated to space travel, and whose many gargoyles include Darth Vader from the *Star Wars* saga. The sixth largest cathedral in the world, Washington National Cathedral is a good place for parents to introduce kids to great architecture. The cathedral sustained substantial damage during an earthquake in 2011. A repair program is currently underway, during which some sections have restricted access.

Washington National Cathedral's west facade

## Key Features

**Bishop's Garden** Modeled on the medieval walled gardens of Europe, this tranquil space is filled with flowers, ornamental plants, fountains, and statuary.

**Children's Chapel** The centerpiece of this chapel is a statue of Christ as a young boy. The chapel has kid-sized dimensions and is filled with carvings of mythical and real baby animals.

**Gargoyles** In medieval times, these were believed to ward off evil. Each of the cathedral's gargoyles is unique – some portray real animals, but most are mythical.

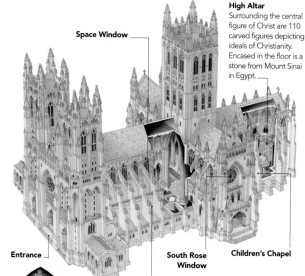

**Space Window**

**High Altar** Surrounding the central figure of Christ are 110 carved figures depicting ideals of Christianity. Encased in the floor is a stone from Mount Sinai in Egypt.

**Entrance**

**South Rose Window**

**Children's Chapel**

**Space Window** This beautiful masterpiece relates mankind's achievements in technology and space travel, including the voyage of Apollo 11. A real Moon rock has been worked into the window's design.

**The Lewis and Clark Window** Look at scenes depicting the landscapes, animals, and peoples that explorers Lewis and Clark encountered on their trek west across the US in 1804–6.

**South Rose Window** A creation of Joseph Reynolds and Wilbur Burnham, this stained-glass window depicts "The Church Triumphant."

## Letting off steam

The **Close**, as the cathedral's grounds are called, offers 59 acres (24 ha) of space for kids to explore. There is a trail that leads through the Olmsted Woods (named after Frederick Law Olmsted, the cathedral's first landscape architect) where one of the last remaining stands of old growth hardwoods in Washington can be found. Also part of the Close is the delightful **Bishop's Garden**, where flower and herb gardens and ivy-covered walls transport visitors back to the gardens of the Middle Ages.

## Eat and drink

Picnic: under $30; Snacks: $30–40; Real meal: $40–75; Family treat: over $75 (based on a family of four)

**PICNIC Rocklands Barbeque and Grilling Company** (2418 Wisconsin Ave NW, 20007; 202 333 2558; www.rocklands.com) is a small barbecue place that offers chopped

**Prices given are for a family of four**

The popular Cafe Deluxe near Washington National Cathedral

# The Lowdown

🌐 **Address** 3101 Wisconsin Ave NW, 20016; 202 537 6200; *www.cathedral.org*

🚗 **Metro** Cleveland Park. **Bus** N2, N3, N4, or N6 from Dupont Circle to the corner of Massachusetts Ave & Wisconsin Ave; 96, 97, or X3 from Woodley Park to the corner of Woodley Road & Wisconsin Ave

🕐 **Open** 10am–5:30pm Mon–Fri (to 8pm Tue & Thu in summer), 10am–4:30pm Sat, 1–4pm Sun

💲 **Price** $10; kids between 5 and 12 $6; under 4s free

🏹 **Guided tours** 10–11:30am, 1–3:30pm Mon–Fri, 10–11:30am, 1–3pm Sat, 1–2:30pm Sun; variety of themed tours available, call or see website for details. 75-minute self-paced audio tour available for $20.

🧗 **Activities** Download Explore the Cathedral with Children from *www.nationalcathedral. org/pdfs/families.pdf*. A scavenger hunt helps families find the cathedral's highlights. For a schedule of services, visit *www.nationalcathedral.org/ worship/services.shtml*

♿ **Wheelchair access** Yes

☕ **Café** Open City in the cathedral's former bapistry

🏷 **Shops** Herb Cottage, by the Bishop's Garden, and the Cathedral Store *(see below)*

🚻 **Restrooms** In northwest cloister

## Good family value?

This is one of the greatest architectural masterpieces in the US and there are plenty of interesting things for kids of all ages to see.

---

or sliced pork, pulled chicken, beef brisket, sirloin, grilled lamb, and Italian sausage. Order to go, and picnic in Bryce Park across the street. **SNACKS Cactus Cantina** *(3300 Wisconsin Ave NW, 20016; 202 686 7222; www.cactuscantina.com)* offers a kids' menu with chicken nuggets and French fries as well as Tex-Mex. Fajitas and margaritas are adult favorites at this popular restaurant. **REAL MEAL Cafe Deluxe** *(3228 Wisconsin Ave NW, 20016; 202 686 2233; www.cafedeluxe. com)* is a cheerful restaurant with reasonably priced food, including grilled sandwiches, juicy burgers, grilled meatloaf with spicy Creole sauce, grilled salmon, and herb-roasted chicken with mashed potatoes. **FAMILY TREAT Heritage India** *(2400 Wisconsin Ave NW, 20007; 202 333 3120; www.heritageindiausa.com)* offers Indian cuisine including tandoori entrées, lamb vindaloo, and vegetarian dishes in a family-friendly setting. Their curries and specials are exceptional.

## Shopping

The **Cathedral Store** has gifts, books, calendars, and clothing that are themed on Gothic architecture and cathedrals worldwide.

## Find out more

**DIGITAL** Watch the 11:15am Holy Eucharist webcast live each week from the homepage. Discover more about the towers, chapels, and organ through online tours at *www.nationalcathedral.org/visit/ onlineTours.shtml*.

**FILM** *Washington National Cathedral* (1993), a PBS special, tells the history of the building through interviews and music.

*Animal models and flowers at the zoo entrance*

## Next stop...

**SMITHSONIAN'S NATIONAL ZOOLOGICAL PARK** A short distance from the cathedral but a world away in atmosphere, the National Zoological Park *(see pp168–9)* is noisy, boisterous, and a barrel of fun. It is a great place to pop into for half an hour or half a day. If time is short, be sure to visit the pandas, elephants, and big cats.

---

# ⑥ Dupont Circle

### Once a brickyard, now a trendy neighborhood

When it is time for tweens and teens to have an urban adventure that involves interesting shops and great restaurants, Dupont Circle is a good bet. Twenty years ago this was a down-on-its-heels neighborhood, but gentrification arrived and it

*The Francis Dupont Memorial Fountain at the Dupont Circle*

## The Lowdown

🌐 **Map reference** 2 G4
   **Address** New Hampshire Ave NW & Connecticut Ave NW, 20036

🚇 **Metro** Dupont Circle

👫 **Age range** All ages

🤸 **Activities** Shopping and dining

⏱️ **Allow** 30 minutes; more if shopping and dining

♿ **Wheelchair access** Yes

🍽️ **Eat and drink** *Real meal* Kramerbooks & Afterwords Cafe & Grill (*1517 Connecticut Ave NW, 20036; 202 387 1400; www.kramers.com*) is a very popular restaurant with an extensive menu offering sand-wiches, salads, desserts, specialty beers, and cocktails. There is live music on some nights and pleasant outdoor seating. *Family treat* Marrakesh Palace (*2147 P St NW, 20037; 202 775 1882; www.marrakeshpstreetdc.com*) serves Moroccan cuisine in an exotic setting. Favorites include chicken pastry, braised lamb with pears, and seafood kebab.

🚻 **Restrooms** No, best bet are the coffee shops and restaurants

quickly became one of the trendiest and most popular places to live in DC. Book lovers will like the fun and funky **Kramerbooks & Afterwords** (*1517 Connecticut Ave, 20036; 202 387 1400*), which also has a good restaurant. Anyone who strings beads should not miss the incredible **Beadazzled** (*1507 Connecticut Ave, 20036; 202 265 2323*), and teenage girls may enjoy a leisurely peruse of the accessories available at **LouLou** (*1601 Connecticut Ave, 20009; 202 588 0027*).

A great picnic lunch can be created by shopping around the food stores, and then enjoyed sitting by the lovely fountain that marks the center of Dupont Circle. Here, enjoy people-watching and maybe catch street musicians who often perform, while out-of-towners and locals alike lounge in the sun or play chess on the permanent stone chessboards.

### Take cover

**The Phillips Collection** (*see opposite*) is America's oldest museum dedicated to modern art, with a remarkable collection of paintings and sculptures from the 20th and 21st centuries.

# ⑦ National Geographic Museum

### Is that the Grand Canyon on the ceiling?

Looking like a small, exotic circus, this museum serves up visual delights such as the scale model of the Grand Canyon that adorns the ceiling, making it very popular with kids. Much of the museum's space is given over to changing exhibits that are often related to subjects from National Geographic TV specials. These are always colorful and kid-oriented, and have included "Geckos," a special that highlighted the world of these fascinating lizards. The photographs on display are always extraordinary, and have included remarkable exhibits such as *Crittercam: the World Through Animal Eyes* and *National Geographic Maps: Tools for Adventure.*

## The Lowdown

🌐 **Map reference** 2 H5
   **Address** 1145 17th St NW, 20036; 202 857 7588; www.ngmuseum.org

🚇 **Metro** Farragut North & Farragut West

🕐 **Open** 10am–6pm daily, closed Dec 25

💲 **Price** $36–46, under 5s free; special exhibits may carry a fee.

👫 **Cutting the line** Usually not crowded

👫 **Age range** All ages

⏱️ **Allow** 30 minutes–1 hour

♿ **Wheelchair access** Yes

🍽️ **Eat and drink** *Snacks* Julia's Empanadas (*1221 Connecticut Ave NW, 20036; 202 861 8828; www.juliasempanadas.com*) offers handmade baked sandwiches. *Real meal* Tabard Inn Restaurant (*Hotel Tabard Inn, 1739 N St NW, 20036; 202 331 8528; www.tabardinn.com/restaurant; reserve in advance for weekend brunches*) serves grilled chicken breast, Black Angus burgers, and crab cakes.

🚻 **Restrooms** In the museum

### Letting off steam

A pretty, green space that has room for kids to work off some energy, **Farragut Square** (*17th St NW & I NW*) was created as part of the original plans for Washington. It can get busy here around noon when workers from the surrounding offices arrive in droves to have lunch in the open air.

*The statue of Admiral David G. Farragut at Farragut Square*

**Above** Exhibits on display in the National Geographic Museum
**Below** Renoir's Luncheon of the Boating Party (1881), the Phillips Collection

## ⑧ The Phillips Collection

### A squashed tomato or a modern masterpiece?

The oldest modern art museum in America, the Phillips Collection is one of Washington's hidden treasures. The works of many gifted modern artists can be found here, including the colorful post-Impressionism of Vincent van Gogh and the empty, disconcerting landscapes of Edward Hopper, a prominent American Realist painter and printmaker. The museum's star attraction is the remarkable Luncheon of the Boating Party (1881) by Pierre-Auguste Renoir. Considered one of the finest masterpieces of French Impressionism, it depicts a group of Renoir's friends sharing lunch after boating on the River Seine. Another major attraction is the Rothko Room, a small gallery where one large work by Mark Rothko hangs on each wall.

### Letting off steam

The park-like environs of **Dupont Circle** (see opposite), though small, offer plenty of space for kids to play.

## The Lowdown

- 🌐 **Map reference** 2 F4
  **Address** 1600 21st St NW, 20009; 202 387 2151; www.phillipscollection.org
- 🚗 **Metro** Dupont Circle
- 🕐 **Open** 10am–5pm Tue–Sat, (until 8:30pm Thu), 11am–6pm Sun, closed Jan 1, Jul 4, Thanksgiving Day & Dec 25
- 💲 **Price** Tue–Fri: adult donation for permanent exhibits, special exhibition fees vary; Sat & Sun: adults pay special exhibition fee starting at $10; under 18s free
- 🚶 **Cutting the line** There is rarely a line to get in.
- 👫 **Age range** 12 plus
- 🤸 **Activities** Live jazz and gallery talks; post 5pm first Thu of every month. Classical chamber music concerts; Oct–May: 4pm Sun; $20; first-come, first-served basis
- ⏱ **Allow** 1 hour
- ♿ **Wheelchair access** Yes
- ☕ **Eat and drink** Snacks Dupont Market (1807 18th St NW, 20009; 202 797 0222) is a small neighborhood store offering some of DC's most raved-about sandwiches, including their famed Borracho Italiano sandwiches. Real meal Tryst at the Phillips (in the museum) has indoor and courtyard seating, with a selection of fine pastries, sandwiches, and salads, and a pleasant ambience.
- 🚻 **Restrooms** On each floor

In the center of the circle, a magnificent fountain, is surrounded by a plaza. There are shady benches, pretty flower beds, and a green lawn, perfect for an impromptu picnic on a sunny day.

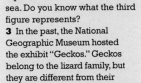

# US National Arboretum and around

The sights in the eastern and southeastern corners of the city are easy to reach by car, but difficult to reach without. The Arboretum, along with Kenilworth Park and Aquatic Gardens, and Oxon Hill Farm should not be missed by families who love nature and the outdoors. The neighborhoods here are improving, but restaurants are scarce, and caution is required when venturing beyond the major attractions in the area.

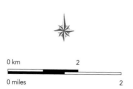

## Places of interest

**SIGHTS**
1. United States National Arboretum
2. Kenilworth Park and Aquatic Gardens
3. Frederick Douglass House
4. Oxon Hill Farm

0 km        2

0 miles        2

*Entrance to the Chinese Pavilion at the United States National Arboretum*

*Lush green spaces and lily ponds, Kenilworth Park and Aquatic Gardens*

West
Hyattsville M

501
QUEENS CHAPEL ROAD
1
DAKOTA AVENUE
RHODE ISLAND AVENUE
BLADENSBURG ROAD
KENILWORTH AVENUE
201
405
295
Anacostia
50
JOHN HANSON HIGHWAY
Cheverly M

**1**
United States
National
Arboretum

**2**
Kenilworth Park
and Aquatic
Gardens

Deanwood
M

FAIRMONT
HEIGHTS

Minnesota Ave M
EAST CAPITOL STREET

ium—
mory M

Potomac
Ave

295

Benning
Road M

Capitol
Heights M

CAPITOL
HEIGHTS

NACOSTIA

rederick Douglass
House

4

PENNSYLVANIA AVENUE

5

SUITLAND

PARKWAY

458

ngress
ghts M

Naylor
Road M

Southern
Ave

Suitland M

BRANCH AVENUE

SUITLAND PARKWAY

HILLCREST
HEIGHTS

Branch Ave M

REST
GHTS

CAPITAL BELTWAY
495 95

MARYLAND

## The Lowdown

🚗 **Metro** Stadium-Armory
station on the Blue &
Orange lines. Orange line
to Deanwood and Green
line to Anacostia.

ℹ️ **Visitor information**
www.usna.usda.gov

🏪 **Supermarket** Giant
Supermarket, 1050
Brentwood Road NE, 20018

🎊 **Festivals** Potomac Bonsai
Festival, National Arboretum
(bonsai exhibits and hands-on
workshops, 1st weekend in
May). Lotus Water Lily
Festival, Kenilworth Aquatic
Garden (gardening
demonstrations, crafts,
and activities for kids,
3rd Sat in Jul).

➕ **Pharmacies** US National
Arboretum: CVS Pharmacy,
320 40th St NE, 20019;
202 396 2331; 24 hours
daily. Frederick Douglass
House: CVS Pharmacy,
2646 Naylor Rd SE, 20020;
202 582 4800; 8am–
midnight daily

*One of the many barns at the Oxon Hill Farm*

# ① United States National Arboretum
## Hungry fishes and forgotten plants

Hidden away on the east side of Washington, this 446-acre (180-ha) arboretum dedicated to research and education is big and colorful, and interesting enough to wear out even the most energetic kids. Check out the majestic Dawn Redwoods and the National Bonsai and Penjing Museum with hundreds of carefully shaped miniature trees. Enjoy a picnic lunch in the area around the visitor center and don't forget to feed the hungry koi in the pond before leaving.

The Capitol Columns at the open-air plaza

## Key Sights

① **Visitor Center** This building is surrounded by a pool filled with waterplants and koi that depend on visitors to feed them with special food from a dispenser.

② **Dawn Redwoods** These trees were thought to have become extinct millions of years ago. In 1942, a few were found in a remote valley in China and seeds were distributed to arboretums worldwide.

③ **Azalea Collection** During springtime, a sea of azaleas blanket the woodland area in a dazzling pallet of color.

**Entrance**

④ **National Herb Garden** Look at more than 100 varieties of roses, an elaborate knot garden, fountains, "touch-me" herbs, and a vine-draped arbor trellis that offers cool shade.

**Capitol Columns**

⑤ **Asian Collection** This hilly section has paths that lead through a richly diverse collection of rhododendrons, camellias, and ornamental shrubs and flowers.

⑥ **National Bonsai and Penjing Museum** These miniature trees have been shaped to cascade over their containers or to suggest windswept trees. One Japanese white pine tree is almost 400 years old.

## The Lowdown

🌐 **Address** 3501 New York Ave NE, 20002; 202 245 2726; www.usna.usda.gov

🚇 **Metro** Stadium-Armory

🕐 **Open** Grounds: 8am–5pm, closed Dec 25. Visitor Center: 8am–4:30pm, closed Dec 25 & Federal holidays. National Bonsai and Penjing Museum: 10am–4pm daily, closed Federal holidays. Arbor House Gift Shop: Mar–mid-Dec: 10am–3:30pm daily, till 5pm Sat & Sun from Apr–Sep

💲 **Price** Free

🚩 **Guided tours** Tram tours are available seasonally and on weekends and holidays. Timings vary accordingly; check the website for more information on schedules and fees.

👫 **Age range** All ages

👟 **Activities** Check website for family events, moonlight hikes, and docent-led tours.

⏱ **Allow** 3 hours to all day; 40 minutes for the tram tour

♿ **Wheelchair access** Yes, partial

☕ **Café** No, snacks in the Arbor House Gift Shop near the visitor center

🛍 **Shop** Arbor House Gift Shop (see p179)

🚻 **Restrooms** In the Administration Building and at the Arbor House

**Good family value?**
A bit off the beaten path, but free and with great attractions for the entire family.

*Relaxing around the fountain at the National Herb Garden, US National Arboretum*

## Take cover

In case of cold weather or rain, step into **Frederick Douglass House** (see p180), which was the home of the African-American statesman and orator from 1878 until his death in 1895. A self-educated man who was born a slave, Frederick Douglass spent his life advancing the cause of African Americans after the Civil War. Today, the house is filled with his possessions and mementos from his fascinating life.

## Eat and drink

*Picnic: under $30; Snacks: $30–40; Real meal: $40–75; Family treat: over $75 (based on a family of four)*

**PICNIC Hogs On The Hill Restaurant** (2003 Bladensburg Rd NE, 20018; 202 526 2027), a take-out BBQ spot, serves pulled-pork sandwiches and sides that can be enjoyed outside the visitor center.

*Hogs On The Hill Restaurant, a barbeque shack off New York Avenue*

**SNACKS Deli City Restaurant** (2200 Bladensburg Rd NE, 20018; 202 526 1800) has soul food and subs. Try their much-loved "Reuben", a hot sandwich of corned beef, Russian dressing, and sauerkraut (see p180). **REAL MEAL Taylor Gourmet** (1116 H St NE, 20002; 202 684 7001; www.taylorgourmet.com), an Italian deli and market, has meal-sized submarine sandwiches served on Italian bread with chicken, pork, and vegetarian options. Try the *cannoli* (cheese-filled pastry) for dessert. **FAMILY TREAT Sticky Rice** (1224 H St NE, 20002; 202 397 7655; www.stickyricedc.com) has a kids' menu and other dishes including sushi rolls, spring rolls, noodles, sandwiches, and American and Pan-American entrées.

## Shopping

The **Arbor House Gift Shop** (US National Arboretum) sells gifts, books, and souvenirs.

## Find out more

**DIGITAL** Check out www.usna. usda.gov/Gardens/collections/ VirtualTours/index.html for a virtual tour for kids and in-depth tours of the arboretum's major collections.

## Next stop...

**OXON HILL FARM** Just outside the city, Oxon Hill Farm (see p181) is designed to let children have hands-on farm experiences. They can try their hand at milking a cow, feeding chickens, or carrying out other tasks under the guidance of National Park personnel.

*Shingled houses and barns at the Oxon Hill Farm*

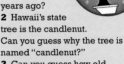

# ② Kenilworth Park and Aquatic Gardens

## Water, water, everywhere...

A great place to escape the hubbub of the city, these gardens were started around 1880 when a government worker, William B. Shaw, bought a 37-acre (15-ha) farm, surrounded by the marshes of the Anacostia, and ordered 12 lilies for the farm pond. His daughter continued to develop the gardens, eventually opening the ponds to the public. Today, this park offers 12 acres (5 ha) of ponds filled with water lilies and other aquatic plants from around the world. In late summer, the garden's Lotus Pond is blanketed with pink lotus blossoms. Kids will enjoy the ponds and the grounds, where turtles, ducks, and salamanders abound. The kids' display in the visitor center offers an overview of the gardens.

Water lily leaves in a pond at Kenilworth Aquatic Gardens

### Letting off steam

If the weather becomes inclement, head to the visitor center at Kenilworth, which has exhibits on the natural history of water lilies and other water plants, as well as on the history of the gardens.

## ③ Frederick Douglass House

### The story of a runaway slave

Born into slavery, Frederick Douglass taught himself how to write and learned how to speak in public, eventually escaping bondage and becoming one of the leaders of the Abolitionist movement. This elegant house was his home from 1878 until his death in 1895, and is a good destination for families with an interest in history. Today, the rooms have been restored and furnished to reflect the way they would have looked when Douglass lived here. Admire photographs of his life and his personal possessions, including a prized walking stick given to him by First Lady Mary Lincoln in memory of President Lincoln.

## The Lowdown

- 🌐 **Address** 1550 Anacostia Ave NE, 20019; 202 426 6905; www.nps.gov/keaq
- 🚇 **Metro** Orange line to Deanwood, then go through the Polk St tunnel to the pedestrian overpass and cross Kenilworth Ave. Make a left on Douglas St and go about two blocks to the end of the street. Turn right onto Anacostia Ave and enter any open gate on the left.
- 🕐 **Open** May–Sep: 7am–5pm daily; Oct–Apr: 7am–4pm daily; closed Jan 1, Thanksgiving Day & Dec 25
- 💲 **Price** Free
- 🚩 **Guided tours** Summer garden tours at 9am & 11am on Sat & Sun, Memorial Day through Labor Day.
- 👫 **Age range** All ages
- 🏃 **Activities** Nature walks are offered on some days; check online calendar for details.
- ⏱ **Allow** 1–3 hours
- ☕ **Eat and drink** Picnic Deli City Restaurant (2200 Bladensburg Rd NE, 20018; 202 526 1800; credit cards not accepted) is a great place to pick up snacks for a picnic in the park (see p179). Real meal El Tapatio (4309 Kenilworth Ave, Bladensburg, MD 20783; 301 403 8882), a popular place for authentic Mexican, offers homemade white corn tortillas, tacos, chile rellenos (stuffed peppers), and horchatas (rice drinks).
- 👫 **Restrooms** In the visitor center

## The Lowdown

- 🌐 **Address** 1411 W St SE, 20020; 202 426 5960; www.nps.gov/frdo
- 🚌 **Metro** Green line to Anacostia, then take the B2 bus in the direction of Mt. Rainier. Get off at the bus stop on the corner of 14th St & W St
- 🕐 **Open** Mid-Apr–mid-Oct: 9am–5pm daily; mid-Oct–mid-Apr: 9am–4:30pm daily; closed Jan 1, Thanksgiving Day & Dec 25
- 💲 **Price** $6–12 advance reservation fee to tour the house
- 👫 **Cutting the line** Call ahead for tour tickets; arrive 20 minutes before tour time.
- 🚩 **Guided tours** 30-minute house tours; check website for timings.
- 👫 **Age range** Grounds: all ages. House tours: 8 plus
- 🏃 **Activities** Self-guided walking tour of the grounds, visitor center exhibits, and a 17-minute film
- ⏱ **Allow** 90 minutes–2 hours
- ♿ **Wheelchair access** On first floor and visitor center
- ☕ **Eat and drink** Picnic Restaurants are small and casual here, so best to get a picnic lunch from near your hotel or in central DC and picnic in the house's grounds. Snacks Big Chair Coffee and Grill (2122 Martin Luther King, Jr. Ave SE, 20020; 202 525 4287; www.bigchaircoffeeshop.com) offers classic American hand-cooked meals.
- 👫 **Restrooms** In the visitor center

Restored and furnished study at the Frederick Douglass House

**Above** *Frederick Douglass House and surrounding grounds*
**Below** *Children feeding chickens at Oxon Hill Farm*

## Letting off steam

The grounds of the Frederick Douglass House offer enough open space to let kids burn some energy. Encourage them to find the Growlery, a reproduction of Douglass's one-room writing studio, where he would go for quiet time.

## ④ Oxon Hill Farm

### A farmer's life for me

Operated by the National Park Service and located just outside the urban environs, Oxon Hill Farm is designed to give city kids a chance to experience farm life first-hand. Children are encouraged to try their hand at farm chores such as feeding chickens and milking the dairy cows. Regularly scheduled events held throughout the day include wagon rides around the farm. Visitors can also simply tour the facilities, visiting the barns and outbuildings to get a feel for traditional farm life. The visitor center has displays on farming and on the agricultural history of this area.

### Take cover

If it rains, take shelter in the visitor center, where kids can enjoy coloring books, games, puzzles, and toys with farming and historic themes. The park rangers are often available to regale visitors with stories of the region's tumultuous past.

## The Lowdown

- **Address** 6411 Oxon Hill Rd, Oxon Hill, MD 20745; 301 839 1176; www.nps.gov/oxhi
- **Car** See the website for driving directions.
- **Open** 8am–4:30pm daily, closed Jan 1, Thanksgiving Day & Dec 25
- **Price** Free
- **Guided tours** No, tours are self-guided. For a group of five or more, check website to make reservations at least two weeks in advance.
- **Age range** All ages
- **Activities** Check website for schedule of ranger-led activities. The activity room in the visitor center has games, puzzles, and books. Ask for the Junior Ranger Program Booklet, for kids aged 9–13, at the visitor center. Kids who complete the activities earn a badge and a patch.
- **Allow** 30 minutes to several hours
- **Eat and drink** *Snacks* Desserts by Gerard *(6341 Livingston Rd, Oxon Hill, MD 20745; 301 839 2185; www.dessertsbygerard.com; closed Mon)* is a fine bakery with pastries, cakes, pies, and gourmet sandwiches available for breakfast and lunch. *Real meal* Pizza Italia *(6308 Livingston Rd, Oxon Hill, MD 20745; 301 839 3446)* serves pizza, pasta dishes such as baked ziti, chicken marsala, crab cakes, and spiced shrimp.
- **Restrooms** In the visitor center

# Day Trips
## and Excursions

Located in the heart of the mid-Atlantic states, Washington, DC is surrounded by historic and natural places to visit, all within driving distance of the city. To the east lie Chesapeake Bay and the Atlantic beaches of Delaware, Maryland, and Virginia, and to the west the Appalachian Mountains rise above fertile valleys. Toward the south are Virginia's rolling hills and the Colonial-era towns where many Founding Fathers lived.

## Highlights

**George Washington's Mount Vernon Estate**
Explore this plantation house and its grounds, restored to look as they did when George Washington lived here (see pp186–7).

**Old Town Alexandria**
Head to this riverfront town, home to attractions like the Torpedo Factory and the historic 18th-century Stabler-Leadbeater Apothecary (see pp188–9).

**Monticello**
Delight in the inventions and innovations at Thomas Jefferson's home. The house is surrounded by pretty flower and vegetable gardens (see pp204–205).

**Colonial Williamsburg™**
Step back in time to the eve of the Revolutionary War at this living history museum, which features over 500 restored 18th-century buildings (see pp208–209).

**Baltimore's Inner Harbor**
Don't miss the awesome National Aquarium and the fun Port Discovery Children's Museum. The harbor is lined with shops and restaurants (see pp218–19).

**Chesapeake Bay Driving Tour**
Enjoy this great bay surrounded by charming historic towns and cities. The beaches and coastal roads here beg to be explored (see pp222–3).

**Left** Riverboat tour on Spa Creek in Annapolis's harbor
**Above left** The popular Loch Ness Monster® ride in Busch Gardens®, Williamsburg

# Day Trips and Excursions

There are many beautiful towns and suburbs surrounding Washington, DC. Places like George Washington's Mount Vernon Estate are an hour away while others require an entire day or weekend to visit. The best way to travel to these is by car, but many are accessible by train or bus too. The Atlantic beaches, Chesapeake Bay, and Shenandoah National Park require a car, which can be rented at Union Station or at Reagan National Airport. Take Amtrak trains for Maryland and Virginia, or MARC for Maryland. Private tour operators offer tours from Washington, DC to Annapolis, Colonial Williamsburg™, and Monticello.

## Places of interest

**SIGHTS**

1. George Washington's Mount Vernon Estate
2. Old Town Alexandria
3. Gunston Hall
4. The Pentagon
5. Mount Vernon Bike Trail
6. Theodore Roosevelt Island
7. Arlington National Cemetery
8. Steven F. Udvar-Hazy Center
9. Manassas National Battlefield
10. Great Falls Park
11. Wolf Trap National Park for the Performing Arts
12. Harpers Ferry National Historic Park
13. Leesburg
14. White's Ferry
15. Frederick
16. Skyline Drive
17. Monticello
18. Charlottesville
19. Fredericksburg
20. Middleburg
21. Colonial Williamsburg™
22. Jamestown
23. Yorktown Battlefield
24. Yorktown Victory Center
25. Colonial Parkway
26. Busch Gardens®
27. Annapolis
28. Baltimore's Inner Harbor
29. Baltimore & Ohio Railroad Museum
30. Sports Legends Museum/ Geppi's Entertainment Museum
31. The Walters Art Museum
32. Chesapeake Bay Driving Tour
33. A Day at the Beach

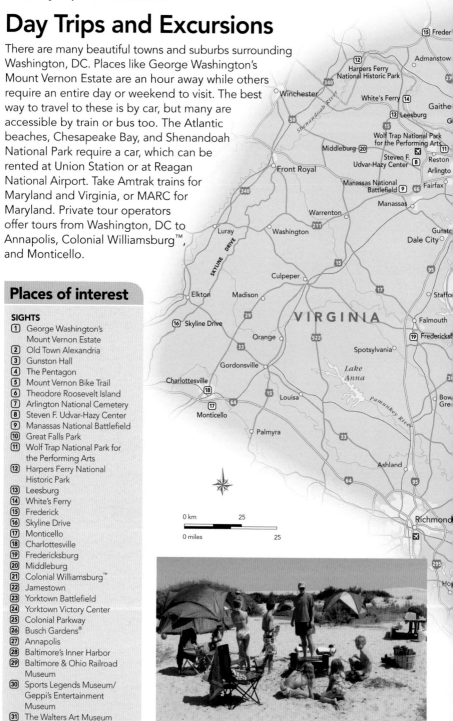

Camping on the sandy beach at Assateague National Seashore in Maryland

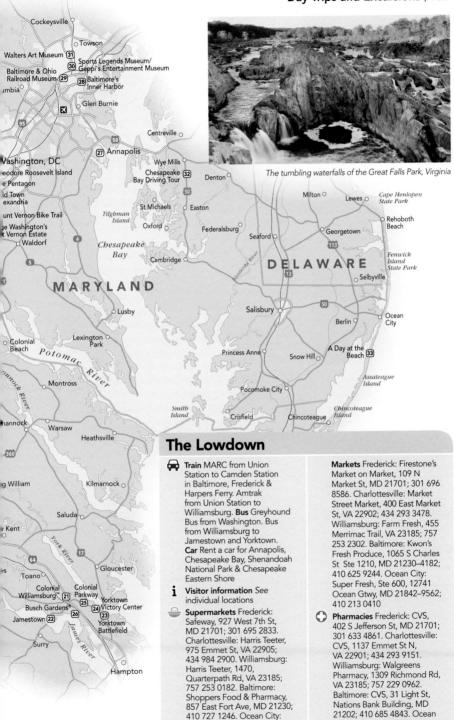

Cockeysville

Towson

Walters Art Museum [31]
[30] Sports Legends Museum/
Geppi's Entertainment Museum
Baltimore & Ohio
Railroad Museum [29]
[28] Baltimore's
Inner Harbor
umbia

Glen Burnie

Centreville

[50]

[27] Annapolis

Washington, DC
eodore Roosevelt Island
e Pentagon
ld Town
exandria

Wye Mills
Chesapeake [32]
Bay Driving Tour

Denton

*The tumbling waterfalls of the Great Falls Park, Virginia*

St Michaels     Easton

Tilghman
Island

Milton     Lewes     Cape Henlopen
State Park

unt Vernon Bike Trail
je Washington's
t Vernon Estate
Waldorf

[4]

Oxford

Federalsburg

Seaford

Georgetown

Rehoboth
Beach

*Chesapeake
Bay*

Cambridge

[115]

D E L A W A R E

[13]

Selbyville

Fenwick
Island
State Park

[5]

M A R Y L A N D

1

Lusby

Salisbury

[50]

Berlin

Ocean
City

Colonial
Beach

Lexington
Park

*Potomac      River*

Princess Anne

Snow Hill

A Day at the
Beach [33]

Assateague
Island

Montross

Pocomoke City

nnock River

Smith
Island

Crisfield

Chincoteague

Chincoteague
Island

hannock

Warsaw

Heathsville

360

g William

Kilmarnock

Saluda

Kent

York River

64

17

s     Toano

Gloucester

Colonial     Colonial
Williamsburg [21]     Parkway
Busch Gardens     [25]     Yorktown
Jamestown [22]     [26]     [24] Victory Center
[23]
Yorktown
Battlefield

James River

Surry

Hampton

## The Lowdown

🚗 **Train** MARC from Union Station to Camden Station in Baltimore, Frederick & Harpers Ferry. Amtrak from Union Station to Williamsburg. **Bus** Greyhound Bus from Washington. Bus from Williamsburg to Jamestown and Yorktown. **Car** Rent a car for Annapolis, Chesapeake Bay, Shenandoah National Park & Chesapeake Eastern Shore

ℹ️ **Visitor information** *See individual locations*

🛒 **Supermarkets** Frederick: Safeway, 927 West 7th St, MD 21701; 301 695 2833. Charlottesville: Harris Teeter, 975 Emmet St, VA 22905; 434 984 2900. Williamsburg: Harris Teeter, 1470, Quarterpath Rd, VA 23185; 757 253 0182. Baltimore: Shoppers Food & Pharmacy, 857 East Fort Ave, MD 21230; 410 727 1246. Ocean City: Food Lion, 9936 Stephen Decatur Hwy # 302; MD 21842–9580; 410 213 0166

**Markets** Frederick: Firestone's Market on Market, 109 N Market St, MD 21701; 301 696 8586. Charlottesville: Market Street Market, 400 East Market St, VA 22902; 434 293 3478. Williamsburg: Farm Fresh, 455 Merrimac Trail, VA 23185; 757 253 2302. Baltimore: Kwon's Fresh Produce, 1065 S Charles St Ste 1210, MD 21230–4182; 410 625 9244. Ocean City: Super Fresh, Ste 600, 12741 Ocean Gtwy, MD 21842–9562; 410 213 0410

➕ **Pharmacies** Frederick: CVS, 402 S Jefferson St, MD 21701; 301 633 4861. Charlottesville: CVS, 1137 Emmet St N, VA 22901; 434 293 9151. Williamsburg: Walgreens Pharmacy, 1309 Richmond Rd, VA 23185; 757 229 0962. Baltimore: CVS, 31 Light St, Nations Bank Building, MD 21202; 410 685 4843. Ocean City: Walgreens Pharmacy, 11307 Manklin Creek Berlin, MD 21811; 410 208 3811

# ① George Washington's Mount Vernon Estate
## Of Washington, slaves, and false teeth

A great destination for kids, the beloved home of George Washington now features a multi-million-dollar interactive education center, and a museum featuring 25 theaters and exhibits tracing Washington's life from his days as a surveyor to his presidency and return to Mount Vernon.

*Facade of the beautiful Mount Vernon*

## Key Sights

**Museum** Aimed at adults and teens, this museum looks at Washington's life and times through artworks, documents, and artifacts.

**Pioneer Farm** Watch horses and mules tread wheat in a 16-sided barn, and learn about the advanced farming practices Washington introduced here.

**Distillery and Gristmill** See how flour and whisky were produced in Washington's day at this historic distillery and gristmill located 3 miles (5 km) south of Mount Vernon.

**Mansion** The house where Washington lived for 45 years has been restored to look as it did during his presidency. Don't miss the large dining room, the study, and the master bedroom where he died.

**Outdoor Kitchen** To protect the house from fire and to keep it cool in summer, the kitchen was housed in a separate building.

**Pioneer Farm**

**Washington's Tomb** There were plans to bury the former president below the Rotunda of the US Capitol (see pp104–105), but Washington had wanted to be buried at Mount Vernon.

**Distillery and Gristmill**

**Upper Garden** This colorful flower and vegetable garden served as a showplace and also produced food for the house kitchens.

**Museum**

**Education Center**

**Slave Quarters** These housed some of the more than 300 slaves who worked at Mount Vernon.

**Education Center** The interactive exhibits offer an overview of Washington's life. Check out the rather life-like figures of him as surveyor, military man, and president.

## The Lowdown

🌐 **Address** 3200 Mount Vernon Memorial Hwy, Mount Vernon, VA 22309; 703 780 2000; www.mountvernon.org

🚗 **Metro** Yellow line to Huntington Station then Fairfax Connector bus #101. **Bus** Gray Line (202 289 1995; www.graylinedc.com) departs from Union Station. **Boat** (703 684 0580; www.potomacriverboatco.com) leaves from the Washington waterfront, Georgetown, and Old Town, Alexandria.

🕐 **Open** Mar, Sep & Oct: 9am–5pm daily; Apr–Aug: 8am–5pm daily; Nov–Feb: 9am–4pm daily

💲 **Price** $50–60; under 6s free; includes admission to George Washington's Distillery & Gristmill

👥 **Cutting the line** Purchase tickets online ($2 fee) to avoid waiting in line. Buy tickets for the National Treasure tour ahead.

🚩 **Guided tours** Hour-long National Treasure tours; $20. Check

website for other tours (www.mountvernon.org/visit-his-estate/plan-your-visit/activities-tours).

👫 **Age range** 4 plus

🏃 **Activities** Kids receive a free Adventure Map. The hands-on History exhibit offers interactive games and activities; late May–early Sep. Wagon rides in Pioneer Farm; Apr: 10am–2pm Fri–Sun.

⏱ **Allow** 3 hours to all day

*Prices given are for a family of four*

## Letting off steam

There is plenty of room in Mount Vernon's grounds for kids to run around and play till they drop. The Upper Garden offers lots of paths and the front lawn has space to run, skip, cartwheel, and tumble, complete with a spectacular view of the Potomac River.

## Eat and drink

*Picnic: under $30; Snacks: $30–40; Real meal: $40–75; Family treat: over $75 (based on a family of four)*

**PICNIC Mount Vernon Food Court** *(Mount Vernon estate)* serves pizzas, burgers, and salads. Take food from here and enjoy it on the grounds.

**SNACKS Eamonn's, A Dublin Chipper** *(728 King St, Alexandria, VA 22314; 703 299 8384; www. eamonnsdublinchipper.com)* is popular for its fresh fish and hand-cut fries. Choose from cod, prawns, grouper, or fish of the day.

*Exterior of the charming Colonial-style Mount Vernon Inn*

**REAL MEAL Mount Vernon Inn** *(Mount Vernon estate)* offers fine dining in a Colonial-style setting with period-costumed servers. The regional and Colonial food includes a broad variety of entrées, salads, and sandwiches at lunchtime. Candlelit dinners are served every night except Sunday.

 **Wheelchair access** On the first floor of the mansion

**Cafés** Restaurant and food court

**Shops** At various locations

**Restrooms** In the Museum, Education Center, visitor center, and restaurant

**Good family value?**
Offering a good variety of activities and a great insight into George Washington's life and times, Mount Vernon is popular with kids.

**FAMILY TREAT Vermilion** *(1120 King St, Alexandria, VA 22314; 703 684 9669; www.vermilion restaurant.com)*, one of Washington, DC's finest restaurants, offers New American cuisine in a casual, yet refined old-town restaurant with exposed brick walls. Enjoy soups, salads, burgers, sandwiches, fried chicken, hanger steak, and great desserts.

## Shopping

Mount Vernon has four shops. **The Shops at Mount Vernon** *(near the exit)* offer gifts, housewares, clothing, and books, all with a Colonial theme. The **Lady Washington Shop** *(near the Upper Garden)* has gifts reflecting Martha Washington's tastes and interests. The **Wharf Shop** sells toys, while the **Gristmill Shop** offers Virginia-made jams, jellies, peanuts, ciders, teas, and coffees.

## Find out more

**DIGITAL** Explore Mount Vernon and search for artifacts, play the harpsichord as Washington dances with his wife, and serve as a gun captain during the siege of Yorktown at www.washingtonsworld.org and www.mountvernon.org/media.
**FILM** Scenes from *National Treasure 2: Book of Secrets* (2007), including the president's birthday party, were filmed at Mount Vernon.

*Biking trail through the lush Dyke Marsh Wildlife Preserve*

## Next stop...

**DYKE MARSH WILDLIFE PRESERVE** Halfway between Old Town Alexandria and Mount Vernon, Dyke Marsh Wildlife Preserve *(west bank of Potomac River)* is home to over 350 plant and 300 bird species, making it a good place for bird- and nature-watching. Kids will enjoy the trails and boardwalk.

# KIDS' CORNER

**Look out for...**
1 Washington introduced the use of certain draft animals for farming in America. Can you guess which they were?
2 What was the main crop raised at Mount Vernon?
3 What was George Washington's first occupation?
4 There were 13 stars on the American flag, one for each state, when Washington became president. Do you know how many states were added during his presidency?

*Answers at the bottom of the page.*

---

**Willed free**
*Washington set his slaves free in his will. He was the only Founding Father to do so.*

### ARMED TO THE TEETH
Contrary to popular myth, Washington never had wooden teeth. He had several sets of dentures made from a variety of materials including human teeth, bone, and both elephant and hippopotamus ivory.

### Far from the city lights
Washington was the only president who didn't live in Washington, DC. The city didn't exist when he was elected. In fact, it was during his presidency that he laid out plans for the future capital city of Washington, DC.

---

**Answers: 1** Mules. **2** Wheat. **3** Surveyor. **4** Five; North Carolina (1789), Rhode Island (1790), Vermont (1791), Kentucky (1792), and Tennessee (1796).

# ② Old Town Alexandria
## Welcome to George Washington's party town

Long before Washington, DC existed, Old Town Alexandria served as the area's main port and commercial center. Today, its streets are lined with boutiques, restaurants, and historic sights, making it a fun place for families. Raise a pint at Gadsby's Tavern, where George Washington celebrated his birthday in 1799, or go back to the 19th century at the Lee-Fendall House, where 37 members of the Lee family resided. Don't miss the Torpedo Factory, which is filled with artisans' studios.

*The Palladian-style Carlyle House*

## Key Sights

① **Market Square** The oldest continually operating public marketplace in the US, this hosts a bustling Saturday farmers' market.

② **Gadsby's Tavern** Presidents George Washington, Thomas Jefferson, and James Madison all drank here. Today, it is both a museum offering a look at Revolutionary War-era Alexandria and a restaurant.

③ **Stabler-Leadbeater Apothecary Museum** For an insight into medicine as it was practiced in the 18th and 19th centuries, visit this historic shop, which sold pills and potions from 1792 to 1933.

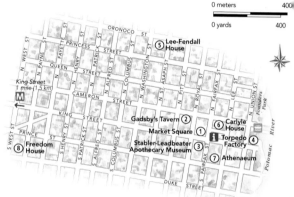

④ **Torpedo Factory** Once a busy munitions factory, this industrial Art Deco building now houses the working studios of over 150 artists. Visitors can stroll from studio to studio to watch artists work, and purchase any piece that catches their eye.

⑤ **Lee-Fendall House** Built by a cousin of Henry "Light Horse" Lee (father of Confederate General Robert E. Lee), this house was regularly visited by George Washington. Children should look out for the wonderful display of antique dollhouses on the third floor.

⑥ **Carlyle House** This Palladian-style stone home was built by Scottish merchant John Carlyle in 1753. During the French and Indian War (1754–63), it served as the headquarters of British General Braddock, who planned his campaigns from here.

⑦ **Athenaeum** Built in 1852 as the Bank of the Old Dominion, this Neo-Classical building houses a fine art gallery today.

⑧ **Freedom House** Once the headquarters of Franklin and Armfield, the most successful slave-trading company in the south, this building is now a museum offering a fascinating look at the slave trade from the early to mid-19th century.

## Letting off steam

Stretching along the banks of the Potomac, **Founders Park** (N Union St, VA 22314) is just a short stroll north of the Torpedo Factory. In addition to pretty gardens and a splendid river view, the park offers benches, lawns, and broad grassy areas that invite kids to kick off their shoes and run around. This is also a good place for a picnic lunch.

**Prices given are for a family of four**

*Lawns and colorful flower beds at the riverfront Founders Park*

## Eat and drink

*Picnic: under $30; Snacks: $30–40; Real meal: $40–75; Family treat: over $75 (based on a family of four)*

**PICNIC Old Town Deli** (*109 North Washington St, VA 22314; 703 836 8028; www.oldtowndeli alexandria.com*) has a huge range of sandwiches (both hot and cold), gyros, and salads. Order to go and then head to the riverfront for dining alfresco by the water.

# The Lowdown

🌐 **Address** Alexandria, VA 22314. Market Square: 301 King St; 703 746 3200. Gadsby's Tavern: 134 N Royal St; 707 746 4242; *www.alexandriava.gov/Gadsbys Tavern*. Stabler-Leadbeater Apothecary Museum: 105–107 S Fairfax St; *www.alexandriava. gov/Apothecary*. Torpedo Factory: 105 N Union St; *www. torpedofactory.org*. Lee-Fendall House: 614 Oronoco St; *www. leefendallhouse.org*. Carlyle House: 121 N Fairfax St; *www. nvrpa.org/park/carlyle_house_ historic_park*. Athenaeum: 201 Prince St; *www.nvfaa.org*. Freedom House: 1315 Duke St; *www.nvul.org/freedomhouse*.

🚗 **Metro** King Street then free King Street Trolley with 20 hop-on hop-off stops along King St (11:30am–10pm daily)

ℹ️ **Visitor information** Visitor center: 221 King St, VA 22314; *www.visitalexandriava.com*.

🕐 **Open** Market Square: 7am–noon Sat. Gadsby's Tavern: Apr–Oct: 10am–5pm Tue–Sat, 1–5pm Sun & Mon; Nov–Mar: 11am–4pm Wed–Sat, 1–4pm Sun. Stabler-Leadbeater Apothecary Museum: Apr–Oct: 10am–5pm Tue–Sat, 1–5pm Sun & Mon; Nov–Mar: 11am–4pm Wed–Sat, 1–4pm Sun. Torpedo Factory: 10am–6pm daily, until 9pm Thu. Lee-Fendall House: 10am–3pm Wed–Sat, 1–3pm Sun. Carlyle House: 10am–4pm Tue–Sat, noon–4pm Sun. Athenaeum: noon–4pm Thu, Fri & Sun, 1–4pm Sat. Freedom House: 9am–4pm Mon–Fri.

💲 **Price** Stabler-Leadbeater Apothecary Museum: $16–26; under 5s free. Lee-Fendall House: $16–26; under 5s free. Carlyle House: $16–26; under 4s free.

🚩 **Guided tours** Historical walking and ghost tours available; check individual websites for details.

👫 **Age range** All ages

🤸 **Activities** Historical and cultural attractions, shopping & dining

⏱️ **Allow** 4 hours to all day

☕ **Cafés** Dozens of restaurants and casual eateries

🛍️ **Shops** Boutiques, antique stores, galleries, and gift shops

🚻 **Restrooms** At visitor center, most sights, and restaurants

### Good family value?

It doesn't cost a thing to explore the historic streets of Alexandria, and can be an entertaining day out for the entire family.

**SNACKS Bittersweet Bakery and Cafe** *(823 King St, VA 22314; 703 549 1028; www.bittersweetcatering. com)* has cupcakes, sweets, and kid-sized lunches too.

**REAL MEAL Bilbo Baggins** *(208 Queen St, VA 22314; 703 683 0300; www.bilbobaggins.net)* serves lunch entrées such as Thai salad, as well as the Bilbo's burger or Bilbo's pizza for the kids.

**FAMILY TREAT Gadsby's Tavern** *(138 N Royal St, VA 22314; 703 548 1288; www.gadsbystavern restaurant.com)* serves American fare in Colonial-style dining rooms.

## Shopping

Children of all ages will enjoy **Hooray for Books** *(1555 King St, VA 22314)* and **Alexandria Cupcake** *(1022 King St, VA 22314)*, while **An American in Paris** *(1225 King St, VA 22314)* is a great place to shop for clothes.

## Find out more

**DIGITAL** A Remarkable and Courageous Journey *(http://alexandriava. gov/uploadedFiles/historic/info/black history/BHCourageousJourney.pdf)* tells the story of the accomplishments of Alexandria's African Americans from the 18th to the 20th centuries.

*Tomb of the Unknowns at Arlington National Cemetery*

## Next stop...

**ARLINGTON NATIONAL CEMETERY** Soldiers and presidents are laid to rest at Arlington National Cemetery (see pp192–3). Most visitors come to see the graves of the famous or visit the many memorials.

---

# KIDS' CORNER

### Do you know...

**1** In the 1830s, Market Square was where people came to buy fresh fruit, vegetables, and meats from local farms. This was also the site of which other less respectable business?
**2** Which wars did the Torpedo Factory build torpedoes for?
**3** How many slaves did Franklin and Armfield send south each month at the height of their business?

Answers at the bottom of the page.

### WASHINGTON, THE PARTY DUDE

In George Washington's day, Alexandria was the closest town to Mount Vernon, and it was here that he came to have dinner, a few drinks, dance (which he loved), and play cards with friends.

### Too loud for the president

When 20,000 revellers showed up at the White House to celebrate Andrew Jackson's inauguration in 1829, the party quickly got out of hand. Jackson escaped through a window, and spent the first night of his presidency at the hotel at Gadsby's Tavern.

**Answers: 1** The second largest public slave market in America. **2** World Wars I and II. **3** 1,000–1,200.

*The restored Georgian-style Gunston Hall and its grounds*

# ③ Gunston Hall

### Home of the "unknown" Founding Father

This is the home of George Mason, who is sometimes called the unknown Founding Father. Mason was the first statesman to call for freedom of the press, religious tolerance, and trial by jury. Although part of the Continental Congress, he refused to sign the Constitution because it did not limit slavery and did not contain a Declaration of Rights. This refusal eventually cooled his friendship with Washington, but his political action was essential to the creation of the

## The Lowdown

🌐 **Address** 10709 Gunston Rd, Mason Neck, VA 22079; www.gunstonhall.org

🚗 **Car** 40-minute 20-mile (32-km) drive; see website for driving directions

🕐 **Open** 9:30am–5pm daily, closed Jan 1, Thanksgiving Day & Dec 25

💲 **Price** $30–40, under 6s free

👫 **Cutting the line** Purchase tickets online and save $1 on adult tickets.

🚩 **Guided tours** House tours every 30 minutes from 9:30am–4:30pm

👫 **Age range** 8 plus

🕐 **Allow** 90 minutes

♿ **Wheelchair access** Yes

🍴 **Eat and drink** *Snacks* Five Guys Burgers and Fries (6210 Quander Rd, Alexandria, VA 22306; 703 768 4700; www.fiveguys.com) has small- and jumbo-sized burgers, fries, and hot dogs. *Real meal* Faccia Luna (823 S Washington St, Alexandria, VA 22314; 703 838 5998; www.faccialuna.com) is a wood-fired pizza place with pasta, desserts, and a kids' menu.

🚻 **Restrooms** In the visitor center

Bill of Rights. Today, the house has been restored to reflect the period in which he lived here (1759–92). A visitor center offers an introductory film and exhibits on his life.

### Letting off steam

Right beside Gunston Hall, **Mason Neck State Park** (7301 High Point Rd, VA 22079) offers hiking trails, as well as canoe and kayak rentals for exploring the wildlife-filled tidal waters of the Potomac. Younger kids will enjoy the playground.

# ④ The Pentagon

### The world's biggest office

With over 17 miles (27 km) of corridors, the headquarters of the US military is the largest office in the world. Tours introduce visitors to the various missions of the branches of service, and important moments in military history. Exhibits that include models of ships and submarines, portraits of Medal of Honor recipients, and paintings depicting

## The Lowdown

🌐 **Address** Army-Navy Dr & S Fern St, Arlington, VA 22202; 703 697 1776; http://pentagontours.osd.mil

🚇 **Metro** Pentagon

🕐 **Open** 9am–2pm Mon–Fri, by advance reservation only, closed Federal holidays

💲 **Price** Free, by reservation only. Reserve online at least 14 days in advance. Foreign nationals should contact their embassy in Washington, DC.

👫 **Cutting the line** Reserve in advance, from 90 days to 8 days ahead; no reservations accepted within 7 days of a visit.

🚩 **Guided tours** Free walking tours Mon–Fri

prisoner of war camps will appeal to adults and teens with an interest in the military.

### Letting off steam

**LBJ Memorial Grove** (George Washington Memorial Parkway, near the Pentagon) is a great place to explore. A trail along the banks of the Potomac offers splendid views of the Washington, DC skyline.

# ⑤ Mount Vernon Bike Trail

### Ride the river road

A real outdoor treasure, this biking, walking, and jogging trail starts at Mount Vernon and follows the Potomac for 18 miles (29 km) north to Theodore Roosevelt Island. Along

*The scenic Mount Vernon Bike Trail along the Potomac River*

👫 **Age range** 14 plus

🕐 **Allow** 1 hour

♿ **Wheelchair access** Yes

🍴 **Eat and drink** *Snacks* Ray's: To The Third (1650 Wilson Blvd, VA 22209; 703 841 0001; open 11am–10pm Sun–Thu, 11am–11pm Fri & Sat; credit cards not accepted) is known for its freshly ground burgers with a selection of toppings. *Real meal* Village Bistro (1723 Wilson Blvd, VA 22209; 703 522 0284; www.villagebistro.com) serves French, Italian, and American entrées.

🚻 **Restrooms** At start and end of tour only

## The Lowdown

🌐 **Address** Mount Vernon in the south to Theodore Roosevelt Island; www.nps.gov/gwmp/planyourvisit/mtvernontrail.htm

🚃 **Metro** Rosslyn Station near north end of trail or Arlington National Cemetery

💲 **Price** Free

👫 **Cutting the line** The trail north of Alexandria is less crowded on busy weekends.

🚩 **Guided tours** Ride With a Ranger; check website for more details and information.

👫 **Age range** All ages

⏱ **Allow** 1–4 hours

🍴 **Eat and drink** *Picnic* Jack's Place (222 N Lee St, Alexandria, VA 22314; 703 684 0372; credit cards not accepted) is a popular local spot for breakfast and lunch. Eat in, or pick up a deli sandwich and head over to Waterfront Park for a picnic. *Real meal* Pita House (719 King St, Alexandria, VA 22314; 703 684 9194; www.the pitahouse.com) serves Lebanese and Mediterranean entrées.

👫 **Restrooms** At numerous locations along route

the way it passes through many parks with a lot to offer, including **Dyke Marsh Wildlife Preserve** (see p187), which is a great birding area, and Lyndon Baines Johnson Memorial Grove, which is among the most scenic on the route. The trail also passes through **Old Town Alexandria** (see pp188–9), which has bicycle rental shops, making it a good starting point for cyclists.

### Take cover
In case of bad weather, head to the **Torpedo Factory** (see p188) in Old Town Alexandria. This kid-friendly art center is home to the working studios of over 150 artists. Browse, buy, or just watch the artists at work.

## ⑥ Theodore Roosevelt Island

### Where the wild things are

Covering 91 acres (37 ha) and offering over 2 miles (4 km) of trails, Roosevelt Island is one of the best family-oriented nature hiking areas close to the capital. The island is surrounded by the tidal waters of the Potomac, and is home to a wide variety of birds, including hawks,

ducks, and geese. In the center of the island is a clearing with a statue of Theodore Roosevelt surrounded by fountains and other water features such as pools.

### Take cover
In case of bad weather, drive 1 mile (1.5 km) south to **Arlington National Cemetery** (see pp192–3), where the Women in Military Service Memorial offers fascinating displays.

*Exploring the wooded areas of Theodore Roosevelt Island*

## The Lowdown

🌐 **Address** Access from George Washington Memorial Parkway, Arlington, VA 20006; www.nps.gov/this

🚃 **Metro** Rosslyn Station and walk two blocks east to Lynn St, then north on pedestrian walkway along Lynn St, crossing 66 & Lee Hwy. Follow the connection to Mount Vernon Trail for about half a mile (1 km) east and south to the entrance of the island.

🕐 **Open** 6am–10pm daily

💲 **Price** Free

🚩 **Guided tours** Check the website for details.

👫 **Age range** All ages

🏃 **Activities** Ranger-led walks and interpretive talks; check website.

⏱ **Allow** 1–2 hours

🍴 **Eat and drink** *Snacks* Best Buns Bread Company (4010 Campbell Ave, VA 22206; 703 578 1500; www.greatamericanrestaurants.com) offers cupcakes, sticky buns, lemon bundt cake, and sandwiches. *Real meal* Pupatella (5104 Wilson Blvd, VA 22205; 571 312 7230; www.pupatella.com) has wood-fired Neapolitan pizza with a thin, soft crust. The kids' special pizza serves two.

👫 **Restrooms** At island's south end

# ⑦ Arlington National Cemetery
## Presidents, heroes, and the unknown soldiers

History and beauty walk hand-in-hand at this cemetery where those who have given exceptional service to their country are laid to rest. A stroll through its park-like grounds reveals the headstones of military heroes such as soldier and actor Audie Murphy as well as the resting places of astronauts, explorers, and other historical figures. Visit a memorial to women in service and watch the moving Changing of the Guard ceremony at the Tomb of the Unknowns.

*The Memorial Amphitheater at Arlington National Cemetery*

## Key Sights

① **Women in Military Service For America Memorial** Displays at this memorial highlight the contributions of women serving in the US military. A walkway along the roof is lined with glass panels etched with quotations about women in service.

② **Kennedy Memorial** Visit this simple and elegant monument that stands in memory of John F. Kennedy, one of America's most beloved presidents. An "eternal flame" burns over his grave.

③ **Arlington House** Once the home of Confederate General Robert E. Lee, the house is now a museum and memorial to the Civil War hero.

④ **Civil War Drummer Boy Grave** John Lincoln Clem served with Union forces as a drummer boy at the age of 10. He fought in the Battle of Chickamauga (1863), wounding a Confederate officer and earning the rank of sergeant.

⑤ **Audie Murphy's Grave** An actor who got his big break in Hollywood by being the most decorated American soldier of World War II, Audie Murphy (1924–71) won the Medal of Honor and 33 other medals, and went on to star in 44 films.

**Entrance**

**The Memorial Amphitheater**

⑥ **Space Shuttle Challenger Memorial** Two panels depict the explosion of the Space Shuttle *Challenger* (Jan 28, 1986) and stand in memory of the astronauts who lost their lives in the disaster.

⑦ **Tomb of the Unknowns** The resting place for unidentified soldiers killed in World Wars I and II, and Vietnam and Korea, is guarded by the 3rd Infantry, the US Army Honor Guard since 1945.

## The Lowdown

🌐 **Address** Near Lincoln Memorial, Arlington, VA 22211; 877 907 8585; www.arlingtoncemetery.mil

🚗 **Metro** Arlington Cemetery

🕐 **Open** Apr–Sep: 8am–7pm daily; Oct–Mar: 8am–5pm daily

💲 **Price** Free; parking for 3 hours $1.75 per hour, over 3 hours $2.50 per hour

🚩 **Guided tours** Narrated hop-on-hop-off ANC Tours by Martz Gray Line; $27–32

👫 **Age range** All ages

👫 **Activities** Check website for special ceremonies and events open to the public. Watch the

Changing of the Guard at the Tomb of the Unknowns; Apr–Sep: every hour on the half hour; Oct–Mar: every hour on the hour.

⏱ **Allow** Several hours

♿ **Wheelchair access** Yes

🛍 **Shop** Bookstore in the visitor center

🚻 **Restrooms** In the visitor center

### Good family value?
Offers beautiful grounds and a unique look at American history. Entrance is free, although many ride the ANC Tours by Martz Gray Line for which there is a charge.

Headstones dotting the sprawling grounds of Arlington National Cemetery

## Take cover
For shelter from heat or rain, head to Arlington House, the Women in Military Service For America Memorial, or the visitor center, which offers displays and a film on the history of the cemetery.

## Eat and drink
Picnic: under $30; Snacks: $30–40; Real meal: $40–75; Family treat: over $75 (based on a family of four)

**PICNIC Rosslyn Coffee & Deli** (1101 Wilson Blvd, VA 22209; 703 522 5387; closed Sat & Sun) offers cold meats, sandwiches, salads, burgers, sweets, snacks, and beverages to go. There is an outdoor seating area next door.

Sleek furnishings and contemporary designs inside Jaleo

**SNACKS Brooklyn Bagel Bakery** (2055 Wilson Blvd, VA 22201; 703 243 4442; www.brooklynbagelva.com; credit cards not accepted) is a New York-inspired deli with breakfast specials, sandwiches, soups, sweets, and authentic bagels.

**REAL MEAL Fashion Centre at Pentagon City – Food Court** (1100 S Hayes St, VA 22202; 703 415 2400; www.simon.com/mall/fashion-centre-at-pentagon-city) is a family-friendly food court inside the shopping mall with a variety of take-out options and a few sit-down restaurants, such as Ruby Tuesday's and Johnny Rockets.

**FAMILY TREAT Jaleo** (2250 A Crystal Dr, VA 22202; 703 413 8181; www.jaleo.com; closed Mon) serves modern yet traditional Spanish cuisine in small-plate tapas-style as well as savory paella (a rice-based dish), and sangria. The lunch menu also has sandwiches and salads.

## Shopping
Arlington is home to **Tysons Corner Mall** (1961 Chain Bridge Rd, VA 22102; 703 847 7300), the first and largest mall in Virginia with over 300 stores, including Apple, Nordstrom, and the first LL Bean opened outside Maine. Across the street, **Tysons Galleria** (2001 International Drive, VA 22102; 703 827 7730) offers even more upscale shops, including Neiman Marcus and Saks Fifth Avenue.

## Find out more
**FILM** The National Geographic DVD Arlington – Field of Honor tells the story of the Arlington National Cemetery, provides true-life accounts of wartime experiences, and looks at the daily activities there.

## Next stop...
**STEVEN F. UDVAR-HAZY CENTER** Head to see the fabulous planes and aircraft at the Steven F. Udvar-Hazy Center (see pp194–5). This huge facility contains hundreds of aircraft including a space shuttle, experimental and military aircrafts, a Concorde jet, and a Lockheed SR-71 Blackbird spy plane.

Spacecraft on display at the Steven F. Udvar-Hazy Center

# ⑧ Steven F. Udvar-Hazy Center
## Biplanes, spy planes, and a real space shuttle

For years, the Smithsonian gathered rare and interesting aircraft that it did not have room to display in the National Air and Space Museum (see pp56–9). Today, these restored aircraft make up the display at this center. Hanging overhead are dozens of aerobatic and historic planes, and filling the hall are rare warplanes, from World War II fighters to the supersonic jets of today. Also here is the Shuttle Discovery, which stands as a symbol of the promise of space exploration.

Aircraft hanging overhead at the Steven F. Udvar-Hazy Center

## Key Features

■ **First Floor** Business Aviation, Commercial Aviation, World War II Aviation, Cold War Aviation, Modern Military Aviation, Human Spaceflight, Space Science, and Rockets and Missiles

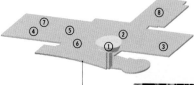

Entrance

① **Donald D. Engen Tower** Displays in the tower explain modern air traffic control systems while the wall of glass offers visitors a panoramic view of the Dulles airport runways.

## The Lowdown

🌐 **Address** 14390 Air and Space Museum Pkwy, Chantilly, VA 20151; 703 572 4118; www.airandspace.si.edu/udvarhazy

🚗 **Metro** Silver line to Wiehle-Reston East then Fairfax Connector bus #983 **Bus** Metro bus from L'Enfant Plaza to Dulles airport then taxi or VTA shuttle to Udvar Hazy

🕐 **Open** 10am–5:30pm daily, closed Dec 25. Times vary yearly; check website.

💲 **Price** Free

👫 **Cutting the line** Plan to visit the shuttle simulator before noon, when lines are shorter.

🔫 **Guided tours** Free guided tours at 10:30am & 1pm

👨‍👧 **Activities** Flight- and space-oriented movies at the IMAX theater (hourly 11am–4pm daily)

⏱️ **Allow** 2–4 hours

♿ **Wheelchair access** Yes

☕ **Café** On first floor (see p195)

🛍️ **Shop** Museum store (see p195)

👬 **Restrooms** At several locations in the museum

### Good family value?
This museum is good for kids who dream of flying or space travel. Entry is free but parking, simulator rides, and movies carry a fee.

② **SR-71 Blackbird** See the super-futuristic-looking spy plane that holds the record as the fastest, jet engine-driven, manned aircraft in the world. One of the world's first stealth aircraft, the SR-71 flew reconnaissance missions in the period of 1964 to 1998.

③ **Modern Military Aviation** Since the 1960s, technology has allowed air forces to build planes that are faster and smarter. Jet fighters and other military aircraft from around the world are on display here.

⑥ **Shuttle Simulator** This sophisticated simulator lets kids try their hand at landing a space shuttle. A museum docent guides the children through the flying and landing processes.

⑦ **Boeing 307 Stratoliner Clipper Flying Cloud** This was the first commercial aircraft to be pressurized, allowing it to fly above weather systems. Still in flying condition, the Clipper Flying Cloud is the last intact 307 in the world.

④ **Concorde** This record-setting commercial plane made the Paris to New York flight at an altitude of 53,000 ft (16,154 m) and at a speed of 1,334 mph (2,140 km/h).

⑤ **Enola Gay** A Boeing B-29 Superfortress Bomber, the Enola Gay dropped the first atomic bomb on Hiroshima, Japan, on August 6, 1945.

⑧ **Space Shuttle Discovery** The centerpiece of the James S. McDonnell space hangar, Discovery looks like one of the most amazing vehicles made on Earth. It flew 39 times from 1984 to 2011.

Prices given are for a family of four

## Letting off steam

From aircraft of the future, head to plantations of the past at **Sully Historic Site** (*3650 Historic Sully Way, Chantilly, VA 20151*), which offers a look into early 19th-century farming in Virginia. Built in 1799, this was the home of Richard Bland Lee, northern Virginia's first congressman. Today, there are hourly tours of the house, which has been furnished with original Lee family possessions. Outside, the grounds feature several outbuildings, including restored slave quarters. The tree-shaded grounds have picnic tables and ample room to play.

## Eat and drink

*Picnic: under $30; Snacks: $30–40; Real meal: $40–75; Family treat: over $75 (based on a family of four)*

**PICNIC** Bring a picnic lunch and enjoy it in the pretty grounds of Sully Historic Site.

**SNACKS** McDonald's and **McCafe** (*first floor of the center*) serve smoked chicken, McDonald's burgers, fries, salads, specialty coffees, muffins, and cakes.

**REAL MEAL** Red Robin (*14450 Chantilly Crossing Lane, Chantilly, VA 20151; 703 961 0620; www. redrobin.com; a car or cab is required to get here from the center*) serves good gourmet burgers, salads, and desserts, and has lots of kids' choices.

*The front entrance of Famous Dave's Barbecue*

**FAMILY TREAT** Famous Dave's **Barbecue** (*14452 Chantilly Crossing Lane, Chantilly, VA 20151; 703 263 7660; www. famousdaves.com; a car or cab is required to get here from the center*) is known for southern barbecue, pulled-pork smoked ribs, brisket, and all the roll-up-your-sleeves accompaniments.

*Still from the movie* The Right Stuff, *starring Sam Shepard*

## Shopping

If the shopping wish list includes a talking Spock bobble-head doll, a model of the space shuttle, or real pilot sunglasses, then the center's store is the place to go. It offers a creative and extensive array of aviation- and space-themed gifts, clothing, calendars, and posters. Kids will like the space-oriented toys and games, as well as the books on every conceivable aviation subject.

## Find out more

**DIGITAL** It is hard to beat the sheer volume of pictures, videos, and entertaining information on space and space travel that can be found on the NASA site *www.nasa.gov.*
**FILMS** The Right Stuff (1983) tells the story of the US development of jet planes and the space program. Watch *Apollo 13* (1995), which details the hair-raising challenges faced by NASA as it brought a damaged spacecraft back home.

## Next stop...

**MANASSAS NATIONAL BATTLEFIELD** The first major land battle of the Civil War occurred at Manassas. Today, Manassas National Battlefield (see p196) has an excellent museum and visitor center. There is also a big, open park with pretty grounds and good picnic facilities.

*The Henry House at the Manassas National Battlefield*

# ⑨ Manassas National Battlefield

## Civil War battlefield twice over

Two great Civil War battles were fought at this site. The First Battle of Bull Run (1861) was a nominal Confederate victory but big losses on both sides convinced all that it was going to be a longer and bloodier conflict than had been imagined. The Second Battle of Bull Run, 13 months after the first, was an overwhelming Confederate victory. Today, an excellent museum and a 45-minute movie at the Henry Hill Visitor Center describe both battles. The battlefield itself is huge, and the best place to see it from is the visitor center, where paths have interpretive signage.

*Cannons on display at the Manassas National Battlefield*

## The Lowdown

🌐 **Address** Henry Hill Visitor Center: 6511 Sudley Rd, VA 20109–2358; 703 361 1339; www.nps.gov/mana

🚗 **Car** No public transportation; see website for driving directions

🕐 **Open** Battlefield: Dawn to dusk daily. Henry Hill Visitor Center: 8:30am–5pm daily, closed Thanksgiving Day & Dec 25

💲 **Price** $12–16; under 16s free

🚩 **Guided tours** Ranger-led walking tours of Henry Hill; 11am & 2pm daily; audio driving CD available at Henry Hill Visitor Center.

👫 **Age range** 8 plus

🏃 **Activities** Living history re-enactments; check website for details.

⏱ **Allow** 1–3 hours to see museum displays and walk interpretive trail at Henry Hill.

🍽 **Eat and drink** *Picnic* Purchase the makings of a picnic from a vendor in DC and enjoy them at the Stuart's Hill Center or Brownsville Picnic Area. *Real meal* Cracker Barrel (10801 Battleview Pkwy, Manassas, VA 20109-2349; 703 369 4641; www.crackerbarrel.com), south of the battlefield, just off Sudley Road, is famous for pot roast, fried catfish, and big breakfasts served all day.

🚻 **Restrooms** At Henry Hill Visitor Center, Brownsville Picnic Area, and the Stuart's Hill Center

### Take cover

Head to the **Manassas Museum System** *(9101 Prince William St, VA 20110)* to take shelter from bad weather. Children are given a questionnaire and have to find the answers among the collection. The museum conducts driving and walking tours of the area, including a visit to the historic 1900 Hopkins Candy Factory. A display inside the building relates the story of the factory which, at its peak, shipped 10 tons (9 tonnes) of candy a day.

# ⑩ Great Falls Park

## Raging river, wild rapids

This excellent park is a great place for families to enjoy the outdoors in close proximity to the city. The falls are the main attraction. More like roaring rapids, they were created by the mighty Potomac River cascading over the geological feature known as the Fall Line which stretches for

*Kayakers riding the rapids at the Great Falls Park*

## The Lowdown

🌐 **Address** 9200 Old Dominion Dr, McLean, VA 22102; 703 285 2965; www.nps.gov/grfa

🚗 **Car** No public transportation; see website for driving directions

🕐 **Open** 7am–dusk daily, closed Dec 25. Visitor center: Spring–Fall 10am–5pm daily

💲 **Price** $12–22 for individuals arriving on foot or bicycle, under 2s free; $5 vehicle pass; both good for 3 consecutive days

🚩 **Guided tours** Ranger-led programs offered throughout the year; call 703 285 2965 for schedule.

👫 **Age range** All ages

🏃 **Activities** A children's room in the visitor center offers games, coloring activities, and puzzles.

⏱ **Allow** 1–3 hours

🍽 **Eat and drink** *Snacks* Deli Italiano (762-B Walker Rd, Village Green Center; 703 759 6782; www.deliitaliano.com) serves dine in or take-out pizzas, wraps, and pastas. *Real meal* The Tavern at Great Falls (9835 Georgetown Pike, Great Falls, VA 22066; 703 757 4770; www.greatfallstavern. com) offers a variety of entrées including fish and chips, prime rib, and crab cakes.

🚻 **Restrooms** At the visitor center

hundreds of miles north and south. This is also a good place to see the remnants of George Washington's "Patowmack Canal," built to get river barges safely around the falls. Head to the overlooks for great views of the falls, and in good weather kayakers can be seen challenging the water. There are also miles of excellent, well-marked hiking trails and picnic facilities.

## Take cover

If it rains, head to the visitor center, where displays on the region's natural history and geology will keep the little ones busy. After that, head for the shopping districts of **Tysons Corner Mall** (1961 Chain Bridge Rd, Arlington VA 22102; 703 893 9400) or Reston, VA, where the vibrant downtown offers shops, theaters, and cafés.

## ⑪ Wolf Trap National Park for the Performing Arts

Music, dance, theater – just another day at Wolf Trap

This is the US's only national park dedicated to the performing arts, and throughout the year it hosts an array of entertainment, from folk, jazz, classical, and pop music, to dance, opera, theater, and multimedia performances. Major artists perform at the Filene Center, which seats 6,800 while smaller names play in the Barns at Wolf Trap. There are also a number of programs for children, mostly on Saturdays, that include ArtPlay for babies and toddlers, ArtPlay for kids, private music lessons, and drumming circles for children of all ages.

## Letting off steam

Wolf Trap is not far from the shopping district of **Tysons Corner Mall**, which offers shopping and family-oriented dining. To get here, take Greenbelt Route 267, exit east to Leesburg Pike Highway 7, and go south and east for 1 mile (1.6 km).

## The Lowdown

🌐 **Address** 1551 Trap Rd, Vienna, VA 22182; 703 255 1868; www.wolftrap.org

🚗 **Bus** Wolf Trap Express Bus provides round-trip service from the West Falls Church-VT/UVA (Orange line) for Filene Center performances; departs every 20 minutes starting 2 hours before showtime

🕐 **Open** 7am–dusk daily, closed during Filene performances and festivals

💲 **Price** Kids' shows from $32, family shows $100 for lawn seats, $200 for orchestra seats

👫 **Cutting the line** Book tickets at www.wolftrap.org/Purchase_Tickets.aspx and arrive at least an hour ahead of showtime.

🚩 **Guided tours** Free programs led by park rangers available year round. Tours usually last one hour. Backstage tours available from Oct–Mar. Check www.nps.gov/wotr for details.

👫 **Activities** Children's Theatre-in-the-Woods shows for kids aged 3–12 Jun 29–Aug 14: 10:30am Tue–Sat

⏱ **Allow** Durations vary depending on performances

🍴 **Eat and drink** Real meal Meals Beneath the Moon (703 255 4017; www.mealsbeneath themoon.com; 10am–5pm Mon–Fri & on performance days) is an online service that will prepare a picnic and have it waiting at Wolf Trap. Orders must be made by 2pm preceding the day of your show. Family treat Ovations (in the Wolf Trap grounds; 703 255 4017; www.mealsbeneath themoon.com; special pricing for under 10s) offers a decadent buffet, salads, and desserts.

👫 **Restrooms** In Filene Center and near Ovations

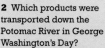

# KIDS' CORNER

## Find out more...

**1** What nickname did a famous Confederate general receive in the First Battle of Bull Run for being harder to move than a stone wall?

**2** Which products were transported down the Potomac River in George Washington's Day?

**3** Who was the oldest casualty in the First Battle of Bull Run?

Answers at the bottom of the page.

## BARGE RIGHT IN

The early riverboats of George Washington's day were keelboats that were only 5 ft (1.5 m) wide but up to 75 ft (23 m) long, and could carry as much as 20 tons (18 tonnes) of cargo. These boats made the voyage downstream in 3–5 days but took up to 12 days to be poled back upriver. Some traders made the journey in simple plank barges that they took apart and sold after reaching Georgetown.

## Trapping wolves

In the mid 1700s, wolves were plentiful and Fairfax County offered a bounty for trapping them. A local waterway was named Wolf Trap Creek and the surrounding area shared the name.

**Answers: 1** General Thomas Jackson became known as "Stonewall Jackson." **2** Tobacco, flour, whisky, and iron. **3** 85-year-old Judith Henry, who was killed by cannon fire that struck Henry House.

Open-air theater performance at Wolf Trap National Park for the Performing Arts

# ⑫ Harpers Ferry National Historic Park
## Mighty muskets and John Brown's war

This historic town is set into a mountain valley at the confluence of the Shenandoah and Potomac rivers. Two dozen buildings in the lower town, spanning the period from Colonial America to the early 20th century, are maintained as a National Historic Park. This is a fun place to explore, with small museums highlighting Civil War history, slavery, early industrial development, and the raid by Abolitionist John Brown on the US arsenal here.

*Artifacts on display at the Black Voices Museum*

## Key Sights

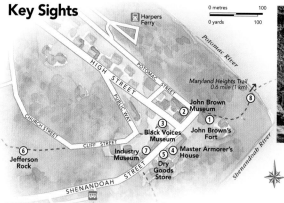

**⑥ Jefferson Rock** A short, steep trail leads to this promontory where, according to his written account, Thomas Jefferson stood in 1783. The view, he claimed, "is worth a voyage across the Atlantic."

**① John Brown's Fort** Period-dressed guides re-enact the story of Abolitionist John Brown. In 1859, he led 21 freed slaves and other volunteers on a raid of the armory at Harpers Ferry. He hoped to gather arms to start a war to free the slaves, but was wounded and captured in this fort.

**② John Brown Museum** Look at the culture of slavery that existed in Brown's day, and discover his life, his raid on army arsenals, and the outcome of this event.

**③ Black Voices Museum** Trace the African-American history of Harpers Ferry. West Virginia was a slave state, but in the mid-19th century the town was home to both free and enslaved African Americans.

**④ Master Armorer's House** This historic building houses exhibits and displays that relate the history of the town of Harpers Ferry.

**⑤ Dry Goods Store** Restored to show a dry goods store of the mid-19th century, this has merchandise that would have arrived daily by railroad and canal.

**⑦ Industry Museum** Harpers Ferry was first settled to take advantage of the water power of the rivers for industry, particularly arms manufacture. Displays here include examples of early machinery.

**⑧ Maryland Heights Trail** Hike the 4-mile (6-km) trail that leads to the Overlook Cliff, which offers a superb view of the town and the two rivers.

## Letting off steam
The **Shenandoah River** banks make a great place for kids to enjoy this spectacular natural setting. Trails here wind along the river's edge, and the shallow banks have smooth rocks and quiet pools. There are wooded and grassy areas that offer a splendid view of the historic town. Groups with younger kids will enjoy flatwater tubing trips on the river.

**Prices given are for a family of four**

*The banks of the Shenandoah River at Harpers Ferry*

## Eat and drink
*Picnic: under $30; Snacks: $30–40; Real meal: $40–75; Family treat: over $75 (based on a family of four)*

**PICNIC Swiss Miss** *(319 Spring St, Harpers Ferry, WV 25425; 304 535 1250)* offers tasty goodies that can be enjoyed in the grounds of the park.
**SNACKS Hannah's Train Depot** *(201 Potomac St, WV 25425; 304 535 1333; www.hannahstraindepot.com)* is a hamburger and snack stand in a colorful, old-fashioned train car.

*Pleasant courtyard seating at the Coach House Grill*

**REAL MEAL Coach House Grill** *(160 High St, WV 25425; 304 535 1257)* offers seating in a tavern setting and a pleasant garden courtyard. Dishes range from pasta and pizza to sandwiches, salads, and desserts.

**FAMILY TREAT The Anvil Restaurant** *(1290 W Washington St, WV 25425; 304 535 2582; www.anvilrestaurant.com)* has lunch selections that include crab and shrimp pasta, pan-seared trout, burgers, sandwiches, and salads.

## Shopping

This historic district offers something for everyone in the family. The **Historical Association Bookshop** *(723 Shenandoah St, WV 25425)* has books for adults and children on early American themes, plus cards and gifts. Fair-trade gifts for kids and the whole family can be found at **Tenfold** *(181A Potomac St, WV 25425)*. **The Village Shop** *(180 High St, WV 25425)* has gifts and souvenirs, as well as a bakery. **The Outfitter** *(189 High St, WV 25425)* features quality hiking and outdoor gear.

## Find out more

**DIGITAL** Visit Harpers Ferry National Parks website at *www.nps. gov/hafe* for a wealth of historical information along with schedules of tours and events. Download the Junior Ranger booklet, full of fun activities, and learn how to become a Junior Park Ranger.

*Overlook at Dickey Ridge Visitor Center, Skyline Drive*

## Next stop...

**SKYLINE DRIVE** Winding lazily through Shenandoah National Park in the Blue Ridge Parkway, Skyline Drive (see pp202–203) is known for dozens of overlooks that provide panoramic views of the pastoral Shenandoah River Valley. The park has hiking trails, waterfalls, and lodges.

# The Lowdown

🌐 **Address** NPS Visitor Center, 171 Shoreline Drive, Harpers Ferry, WV 25425; www.nps. gov/hafe

🚗 **Train** MARC from Union Station to Harpers Ferry in 90 minutes; check www.mta.maryland.gov/marc-train

ℹ️ **Visitor information** Visitor Center: 171 Shoreline Dr, WV 25425; 304 535 6029; www.nps. gov/hafe

🕐 **Open** 8am–5pm daily, closed Jan 1, Thanksgiving Day & Dec 25

💲 **Price** $16–20; $10 per single private vehicle. John Brown Museum: $24–30; under 5s free

👫 **Cutting the line** The park can get crowded after lunch, so plan to visit early and have lunch before noon, or eat after 1:30pm.

🧍 **Activities** Tours, hikes, talks, and events; mid-Jun–mid-Aug: 11am–4pm daily; check the visitor center or website.

⏱️ **Allow** A full day to see the buildings, museums and hike; 3–4 hours for the roundtrip hike to Maryland Heights.

☕ **Cafés** Several restaurants in the lower town

🛍️ **Shops** Numerous shops in the merchants district

🚻 **Restrooms** At the visitor center and the bookshop in lower town

### Good family value?

With something of interest for everyone, this is a beautiful place for a family to spend a full day.

# ⑬ Leesberg

### A lesson in history

This charming southern town is a good family destination for cafés, shopping, and ambience, as well as a handful of historic sites. Prime among these is Dodona Manor, an elegant home built in 1820 that stands within walking distance of downtown Leesburg. A National Historic Landmark, this was the home of General George C. Marshall, a Nobel Peace Prize recipient who was considered the architect of the Allied victory in World War II. Today, the house has been restored to 1950s style to reflect the time that Marshall lived there. Downtown Leesburg is home to the County Courthouse, one of the few buildings in the south not burnt down during the Civil War. Six miles (10 km) south of town, Oatlands Plantation is one of the most magnificent antebellum plantation homes in Virginia.

Shops and restaurants along King Street in downtown Leesburg

## The Lowdown

🌐 **Address** Loudoun County, VA 20175–20178

🚗 **Car** Rent a car from any of the car rental companies *(see p23)*

ℹ️ **Visitor information** Visitor center: Market Station, 112-G South St SE, VA 20175; 703 771 2170 or 800 752 6118; www.visitloudoun.org

🕐 **Open** 9am–5pm daily

🚩 **Guided tours** Walking tours of downtown Leesburg available by reservation at Loudoun Museum: 16 Loudoun St, 10am–5pm Fri & Sat, 1–5pm Sun; $6–16, under 12s free. Oatlands Plantation: house tours on the hour 10am–4pm Mon–Sat, 1–4pm Sun; $40–50, under 6s free; garden and grounds at 11am Mon–Fri; $48–58; combined tour $80–90; check www.oatlands.org for details

👫 **Age range** All ages

🕐 **Allow** 2–4 hours for town and Oatlands Plantation

🍴 **Eat and drink** *Real meal* La Chocita Grill (210 Loudoun St SE, VA 20175; 703 443 2319; www.lachocitagrill.com), a Salvadoran restaurant, serves grilled chicken marinated in spices, and other Central American specialties. *Family treat* Tuscarora Mill Restaurant (203 Harrison St, VA 20175; 703 771 9300; www.tuskies.com; lunch at 11am daily, brunch Sun) offers sit-down dining in an old mill, with spicy lamb burgers and smoked chicken pasta.

👫 **Restrooms** At the visitor center and County Courthouse

## Letting off steam

The site of a Civil War battle, **Ball's Bluff Battlefield Regional Park** *(Ball's Bluff Rd, Leesburg, VA 20176)* offers a scenic trail that winds through old-growth hardwoods from the parking lot to a bluff above the Potomac River.

# ⑭ White's Ferry

### Ride the boat-on-a-rope

The ferry at this remote location has been taking travelers across the Potomac River from Maryland to Virginia and back since 1817 and is the last of its kind. It now carries cars, pedestrians, and bicycles. After the Civil War, the ferry was bought and operated by Elijah V. White, who named the boat after his Confederate commander, General Jubal A. Early, and it remains

Cars crossing the waters of the Potomac on White's Ferry

## The Lowdown

🌐 **Address** 24801 White's Ferry Rd, Dickerson, MD 20842; 301 349 5200

🚗 **Car** Drive 1 mile (1.5 km) N of Leesburg on Hwy 15, turn right on State Route 655

🕐 **Open** 5am–11pm daily

💲 **Price** $5 one way, $8 round trip for cars

👫 **Cutting the line** Lines can be an hour long or more on busy summer weekends. Arrive before noon to beat the crowds.

👫 **Age range** All ages

🕐 **Allow** 30 minutes

🍴 **Eat and drink** *Picnic* Pick up a picnic lunch in Leesburg and enjoy it on the Maryland side of the river, where there is a park-like space with picnic tables. There is a snack shop on the Maryland side as well. *Real meal* Lightfoot Restaurant (11 North King St, Leesburg, VA 20176; 703 771 2233; www.lightfootrestaurant.com) has sandwiches, lobster and shrimp pasta, and a specialty called the Cardini fish taco of Tijuana.

👫 **Restrooms** On the Maryland side of the river

so-named to this day. This is a pretty spot and the Maryland side of the river has a picnic area by the river and ruins of the C&O Canal *(see pp156–7)* that are worth exploring.

## Letting off steam

Families can wander the grounds around lily-filled ponds and enjoy the views of the lazy Monocacy River at the **Lilypons Water Garden** *(6800 Lily Pons Rd, Adamstown, MD 21710)*. The gazebo, surrounded by a water garden, is a good place for a picnic.

# ⑮ Frederick

## The C&O or the B&O?

With lots of interesting shops, cafés, and shady sidewalks, this historic town is perfect for family rambling. The Baltimore and Ohio (B&O) Railroad built a line into town in 1831, entering into competition with the C&O Canal, 10 miles (16 km) west of town. Today, the C&O Canal Visitor Center and the Brunswick Railroad Museum are in the same building, making it a good place to learn about the town's history. Frederick was invaded three times by the Confederacy and was the scene of numerous skirmishes, so it is not surprising that it is home to the National Museum of Civil War Medicine, which has plenty to fascinate both kids and adults. Exhibits show how much of modern medicine owes to advances made during the Civil War.

## Letting off steam

Four miles (6 km) outside of Frederick on Hwy 355, **Monocacy National Battlefield** (*4801 Urbana Pike, MD 21704–7303*) is where the

*Above* Cannon on display at Monocacy National Battlefield, near Frederick
*Below* A gazebo and lily-filled pond at the Lilypons Water Garden

Confederacy won their northernmost victory in July 1864, killing more than 1,200 Union soldiers. Today, this is a tranquil, open area that invites children to play. There are cannons, a trail with interpretive signage, and a museum.

## The Lowdown

🌐 **Address** Maryland. Brunswick Railroad Museum: 40 West Potomac St, Brunswick, MD 21716; *www.brrm.net*. National Museum of Civil War Medicine: 48 East Patrick St, Frederick, MD 21705; 301 695 1864; *www.civilwarmed.org*

🚂 **Train** 90-minute MARC ride from Union Station to Frederick; call 410 539 5000 or check *www.mta. maryland.gov/marc-train*

ℹ️ **Visitor information** Visitor center: 151 SE St, MD 21701; 301 600 4047; *www.visitfrederick.org*

🕐 **Open** Visitor center: 9am–5:30pm daily. Railroad Museum: 10am–2pm Fri, 10am–4pm Sat, 1–4pm Sun. National Museum of Civil War Medicine: 10am–5pm Mon–Sat, 11am–5pm Sun. Monocacy National Battlefield: 8:30am–5pm daily

💲 **Price** Railroad Museum: $25–35; under 4s free. National Museum of Civil War Medicine: $26–36; under 10s free. Monocacy National Battlefield: free

🚩 **Guided tours** Walking history and ghost tours are available; contact visitor center for details.

👫 **Age range** All ages

⏱️ **Allow** 1–4 hours

🍴 **Eat and drink** *Snacks* That Cuban Place (*506 E Church St, Frederick MD 21701; www.thatcubanplace. com*) serves Cuban sandwiches, smoothies, and other light fare. *Real meal* The Orchard (*45 N Market St, MD 21701; 301 663 4912; www.theorchardrestaurant. com*) offers tasty dinners with plenty of vegetarian options.

🚻 **Restrooms** At the visitor center

# ⑯ Skyline Drive

## Tumbling waters and mountain vistas

Tracing the high Appalachian ridges of Shenandoah National Park, the 105-mile (168-km)-long Skyline Drive is one of the most spectacularly scenic drives in the Atlantic region. There are scores of overlooks that offer views across mountain ranges and down to the emerald fields of the Shenandoah Valley. The park also offers a multitude of hiking trails, which range from easy to difficult. Rangers at any of the visitor centers will be glad to suggest hikes and walks appropriate to any age group.

*Colorful trees lining Skyline Drive*

## Key Sights

① **Dickey Ridge Visitor Center (Mile 4.6)** A good first stop for visitors coming from Washington, the center offers maps, information, and a movie describing the history of the park and attractions found along the drive. The picnic area behind the center offers a panoramic view of the pastoral Shenandoah Valley. Beginning here, the Fox Hollow nature trail is an easy 1.2-mile (2-km) hike for families.

⑤ **Dark Hollow Falls Trail (Mile 50.7)** A moderately challenging trail, best for ages 10 and above, this trail offers a short, sometimes steep hike down to the lovely 70-ft (21-m)-high Dark Hollow Falls.

⑥ **Big Meadows (Mile 51.2)** A good family stop, Big Meadows offers a hotel, restaurant, and gift shop, as well as some easy hiking trails. The Byrd Visitor Center here has an excellent exhibit detailing the park's history and the building of Skyline Drive. Starting here, the Story of the Forest nature trail is a gentle 1.8-mile (3-km) hike with signage that relates the natural and cultural history of the forest and swamp.

② **Stony Man Overlook (Mile 38.6)** This short, moderately easy hike gains about 800 ft (244 m) in elevation and leads to a rocky outcropping that offers one of the most spectacular views in the park. The highest point on the drive can be found near the Stony Man overlook at 3,680 ft (1,122 m).

③ **Little Stony Man Cliffs (Mile 39.1)** This 0.9 mile (1.5 km), 1-hour round-trip is an excellent and fairly easy hike with spectacular views of the valley.

④ **Skyland Resort (Mile 41.7)** The historic heart of the park, this attracted the wealthy between the 1890s and the 1920s. Today, part of the original resort has been restored and is open for tours. There is a modern resort and a restaurant here.

⑦ **Loft Mountain (Mile 79.5)** There are several hiking trails in this area, along with a restaurant and a large family campground.

**Prices given are for a family of four**

Front Royal

① Dickey Ridge Visitor Center

Elkwallow Wayside

Stony Man Overlook

Little Stony Man Cliffs ③ ④
Skyland Resort ④
Hawksbill Mountain

Big Meadows ⑥ ⑤ Dark Hollow Falls Trail

SKYLINE DRIVE

Lewis Mountain

33

⑦ Loft Mountain

SKYLINE DRIVE

0 km        15

0 miles        15

64

# The Lowdown

🌐 **Address** 3655 US Hwy 211, East Luray, VA 22835; 540 999 3500; *www.nps.gov/shen*

🚗 **Car** Rent a car from any of the car rental companies (*see p23*)

🕐 **Open** Dickey Ridge Visitor Center and Byrd Visitor Center: Apr–early May: 9am–5pm Sat & Sun, early May–Dec: 9am–5pm daily. Check website as dates vary yearly.

💲 **Price** Mar–Nov: $15 per car; Dec–Feb: $10 per car; visitors coming from Washington pay admission at the park entrance at Front Royal and then continue along Skyline Drive to the Dickey Ridge Visitor Center.

👫 **Cutting the line** Weekend afternoons in summer are busy. Head out in the morning and use the afternoon to explore the area. Book accommodations days or weeks in advance.

🚩 **Guided tours** The ranger offices offer wildlife and nature programs and walks for all ages; check at the visitor centers.

👪 **Age range** All ages

🏃 **Activities** Apr–Oct: Purchase a Junior Ranger explorer notebook from the visitor centers, complete the activities in the book, and earn a sticker, badge, or patch. Walks and programs offered daily at visitor centers.

⏱ **Allow** 3 hours to a full day

☕ **Cafés** From mid-Apr to mid-Nov at Elkwallow Wayside, Skyland Resort, Big Meadows Lodge, and Loft Mountain

🛍 **Shops** All visitor centers and lodges have shops with mountain-themed gifts.

🚻 **Restrooms** At Dickey Ridge, Elkwallow Wayside, Skyland Resort, Big Meadows Lodge, Lewis Mountain (Mile 57.5), and Loft Mountain

## Good family value?
This great outdoor destination close to the city is cheap and offers good hiking and scenery.

## Take cover
If it rains, head to the visitor centers at **Dickey Ridge** or **Big Meadows**. Both offer displays and exhibits on the natural history of the park.

## Eat and drink
*Picnic: under $30; Snacks: $30–40; Real meal: $40–75; Family treat: over $75 (based on a family of four)*

**PICNIC McAlister's Deli** (70 Riverton Commons Dr, Front Royal, VA 22630; 540 631 7277; *www.mcalistersdeli.com*) dishes up tasty sandwiches, salads, meat and cheese plates. It offers both dine-in and take-out services.

**SNACKS Elkwallow Wayside** (Mile 24.1) offers grilled sandwiches, breakfast items, and snacks.

**REAL MEAL Pollock Dining Room** (Mile 41.7; 877 847 1919; *www.goshenandoah.com/Dine.aspx*) serves all-American lunches such as Virginia macaroni and cheese.

**FAMILY TREAT Spottswood Dining Room** (Mile 51.2; 877 847 1919; *www.goshenandoah.com/Dine.aspx*) offers Nouveau takes on traditional American lunches and dinners, including salads and desserts such as the Mile High Blackberry Ice Cream Pie.

## Find out more
**DIGITAL** *www.nps.gov/shen/historyculture/index.htm* and *www.nps.gov/shen/naturescience/index.htm* have kid-friendly information on Shenandoah National Park.
**FILM** The 1965 film *Shenandoah!* depicts the struggle of Shenandoah farm families during the Civil War. Another Civil War film, *Sommersby* (1993), was filmed in the area.

## Next stop...
**MONTICELLO** Built over 40 years, beginning in 1769, **Monticello** (*see pp204–205*) is a short drive from the southern entrance to the park. Today, the house is furnished and looks much as it would have done in Thomas Jefferson's day.

*The well-restored, elegant, and airy tearoom in Monticello*

# ⑰ Monticello
## Back to the future with Thomas Jefferson

A Palladian masterpiece, Thomas Jefferson's house offers an insight into the world of one of the most fascinating Founding Fathers. From the writing desk that could make copies, to hidden closets, Monticello abounds with things that will catch the interest of kids. Outside, the beautiful grounds are filled with Jeffersonian innovations such as the glass-and-brick garden room.

**Gardens** The home is surrounded by flower gardens, but the real business of the plantation was food production, which is still carried on using organic practices in the orchards and vineyards.

## Key Features

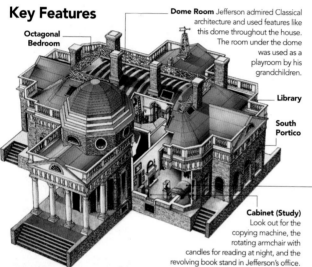

**Octagonal Bedroom**

**Dome Room** Jefferson admired Classical architecture and used features like this dome throughout the house. The room under the dome was used as a playroom by his grandchildren.

**Library**

**South Portico**

**Cabinet (Study)** Look out for the copying machine, the rotating armchair with candles for reading at night, and the revolving book stand in Jefferson's office.

**Octagonal Bedroom** This room was for honored guests, such as the fourth US president James Madison and his wife, Dolley, who were regular visitors.

**Bed Chamber** Jefferson designed his bed so he could exit it either into the bedroom or his study. The wall above the bed has a secret closet.

**South Portico** Jefferson was justifiably proud of his elegant greenhouse, which protected delicate tropical plants and trees such as citrus through the winter.

**Library** Jefferson was an avid reader who knew several languages. His collection of books was one of the finest in the country.

**Kitchen** Cellar tunnels leading to the kitchen allowed prepared food to be brought into the house in all weather, while keeping the danger of kitchen fires away from the main structure.

**Prices given are for a family of four**

## The Lowdown

🌐 **Address** 931 Thomas Jefferson Pkwy, Charlottesville, VA 22902; 434 984 9822; www.monticello.org

🚗 **Transport** No public transportation; several private tour companies offer Monticello tours; call 888 878 9870.

🕐 **Open** 9am–5pm daily, extended hours in summer

💲 **Price** Mar–Oct: $60–70; Nov–Feb: $50–60; under 6s free

👪 **Cutting the line** Arrive early to beat the line-ups as crowds descend during warm weather weekends.

🏳 **Guided tours** House and grounds tours included in the ticket price. Plantation tour and wine tour included with admission Apr–Oct. Behind the scenes tour $220 for family of four; check website for schedule.

👫 **Age range** All ages

🏃 **Activities** 30-minute tours daily for kids 6–11 offer a hands-on look at what life was like here for children in the 18th century. Take in the introductory movie and displays at the visitor center to enhance the visit.

⏱ **Allow** 2–4 hours

♿ **Wheelchair access** Yes

☕ **Café** At the visitor center (see p205)

🛍 **Shop** At the visitor center (see p205)

🚻 **Restrooms** At the visitor center and in the house

### Good family value?
Monticello is elegant, beautiful, and filled with things that will intrigue young minds. Admission is pricey, but helps pay for the upkeep and ongoing research.

## Letting off steam

When it is time to let the kids run, Monticello's gardens and orchards offer lots of paths and open spaces for exploration and play. A walk to Jefferson's grave offers just enough up and down to tire children, without exhausting parents.

## Eat and drink

*Picnic: under $30; Snacks: $30–40; Real meal: $40–75; Family treat: over $75 (based on a family of four)*

**PICNIC Café at Monticello** *(at the visitor center)* offers snacks, drinks, and boxed lunches to take out and enjoy on the deck or in the pretty visitor center courtyard.

*The popular Café at Monticello at the visitor center*

**SNACKS Market Street Market** *(400 E Market St, Charlottesville, VA 22902; 434 293 3478; www.market streetmarket.net)* is a family-run grocery store that carries over 5,000 products, including deli items and delicious made-to-order sandwiches.

**REAL MEAL Michie Tavern** *(683 Thomas Jefferson Pkwy, Charlottesville, VA 22902; 434 977 1234; www.michietavern.com)*, a short drive from Monticello, has been serving visitors since 1784. Today, waiters in period garb serve up 18th-century versions of southern chicken, pork, and veggies, all served buffet-style.

**FAMILY TREAT Aromas Cafe** *(1104 Emmet St, Charlottesville, VA 22903; 434 244 2486; www.aromas cafecville.com)* offers Moroccan-inspired dishes such as chicken Marrakech, or the Casablanca sandwich of lean beef *kofta* (meat-ball) with seven spices on pita.

## Shopping

The museum shop at the visitor center is a celebration of all things Jeffersonian. There are over 250 book titles and reproductions of some of his most innovative gadgets,
such as the rotating book stand. Also on sale here are wines, gourmet foods, artworks, clothing, and jewelry embroidered or engraved with some of Jefferson's most famous quotes. There is a home decor range as well.

## Find out more

**DIGITAL** The official website *www. monticello.org* offers an extensive collection of information, documents, and articles on Jefferson's public service and his life at Monticello. It also has kid-oriented sections. Biography.com offers videos and an extensive biography of Thomas Jefferson at *www.biography.com/ people/thomas-jefferson-9353715*.
**FILM** Watch *Jefferson in Paris* (1995), a period drama about Jefferson's years in Paris on the eve of the French Revolution. The movie, rated PG-13, has some adult themes, but should appeal to older children. The 1996 documentary *Thomas Jefferson: A Film by Ken Burns* takes a penetrating look at Jefferson's life, including at Monticello, and his contributions to America.

## Next stop...

**CHARLOTTESVILLE** Close to Monticello is historic Charlottesville (see p206), a walker's delight. Here, the brick pedestrian mall offers a tree-lined, courtyard-like venue of over 120 boutique and specialty shops, as well as restaurants and a lively collection of street vendors. A few blocks to the east, the University of Virginia, founded by Jefferson, is home to the Rotunda, one of his most exceptional architectural achievements.

*The grave of Thomas Jefferson at Monticello*

# ⑱ Charlottesville

## Thomas Jefferson's convenience store

This charming historic town was where Thomas Jefferson came to buy curtains or a new wagon wheel. Today, the number one attraction here is the brick-paved pedestrian Downtown Mall – a broad, open plaza between two rows of vibrant shops, boutiques, and restaurants. Sit on a bench and relax under the shady trees, enjoy the open-air cafés, and shop from the table-top vendors selling all manner of colorful wares, including clothes and jewelry.

Near the east end of the Downtown Mall, the Virginia Discovery Museum is geared toward kids aged 4 to 8 years, and offers a wealth of hands-on exhibits on

One of the many cafés with outdoor seating in Downtown Mall, Charlottesville

Playground with swings in McIntire Municipal Park, Charlottesville

science, nature, and history. Kids can play in the 18th-century Showalter Cabin, watch bees working in a hive, or send tennis balls flying along see-through pneumatic tubes in the Amazing Airways exhibit. A short distance west of the Mall, the Rotunda at the University of Virginia is an architectural gem designed by Jefferson, who founded the college. However, Jefferson is not the region's only Founding Father. Three miles (5 km) south of town, Ash-Lawn Highland was once home to the fifth US president James Monroe, while 25 miles (40 km) north of town, Montpelier is where the fourth US president James Madison lived.

### Letting off steam

A mile (1.6 km) north of the Downtown Mall, the big **McIntire Municipal Park** (1300 Pen Park Rd, VA 22901) has a modern playground and lots of room for children to run. On a sunny day, enjoy a picnic surrounded by green woods and lawn-like expanses.

# ⑲ Fredericksburg

## George Washington's boyhood hometown

George Washington spent much of his childhood living in Fredericksburg at his family's estate, Ferry Farm. Archaeological excavations have uncovered the foundations of the house where he grew up. Take a walking tour of the property, admire the various exhibits at the visitor center, and see how kids grew up in Colonial Virginia. Downtown Fredericksburg has two more homes that belonged to George Washington's family members – his sister Betty's lovely Georgian home, Kenmore Plantation, and the cottage where his mother, Mary, lived after her husband's death.

Visit the Hugh Mercer Apothecary and the Fredericksburg Area Museum and Cultural Center. A fun stop for kids, the apothecary is a reproduction of a Colonial-period drugstore, complete with jars of leeches used to bleed patients in those days. Later on, shop and dine at Princess Ann Street and Caroline

Home of Mary Washington, George Washington's mother, Fredericksburg

## The Lowdown

🌐 **Address** Virginia. Virginia Discovery Museum: 524 East Main St, VA 22902; 434 977 1025; www.vadm.org

🚃 **Train** Amtrak from Union Station to Charlottesville daily. **Bus** Greyhound Bus from Washington daily. Several private tour companies offer Charlottesville tours; call 888 878 9870.

🕐 **Open** Virginia Discovery Museum: 10am–5pm Mon–Sat

ℹ️ **Visitor information** Visitor center: 610 East Main St, VA 22902; 434 293 6789 or 877 386 1103; www.visitcharlottesville.org; 10am–5pm daily

💲 **Price** Virginia Discovery Museum: $24; under 1s free

🚩 **Guided tours** Montpelier and Ash-Lawn Highland tours

👫 **Age range** All ages

👫 **Activities** The Charlotte Pavilion at the east end of the Downtown Mall offers regular music programs; some are free, while others raise money for worthwhile causes. On summer weekends, buskers perform at the Downtown Mall, providing an extra-festive atmosphere.

🍴 **Eat and drink** Snacks Blue Ridge Country Store (518 E Main St, VA 22902; 434 295 1573) is a fun and funky place with old-fashioned candy and healthy snacks. They also offer sit-down hearty lunches such as meatloaf or Jerk chicken, all at very affordable prices. Real meal Marco and Luca (112 West Main St, VA 22902; 434 295 3855) is a Chinese-fusion noodle house on the Downtown Mall that serves up fresh and delicious dumplings, spring rolls, and sesame noodles in a very family-friendly atmosphere.

👫 **Restrooms** In the visitor center

## The Lowdown

🌐 **Address** Virginia. Ferry Farm: 268 Kings Hwy, VA 22405; www.kenmore.org. Fredericksburg Area Museum and Culture Center: 1001 Princess Anne St, VA 22401; www.famcc.org. Hugh Mercer Apothecary: 1020 Caroline St, VA 22401; www.washingtonheritagemuseums.org

🚆 **Train** Amtrak from Union Station to Fredericksburg daily and then walk to most sights. **Bus** Greyhound Bus from Washington daily. For Ferry Farm, take a cab or book tickets through an organized tour.

🕐 **Open** Ferry Farm: Mar–Oct: 10am–5pm daily, Nov–Dec: 10am–4pm daily. Fredericksburg Area Museum and Culture Center: 10am–5pm Mon–Sat, noon–5pm Sun. Hugh Mercer Apothecary: Mar–Oct: 9am–4pm Mon–Sat, noon–4pm Mon, Nov–Feb: 10am–3pm Mon–Sat, noon–4pm Sun

ℹ️ **Visitor information** Visitor center: 706 Caroline St, VA 22401; 540 373 1776

💲 **Price** Check websites for details

🚶 **Guided tours** Get brochures and map for a self-guided walking tour at the visitor center.

👨‍👧 **Age range** All ages. Ferry Farm: 6 plus. Kenmore Plantation: 10 plus

🏃 **Activities** Watch a 14-minute movie on Fredericksburg's history and attractions at the visitor center.

⏱️ **Allow** 2–4 hours

🍴 **Eat and drink** *Snacks* Olde Towne Wine and Cheese Deli (707 Caroline St, VA 22401; 540 373 7877) offers delicious filling sandwiches made with local ingredients. *Real meal* Sammy T's (801 Caroline St, VA 22401; 540 371 2008; www.sammyts.com) serves pub-style food with a kids' menu and vegetarian offerings.

🚻 **Restrooms** In the visitor center and at Ferry Farm

Street, where many of the original commercial buildings now house interesting shops and restaurants.

### Letting off steam

There is no better place to run and play than where George Washington did – on Ferry Farm. Here, large grassy expanses overlook the lovely Rappahannock River and offer places to explore, and enjoy a picnic lunch.

## 20 Middleburg

### Once famous for foxhunting and steeplechasing

Surrounded by miles of beautiful rolling hills and thoroughbred horse farms, this small historic town is the heart of hunt country. Families can also enjoy a stroll along the charming main street, where old stone buildings house interesting boutique shops and restaurants.

### Take cover

If bad weather threatens, head to the **National Sporting Library and Museum** (102 The Plains Rd, Middleburg, VA 20118; www.nsl.org), to learn about horses, riding, and foxhunting. This may appeal to older kids more than young ones.

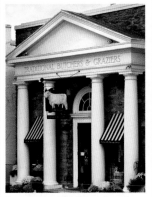

*Front entrance of the Home Farm Store in Middleburg*

## The Lowdown

🌐 **Address** Virginia

🚗 **Car** 42-mile (68-km) drive; see website for driving directions.

🕐 **Open** 11am–3pm Mon–Fri, 11am–4pm Sat & Sun

ℹ️ **Visitor information** Visitor center: 12 Madison St N, VA 20118; 540 687 8888; www.middleburgonline.com

👨‍👧 **Age range** All ages

🏃 **Activities** Self-guided tour map and pamphlet available at the visitor center.

🍴 **Eat and drink** *Snacks* Market Salamander (200 W Washington St, VA 20117; 540 687 9720; www.marketsalamander.com) offers gourmet sandwiches, fresh fruit and veggies, and other goodies. *Family treat* Red Fox Inn and Tavern (2 East Washington St, VA 20117; 540 687 6301; www.redfox.com) has home-style country fare with an upscale twist. Try the Red Fox crab cake sandwich and chicken avocado melt.

🚻 **Restrooms** In the visitor center

# ㉑ Colonial Williamsburg™
## Become part of a revolution

The largest living history museum in America, Colonial Williamsburg™ is a fantastic place for kids to learn what life was like at the time of the American Revolution by exploring the government buildings, shops, homes, gardens, and taverns of the Revolutionary City. The nation's capital during the Revolutionary era, it now gives children a chance to march with the Fife and Drum Corps, play the on-site, citywide spy game, or create a work of art to take home.

Firing cannons during Patrick Henry's speech

## Key Sights

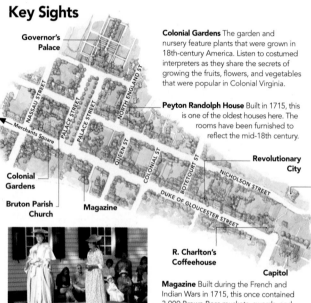

Governor's Palace

NASSAU STREET
PALACE STREET
PALACE STREET
NORTH ENGLAND ST
Merchants Square
QUEEN ST
COLONIAL ST
BOTETOURT ST
NICHOLSON STREET
DUKE OF GLOUCESTER STREET

Colonial Gardens

Bruton Parish Church

Magazine

R. Charlton's Coffeehouse

Capitol

Revolutionary City

**Colonial Gardens** The garden and nursery feature plants that were grown in 18th-century America. Listen to costumed interpreters as they share the secrets of growing the fruits, flowers, and vegetables that were popular in Colonial Virginia.

**Peyton Randolph House** Built in 1715, this is one of the oldest houses here. The rooms have been furnished to reflect the mid-18th century.

**Governor's Palace** Completed in 1722, the home of the Royal Governor of Virginia was one of the finest in the colonies. Visitors can tour the house, kitchen, and gardens.

**Gaol** Dating to 1704, the gaol (or jail) was used to hold criminals and debtors, runaway slaves, and sometimes the criminally insane.

**Magazine** Built during the French and Indian Wars in 1715, this once contained 3,000 Brown Bess muskets, swords, and other arms. Today, many of these still line the walls of the building.

**Revolutionary City** This street theater immerses visitors in the sights and sounds of the Revolutionary War. Watch a Loyalist mother argue with her independence-minded daughter or listen to revolutionary leader Patrick Henry give a rousing speech.

**Bruton Parish Church** Ever since the first service took place in 1715, the likes of George Washington and Thomas Jefferson have attended this church.

**R. Charlton's Coffeehouse** Sit at tables in a large room and listen to costumed guides as they serve coffee (hot chocolate for kids) and discuss the news of the day on the brink of the Revolutionary War.

## Letting off steam
Located in front of the Governor's Palace, Palace Green is an open lawn rimmed by trees. Kids can play here while citizens in 18th-century garb stroll the surrounding lanes.

## Eat and drink
Picnic: under $30; Snacks: $30–40; Real meal: $40–75; Family treat: over $75 (based on a family of four)

**PICNIC Aromas Coffee** (431 Prince George St, VA 23185; 757 221 6676; www.aromasworld.com) is an

Prices given are for a family of four

inviting coffee shop offering drinks, sandwiches, soups, and pastries to eat in or take out. For a picnic, take the goodies to Palace Green.

The pretty tree-lined Palace Green facing the Governor's Palace

**SNACKS Chowning's Tavern** (109 East Duke of Gloucester St, VA 23185; 757 229 2141; www.colonialwilliamsburg.com/do/restaurants/historic-dining-taverns/chownings) offers snacks and light meals. Eat inside, or take the quick-service option in the garden behind.
**REAL MEAL King's Arms Tavern** (416 East Duke of Gloucester St, VA 23185; 888 965 7254; www.colonialwilliamsburg.com/do/restaurants/historic-dining-taverns/kings-arms; reservations required for dinner) serves traditional Southern fare and

# The Lowdown

🌐 **Address** Virginia

🚗 **Train** Amtrak from Union Station to Williamsburg daily. **Bus** Greyhound Bus from Washington, DC daily; package tours include admission, transport, and accommodations.

ℹ️ **Visitor information** Visitor center: 101 Visitor Center Drive Williamsburg, VA 23185; 800 447 8679; www.colonial williamsburg.com

🕐 **Open** 9am–5pm daily; individual sites and attractions have variable hours.

💲 **Price** One-day ticket: $126–36; under 6s free. Multi-day pass: $150–60; under 6s free

👥 **Cutting the line** Arrive early and see the major sites in the morning, as during warmer months, especially on weekends, Williamsburg can get crowded. Purchase tickets in advance at www. colonialwilliamsburg.com to get a discount.

🚩 **Guided tours** Admission ticket includes guided tours of the Capitol and a free 30-minute

orientation walk around the Revolutionary City.

👫 **Age range** All ages

👫 **Activities** Kids can play Colonial-era games, act in period plays, march with the Fife and Drum Corps, and tend Colonial gardens. Children's Colonial-period costume rentals available in the visitor center and at the booths in Merchants Square; $19.95 daily with $50 refundable deposit. Street theater performances are held from mid-Mar–Oct.

⏱️ **Allow** Half a day to see highlights; 2 days to see in depth

☕ **Cafés** In the Revolutionary City and Merchants Square

🛍️ **Shops** In Merchants Square and the Revolutionary City

👫 **Restrooms** At the visitor center and in the Revolutionary City

**Good family value?**
Colonial Williamsburg™ does a great job of re-creating the day-to-day issues of the Revolutionary War and making history fun for children.

desserts. Lunch specials feature Colonial dishes such as Norfolk pottage pye, a chicken pot pie, or a bowl of beef (a savory beef stew). **FAMILY TREAT Christiana Campbell's Tavern** *(101 South Waller St, VA 23185; 999 965 7254; www.colonialwilliamsburg.com/do/ restaurants/historic-dining-taverns/ christiana-campbells; from 5pm Tue–Sat; reservations required)* has specialties such as a fricassee of shrimp, scallops, lobster, and grilled tenderloin of beef and crab cake.

## Shopping
There are many shops both in the Revolutionary City and in Merchants Square. Children and adults will like **Prentis Store** *(in the Revolutionary City)*, where artisans sell wares made using 18th-century techniques and tools. **Tarpley, Thompson & Co.** *(in the Revolutionary City)* offers tavernware, games, and candies. **Toymaker of Williamsburg** *(in Merchants Square)* has modern and historic toys for all ages. **Everything Williamsburg** *(in Merchants Square)* sells official Colonial Williamsburg™ clothing and souvenirs.

## Find out more
**DIGITAL** Williamsburg's official history website, www.history.org/ history has lots of resources for kids. **FILM** Williamsburg was the backdrop for many scenes in the 1984 miniseries *George Washington*, as well as in the 1987 sequel.

*Exhibits on display in the Education Center, Jamestown Settlement*

## Next stop...
**JAMESTOWN** Just 11 miles (18 km) southwest of the center of Colonial Williamsburg™ are two distinct areas of Jamestown *(see pp210–11)*. Historic Jamestowne is the archaeological excavation of the original town, and Jamestown Settlement is a living history museum that re-creates everyday life in this 17th-century settlement.

(see pp210–11)

# KIDS' CORNER

### Find out more...
**1** Williamsburg was the first capital of Virginia. True or false?
**2** What first brought Thomas Jefferson to Williamsburg?
**3** In Colonial America, adults and even children drank a lot of beer, wine, and liquor. But in the 18th century, Dutch traders brought three new drinks to the colonies that changed drinking habits for the better. What were these new-fangled drinks?
**4** What was one of the major reasons for relocating the capital of Virginia from Jamestown to Williamsburg?

Answers at the bottom of the page.

### Place of the paranormal
The Peyton Randolph House is considered one of the most haunted houses in America. According to claims, many spirits reside in its rooms, including a Colonial-era soldier and a young girl who is said to have died after falling down the stairs.

### BRANDED FOR LIFE
In 18th-century Williamsburg, many of the prisoners held in the gaol were awaiting one of three big punishments: branding, whipping, or being hanged. During the Revolutionary War, spies, traitors, and deserters were imprisoned there.

*Pirates of the Caribbean*
*In 1718, the Williamsburg gaol held 15 members of the crew of the infamous pirate, Blackbeard.*

**Answers: 1** False – the first capital of Virginia was Jamestown. **2** He was a student at William and Mary College. **3** Coffee, tea, and hot chocolate. **4** Fear of malaria.

# ㉒ Jamestown
## The early days of Colonial America

The first successful English colony in America, Jamestown has two major attractions. Jamestown Settlement re-creates life in the early 1600s. Visitors can explore re-creations of Jamestown Fort and a Powhatan village or take part in demonstrations of 17th-century shipboard activities and daily chores. Historic Jamestowne is the actual site of the colony, where archaeological excavations are ongoing. See a replica of an early Jamestown church and watch glass-blowing in a reconstruction of the 17th-century glass factory.

*Period-costumed historical interpreter with a young visitor*

## Key Sights

① **Archaeological sites** Interpretive signage describes the archaeological sites that have been excavated to date. Guided tours visit and explain current digs.

Williamsburg 5 miles (8 km)

0 meters 500
0 yards 500

⑦ Exhibition Galleries
JAMESTOWN SETTLEMENT
⑥ Powhatan Village
Colonial Fort ⑤
Three Ships ④
Glasshouse ③
Archearium ②
HISTORIC JAMESTOWNE
①
Archaeological Sites
James River
Sandy Bay
Back River

② **Archearium** This museum displays some of the thousands of artifacts that have been recovered at Jamestown. Exhibits describe life in the early colony, as well as the archaeological processes that have uncovered its history.

③ **Glasshouse** Watch artisans create blown-glass bottles with the same tools and processes that were used in the 17th century. A primitive glass factory was the first industry in the new colony.

④ **Three Ships** Tour the replicas of the three ships that brought the first 104 men from England to create Jamestown. Historical interpreters discuss life aboard ship and the voyage to Virginia.

⑤ **Colonial Fort** In this reproduction of the Jamestown fort, period-costumed interpreters re-enact daily life in the settlement. Enjoy the live musket firings and get a chance to participate in hands-on Colonial activities.

⑥ **Powhatan Village** This replica of a 17th-century Powhatan village lets visitors take a close look at the Virginia Indian culture that existed here before the colonists arrived in 1607.

⑦ **Exhibition Galleries** Trace the development of Jamestown from the arrival of the first English settlers to the hardships of the early years in America in this interactive museum. Powhatan Indian culture and Jamestown's role as Virginia's first capital are also highlighted.

## The Lowdown

🌐 **Address** Virginia. Jamestown Settlement: 2110 Jamestown Rd, Route 31 S, Williamsburg, VA 23185; www.historyisfun.org

🚗 **Train** Amtrak from Union Station to Williamsburg daily. **Bus** Greyhound Bus from Washington daily. Free Historic Triangle Shuttle from Colonial Williamsburg Visitor Center to Jamestown and Yorktown operates spring through fall

ℹ **Visitor information** Historic Jamestowne Visitor Center: 1368 Colonial Parkway, Jamestown, VA 23081; www.historicjamestowne. org, www.nps.gov/jame

🕐 **Open** Jamestown Settlement: 9am–5pm daily; Jun 15–Aug 15: 9am–6pm daily. Historic Jamestowne: 8:30am–4:30pm daily

💲 **Price** Jamestown Settlement: $46–56; under 6s free. Jamestown Settlement/Yorktown Victory Center $60–70; under 6s free. Historic Jamestowne: $30–40; under 15s free; good for 7 days at Historic Jamestowne and Yorktown Battlefield

👫 **Cutting the line** Combination ticket to Historic Jamestowne,

Jamestown Settlement, Yorktown Battlefield, and Yorktown Victory Center allows unlimited visits for 7 days; check individual websites (see p212).

🚩 **Guided tours** Jamestown Settlement: tours daily; check website for details. Historic Jamestowne: ranger-led tours throughout the day

👫 **Age range** All ages, but both sites require significant walking

👫 **Activities** Jamestown Settlement: watch musket firings and dress in kid-size armor. Historic Jamestowne: meet an

Prices given are for a family of four

*Kids pretending to row a dugout canoe at Jamestown Settlement*

## Letting off steam

Both Jamestown Settlement and Historic Jamestowne are large, mostly outdoor sites that host many visitors every day. At Historic Jamestowne, families can discover walking trails or take the island loop drive, a 5-mile (8-km) driving tour that explores the natural environment. If inclement weather threatens at either site, head for the museums, where there are plenty of fun, interesting exhibits to keep young minds busy.

## Eat and drink

*Picnic: under $30; Snacks: $30–40; Real meal: $40–75; Family treat: over $75 (based on a family of four)*

**PICNIC** Shop for goodies at the **Merchants Square** (*Colonial Williamsburg™, see p209*), and enjoy them at Sandy Bay Park (*see p213*), a small park with a sandy beach on the James River.

archaeologist and earn a Junior Ranger badge.

⏱ **Allow** Jamestown Settlement: 3–4 hours. Historic Jamestowne: 2–3 hours

☕ **Café** At both sites

🛍 **Shops** At both sites

🚻 **Restrooms** In the visitor center in Historic Jamestowne and museums at both sites

### Good family value?

Kids and adults will learn some history and get a glimpse into the earliest days of colonization.

**SNACKS Jamestown Settlement Cafe** (*1760 Jamestown Rd, Williamsburg, VA 23185; 757 253 2571; www.jamestowncafe.com*) offers Brunswick stew, burgers, pizzas, and desserts.

**REAL MEAL Second Street Williamsburg** (*140 2nd St, Williamsburg, VA 23185; 757 220 2286; www.secondst.com*) is a lively American bistro with salads, soups, and lunch specials that include bison meatloaf. A kids' menu is available.

**FAMILY TREAT Christiana Campbell's Tavern** (*101 South Waller St, VA 23185; 757 229 2141; www.colonialwilliamsburg.com/do/restaurants/historic-dining-taverns/christiana-campbells; from 5pm Tue–Sat; reservations required*) serves traditional food in a historical setting. Popular items include fried chicken, spoonbread, and crab cakes.

## Find out more

**DIGITAL** The official Jamestown Settlement site, *www.historyisfun.org*, has lots of information on the original settlement, as well as things to see and do. To get the scoop on what the archaeologists are digging at Historic Jamestowne, see *www.historicjamestowne.org/the_dig*.

**FILM** The 2005 epic *The New World*, with Colin Farrell as John Smith (*see p42*), shows the British and Powhatan cultures coming together in the first English colony.

*Families taking a rollercoaster ride in Busch Gardens®*

## Next stop...

**BUSCH GARDENS®** For a complete change of scene from Historic Jamestowne, head to the colorful and exciting Busch Gardens® (*see pp214–15*). This upscale and extravagant theme park offers family fun on gigantic roller coasters and other rides, along with European-themed sections that transport visitors to Ireland, Italy, France, and Germany.

(*see p42*), (*see pp214–15*), (*see p213*), (*see p209*)

# KIDS' CORNER

### Find out more...

**1** A small number of older boys came to Virginia in the first few years of settlement. What was a role some of them were given?

**2** In the winter of 1609–10, the crops failed and the colonists were afraid to leave the fort to look for food, fearing Powhatan attack. Only 60 of the 220 settlers survived. Do you know what they called this winter?

**3** What did both boys and girls in Colonial America wear until they were 6 years old?

Answers at the bottom of the page.

### LOST VIRGINIANS

Jamestown was the first successful English colony, but not the first colony. In 1587, 150 English colonists arrived to establish the colony of Roanoke. A relief ship ariving with supplies 3 years later found the colony deserted. The fate of the 150 colonists has never been discovered.

### Count the lines to know the time

Early colonists used special candles to tell the time. These candles had a uniform width and were marked with lines. It took one hour for the candle to burn down from one line to the next.

**Answers: 1** They were left with the Powhatans to learn their language. **2** "The Starving Time." **3** Dresses.

## ㉓ Yorktown Battlefield

### America wins the revolution

In 1781, English forces under General Charles Cornwallis surrendered to the combined Continental and French forces under General George Washington and Lieutenant General Comte de Rochambeau at Yorktown. This battle effectively ended British rule over America and marked the birth of a new nation.

Also part of the battlefield, Historic Yorktown is where many original 18th-century buildings can be seen. These include Moore House, where the surrender was

### The Lowdown

🌐 **Address** 1000 Colonial Pkwy, VA 23690; 757 898 2410; *www. nps.gov/yonb*

🚆 **Train** Amtrak from Union Station to Williamsburg daily in 3 hours and 30 minutes. **Bus** Greyhound Bus from Washington daily in 4 hours and 30 minutes; Historic Triangle Shuttle from Williamsburg Visitor Center to Historic Yorktown Mar 22–Oct 31: 9am–3:30pm

🕐 **Open** Visitor center: 9am–5pm daily; closed Jan 1, Thanksgiving Day & Dec 25. Historic homes: varying schedules as staffing permits; see website

💲 **Price** $14–24; under 16s free; ticket good for 7 days at Yorktown Battlefield

👫 **Cutting the line** Four-site combination ticket valid for 7 days allows unlimited visits to Jamestown Settlement, Historic Jamestowne, Yorktown Battlefield, and Yorktown Victory Center; check individual websites.

👣 **Guided tours** Ranger-led tours at varying times during the day; check at the visitor center.

👫 **Age range** 8 plus

🏃 **Activities** Pick up a Junior Ranger activity booklet at the visitor center and complete all the activities to receive a merit badge.

🕐 **Allow** 1 hour for visitor center & 1 hour for driving tour

🍴 **Eat and drink** *Snacks* Beach Delly (*524 Water St, VA 23690; 757 886 5890*) offers burgers, pizzas, and sandwiches. *Real meal* Carrot Tree (*323 Water St, Yorktown, VA; 757 988 1999; www.carrottree kitchens.com/yorktown; closed for dinner*) serves soups, salads, wraps, and sandwiches in a lovely waterfront location.

🚻 **Restrooms** In the visitor center, battlefield, and Historic Yorktown

*The front entrance of the historic Moore House at Yorktown Battlefield*

negotiated and the beautiful Georgian mansion of Thomas Nelson, a signatory to the Declaration of Independence.

### Take cover

If the skies darken, head to the **Yorktown Visitor Center**, which screens a 15-minute movie every hour and half hour, and has displays and exhibits on the historic Siege of Yorktown (1781) and its aftermath. Booklets available at the visitor center provide information on two driving tours that lead to points of interest around the battlefield.

## ㉔ Yorktown Victory Center

### Muskets and cannons, and ... squash

Colonial Virginia during the Siege of Yorktown is brought to life at this vibrant, family-oriented, and highly interactive museum. Displays here highlight the era of the revolutionary war. One particularly evocative

### The Lowdown

🌐 **Address** Route 1020, Yorktown, VA 23692; 757 253 4838; *www. historyisfun.org*

🚆 **Train** Amtrak from Union Station to Williamsburg daily in 3 hours and 30 minutes. **Bus** Greyhound Bus from Washington daily in 4 hours and 30 minutes; Historic Triangle Shuttle from Williamsburg Visitor Center to Yorktown Victory Center Mar 22–Oct 31: 9am–3:30pm

🕐 **Open** 9am–5pm daily

💲 **Price** $31–41; under 6s free. 1-day admission to Jamestown Settlement and Yorktown Victory Center (tickets may be used on different days) $60–70; under 6s free

👫 **Cutting the line** There is rarely a line to get in.

👫 **Age range** 6 plus

🏃 **Activities** Participate in military activities in the Continental Army Encampment, and farm activities in the working 1780s farm.

🕐 **Allow** 2–3 hours

♿ **Wheelchair access** Yes

🍴 **Eat and drink** *Snacks* Riverwalk Restaurant (*323 Water St, VA 23690; 757 875 1522; www. riverwalkrestaurant.net*) offers sandwiches and entrées that feature fresh Chesapeake Bay seafood. *Real meal* County Grill & Smokehouse (*1215 George Washington Memorial Hwy, VA 23693; 757 591 0600; http:// countygrill.net*) serves smoked ribs, beef brisket, and pork chops.

🚻 **Restrooms** In the visitor center

exhibit tells the stories of 10 men and women through the words they wrote at the time. There is also a Discovery Room, where children can dress in period costumes such as

*Kids preparing cannons for firing at the Yorktown Victory Center*

**Above** People fishing at Sandy Bay Park near Jamestown
**Below** A guide chops wood at a re-created 1780s farm, Yorktown Victory Center

tricorne hats, bonnets, and dresses. Outside, a re-creation of a Continental Army encampment offers a peek into army life during the revolution. Kids can take part in marching drills and even work with an artillery crew to prepare cannons for firing – they will be back with parents, well behind the safety lines, when the cannons are fired.

### Letting off steam

Part of the Yorktown Victory Center, the 1780s Virginia Farm re-creates the ways in which ordinary people lived in Virginia during the revolution. Visitors can water or weed the squash, corn, and tobacco, as well as participate in other farm activities.

### ㉕ Colonial Parkway

#### Scenic highway through history

Part of the National Park Service system, this 23-mile (37-km)-long National Scenic Byway loops around the historic triangle, linking Colonial Williamsburg™, Jamestown, and Yorktown. As well as being the best way to get from one attraction to another, it offers magnificent panoramas of the rolling farmland, wetlands, and tidal areas along the rivers York and James. Pull-offs along the waterfront are great places to stop and enjoy the views.

### Letting off steam

**Sandy Bay Park** (2 miles, 3 km east of Historic Jamestowne) is a pretty spot on the banks of the James River. It has picnic facilities on a stretch of sandy beach where families can beachcomb.

### The Lowdown

- 🌐 **Address** Virginia. 23-mile (37-km) roadway stretching from York River at Yorktown to James River at Jamestown and connecting Jamestown, Williamsburg, and Yorktown

- 🚃 **Train** Amtrak from Union Station to Williamsburg daily in 3 hours and 30 minutes. **Bus** Greyhound Bus from Washington daily in 4 hours and 30 minutes. Historic Triangle Shuttle from Williamsburg Visitor Center to Jamestown Settlement, Historic Jamestowne, Yorktown Victory Center, and Historic Yorktown Mar 22–Oct 31: 9am–3:30pm

- 🕐 **Open** 24 hours daily

- 🚻 **Age range** All ages

- ⏱ **Allow** 1–2 hours from one end to the other and back

- ♿ **Wheelchair access** Yes

- 🍴 **Eat and drink** Snacks Five Forks Cafe (4456 John Tyler Hwy Williamsburg, VA 23185; 757 221 0484; www.fiveforkscafe.com) serves pancakes, burgers, fries, and milkshakes. Real meal La Tolteca (3048 Richmond Rd, Williamsburg, VA 23185; 757 253 2939; www.latolteca2.com) has Mexican food and a kids' menu.

- 🚹 **Restrooms** At the visitor centers in Williamsburg, Jamestown, and Yorktown

# ㉖ Busch Gardens®

## Screams, laughter, and monster rides

The remarkably bright, colorful, and family-oriented Busch Gardens®
has over 50 exciting rides, all geared toward specific age groups.
Older children will want to ride Griffon®, Alpengeist®, and Mäch Tower®,
while younger kids will get a kick out of Loch Ness Monster® and
Verbolten®. The Sesame Street®-themed Prince Elmo's Spire will
appeal to the youngest ones. Divided into areas with European country
themes, the park is a visual feast of flowers and lush landscapes.

The mythological Land of
the Dragons®

## Key Features

① **Alpengeist®** Just slightly smaller than
Griffon®, this ride twists, turns, and serves
up surprises, and is the tallest full-circuit
inverted roller coaster in the world.

② **Loch Ness Monster®** Slightly tamer
than Alpengeist®, this is still a serious roller
coaster with tight, interlocking loops and
leave-your-stomach-behind drops.

③ **Mäch Tower®** The closest to skydiving
without a plane, this ride lifts visitors
240 ft (73 m) high. Then the locks release,
gravity rules, and the riders rocket toward
the ground.

④ **Animal Encounters** Wolf Training
is a behind-the-scenes tour that reveals
how graceful and intelligent these
beautiful animals can be. Kids will also
enjoy Lorikeet Glen where they get a
chance to feed colorful birds.

⑤ **Verbolten®**
The indoor/outdoor
roller coaster at Busch
Gardens® sends guests
on a fun and mystifying
family adventure through
Germany's Black Forest.

⑥ **Sesame
Street® Forest
of Fun™** This area
is chock-full of
colorful rides such
as Prince Elmo's
Spire. It also offers
kids a chance to
meet their favorite
*Sesame Street®*
characters and
have their pictures
taken with them.

Entrance

⑦ **Griffon®** Named after the griffin, a
half-lion/half-eagle mythological creature,
this 205-ft (62-m)-drop roller coaster stops
at the top for a heart-stopping moment
before rocketing down the track at speeds
of over 70 miles/hr (113 km/hr).

## The Lowdown

🌐 **Address** 1 Busch Gardens
Blvd, VA 23185; 800 343 7946;
*http://seaworldparks.com/en/
buschgardens-williamsburg*

🚗 **Train** Amtrak from Union
Station to Williamsburg daily.
**Bus** Greyhound Bus from
Washington to Williamsburg
daily; no public transport from
Williamsburg to Busch Gardens.
**Taxi** Taxicabs available from bus
and train stations in Williamsburg

🕐 **Open** Mar–Dec; check website
for details of opening hours.

💲 **Price** Single day ticket $260–
270, under 3s free, additional fee

for parking. Prices vary for other
tickets and packages; check
website for details

👫 **Cutting the line** Special passes,
specially priced packages,
single park and multiple park
tickets, fun cards, and annual
passes available; check website
for details.

🚩 **Guided tours** Several behind-
the-scenes tours (additional fee)

👫 **Age range** Most rides have
height requirements; there
are also KIDsiderate rides for
toddlers accompanied
by parents.

🤸 **Activities** Rides, theatrical shows,
and behind-the-scenes tours

🕐 **Allow** A full day

🍽 **Cafés** Restaurants, cafés, and
snack shops throughout the park
(see p215)

🛍 **Shops** 25 shops are located in the
park (see p215)

🚻 **Restrooms** Located throughout
the park

**Good family value?**
The entrance fee is not cheap, but
the tickets cover almost everything
the park offers. Come early, stay all
day, and enjoy family time.

**Prices given are for a family of four**

## Take cover

If rain threatens, head for one of the theatrical performances that are held under a roof in the complex, or take a break for a snack. Another great activity is the gentle, and covered, riverboat tour on the Rhine River that gets even prettier when it rains.

## Eat and drink

*Picnic: under $30; Snacks: $30–40; Real meal: $40–75; Family treat: over $75 (based on a family of four)*

**PICNIC** Carry goodies and enjoy them at one of the picnic areas adjacent to the parking lots. Picnic baskets and other large tote bags cannot be brought into the park.
**SNACKS Cafe Lulu** *(in the New France area)* is a great place to get a quick energy shot from a big smoked turkey leg, jumbo soft pretzels, or fresh fruit smoothies.
**REAL MEAL Grogan's Grill** *(in the Ireland area)* is a small Irish café with delicious pub-style food. Try the seasoned pork loin with red onion marmalade or the tomato basil ham wrap, and make sure to leave room for cherry cheesecake for dessert.
**FAMILY TREAT Trapper's Smokehouse** *(in the New France area)* offers traditional smoked meats with a French twist. Smoked chicken and sliced beef brisket are among the favorites.

*The pretty courtyard outside Grogan's Pub in Busch Gardens®*

## Shopping

There are 25 shops located strategically around the park that sell every imaginable type of apparel, toy, and gift. From the coolest in tween clothing to amazing magic tricks and wizardly paraphernalia, there is something available for every taste. Each shop is unique, and many are themed to the

*Riverboat cruise on the Rhine River in Busch Gardens®*

European area in which they are located.

## Find out more

**DIGITAL** The official Busch Gardens® Williamsburg site, *http://seaworld parks.com/en/buschgardens-williams burg*, has all the necessary information to help families plan their visit.
**FILM** The first Busch Gardens® park was developed in Pasadena, California. For a while, movies were made there, including *Gone with the Wind* (1939) and the 1938 Errol Flynn classic *The Adventures of Robin Hood*.

## Next stop...

**YORKTOWN** Visit Yorktown *(see pp212–13)*, the site of the decisive battle of the Revolutionary War. After the battle of Yorktown, America ceased to be a British colony and became the United States of America. Just 10 miles (16 km) east of Busch Gardens®, there are two major attractions here: Yorktown Battlefield, a National Park System-operated historic site, and Yorktown Victory Center, a living history museum that brings the final days of the Revolutionary War to life.

*A re-enactment of the Revolutionary War at the Yorktown Victory Center*

# ㉗ Annapolis
## Welcome to America's "crabbiest" town

Charming, highly walkable, and with plenty to see and do, Annapolis is a great family destination. Fascinating Main Street is lined with 18th- and 19th-century buildings that house unique shops, as well as restaurants serving Chesapeake's legendary steamed blue crabs. Head to the waterfront to watch the endless parade of yachts that make Annapolis one of America's great sailing towns, or explore historic sights such as the Banneker Douglass Museum and the 18th-century William Paca House.

Baked goods for sale at a farmers' market in Annapolis

## Key Sights

0 meters 300

0 yards 300

① **City Dock** Surrounded by shops, ice-cream parlors, and restaurants, this plaza-like waterfront offers open spaces where kids can play. Quaint boats offer 45-minute trips that explore the pretty and historic harbor.

④ **Carroll House** Visit the simple yet elegant house of Charles Carroll, who was the only Catholic to sign the Declaration of Independence.

⑤ **Maryland State House** The oldest state house still in use in the US, this is where George Washington resigned his commission as commander-in-chief in 1783.

⑥ **Banneker Douglass Museum** Learn about Maryland's first black settler, and see an advertisement for the slave auction that Kunta Kinte was sold in at this fascinating museum dedicated to the history of African-Americans in Maryland.

⑦ **United States Naval Academy** The visitor center here has exhibits that cover the history of the academy. Among the artifacts on display is the Freedom 7 space capsule piloted by Alan Shepard in 1961. Visitors can stroll through the academy's beautiful grounds.

② **Alex Haley Memorial** In Alex Haley's book, *Roots* (1976), his ancestor Kunta Kinte is brought to Annapolis to be sold into slavery. This memorial features a bronze statue of Haley reading to kids.

③ **William Paca House** Built between 1763 and 1765 for William Paca, a signatory of the Declaration of Independence, this beautiful Georgian home has been immaculately restored and is surrounded by lovely Colonial-era gardens.

## Letting off steam

There is plenty of room in the plaza-like stretches of the City Dock for kids to run around. For more space, drive

Boat cruising in the bustling City Dock, Annapolis

**Prices given are for a family of four**

to **Sandy Point State Park** (*1100 East College Pkwy, MD 21409*), where there are acres to play on, a sandy beach, and a great view of the Chesapeake Bay Bridge.

## Eat and drink

*Picnic: under $30; Snacks: $30–40; Real meal: $40–75; Family treat: over $75 (based on a family of four)*

**PICNIC Market House** (*25 Market Space, MD 21401; 410 263 3154*) is a good place to grab a sandwich,

salad, *cannolo* (Italian pastry), and other picnic goodies before heading to City Dock for a picnic. **SNACKS Sofi's Crepes** (*1 Craig St, MD 21401; 410 990 0929; www. sofiscrepes.com*) offers savoury and sweet crepes made with fresh local ingredients. Sweet crepes feature a delicious chocolate and hazelnut filled surprise.

**REAL MEAL Red Hot and Blue** (*200 Old Mill Bottom Rd, MD 21409; 410 626 7427; www. redhotandblue.com*), one of the best barbecue joints in the mid-Atlantic, serves smoked ribs, brisket, and sausage. **FAMILY TREAT Middleton Tavern** *(2 Market Space, MD 21401; 410 263 3323; www.middletontavern.com)* has been serving quality seafood since 1750. It has oysters, lobster ravioli, as well as a kids' menu.

*Diners at the popular 18th-century Middleton Tavern*

## Shopping

Downtown Annapolis has many shops, including some that appeal to kids. **The Pink Crab** *(16 Market Space, MD 21401)* has fashions for women and kids, as does **Giant**

Peach *(17 Annapolis St, MD 21401)*. **Annapolis Bookstore** *(35 Maryland Ave, Annapolis, MD 21401)* has a wonderful children's section, while **The Museum Store** *(77 Main St, MD 21401)* offers historic toys and books.

## Find out more

**DIGITAL** The Historic Annapolis Foundation has tons of tales about the town's long history at *www.annapolis.org*.
**FILM** The TV miniseries *Roots* (1977), based on Alex Haley's book, tells the story of Kunta Kinte, who was sold as a slave in Annapolis.

## Next stop...

**Baltimore's Inner Harbor** Pulsing with excitement, Baltimore's Inner Harbor *(see pp218–19)* appeals to families. Enjoy the hands-on Maryland Science Center, the Port Discovery Children's Museum, and the National Aquarium.

## The Lowdown

🌐 **Address** Maryland. William Paca House: 186 Prince George St, MD 21401; 410 990 4543. Maryland State House: 100 State Circle, MD 21401; *www.msa.md.gov/msa/mdstatehouse/html/home.html*. Banneker Douglass Museum: 84 Franklin St, MD 21401; *www.bdmuseum.com*. Carroll House: 107 Duke of Gloucester St, MD 21401; *www.charlescarrollhouse.org*. US Naval Academy: 121 Blake Rd, MD 21402; *www.usna.edu*

🚗 **Bus** Greyhound Bus has round trips from Washington to Annapolis daily.

ℹ **Visitor information** Visitor center: 26 West St, MD 21401; 410 280 0445; *www.visitannapolis.org*

🕐 **Open** William Paca House: 10am–5pm Mon–Sat, noon–5pm Sun. Maryland State House: self-guided tours 9am–5pm daily, closed Dec 25 & Jan 1. Banneker Douglass Museum: 10am–4pm Tue–Sat; Memorial Day–Labor Day: 10am–4pm Tue–Sat (to 5pm Thu), 1–5pm first Sundays. Carroll House: Jun–Sep: noon–4pm Sat & Sun. US Naval Academy: check website for seasonal timings.

💲 **Price** William Paca House: $30–40; under 5s free. Carroll House: free. Maryland State House: free. Banneker Douglass Museum: free. US Naval Academy: $34–44

👫 **Cutting the line** Annapolis can get crowded on warm summer weekends, particularly in the late afternoon/evening, but this is part of the festive fun.

🚩 **Guided tours** Walking history tours, ghost tours, and sailing tours. Pirates of the Chesapeake tour; check *www.chesapeakepirates.com* or ask at the visitor center.

👫 **Age range** 8 plus

🏃 **Activities** Self-guided walking tour brochures and audio tours available at the visitor center. Horse-drawn carriage tours are also popular.

⏱ **Allow** Half a day to a full day

☕ **Cafés** Throughout town

🛍 **Shops** Along City Dock and Main St

🚻 **Restrooms** At the visitor center, historic homes, and City Dock

### Good family value?

Historic, beautiful Annapolis offers something to interest every family member over 8 years.

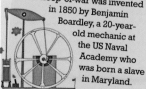

# ㉘ Baltimore's Inner Harbor
## Submarines, sharks, and sailing ships

Baltimore's dazzling social and entertainment center, the Inner Harbor has plenty to interest families. At the head of the list is the National Aquarium, where fish of every type swim behind curved-glass walls. Maryland Science Center delights with experiences such as digging for dinosaur fossils, while Port Discovery is a lively children's museum. On the waterfront, step aboard historic ships including the last sailing US Navy warship, the USS *Constellation*.

## Key Sights

[Map showing: Port Discovery Children's Museum ⑥, Camden Yards ①, Historic Ships ②, National Aquarium ⑤, Maryland Science Center ③, Visionary Art Museum ④, Fells Point ⑦, Fort McHenry ⑧. WEST LOMBARD ST, E PRATT STREET, W CONWAY ST, FLEET STREET, KEY HIGHWAY, EAST FORT AVENUE. 0 meters 500, 0 yards 500]

① **Camden Yards** Sports fans will enjoy a trip to the beautiful home field of the Baltimore Orioles, who first signed baseball legend "Babe" Ruth to their team in 1913. Don't miss the Sports Legends Museum.

② **Historic ships** Tour the Civil War ship USS *Constellation*, the World War II submarine USS *Torsk*, and the last surviving warship of Pearl Harbor.

④ **Visionary Art Museum** Weird, wacky, and fun, this museum focuses on the works of untrained artists. Two of its best-known creations are the *Whirligig*, a giant mechanical wind vane made from metal parts, and *Gallery Go-Go*, a bus decorated with mirrors and ceramic pieces.

⑤ **National Aquarium** This waterfront building is home to over 16,000 marine creatures, from stingrays, glowing jellyfish, and sharks to pods of leaping dolphins.

⑥ **Port Discovery Children's Museum** Play-and-learn experiences for ages 2 to 10 include learning about life on a farm, deciphering hieroglyphics, or climbing a multistory, treehouse-rope-bridge-tube-slide-tower called KidWorks.

⑦ **Fells Point** This funky, historic waterfront is loaded with interesting shops and restaurants, and colorful 18th- and 19th-century row houses.

⑧ **Fort McHenry** This fort, whose "flag was still there" after a night of bombardment by the British in 1812, inspired lawyer Francis Scott Key to pen the US national anthem.

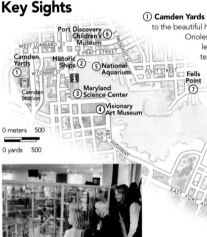

③ **Maryland Science Center** Create a tornado with one hand, look at real DNA, or try docking a space shuttle. The special kids' room is a scientific play space for kids up to 8 years old.

## The Lowdown

🌐 **Address** Maryland 21202. Camden Yards: 333 West Camden St, MD 21201; 410 685 9800. Maryland Science Center: 601 Light St, MD 21230; www.mdsci.org. Historic Ships: 301 East Pratt St, MD 21202; www.historicships.org. Visionary Art Museum: 800 Key Hwy, MD 21230; www.avam.org. National Aquarium: 501 East Pratt St, MD 21202; www.aqua.org. Port Discovery Children's Museum: 35 Market Place, MD 21202; www.portdiscovery.org. Fort McHenry: 2400 East Fort Ave, MD 21230; www.nps.gov/fomc

🚗 **Train** The MARC Camden line runs from Union Station to Camden Station, two blocks east of the Inner Harbor; 1 hour 30 minutes

ℹ️ **Visitor information** Visitor center: 401 Light St, MD 21202; 410 659 7300; www.baltimore.org

🕐 **Open** Visitor center: timings vary, check www.baltimore.org/visitor-center. See individual websites of the sights for specific timings.

💲 **Price** Historic Ships: $50–60, under 6s free. Maryland Science Center: $54–64. Visionary Art Museum: $50–60; under 6s free. National Aquarium: $90–100; additional $100–110 for dolphin show and 4-D movie. Port Discovery Children's Museum: $52–62. Fort McHenry: $28–38; under 15s free.

🧑‍🤝‍🧑 **Cutting the line** Reach the National Aquarium before 11am if possible. The National Aquarium, Maryland Science Center, and Port Discovery Children's Museum offer online tickets, which also save money.

🚩 **Guided tours** All sights offer guided tours; see individual websites for details. The visitor center offers city and Inner Harbor tours.

👫 **Age range** Inner Harbor: 8 plus; National Aquarium and Maryland Science Center: 5 plus. Port Discovery Children's Museum: up to 10 years

# Letting off steam

Except on busy summer days, there is ample room on the wide walkways and plazas around the Inner Harbor for kids to play. For more space, head to the park that runs along the west side of the Inner Harbor beside the visitor center.

# Eat and drink

*View of Baltimore's picturesque Inner Harbor*

*Picnic: under $30; Snacks: $30–40; Real meal: $40–75; Family treat: over $75 (based on a family of four)*

**PICNIC** Pick up goodies at the **Gallery Food Court** *(Gallery mall, next to the harbor)* and head to the park by the visitor center for a picnic lunch with splendid views.

**SNACKS Five Guys Burgers and Fries** *(201 E Pratt St, MD 21202; 410 244 7175; www.fiveguys.com)* draws crowds for its big burgers, hearty fries, and chilled shakes.

**REAL MEAL Phillips Seafood** *(601 E Pratt St, MD 21202; 410 685 6600; www.phillipsseafood.com)*

*Signage and exterior of Phillips Seafood restaurant*

 **Activities** Boat tours around the harbor are offered. Museums offer many activities; see websites.

**Allow** All day

**Cafés** In all museums and around the Inner Harbor

**Shops** In all museums and at Harborplace

**Restrooms** At the visitor center and at all attractions

### Good family value?

Baltimore's Inner Harbor offers several kid-oriented and interactive museums and attractions, all within walking distance of each other.

features a buffet of fresh seafood, salads, soups, and desserts; it also has a kids' menu.

**FAMILY TREAT Charleston** *(1000 Lancaster St, MD 21202; 410 332 7373; www.charlestonrestaurant. com; dinner only)*, an award-winning restaurant, is where classic French cuisine meets South Carolina Low Country cooking.

# Shopping

**Harborplace** *(northeast corner of the Inner Harbor)* is a mall filled with shops and restaurants, but kids may find the most interesting shopping experiences at the National Aquarium, Maryland Science Center, and Fort McHenry, where there are lots of toys, games, apparel, gifts, and souvenirs. The gift shop of the Visionary Art Museum also has some rather offbeat offerings.

# Find out more

**DIGITAL** www.mdsci.org/science-encounters/index.html has a wealth of science information and experiments that can be tried at home. For interesting stories on the environment, see www.aqua.org/care.

**FILM** The 2007 musical *Hairspray* is a silly and exuberant celebration of all things Baltimore in the 1960s, with an all-star cast, including John Travolta.

# Next stop...

**WORLD TRADE BUILDING** The 27th floor of the World Trade Building *(edge of the Inner Harbor; 10am–6pm Mon–Thu, 10am–7pm Fri & Sat, 11am–6pm Sun; $16–26)* offers a spellbinding view of the city and the Inner Harbor, as well as a wide swath of the Chesapeake Bay.

*The Roundhouse, forming a backdrop to a locomotive at the B&O Railroad Museum*

# 29 Baltimore & Ohio Railroad Museum

**Birthplace of American railroading**

Begun in 1828, the Baltimore & Ohio (B&O) Railroad was the first commercial railroad in America. During its heyday, this 40-acre (16-ha) site served as a major railroad hub. Today, it is one of America's best railroad museums and a great place for kids who are interested in machines and trains, and their history. The centerpiece of the museum is the 1884 Roundhouse, which contains an unparalleled collection of restored steam engines and railcars from the early days of train travel. The museum displays over 200 pieces of locomotives and rolling stock –

anything that rolled along the rails. The galleries near the entrance have thousands of small artifacts that span two centuries of railroad history.

**Letting off steam**

In the museum itself, just west of the Roundhouse, is a family activity area that includes a well-equipped playground for kids.

# 30 Sports Legends Museum/Geppi's Entertainment Museum

**From sports to *Star Wars***

Located in Camden Station, Camden Yards, the **Sports Legends Museum** began with a collection of Baltimore Orioles and Colts memorabilia in the Babe Ruth Museum, which was

originally two blocks away. Today, the collection has expanded to include memorabilia and displays on famous Maryland sports heroes such as baseball star George "Babe" Ruth and football star Johnny Unitas. Children can try on authentic college or major league uniforms, sign a giant baseball, and answer trivia questions in the Locker Room: Kids' Discovery Zone.

Also in Camden Station, **Geppi's Entertainment Museum** features popular culture images advertised in newspapers from the 1700s to *Star Wars*. This vast and entertaining collection features pop culture and

## The Lowdown

- 🌐 **Address** 301 W Camden St, MD 21201. Sports Legends Museum: *http://baberuthmuseum.org*. Geppi's Entertainment Museum: 410 625 7060; *www.geppis museum.com*
- 🚆 **Train** MARC Camden line from Union Station to Camden Station in 1 hour 30 minutes
- 🕐 **Open** Sports Legends Museum: 10am–5pm daily. Geppi's Entertainment Museum: 10am–6pm Tue–Sun, closed Jan 1, Thanksgiving Day & Dec 25
- 💲 **Price** Sports Legends Museum: $18–24; under 2s free. Geppi's Entertainment Museum: $24–32; under 4s free. Both: $34–48
- 👥 **Cutting the line** Buy tickets for Sports Legends Museum online or call 410 727 1539.
- 🚩 **Guided tours** Geppi's Entertainment Museum offers 1-hour tours on request with admission.
- 👪 **Age range** Sports Legends Museum: 10 plus. Geppi's Entertainment Museum: 7 plus
- 👪 **Activities** Geppi's Entertainment Museum: Find things on the treasure hunt cards. Kids with a good score get comic books.
- 🕐 **Allow** Sports Legends Museum: 1–2 hours. Geppi's Entertainment Museum: 1–2 hours
- ♿ **Wheelchair access** Yes
- 🍵 **Eat and drink** *Snacks* Edie's Deli and Grill (*250 W Pratt St, MD 21201; 410 837 9131; breakfast & lunch*) is a great diner and good alternative to fast food. *Real meal* Luna del Sea (*300 W Pratt St, MD 21201; 410 752 8383*) offers steaks, and seafood, it also has a kids' menu.
- 👥 **Restrooms** Sports Legends Museum: on the lower floor. Geppi's Entertainment Museum: on the main floor near the first gallery.

## The Lowdown

- 🌐 **Address** 901 West Pratt St, Baltimore, MD 21223; 410 752 2490; *www.borail.org*
- 🚆 **Train** MARC Camden line from Union Station to Camden Station in 1 hour 30 minutes. Then walk two blocks north on Howard St to Pratt St, take the Charm City Circulator Orange line westbound to museum.
- 🕐 **Open** 10am–4pm Mon–Sat, 11am–4pm Sun
- 💲 **Price** $44–54, under 1s free; additional fee for train rides
- 👥 **Cutting the line** Plan a visit for Wed–Fri, as weekends in summer are most crowded. Crowds thin out when train tours take place.
- 🚩 **Guided tours** Narrated 20-minute train tours 11:30am Wed–Fri,

11am, 1pm, 3pm Sat, 12:30pm, 2:30pm Sun

- 👪 **Age range** 6 plus
- 👪 **Activities** A variety of programs, including train rides, offered throughout the year; check with docents for details.
- 🕐 **Allow** 2–4 hours
- ♿ **Wheelchair access** Yes
- 🍵 **Eat and drink** *Snacks* Zella's Pizzeria (*1145 Hollins St, MD 21223; 410 685 6999; www. zellaspizzeria.com*) offers pizzas, sandwiches, and pasta. *Real meal* Frank and Nic's West End Grille (*511 W Pratt St, MD 21201; 410 685 6800; www.frankandnics.com*) is a slightly upscale sports bar with a good kids' menu.
- 👥 **Restrooms** Near the entrance

Prices given are for a family of four

*The entrance of Geppi's Entertainment Museum in Camden Station*

comic-book images as they appeared in print and on everyday items such as juice and bread, PEZ candy dispensers, and a bewildering array of other items, including toy cars, games, and Disney collectibles.

## Letting off steam

Just three blocks east, there is a lovely park beside the **Baltimore Visitor Center** (see p218) on the Inner Harbor. There is a splendid view of the harbor from here, as well as paths, fountains, and lots of space for kids to play.

## ③ The Walters Art Museum

### Fancy eggs and alligators

Displaying around 5,000 artworks spanning 5,000 years, this museum has enough stuff to enthrall children of all ages. Exhibits include an Egyptian mummy, ancient Greek statues and pottery, lots of medieval armor and swords, and jeweled Fabergé eggs, as well as room after room of superb paintings and

## The Lowdown

- 🌐 **Address** 600 N Charles St, MD 21201; 410 547 9000; http://thewalters.org
- 🚌 **Bus** Take the northbound Charm City Circulator Purple line from Harborplace (E Pratt St & S Calvert St) to Centre St
- 🕐 **Open** 10am–5pm Wed–Sun (to 9pm Thu)
- 💲 **Price** Free; fee for special exhibitions
- 👫 **Cutting the line** Visit in the morning or on a weekday as weekends get busy after noon.
- 👪 **Age range** 8 plus
- 🚶 **Activities** Free audio tours available at the visitor center; free walk-in tours on various subjects offered at 2pm Sun; check website for details.
- 🕐 **Allow** 2–3 hours
- 🍴 **Eat and drink** *Real meal* The Museum Café (*in The Walters Art Museum*) serves soups, salads, sandwiches, drinks, and desserts. *Family treat* Sascha's 527 Café (527 North Charles St, MD 21201; 410 539 8880; www.saschas.com) offers salads, grilled and sauted entrées, and tapas-style "taste plates."
- 🚻 **Restrooms** On the first floor

sculptures, ranging from Byzantine to Post-modern. Kids will love the Chamber of Arts and Wonder, which is filled with antique globes and maps, beautiful 18th- and 19th-century paintings, and marvels of nature including a 12-ft (4-m)-long stuffed alligator, and collections of animal skulls and bugs.

## Letting off steam

One block north, Baltimore's **Washington Monument** (699 North Charles St, MD 21201) has lots of green space where children can run and enjoy themselves.

*Paintings on display at the Chamber of Art and Wonders, The Walters Art Museum*

**Picnic** under $30; **Snacks** $30–40; **Real meal** $40–75; **Family treat** over $75 (based on a family of four)

# ㉜ Chesapeake Bay Driving Tour
## Schooners, blue crabs, and salty towns

Just an hour from Washington, Chesapeake's Eastern Shore feels like it is half a century back in time. Here, narrow roads pass the farm fields and woodlands on their way to small towns that date to the American Revolution. The area is filled with bridges, inlets, and marinas, but there is more to it than just bay and country. Easton is an 18th-century town bustling with restaurants and shops, while St. Michaels is home to Chesapeake Bay Maritime Museum, whose waterfront buildings include Hooper Strait Lighthouse.

Hooper Strait Lighthouse at the Maritime Museum

## Key Sights

① **Chesapeake Bay Bridge** When it was constructed in 1952, this 4.3-mile (7-km) bridge was the longest continuous steel over-water structure in the world. Today, it offers a spectacular view of the bay.

② **Wye Grist Mill** Dating to 1668, this mill supplied flour to George Washington's troops during the Revolutionary War. Still a working mill, visitors can watch the waterwheel turn and the mill stones grind wheat into flour.

0 km 10

0 miles 10

③ **Easton** A busy commercial and cultural center, Easton is known for its 18th- and 19th-century brick buildings housing unique shops and restaurants.

④ **Oxford Bellevue Ferry** Begun in 1683, this is the oldest continually operated ferry service in America. The ferry holds nine cars and takes passengers on a 12-minute pastoral voyage across the Tred Avon River.

⑤ **Chesapeake Bay Maritime Museum** This museum is filled with historic boats and exhibits that highlight the long commercial and natural history of the bay. Explore the 1879 Hooper Strait Lighthouse, and step aboard the Chesapeake buy boat *Mister Jim*.

⑥ **St. Michaels** Offering plenty of shops, inns, and restaurants, this historic town makes an ideal base to explore the area.

⑦ **Skipjacks** The last working sailboats in the US, a dozen of these skipjacks are still used to harvest oysters. Several dock in the southern harbor of Tilghman Island.

---

## Letting off Steam

Five miles (8 km) north of Easton, **Pickering Creek Audubon Center** (11450 Audubon Lane, MD 21601) has plenty of trails to hike. **Perry Cabin Park & Sports Complex** (710 Talbot St N, St. Michaels, MD 21663) has a small playground and open spaces.

Crabs served at The Crab Claw Restaurant

## Eat and drink

*Picnic: under $30; Snacks: $30–40; Real meal: $40–75; Family treat: over $75 (based on a family of four)*

**PICNIC** Amish Country Market (101 Marlboro Ave, MD 21601; 410 822 8989) offers fresh produce, cooked chickens, and baked goods. Take food from here to St. Michaels and enjoy it in the Church Cove Park on Water Street.

**SNACKS** Ava's Pizzeria and Wine Bar (409 S Talbot St, MD 21663; 410 745 3081) serves pizzas made with fresh local ingredients.

**REAL MEAL** The Crab Claw Restaurant (304 Burns St, MD 21663; 410 745 2900; www. thecrabclaw.com) is a legendary waterfront crab restaurant with indoor and outdoor seating.

**FAMILY TREAT** 208 Talbot (208 N Talbot St, MD 21663; 410 745 3838; www.208talbot.com; dinner

Prices given are for a family of four

*only)* is a stellar bistro that serves dishes featuring fresh seafood and local farm ingredients.

## Shopping

In St. Michaels, shop at **Calico Toys and Games** *(212 N Talbot St, MD 21663)* for games, puzzles, and stuffed toys. **Chesapeake Bay Outfitters** *(100 N Talbot St, MD 21663)* has gifts and clothing for all ages. In Easton, go to **Crackerjacks Toys and Children's**

*Art gallery and clothes shops in Easton, Chesapeake*

Books *(7 S Washington St, MD 21601)* for toys, games, books, and collectors' dolls.

## Find out more

**DIGITAL** *www.cbf.org* offers information on the bay, its natural history, and the environmental issues it faces.
**FILM** *The New World* (2005) tells the story of explorer John Smith *(see p42)*, Pocahontas, and America's first English settlement on the banks of Chesapeake Bay.

## Take cover

In case of bad weather, head to the barn-shaped building near the entrance of Chesapeake Bay Maritime Museum, which has exhibits on the history of the bay.

## Next stop...

**SMITH ISLAND** Drive south from Easton on state routes 50 to 13 to 413 ending in Crisfield, and take a 40-minute boat ride to historic Smith Island. Tours leave at 12:30pm from Somers Cove Marina in Crisfield.

## KIDS' CORNER

### Do you know...

**1** This shellfish has claws, and is fished in every part of the Chesapeake Bay. Served steamed with spices, the claws are opened by hitting them with a small mallet. What is this shellfish called?

**2** These boats are the last working sailboats in America and are used to harvest oysters from the Chesapeake Bay. Do you know their name?

**3** The octagonal lighthouses that stand in the shallow waters of the bay have a unique name. What is it?

Answers at the bottom of the page.

### Name games

The scientific name for blue crabs is *Callinectes Sapidus.* The word *Callinectes* originates from Greek, and means beautiful swimmer. *Sapidus* is Latin for savory or delicious.

### CHESAPEAKE CHALLENGES

Chesapeake Bay is an estuary, a place where salt and freshwater mix. It is an important habitat for fish, shellfish, birds, and wildlife. In the 1960s and 70s, pollution from industry was a problem. People had to work hard to clean up the bay. But today it faces a new problem. The bay's waters are becoming murky due to algae that grows fast because of fertilizer running into the bay from farms and suburban lawns.

**Answers: 1** Blue crab. **2** Skipjack. **3** Screw-pile lighthouses.

## The Lowdown

🌐 **Address** Maryland. Wye Grist Mill: 14296 Old Wye Mills Rd (Rt 662), Wye Mills, MD 21679; *www.oldwyemill.org.* Chesapeake Bay Maritime Museum: 213 N Talbot St, MD 21663; *www.cbmm.org*

🚗 **Car** Rent a car from any of the car rental companies *(see p23)*

ℹ **Visitor information** Talbot County Visitor Center: 11 S Harrison St, MD 21601; *www.tourtalbot.org, www. eastonmd.org*

🕐 **Open** Wye Grist Mill: mid-Apr–mid-Nov: 10am–4pm Mon–Sat, 1pm–4pm Sun. Chesapeake Bay Maritime Museum: check website for timings.

💲 **Price** Wye Grist Mill: $2 donation. Chesapeake Bay Maritime Museum: $38–48; under 6s free

👥 **Cutting the line** St. Michaels: visit midweek when the town is quieter. Chesapeake Bay Maritime Museum: $3 discount to visitors showing a same-day receipt from a local merchant for $20 or more; limit one receipt per guest.

🪧 **Guided tours** Self-guided tour brochures for Easton and St. Michaels are available at Talbot County Visitor Center.

👫 **Age range** 6 plus

🧑‍🤝‍🧑 **Activities** Chesapeake Bay Maritime Museum offers several on-the-water tours, including tours of the bay onboard the museum's replica buy boat, *Mister Jim.*

🕐 **Allow** 1 to 2 days

☕ **Cafés** Restaurants and cafés in Easton and St. Michaels

🛍 **Shops** Easton and St. Michaels have interesting shops. The Chesapeake Bay Maritime Museum shop has lots of toys and games for kids.

👫 **Restrooms** At Chesapeake Bay Maritime Museum, Talbot County Visitor Center, and near the corner of Talbot St and Carpenter St in St. Michaels

### Good family value?

This tour features charming historic towns and waterfront scenery. Kids will enjoy the Chesapeake Bay Maritime Museum.

# ㉝ A Day at the Beach
## Sand, ponies, and boardwalks

A 3-hour drive east of Washington takes visitors to endless miles of Atlantic ocean beaches. If the kids are dreaming of building sand castles, then this is the place to head to. Rehoboth and Ocean City offer beaches and boardwalks lined with restaurants and shops, while Cape Henlopen and Delaware are popular for swimming and beachcombing. For surf fishing, or just a stroll along the surf's edge, visit Assateague and Chincoteague.

Surfers at the beach in
Delaware Seashore State Park

## Key Sights

① **Cape Henlopen State Park** Featuring 4 miles (6 km) of surf-carved sand beach, this park is great for camping, bird-watching, beachcombing, and hiking.

② **Rehoboth Beach** With sandy lanes lined with pastel-colored cottages, Rehoboth is a genteel beach town that offers a wealth of restaurants and shops.

③ **Delaware Seashore State Park** Spanning a barrier island, this park offers a 6-mile (10-km)-long strand of pristine Atlantic beach on one side and wild salt marshes on the other.

④ **Fenwick Island State Park** A wild stretch of sand and waves, this is a haven for surfers and bird-watchers. Walk along stretches of beach where shorebirds skitter and shells lie in the sand for the taking.

⑤ **Ocean City** A family destination with a 3-mile (5-km) boardwalk – lined with bustling hamburger joints, shops, and beachfront restaurants and hotels.

⑥ **Assateague Island** This stretch of the National Seashore is famous for the wild Chincoteague ponies that can be seen grazing on the dunes and beside roadways. Assateague also offers camping, hiking trails, surf fishing, and kayaking.

⑦ **Chincoteague Island** The Virginia section of the National Seashore offers miles of beaches, and salt marshes that can be explored by kayak or canoe.

## The Lowdown

**Address** Delaware, Maryland & Virginia

**Buses** BestBus (www.bestbus.com) runs from DC to Rehoboth and Dewey Beach Fri–Mon.

**Visitor information** Cape Henlopen State Park Visitor Center: 15099 Cape Henlopen Dr, DE 19958; www.destateparks.com. Rehoboth Beach Visitor Center: 501 Rehoboth Ave, DE 19971; www.beach-fun.com. Delaware Seashore State Park & Fenwick Island State Park: 39415 Inlet Rd, DE 19971; www.destateparks.com. Ocean City Visitor Center: 4001 Coastal Hwy; MD 21842; www.ococean.com.

Assateague Island Visitor Center: 7206 National Seashore Lane, MD 21811; www.nps.gov/asis

**Open** Cape Henlopen State Park: 8am–dusk daily. Rehoboth Beach Visitor Center: 8am–4:30pm Mon–Sat, 9am–4:30pm Sun. Delaware Seashore State Park & Fenwick Island State Park: 8am–dusk daily. Ocean City Visitor Center: 8am–4:30pm Mon–Sat, 9am–4:30pm Sun. Assateague Island Visitor Center: 9am–5pm daily

**Price** Delaware State parks: state registered vehicle $4 per per day, out-of-state registered vehicle $8 per day. Assateague/

Chincoteague Islands: $15 per vehicle, good for seven days in both parks.

**Cutting the line** Ocean City: visit during the week or before 11am on summer weekends. Rehoboth Beach: best during the week. An annual unlimited pass to all US National Parks is $80 and available at www.store.usgs.gov/pass.

**Guided tours** Rehoboth Beach and Ocean City offer boat, city, and adventure tours; check at the visitor centers for details.

**Age range** 6 plus

**Activities** National and State Parks

Prices given are for a family of four

*The entrance to Indian River Life-Saving Station at Delaware Seashore State Park*

## Take cover

If inclement weather threatens, head to the **Seaside Nature Center** (15099 Cape Henlopen Dr, DE 19958) at Cape Henlopen or the **Indian River Life-Saving Station** (25039 Coastal Hwy, DE 19971) at Delaware Seashore State Park. At Assateague or Chincoteague, spend time at the visitor centers, which have displays on the flora and fauna of Atlantic coast beaches.

## Eat and drink

Picnic: under $30; Snacks: $30–40; Real meal: $40–75; Family treat: over $75 (based on a family of four)

**SNACKS Green Man Juice Bar and Bistro** (12 Wilmington Ave, Rehoboth Beach, DE 19971; 302 227 4909; www.greenmanjuicebar. com) serves beverages and snacks in a beachside cottage.

**REAL MEAL The Pig + Fish Restaurant Company** (236 Rehoboth Ave, DE 19971; 302 227 7770; www.thepigandfish.com)

---

offers inexpensive fresh seafood and meat dishes. There is a kids' menu as well.

**Fish Tales Restaurant** (2207 Herring Way, Ocean City, MD 21842; 410 289 0990; www.ocfishtales.com) is a marina restaurant serving seafood, pizzas, salads, and meat dishes. There is also a good kids' menu.

**FAMILY TREAT Liquid Assets** (9301 Coastal Hwy, Ocean City, MD 21842; 410 524 7037; www.ocliquid assets.com), a kid-friendly bistro in the center of a wine store, has fresh local foods, gourmet burgers, pastas, salads, and lunch specials.

## Shopping

In Rehoboth Beach, pick up kites and other fun stuff for the beaches from **Chesapeake Flag, Kite and Yo-Yo Company** (122 C Rehoboth Ave, DE 19971) and **Rehoboth Toy & Kite Company** (1 Virginia Ave & Boardwalk, DE 19971). **Fun for all Toys** (42 Rehoboth Ave, DE 19971; 302 227 1015) is stocked with classic toys and games. In Ocean City Maryland, find kites, beach toys, and clothes at **Kite Loft** (511 Boardwalk, MD 21842).

*Outdoor seating at Fish Tales Restaurant in Ocean City, Delaware*

## Find out more

**DIGITAL** Find information on these beaches, and the birds and wildlife at www.assateagueisland.com.
**FILM** The film Misty (1961) is a kids' classic about the annual roundup of wild ponies on Assateague Island.

## Next stop...

**COLONIAL WILLIAMSBURG™** Take a scenic drive south along Delmarva Peninsula from Chincoteague Island through Chesapeake Bay to reach Colonial Williamsburg™ (see pp208–209), which is the largest living-history museum in the US.

---

have regular tours, check at the park office for details

⏱ **Allow** Half to 1 day per beach

☕ **Café** Rehoboth Beach and Ocean City restaurants

🛍 **Shops** Many shops in Rehoboth Beach and Ocean City

🚻 **Restrooms** In the visitor centers, at the main visitor entrances to beaches, and in the National Seashore and State Parks

**Good family value?**
The beaches are lovely and, outside of Ocean City, uncrowded. The programs in the State Parks and National Seashore are first class.

---

# Where to Stay in Washington, DC

Families can find historic inns, all-suites hotels, modern high-rises, and hip boutiques near the metro stations and main sights in central Washington. Hotels welcome families and often offer weekend packages. Self-catering private apartments, townhouses, and B&Bs are available outside the city center.

## AGENCIES

### Bed and Breakfast Accommodations, LTD
www.bedandbreakfastdc.com
The website offers a selection of B&Bs and self-catering apartments in neighborhoods to the north and east of central Washington.

### Vacation Rentals by Owner
www.vrbo.com
An international online service, this offers privately owned homes, condos, and apartments in Washington, DC, Virginia, Maryland, and West Virginia.

## National Mall

### HOTELS
### Holiday Inn Capitol   Map 7 D4
550 C St SW, 20024; 202 479 4000; www.hicapitoldc.com; Metro: L'Enfant Plaza
Located a block south of the National Air and Space Museum, this family-friendly hotel provides tour and sightseeing information and offers a range of on-site restaurants. All rooms have fridges, and suites come with microwaves. Pay movies are available.
🌁 🍴 P 🅿️   $

### L'Enfant Plaza Hotel   Map 7 C5
480 L'Enfant Plaza SW, 20024; 202 484 1000; www.lenfantplazahotel. com; Metro: L'Enfant Plaza
This hotel has direct access to a metro station and is a short walk from the National Air and Space Museum. There is a fitness center, and special packages that include metro and sight tickets.
🌁 🍴 P 🅿️   $$

### Residence Inn Marriott  Map 7 D5
333 E St SW, 20024; 202 484 8280; www.capitolmarriott.com; Metro: Smithsonian
Spacious suites with kitchens, self-service laundry, free breakfast, and a complimentary grocery shopping service make this a family

favorite. Close to the metro, the National Air and Space Museum, and the US Capitol. Pets welcome.
🌁 P 🗄️   $$

### Mandarin Oriental, Washington DC   Map 7 B5
1330 Maryland Ave SW, 20024; 202 554 8588; www.mandarinoriental. com/washington; Metro: Smithsonian
An elegant hotel with large rooms, the Mandarin Oriental is located a short distance south of the National Mall and within walking distance of the Tidal Basin and Washington Monument. The spa is luxurious, many rooms offer water or monument views, and there is a fitness center as well.
🌁 🍴 P 🅿️   $$$

*Guests in the lobby of the Mandarin Oriental, Washington, DC*

## Capitol Hill

### HOTELS
### Hyatt Regency Washington on Capitol Hill   Map 8 E2
400 New Jersey Ave NW, 20001; 202 737 1234; www.washington regency.hyatt.com; Metro: Union Station
Comfortable and moderately upscale, this hotel is within walking distance of the Capitol. Cribs and rollaway beds are available when

asked for in advance, and there is an on-site gym facility.
🌁 🍴 P 🅿️   $$

### The Liaison   Map 8 E2
415 New Jersey Ave NW, 20001; 202 638 1616; www.affinia.com; Metro: Judiciary Square
Family-friendly hotel with complimentary bikes and Walking Tour Kit with iPod, guidebook and pedometer. It also provides Experience Kits, such as the kids' backpack with a digital camera and sticker book, and provides cribs, strollers, or high chairs on request.
🌁 🍴 P 🅿️   $$

### Phoenix Park Hotel   Map 8 E1
520 N Capitol St NW, 20001; 202 638 6900; www.phoenixparkhotel. com; Metro: Union Station
This historic Irish country-styled hotel with helpful service offers cozy rooms with fine Irish linen and toiletries, pay-per-view movies, and a flatscreen TV. Special packages may include trolley passes or Newseum tickets.
🌁 🍴 P   $$

### Washington Court Hotel   Map 8 E2
525 New Jersey Ave NW, 20001; 202 628 2100; www.washington courthotel.com; Metro: Union Station
Three blocks from the US Capitol, this pet-friendly hotel has a fitness room, and comfortable rooms with modern baths, LCD TVs, and video on demand. Family packages may include discount tickets, food and beverage credit, and free parking.
🌁 🍴 P   $$

### Capitol Hill Suites   Map 8 G4
200 C St SE, 20003; 202 543 6000; www.capitolhillhotel-dc.com; Metro: Capitol South
Each suite offers TV, DVD player, and work desk. Most have a kitchen. A fitness room, complimentary breakfast, and laundry service is available. Minimum stay of 2–3 nights.
🌁 🍴 P 🗄️   $$$

*The entrance and facade of The Liaison in Capitol Hill*

### Hotel George          Map 8 E2
*15 E St NW, 20001; 202 347 4200; www.hotelgeorge.com; Metro: Union Station*
This ultra-modern and eco-friendly boutique hotel has comfortable rooms and attentive staff. Each child is welcomed with a gift; cribs and high chairs are available on request, as are in-room child safety kits. There is also a 24-hour fitness center.

📶 ⍥ 🍽 P                                $$$

## The White House and Foggy Bottom
### HOTELS
### Hotel Lombardy          Map 2 F6
*2019 Pennsylvania Ave NW, 20006; 202 828 2600; www.hotellombardy.com; Metro: Farragut West & Foggy Bottom*
A boutique hotel close to the White House, the Lombardy has a friendly multilingual staff, and features classic 1920s decor. Rooms are decorated with imported fabrics and original art.

⍥ 🍽 P                                   $

### State Plaza Hotel          Map 6 F2
*2117 E St NW, 20037; 202 861 8200; www.stateplaza.com; Metro: Foggy Bottom*
This all-suites hotel, with kitchenettes or full kitchens in most rooms, is located on the campus of George Washington University. Amenities include a complimentary fitness center, a business center with Internet access, and multilingual information packs for international visitors.

🍽 P 🛏                                   $

### Capital Hilton          Map 2 H6
*1001 16th St NW, 20036; 202 393 1000; www3.hilton.com; Metro: Farragut North*
A family hotel just two blocks north of the White House and near three metro stations. The rooms feature comfortable furnishings, TVs, and plush beds. There is a fine health club and spa on site as well.

⍥ 🍽 P                                   $$

### Embassy Suites Washington DC          Map 2 F5
*1250 22nd St NW, 20037; 202 857 3388; http://embassysuites3.hilton.com; Metro: Dupont Circle*
This modern, family-friendly hotel is located a few blocks from Georgetown and Dupont Circle. Suites come with two TVs, mini-refrigerators, and microwaves. Complimentary breakfast is provided.

⍥ 🍽 P ⊘                                 $$

### The George Washington University Inn          Map 2 E6
*824 New Hampshire Ave NW, 20037; 202 337 6620; www.gwuinn.com; Metro: Foggy Bottom*
Close to the Kennedy Center and Georgetown University, this hotel is a popular choice for families. Spacious suites come with fridge,

microwave, TV, and high-speed Internet. Ask about family packages.

🍽 P                                     $$

### Hilton Garden Inn Washington DC Downtown          Map 3 A6
*815 14th St NW, 20005; 844 421 4604; http://hiltongardeninn3.hilton.com; Metro: McPherson Square*
This hotel is located close to the White House. Ask for the family package, and enjoy the on-demand movies, Nintendo, microwave, refrigerator, and a convenience mart off the lobby. Cribs are available and the restaurant has a kids' menu.

⍥ 🍽 P ⊘                                 $$

### The Mayflower Renaissance Washington, DC          Map 2 H5
*1127 Connecticut Ave NW, 20036; 202 347 3000; www.marriott.com; Metro: Farragut North*
Built in 1925, this elegant hotel welcomes children and pets. The rooms are spacious, with luxury bedding, Aveda bath products, and cable TV with on-demand movies. There is also a fitness center on site.

⍥ 🍽 P                                   $$

### The Quincy          Map 2 G5
*1823 L St NW, 20036; 202 223 4320; www.thequincy.com; Metro: Farragut West & Farragut North*
A boutique hotel, the Quincy boasts fine decor, rooms with a TV, and either a kitchen or a refrigerator and microwave. Located between the White House and Dupont Circle, it is close to places to shop and dine, as well as to the metro.

⍥ 🍽 P                                   $$

### The River Inn          Map 2 E6
*924 25th St NW, 20037; 202 337 7600, www.theriverinn.com; Metro: Foggy Bottom*
This boutique pet-friendly hotel has rooms with modern furnishings and sofa beds. Suites have equipped kitchens, and amenities include fitness facilities, Internet, laundry service, and complimentary bikes rentals. Weekend rates and special packages offer great value.

⍥ 🍽 P 🛏                                 $$

> ### Price Guide
> The following price ranges are based on one night's accommodation in high season for a family of four, inclusive of service charges and additional taxes.
>
> **$** under $225  **$$** $225–425  **$$$** over $425

*The Hyatt Regency, with the dome of the US Capitol rising in the distance*

**Key to symbols** *see back cover flap*

## W Washington DC    Map 7 A2
*515 15th St NW, 20004; 202 661 2400; www.wwashingtondc.com;*
*Metro: McPherson Square*
A block from the White House, this child-friendly hotel has attentive staff and a rooftop restaurant with fabulous views. The rooms are modern chic, with the signature W bed, TVs, movies on demand, iPod docks, and spacious work desks.
🔊 🍽 P    $$

## Washington Guest Suites    Map 2 E6
*801 New Hampshire Ave NW, 20037; 202 785 2000; www.washingtonguestsuites.com; Metro: Foggy Bottom*
Kids love the chocolate chip cookies and rooftop pool, while parents appreciate the bedroom suites with a living room and equipped kitchen at this hotel conveniently located near the Kennedy Center.
🔊 P 🅿 🗖    $$

## Washington Plaza    Map 3 A5
*10 Thomas Circle NW, 20005; 202 842 1300; www.washingtonplazahotel.com; Metro: McPherson Square*
Modern and casual, this resort-style hotel with beautiful landscaping is wrapped around an outdoor pool. The spacious rooms are perfect for a family evening with an in-room movie and room-service dinner. It is located near the chic Thomas Circle.
🔊 🍽 P 🅾    $$

## Fairmont Washington    Map 2 E5
*2401 M St NW, 20037; 202 429 2400; www.fairmont.com; Metro: Foggy Bottom*
An elegant place with a glassed-in lobby, courtyard, and gardens, Fairmont is located near Rock Creek Park. Family packages vary from one that includes breakfast to a Zoo Welcome Kit, which includes a toy panda, scavenger hunt, and computer game.
♿ 🔊 🍽 P 🅾 🐾    $$$

## Hotel Helix Dupont    Map 3 A4
*1430 Rhode Island Ave NW, 20005; 202 462 9001; www.hotelhelix.com; Metro: Dupont Circle*
Hip and trendy, this upscale hotel features splashes of bright shades of green and orange with pop culture artworks. Opt for the bunk-bed room with a king-sized bed

*A lavishly decorated sitting area in the renowned Williard InterContinental*

for the adults and bunk beds for the kids, or the large Helix Suite with a sitting room and master bedroom. Ask about family packages and the Kimpton Kids program.
🔊 🍽 P    $$$

## St. Regis Hotel    Map 3 A6
*923 16th St NW & K St NW, 20006; 202 638 2626; www.stregiswashingtondc.com;*
*Metro: Farragut North*
Splurge on luxury accommodations two blocks from the White House. The hotel provides a family package that includes a teddy bear for each child, DVDs, and snacks on arrival. Complimentary breakfast and access to the fitness center.
♿ 🔊 🍽 P    $$$

## Sofitel Washington DC Lafayette Square    Map 3 A6
*806 15th St NW, 20005; 202 730 8800; www.sofitel.com;*
*Metro: McPherson Square*
A luxury hotel with European flair and high service standards, the Sofitel is located near the White House. Rooms have modern decor, the staff is multilingual, and there is a gym. Special packages often offer discounts for longer stays.
♿ 🔊 🍽 P    $$$

## Willard InterContinental    Map 7 A2
*1401 Pennsylvania Ave NW, 20004; 202 628 9100; www.washington.intercontinental.com;*
*Metro: McPherson Square*
This famous place has hosted US presidents and dignitaries for more than 150 years. The hotel is luxurious, the service outstanding, and the rooms spacious and well appointed.

The Red Door Spa, the stately Round Robin Bar, luxury shops, and a fitness center are on site.
♿ 🔊 🍽 P    $$$

# Penn Quarter

HOTELS
## Hotel Harrington    Map 7 B2
*436 11th St NW, 20004; 202 628 8140; www.hotel-harrington.com;*
*Metro: Metro Center*
Operating since 1914, this no-frills hotel offers basic accommodations, friendly service, and double, triple, quad, or family deluxe rooms with varied bed and bathroom configurations. It is just a few blocks from the Mall and the White House.
🔊 🍽 P    $

## Embassy Suites Washington DC – Convention Center    Map 3 B6
*900 10th St NW, 20001; 202 739 2001; http://embassysuites3.hilton.com; Metro: Union Station*
This modern high-rise, all-suites hotel is popular with families and business travelers. Guest suites have a bedroom and living room with a sofa-bed for the kids, two TVs, a microwave, and a refrigerator. There is complimentary breakfast, and kids are provided with evening snacks.
🔊 🍽 P 🅾    $$

## Fairfield Inn & Suites Washington, DC/Downtown    Map 7 D1
*500 H St NW, 20001; 202 289 5959; www.marriott.com;*
*Metro: Gallery Place–Chinatown*
A renovated family-friendly hotel in Chinatown, Fairfield has an Asian-themed decor, complete with a jar

of fortune cookies at the front desk. The complimentary breakfast includes fresh waffles and there is a fitness room and business center.

🌐 ⏸️ P                                $$

### Hilton Garden Inn    Map 3 A6
*815 14th St NW, 20005; 844 223 9008; www.hiltongardeninn.com; Metro: Metro Center*
Close to the White House, Ford's Theatre, and the National Museum of Women in the Arts, this hotel features 300 rooms with refrigerators, microwaves, and complimentary Wi-Fi. A good, moderate choice for families in a downtown location. Hotel amenities include an indoor pool, fitness center, and room service.

🌐 ⏸️ ⊘                               $$

### Marriott Courtyard Washington Convention Center    Map 7 C1
*900 F St NW, 20004; 202 638 4600; www.marriott.com; Metro: Gallery Place–Chinatown*
This hotel is housed in a modernized 10-story bank building, just two blocks from the International Spy Museum. The decor is a mix of historic and contemporary, and the atmosphere is relaxed.

🌐 ⏸️ P ⊘                             $$

### Grand Hyatt Washington    Map 3 B6
*1000 H St NW, 20001; 202 582 1234; www.grandwashington. hyatt.com; Metro: Metro Center*
Located near the Convention Center, this elegant hotel has a soaring 12-story, glass-enclosed atrium lobby that offers direct access to the Metro Center station. Guest rooms have comfortable beds, large workspaces, and flatscreen TVs. Family-friendly packages may include special weekend rates or dining discounts.

♿ 🌐 ⏸️ P ⊘                          $$$

*A well-appointed room at the Fairmont Washington hotel*

### Henley Park Hotel    Map 3 C6
*926 Massachusetts Ave NW, 20001; 202 638 5200; www.henleypark.com; Metro: Mt. Vernon Square*
Built in 1918, this Tudor-style boutique hotel is a member of the Historic Hotels of America. The place feels like an English country manor and does a fine British high tea. Guest rooms are decorated with antique furnishings, fine linens, and have flatscreen TVs and free Wi-Fi.

🌐 ⏸️ P                               $$$

### Hotel Monaco Washington DC    Map 7 C1
*700 F St NW, 20004; 202 628 7177; www.monaco-dc.com; Metro: Gallery Place–Chinatown*
Next to the International Spy Museum, this historic hotel offers a luxurious, fun environment for families. The decor combines historic elements and bright colors with contemporary furnishings. The Kimpton Kids program offers complimentary cribs, playpens, child-safety kits, and a welcome gift for each child. Family packages offer nightly cookies and milk or breakfast.

♿ 🌐 ⏸️ P                            $$$

### JW Marriott on Pennsylvania    Map 7 A2
*1331 Pennsylvania Ave NW, 20004; 202 393 2000; www.marriott.com Metro: Metro Center*
This hotel offers luxurious rooms close to the White House, National Mall, Washington Monument, and the metro. Cribs and rollaway beds are available on request. Family packages often include breakfast, lunch, and dinner for up to four kids aged 12 and under.

🌐 ⏸️ P ⊘                            $$$

## INNS
### Morrison-Clark Historic Inn    Map 3 B5
*1015 L St NW, 20001; 202 898 1200; www.morrisonclark.com; Metro: Metro Center*
This charming historic inn housed in a restored 19th-century Victorian mansion with antique-filled rooms and modern conveniences is located a block from the Convention Center. The two-room parlor suites offer comfortable French country-style decor with a pull-out couch in the living room. There is a park across the street.

🌐 ⏸️ P                               $$

# Georgetown
## HOTELS
### Georgetown Suites    Map 1 D5
*1111 30th St NW & 1000 29th St NW, 20007; 202 298 7800; www.georgetownsuites.com; Metro: Foggy Bottom*
Families enjoy this two-building all-suites hotel for the great location, huge guest rooms, good value, and friendly service. The suites vary in size, but all have kitchens and separate sitting rooms, with continental breakfast included. The C&O Canal and M Street are less than a block away.

🌐 P 🛏️                               $

*Visitors walking up to the Hotel Monaco Washington DC*

### Avenue Suites Georgetown    Map 2 E5
*2500 Pennsylvania Ave NW, 20037; 202 333 8060; www.avenuesuites. com; Metro: Foggy Bottom*
The spacious family suites here offer a private bedroom, comfortable living room with a sleeper couch, and kitchen. Freshly baked cookies at check-in, laundry service, and complimentary breakfast are a few of the amenities. Family specials are available on most weekends.

🌐 P ⏸️ 🛏️                            $$

### The Georgetown Inn    Map 1 C5
*1310 Wisconsin Ave, 20007; 202 333 8900; www.georgetowninn.com; Metro: Foggy Bottom*
This hotel is close to Georgetown's attractions. The Colonial-styled guest rooms are spacious, the mini-suites have a sitting area, and the pay-per-view in-room movies and video games keep kids busy. The on-site restaurant Daily Grill has a good kids menu.

🌐 ⏸️ P                               $$

Key to symbols *see back cover flap*

## Holiday Inn Washington - Georgetown
Map 1 B2
*2101 Wisconsin Ave NW, 20007; 202 338 4600; www.ihg.com/holidayinn; Metro: Woodley Park-Zoo*
Located near Dumbarton Oaks and Washington National Cathedral, this hotel has a free shuttle service to the metro station and access to the DC Circulator. Rooms offer plush bedding, a lounge chair, desk, and cable TV. Kids under 12 eat free at the breakfast buffet in Market Café.

꠵ ⃝ P ✹     $$

## Capella
Map 1 D5
*1050 31st St NW, 20007; 202 617 2400; www.capellahotels.com; Metro: Foggy Bottom*
A luxury boutique hotel in Georgetown, Capella boasts a rooftop infinity pool overlooking the Potomac, fitness center and in-hotel childcare services. All the amenities you'd expect for a luxury hotel are available (for a price).

⚅ ꠵ ⃝ P ✹     $$$

## Four Seasons Hotel
Map 1 D5
*2800 Pennsylvania Ave NW, 20007; 202 342 0444; www.fourseasons.com; Metro: Foggy Bottom*
This high-end luxury hotel is known for its family-friendly amenities. Each child receives a personalized gift, chocolate chip cookies, and age-appropriate toys, magazines, and books. There are child-sized bathrobes, water toys, and floats at the pool, and children under 18 share their parents' room for no extra charge. The hotel also boasts luxurious steam rooms, saunas and an aerobics fitness studio.

⚅ ꠵ ⃝ P ✹     $$$

*Guests dining alfresco on the deck of the luxury Four Seasons Hotel*

---

*The driveway leading to the Fairfield Inn & Suites*

# Beyond Central Washington

## HOTELS

## Holiday Inn Express Washington DC - Northeast
Map 2 H4
*1917 Bladensburg Rd NE, 20002; 202 266 9000; www.ihg.com/holidayinn; Metro: New York Ave*
Comfortable and good-sized rooms with a microwave and mini-refrigerator, TVs with a Nintendo console, and crib or rollaway beds are available. The hotel is located near the National Arboretum and provides a free shuttle service to Union station and the Convention Center. There is free breakfast, a self-service laundry, an indoor pool, and a well-equipped exercise room.

꠵ P ✹     $

## Beacon Hotel & Corporate Quarters
Map 2 H5
*1615 Rhode Island Ave NW, 20036; 202 296 2100; www.beaconhotelwdc.com; Metro: Dupont Circle*
Located near the metro station, this boutique hotel is popular with family and business travelers. The decor is modern, with a range of guest rooms. The suites offer kitchens, sitting rooms, and desk space options, and come with complimentary access to the YMCA across the street. Check the website for promotional rates.

꠵ ⃝ P     $$

## Carlyle Suites Hotel
Map 2 H3
*1731 New Hampshire Ave NW, 20009; 202 234 3200; www.carlylesuites.com; Metro: Dupont Circle*
With modern amenities and Art Deco decor, this all-suites hotel is located three blocks from Dupont Circle. The comfortable and large rooms have plush bedding,

---

kitchenettes, TVs, and eco-friendly bath amenities. The special deals and packages are worth checking out.

꠵ ⃝ P 🛏     $$

## Courtyard Marriott Washington, DC/ Dupont Circle
Map 2 F2
*1900 Connecticut Ave NW, 20009, 202 332 9300; www.marriott.com; Metro: Dupont Circle*
This refurbished hotel offers floor-to-ceiling windows, an elegant lobby, and guest rooms with luxury bedding, mini-refrigerators, TVs, and pay-per-view movies and video games. The Nickelodeon Your Stay program is a favorite with kids. There is an exercise room, outdoor pool, laundry service, and a café.

꠵ ⃝ P ✹     $$

## The Dupont Circle Hotel
Map 2 G4
*1500 New Hampshire Ave NW, 20036; 202 483 6000; www.doylecollection.com; Metro: Dupont Circle*
Elegance and minimalist decor combine to create a sophisticated yet homely vibe at this hotel. The staff is courteous and the rooms are comfortable. Some packages include free breakfast, and kids 11 and under stay free with parents.

⚅ ꠵ ⃝ P     $$

## Fairfax Hotel at Embassy Row
Map 2 F4
*2100 Massachusetts Ave NW, 20008; 202 293 2100; www.fairfaxhoteldc.com; Metro: Dupont Circle*
A gracious, historic hotel, Fairfax is nestled among stately mansions, with a metro station, restaurants, shops, and nightlife nearby. Families enjoy contemporary, luxury accommodations and excellent, personalized service.

⚅ ꠵ ⃝ P     $$

## Fairfield Inn & Suites Washington DC
*2305 New York Ave NE, 20002; 202 266 3000; www.marriott.com; Metro: New York Ave*
This hotel is located near the National Arboretum and provides a free shuttle service to Union Station and the Convention Center. The comfortable rooms have TVs and local calls are free. The

complimentary breakfast includes make-your-own waffles; there is a fitness center and a weights room.

🔊 P ⊘                          $$

## Holiday Inn Hotel Washington - Central   Map 2 H5
1501 Rhode Island Ave NW, 20005; 202 483 2000; www.inndc.com; Metro: Dupont Circle
Just east of Dupont Circle, this full-service hotel is within walking distance of two metro stations. Dine at the Avenue Café, where children eat free; take the kids to the rooftop seasonal pool and admire the panoramic view of the city; or enjoy cable TV and in-room movies.

🔊 🍴 P ⊘                       $$

## Homewood Suites by Hilton   Map 3 A5
1475 Massachusetts Ave NW, 20005; 202 265 8000; http://homewoodsuites3.hilton.com; Metro: McPherson Square
This comfortable all-suites hotel, close to the White House, is popular with families and business travelers. The suites provide a living area with sleeper-sofa, kitchen, and Internet. Complimentary services include buffet breakfast and fitness center.

🔊 🍽 P                         $$

## Marriott Residence Inn Washington DC Dupont Circle   Map 2 F4
2120 P St NW, 20037; 202 466 6800; www.marriott.com; Metro: Dupont Circle
The Marriott has spacious bedroom suites with kitchens and separate areas for sleeping, working, eating, and relaxing. Guests can request a crib or rollaway bed. Cable TV and movies are available, as well as video games for rent. Gorge on the included American breakfast buffet, then work it off in the fitness center.

🔊 P                            $$

## Omni Shoreham Hotel   Map 2 E1
2500 Calvert St NW, 20008; 202 234 0700; www.omnihotels.com; Metro: Woodley Park-Zoo
Situated in Rock Creek Park, this grand luxury hotel is close to the metro and a short walk from the zoo. It has an elegant lobby, a spa, and spacious modern rooms with on-demand movies, Nintendo, and cable TV. Kids receive games, books, and a backpack. Stroll

through the gardens, swim, or head out the back door to hike, bike, or jog in Rock Creek Park.

🔊🔊🍽 P ⊘                      $$

## Savoy Suites Hotel   Map 1 B1
2505 Wisconsin Ave NW, 20007; 202 337 9700; www.savoysuites.com; Metro: Woodley Park-Zoo
Off the beaten path on the northern side of Georgetown, this boutique hotel offers a free shuttle to and from the Woodley Park-Zoo metro station and Georgetown University. Guest rooms have comfortable furnishings and some suites offer full kitchens. It also has a fitness center.

🔊 🍽 P                         $$

The Fairfax Hotel at Embassy Row on Massachusetts Avenue

## Washington Doubletree
Map 3 A4
1515 Rhode Island Ave NW, 20005; 202 232 7000; http://doubletree3.hilton.com; Metro: Dupont Circle
Located in a quiet neighborhood near Scott Circle, this large family-friendly hotel is known for its good service. The rooms have modern furnishings, comfortable beds, and cable TV. Cribs and high chairs are available, as are family packages. Dupont Circle is a short walk away.

🔊 🍽 P                         $$

## Washington Marriott Wardman Park   Map 2 E1
2660 Woodley Rd NW, 20008; 202 328 2000; www.marriott.com; Metro: Woodley Park-Zoo
Washington, DC's largest hotel is within walking distance of the zoo. It is modern, with a vast lobby, convention center, and guest rooms with Marriott Revive bedding, pay-per-view movies, and cable TV. Rooms in the quieter Wardman Tower are popular with families.

🔊 🍽 P ⊘                       $$

## The Embassy Row Hotel   Map 2 G4
2015 Massachusetts Ave NW, 20036; 202 265 1600; www.embassyrowhotel.com; Metro: Dupont Circle
Housed in a richly renovated 10-story building, this hotel has modern guest rooms with luxurious pillow-top mattresses. Connecting rooms, cribs, and playpens are available on request. The Dupont Circle metro station, embassies, museums, and restaurants are close by. Ask about the family packages and board games for the kids.

🔊 🍽 P ⊘                       $$$

## BED & BREAKFAST
### Ivy Mansion at Dupont Circle   Map 2 F3
21st St NW & R St NW, 20005; 202 302 0242; www.theivymansion.com; Metro: Dupont Circle
The garden apartment at this B&B offers a bedroom with a queen-sized bed and private bath, a living room with a double-sized sleeper couch, a fully equipped kitchen, and a private patio. Cable TV is available, but breakfast is not included. It is close to the metro, and to the Connecticut Avenue shops.

🔊 🍽                            $$

### Swann House   Map 2 H3
1808 New Hampshire Ave NW, 20009; 202 265 4414; www.swannhouse.com; Metro: Dupont Circle
Housed in a grand mansion, this B&B offers modern amenities in a 19th-century setting. Enjoy the private two-bedroom suite with a sitting room and courtyard entrance. The complimentary breakfast with cereal, gourmet entrées, and home-made pastries receives rave reviews, and kids like the afternoon cookies served with tea and lemonade.

🔊 ⊘                            $$

## CAMPING
### Cherry Hill Park
9800 Cherry Hill Rd, College Park, MD 20740; 800 801 6449; www.cherryhillpark.com
A large campground for RVs and tents, Cherry Hill Park also has trailers and cabins for rent. It is located 10 miles (16 km) north of Washington, DC; a bus service is available. Around 400 sites with amenities such as a seasonal café, movies, laundry room, game room, hot tub, and sauna.

🔊 P ⊘ ⚓                        $

Key to symbols see back cover flap

### Greenbelt Park
*6565 Greenbelt Rd, Greenbelt, MD 20770; 301 344 3948; www.nps.gov/gree; Metro: College Park-U of MD*
This National Park campground for RVs and tents is 12 miles (19 km) northeast of Washington. The park offers nature trails and ranger-led programs for kids. There is a metro station 3 miles (5 km) away. There are no electrical or water hookups.
⛺ P ♿                                    $

## Day Trips and Excursions – Mount Vernon

### CAMPING
### Pohick Bay Regional Park Campground
*6501 Pohick Bay Drive, Lorton, VA 22079; 703 339 6104; www.nvrpa.org/park/pohick_bay*
Located 11 miles (17 km) south of the Franconia Springfield metro station and Mount Vernon, this campground has 150 sites, 100 with electric hookups, 50 tent sites, plus two-room rustic cabins for rent. Nature trails, paddleboats, kayaks for rent, and a water park are available.
P ⊕ ♿                                    $

## Alexandria

### HOTELS
### Embassy Suites Alexandria - Old Town
*1900 Diagonal Rd, Alexandria, VA 22314; 703 684 5900; http://embassysuites3.hilton.com; Metro: King Street*
Set across from a metro station, this hotel offers suites that have a sitting area with two TVs, a microwave, and a refrigerator. Free breakfast and a nightly manager's reception with beverages and snacks. Ask about kids' activities and family packages.
⌂ ⦿ P ⊕                                    $$

### Hotel Monaco Alexandria
*480 King St, Alexandria, VA 22314; 703 549 6080; www.monaco-alexandria.com*
This colorful, whimsical, pet- and family-friendly boutique hotel has a daily kids' hour with games, toys, and snacks, free bike use, and a Drive In Movie Night at the pool on Saturdays. The Kimpton Kids program has a gift for each child.
⌂ ⦿ P ⊕                                    $$

### Morrison House
*116 S Alfred St, Alexandria, VA 22314; 703 838 8000; www.morrisonhouse.com*
Housed in a Federal-style building, this four-star boutique hotel is elegant and sophisticated. The lobby is welcoming, the parlor comfortable, the rooms have period furnishings, and the Kimpton Kids program welcomes each child with a gift.
♿ ⌂ ⦿ P ⊕                                    $$

## Arlington

### HOTELS
### The Virginian Suites
*1500 Arlington Blvd, Arlington, VA 22209; 866 371 1446; www.virginiansuites.com; Metro: Rosslyn*
This family-friendly apartment-style hotel offers studios and one-bedroom suites with kitchens. Rooms have convertible sofas and plush top mattresses. The metro is within walking distance and there is a fitness center with saunas. There is a grocery delivery service, and a variety of local restaurants provide room service.
⌂ P ⊕ 🛏                                    $

### Hyatt Arlington
*1325 Wilson Blvd, Arlington, VA 22209; 703 525 1234; www.arlington.hyatt.com; Metro: Rosslyn*
The renovated Hyatt Arlington is located across from the metro station. The rooms are large, modern, and comfortable with Hyatt Grand Beds, granite baths and spa products, and iPod docks. There are golf courses, jogging paths, and bike trails nearby.
⌂ ⦿ P                                    $$

### Key Bridge Marriott
*1401 Lee Hwy, Arlington, VA 22209; 703 524 6400; www.marriott.com; Metro: Rosslyn*
This family-friendly, high-rise hotel is located just a walk or shuttle ride from Georgetown, and three blocks from the metro station. There is a fitness center and sauna, and an indoor/outdoor connected pool with a whirlpool. Ask about special family packages.
⌂ ⦿ P ⊕                                    $$

## Harpers Ferry

### HOTELS
### Quality Hotel Conference Center
*4328 William L Wilson FWY, Harpers Ferry, WV 25425; 304 535 6302; www.qualityinn.com*
Located near the Harpers Ferry National Historic Park, this hotel is popular with families. Rooms have a refrigerator, microwave, and cable TV. There is free breakfast and local calls, coin-operated laundry, and access to a fitness room and business center.
⌂ ⦿ P ⊕                                    $

### BED AND BREAKFAST
### Jackson Rose Bed & Breakfast
*1167 W Washington St, Harpers Ferry, WV 25425; 304 535 1528; www.thejacksonrose.com*
The pace is relaxed at this historic home, which Confederate General Stonewall Jackson chose as his temporary headquarters during the Civil War. The Federal-style home has been restored and tastefully decorated. Families with kids aged 12 and above may enjoy the third-floor suite with two bedrooms.

*Stunning views from the Skyland Resort in Shenandoah National Park*

Key to Price Guide see p227

*The dining room at the Jackson Rose Bed & Breakfast in Harpers Ferry*

The innkeepers are hospitable and serve a full breakfast. There is a charming rose garden outside.

🔲 P                                    $$

# Frederick

## HOTELS
### Comfort Inn Red Horse
*998 W Patrick St, Frederick, MD 21703; 301 662 0281; www.comfortinn.com*
A no-frills hotel, the Red Horse offers tastefully decorated guest rooms with microwaves and refrigerators. There is free breakfast and Internet, local calls, and a weekday newspaper.

P                                    $

## BED AND BREAKFAST
### Hill House
*12 W 3rd St, Frederick, MD 21705; 301 682 4111; www.hillhouse frederick.com*
Housed in a renovated Victorian townhouse, this B&B offers four guest rooms furnished with a mix of styles. The gourmet breakfast is served in the dining room, or the garden, weather permitting. The shops and restaurants of Frederick are only a short distance away.

🔲 P                                    $$

# Skyline Drive

## HOTELS
### Big Meadows Lodge
*Mile 51.2 Skyline Drive, Shenandoah National Park, Virginia; 877 247 9261; www.nationalparkreservations. com; open mid-May–early-Nov*
Built in 1939, this stone lodge offers small rooms, as well as rustic cabins. Rooms have no phones or Wi-Fi, and most do not have a TV. Activities include walking to the waterfall, deer-watching, and hiking.

🍴 P                                    $

### Skyland Resort
*Mile 41.7 Skyline Drive, Shenandoah National Park, Virginia; 540 999 2212; www.nationalparkreservations. com; open Apr–Nov*
Along a mountain crest, this resort offers modern hotel-style rooms. Rooms either have balconies with views into the valley or windows facing the woods. Rooms vary in size and configuration with no telephones or Wi-Fi, and most do not have a TV. There is easy access to nature trails and great views.

🍴 P                                    $

## CAMPING
### Shenandoah National Park
*Mathews Arm, Big Meadows, Lewis Mountain, and Loft Mountain Campgrounds, Skyline Drive; 877 444 6777; www.nps.gov/shen/ planyourvisit/campgrounds.htm*
The four campgrounds here do not have RV hookups, but all except Lewis Mountain Campground accept RVs. Tents are allowed in all four as well as in some other areas of the park. Some sites have views, but most are in the woods. Each campground provides access to hiking trails, and most have waterfalls nearby. Check the website for opening and closing dates.

P                                    $

# Charlottesville

## HOTELS
### Omni Charlottesville Hotel
*212 Ridge Rd, Charlottesville, VA 22903; 434 971 5500; www.omnihotels.com*
Just next to Downtown Mall, this comfortable hotel has a seven-story atrium lobby. The rooms are decorated in relaxing colors with cable TV, on-demand movies, and Nintendo. Kids are welcomed with a backpack, books, and games.

🔲 🍴 P 🔄                              $$

# Fredericksburg

## HOTELS
### Courtyard Marriott Fredericksburg
*620 Caroline St, Fredericksburg, VA 22401; 540 373 8300; www.marriott.com*
The only hotel located in the historic district is part of a chain with reliable service and amenities. The guest rooms are comfortable with contemporary decor, flatscreen TVs, and large desks. Restaurants, and shops including boutiques, antique stores, and second-hand places, are within walking distance of the hotel.

🔲 🍴 P 🔄                              $

## INNS
### Richard Johnston Inn
*711 Caroline St, Fredericksburg, VA 22401; 540 899 7606; www.therichardjohnstoninn.com*
An immaculate inn housed in two 18th-century homes, the Richard Johnston Inn is located in the heart of historic Fredericksburg. Each room is unique, with furnishings and decor ranging from relaxed contemporary to formal rooms with a canopy bed. Full breakfast on weekends, and an extended continental breakfast on weekdays is included.

🔲 P                                    $

*Exterior of the multi-storied Omni Charlottesville Hotel*

## CAMPING
### Aquia Pines Resort
*3071 Jefferson Davis Hwy, Stafford, VA 22554; 540 659 3447; www.aquiapines.com*
This family-friendly campground in a wooded area offers a variety of sites, from full-service sites with Wi-Fi, cable TV, and telephone to wooded sites for tents. Kids enjoy the miniature golf, basketball court, and the large swimming pool. Information on getting to Washington, DC, Mount Vernon, and Fredericksburg is available.

🔲 P 🔄 🦽                              $

**Key to symbols** *see back cover flap*

# Middleburg

## INNS

### Middleburg Country Inn
*209 East Washington St, Middleburg, VA 20117; 540 687 6082; www.middleburgcountry inn.com*

Charming and comfortable, this inn offers modern conveniences. There are eight country-style guest rooms, each uniquely decorated, and with cable TV, VCR, and a private bath. Two spacious suites are designed for families. The made-to-order country breakfast offers several choices. Ice cream and wine are available in the evenings. Boutique shops and restaurants are close by.

🔊 P $$

### Red Fox Inn and Tavern
*2 East Washington St, Middleburg VA 20117; 540 687 6301; www. redfox.com*

Dating from 1728, Red Fox Inn and Tavern is known as Virginia's oldest country inn and many famous people, including George Washington and Jacqueline Kennedy Onassis have stayed here. Built with local fieldstone, the inn comprises three buildings. Each guest room is unique in size and decor, with comfortable bedding and cable TV.

🔊 IOI P $$

# Williamsburg

## HOTELS

### Williamsburg Lodge
*310 South England St, Williamsburg, VA 23185; 757 220 7976; www.colonialwilliamsburg.com*

A popular family cabin, this lodge is a short walk from historic Williamsburg. Rooms are located in eight buildings, and many furnishings are inspired by art from the nearby Abby Aldrich Rockefeller Folk Art Museum. Cable TV is also available.

♿ 🔊 IOI P ⊘ $$

### Williamsburg Inn
*136 East Francis St, Williamsburg, VA 23185; 757 220 7978; www.colonialwilliamsburg.com*

This Regency-style inn offers all the luxuries of a modern hotel, has spacious rooms, and welcomes families. There is a fitness center and spa, and access to a tennis court and golf course.

♿ 🔊 IOI P ⊘ $$$

*Pretty flowers outside the inviting Middleburg Country Inn*

# Annapolis

## HOTELS

### Loews Hotel
*126 West St, Annapolis, MD 21401; 410 263 7777; www.loewshotels.com*

This hotel offers several amenities in a family-friendly atmosphere. The nautical-themed rooms are spacious, with a workspace, and there is a fitness room and spa on site. Check out the Loews Loves Kids and Teens programs, with special services, toys, entertainment, and family packages.

🔊 IOI P $$

## BED AND BREAKFAST

### Flag House Inn
*26 Randall St, Annapolis, MD 21401; 410 280 2721*

Welcoming families with children aged 13 and above, this tastefully furnished 1870s Victorian home is located near the waterfront. The innkeepers are well informed about the area. A full hot breakfast with freshly baked goods is served in the dining room. Guests receive their country's flag on arrival.

P $$

# Baltimore

## HOTELS

### Fairfield Inn & Suites – Baltimore Inner Harbor
*101 President St, Baltimore, MD 21202; 410 837 9900; www.greenfairfieldinn.com*

Housed in a re-purposed industrial warehouse, Baltimore's first green hotel is modern and close to the Inner Harbor. The comfortable rooms and suites feature pillow-top mattresses, TVs, and large desks. The deluxe continental breakfast is free.

🔊 IOI P $$

### Pier 5 Hotel
*711 Eastern Ave, Baltimore, MD 21202; 410 539 2000; www.harbormagic.com*

Located on its own pier in Baltimore's Inner Harbor, this whimsical hotel offers comfortable, fun, and colorful rooms. Hues of purple, green, red, and yellow abound, yet the suites and standard rooms are relaxing. Special themed events for families include Crabby Hour and the Chocolate Event.

🔊 IOI P $$

## INNS

### Admiral Fell Inn
*888 South Broadway, Baltimore MD 21231; 410 522 7380; www.harbormagic.com*

This European-style, historic hotel is located in the waterfront village of Fells Point. Each of the stately guest rooms is unique, with movies-on-demand, bottled water, and green toiletries. There are ghost tours on Friday and Saturday evenings.

🔊 IOI P $

### Inn at Henderson's Wharf
*1000 Fell St, Baltimore, MD 21231; 410 522 7777; www.hendersons wharf.com*

European charm and modern comforts blend in this waterfront inn at Fells Point. The rooms have

*Outdoor pool at the Sea Hawk Motel in Ocean City, Maryland*

fine furnishings and feather beds, and complimentary luxuries include a check-in bottle of wine, continental breakfast, and use of a fitness center.

🛜 P                            $$

# Chesapeake Bay

## INNS
### The Old Brick Inn
*401 S Talbot St, St. Michaels, MD 21663; 410 745 3323; www.oldbrickinn.com*
Located near several shops and restaurants in the center of St. Michaels, this inn offers 20 unique rooms in three separate buildings. Elegant and comfortable rooms, friendly service, and excellent breakfasts set the stage for a pampered stay. Many of the tastefully decorated guest rooms have fireplaces and whirlpool tubs.

🛜 P ✪                          $$

## MOTELS
### Best Western St. Michaels Motor Inn
*1228 S Talbot St, St. Michaels, MD 21663; 410 745 3333; www.bestwestern.com*
This bright and clean motor inn is located close to shops, museums, and restaurants. Rooms have cable TV and cribs. Children aged 17 and under can stay free in their parents' room. There is a complimentary continental breakfast, free local calls under 30 minutes, and some business services.

🛜 P ✪                           $

# Assateague

## CAMPING
### Assateague Island National Seashore Campgrounds
*7206 National Seashore Lane, Berlin, MD 21811; 410 641 3030; www.nps.gov/asis*
These oceanside and bayside drive-in campgrounds are suitable for tents, trailers, and recreation vehicles, although there are no electrical, sewage, or water hookups. There is also an oceanside walk-in campground for tents only. Each site provides a picnic table and an upright grill. Bring firewood, sunscreen, insect repellent, and long tent stakes to anchor tents in the sand. There are cold water showers and chemical toilets.

P                               $

### Assateague Maryland State Park Campground
*7307 Stephen Decatur Hwy, Berlin, MD 21811; 410 641 2120; www.dnr.state.md.us/publiclands/eastern/assateaguecamping.asp*
Campsites for tents, trailers, and recreational vehicles are separated from the beach by a dune, and a few sites with electricity are also available. There are picnic tables, fire rings, and restrooms with warm showers.

*RV at Assateague Maryland State Park Campground*

P ☾                             $

# Ocean City

## HOTELS
### Castle in the Sand Hotel
*3701 Atlantic Ave, Ocean City, MD 21842; 410 289 6846; www.castleinthesand.com*
This oceanfront hotel and resort offers standard rooms, efficiency apartments, and suites. There is no extra charge for kids aged 11 and under. Free activities for kids include arts and crafts projects, and shows with clowns, mermaids, and pirates.

🛜 🍽 P ✪                         $$

*Facade of the Victorian-style Dunes Manor Hotel*

### Dunes Manor Hotel
*2800 N Baltimore Ave, Ocean City, MD 21842; 410 289 1100; www.dunesmanor.com*
Just a block from the Ocean City boardwalk, this grand hotel offers ocean views from the lobby and every room. Complimentary tea and crumpets are served in the afternoon. Head out to the beach, sunbathe on the sundeck, or lounge on the verandah overlooking the ocean.

🛜 🍽 P ✪ ☾                       $$

## MOTELS
### Sea Hawk Motel
*12410 Coastal Hwy, Ocean City, MD 21842; 410 250 3191; www.seahawkmotel.com*
Popular with families, this older hotel is clean, comfortable, and just a block from the beach. Rooms have two beds and a sofa bed; some units are efficiency apartments with kitchens. The hotel does not charge extra for up to two children aged 10 years and under staying with parents. Restaurants, shops, and entertainment are close by.

P ✪                             $

# Rehoboth Beach

## HOTELS
### Avenue Inn
*33 Wilmington Ave, Rehoboth Beach, DE 19971; 1800 433 5870; www.avenueinn.com*
Relax and enjoy the beach and boardwalk, just a block from this hotel. Avenue Inn also offers many amenities such as a day spa, hot tub, steam room, sauna, and a fitness room. There is a complimentary full breakfast, afternoon wine and cheese, and evening cookies. The guest rooms have a microwave, small refrigerator, and TV.

🛜 P ✪ ☾                         $$

## MOTELS
### Beach View Motel
*6 Wilmington Ave, Rehoboth Beach, DE 19971; 302 227 2999; www.beachviewmotel.com*
With a great location near the beach and the Rehoboth boardwalk, this hotel has rooms with private balconies or large windows overlooking the pool. There are also refrigerators, microwaves, and cable TVs. Funland, with rides, and video and pinball games, is nearby.

🛜 P ✪ ☾                         $$

**Key to symbols** *see back cover flap*

An aerial view of Washington, DC's most famous monuments, including the United States Capitol and the Washington Monument in the background

# WASHINGTON, DC

## Maps

# Washington, DC City Maps

The map below shows the division of the eight
pages of maps in this section, as well as the main
areas covered in the Exploring section of this book.
The smaller inset map shows Central Washington
and the area covered in Beyond Central Washington.

## KEY TO MAPS 1–8

| | |
|---|---|
| ▢ | Major sight |
| ▢ | Place of interest |
| ▢ | Other building |
| M | Metro station |
| R | Rail station |
| ⛴ | Riverboat boarding point |
| P | Parking |
| i | Visitor information |
| ⛹ | Playground |
| ⚑ | Police station |
| ▤ | Highway |
| ▤ | Pedestrian road |
| ⚊ | Rail road |

0 meters ————————— 400

0 yards ————————— 400

**Beyond Central Washington**
*pp162–181*

Hyattsville

DISTRICT OF
COLUMBIA

Cleveland
Park

Kalorama

Georgetown

**Central
Washington**

Fairmont
Heights

Capitol
Hill

Fort
Dupont

Arlington

Waterfront

MARYLAND

VIRGINIA

Anacostia

Suitland

Potomac

Hillcrest
Heights

Forest
Heights

Alexandria

Camp
Springs

0 Km ————————— 1

0 miles ————————— 1

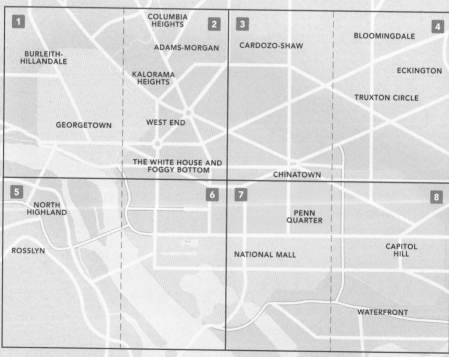

**1**

BURLEITH-
HILLANDALE

GEORGETOWN

COLUMBIA
HEIGHTS

**2**

ADAMS-MORGAN

KALORAMA
HEIGHTS

WEST END

THE WHITE HOUSE AND
FOGGY BOTTOM

**3**

CARDOZO-SHAW

**4**

BLOOMINGDALE

ECKINGTON

TRUXTON CIRCLE

CHINATOWN

**5**

NORTH
HIGHLAND

ROSSLYN

**6**

**7**

PENN
QUARTER

NATIONAL MALL

**8**

CAPITOL
HILL

WATERFRONT

# Selected Washington Maps Index

E  NW  NE  F  G  H  4

1

CHANNING  ST  NW

DOUGLAS  ST  NE

EDGEWOOD  STREET  NE

GLENWOOD
CEMETERY

CHANNING  ST  NE

BRYANT  STREET  NE

Rhode Island Ave-
Brentwood  M  P

ADAMS  STREET  NW

ADAMS  STREET  NE

W  STREET  NW

STREET  NW

V  STREET  NE

2

V  STREET  NW

BLOOMINGDALE

U  STREET  NE

U  STREET  NE

TODD  PLACE  NE

T  STREET  NW

ECKINGTON

T  STREET  NE

SEATON  PLACE  NW

S  STREET  NW

3

RANDOLPH  PLACE  NW

R  STREET  NE

QUINCY  PLACE  NE

STREET  NW

Q  STREET  NE

STREET  NW

STREET  NW

NEW  YORK  AVENUE  NE

P

STREET  NW

RUXTON  CIRCLE

P

BENTWOOD
PARK

O  STREET  NE

PENN  STREET  NE

P

4

HANOVER  PL  NW

New York Ave-
Florida Ave-
Gallaudet  M

N  STREET  NE

P

PATTERSON  ST  NE

FLORIDA  AVENUE  NE

M  STREET  NE

M  STREET  NE

5

MORTON  PL  NE

PIERCE  STREET  NE

ORLEANS  PL  NE

L  STREET  NE

L  STREET

K  STREET  NE

I  STREET  NE

I  STREET

6

G  PLACE  NE

P  E  F  i  8  G  H

H  STREET  NE

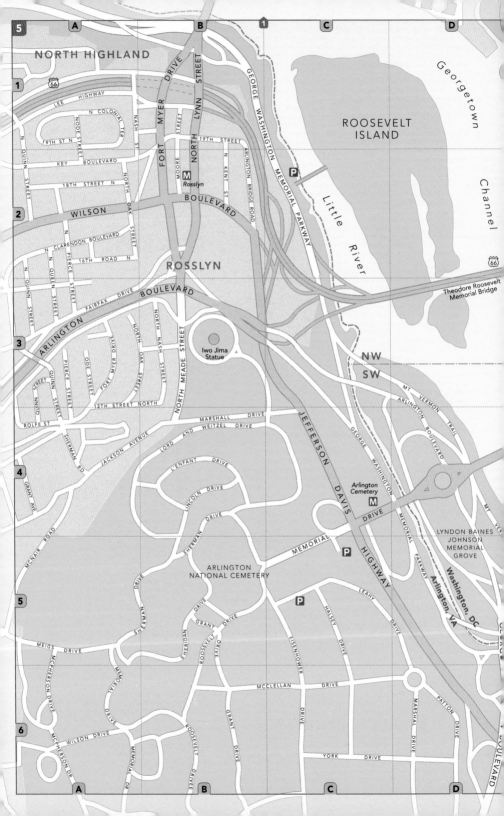

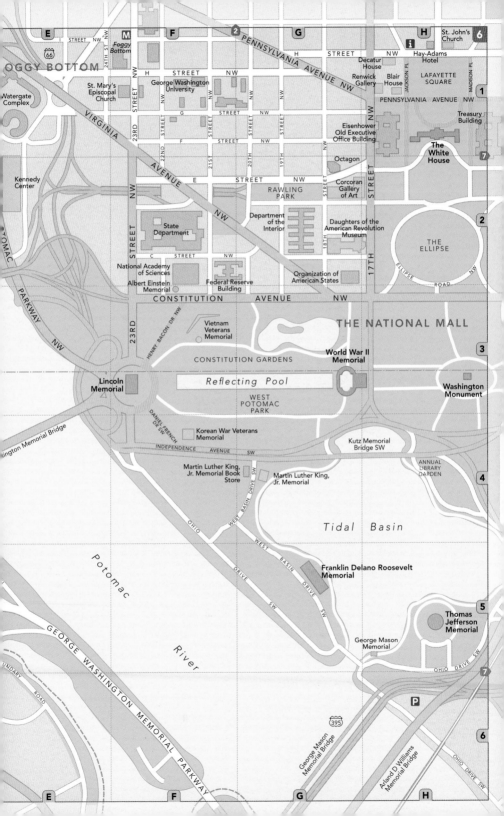

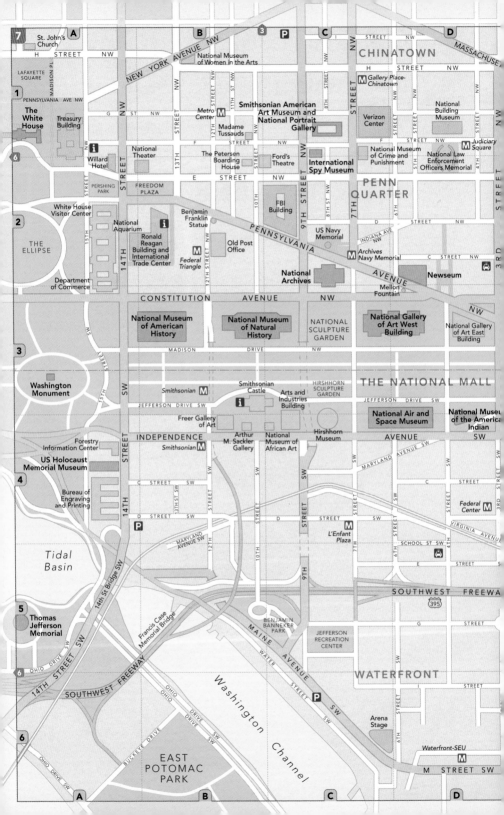

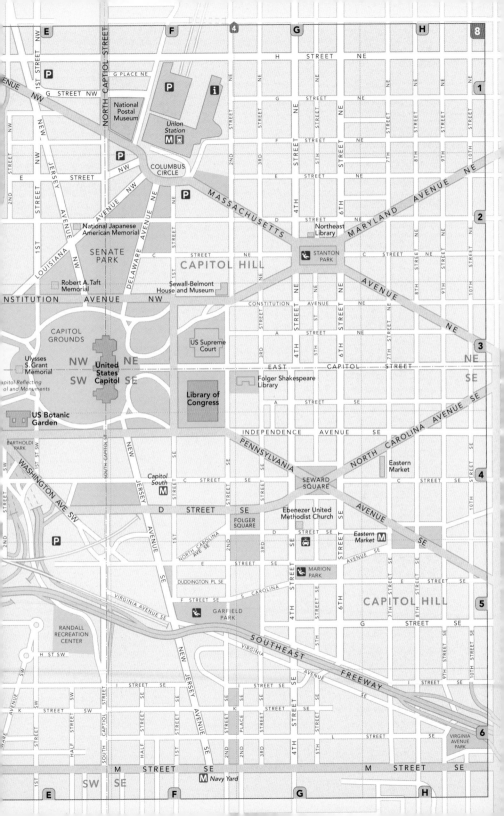

# Index

Page numbers in **bold** type refer to main entries.

# Acknowledgments

Dorling Kindersley would like to thank the following people whose help and assistance contributed to the preparation of this book.

**Main Contributors**
Paul Franklin is an award-winning travel writer and photographer whose work has appeared in over a 100 publications internationally. He has photographed, authored, or co-authored 16 travel books, including Dorling Kindersley's Eyewitness Top 10 guides to Santa Fe, New Mexico, San Antonio, and Texas. After having lived in the Washington, DC area for many years, Paul now resides in the mountains north of Asheville, North Carolina with his wife, and frequent co-author, Nancy Mikula and their cat, Nikko.

Eleanor Berman is a widely published writer for magazines and newspapers, and the author of 14 travel guides. Her books include two other guides for Dorling Kindersley: Eyewitness *Top 10 New York* and the *Eyewitness Guide to New York*, which won the Thomas Cook award as the year's best guidebook.

**Additional Photography**
Peter Dennis; Rough Guides: Angus Osborn,/Paul Whitfield; Kim Sayer; Giles Stokoe.

**Design and Editorial**
PUBLISHER Vivien Antwi
LIST MANAGER Christine Stroyan
SENIOR MANAGING ART EDITOR Mabel Chan
SENIOR CARTOGRAPHIC EDITOR Casper Morris
CARTOGRAPHIC EDITOR Stuart James
SENIOR EDITOR Michelle Crane
JACKET DESIGN Louise Dick, Tessa Bindloss
ICON DESIGN Claire-Louise Armitt
SENIOR DTP DESIGNER Jason Little
PICTURE RESEARCH Ellen Root, Chloe Roberts
PRODUCTION CONTROLLER Rebecca Short
READERS Scarlett O'Hara, Debra Wolter
FACT CHECKER Caitlin Fairchild
PROOFREADER Patrick Newman
INDEXER Hilary Bird
With thanks to Douglas Amrine for his help in developing this series

**Additional Editorial Assistance**
Vicki Allen, Claire Bush

**Revisions Team**
Ashwin Raju Adimari, Shruti Bahl, Emer FitzGerald, Sarah Holland, Bharti Karakoti, Sumita Khatwani, Priyanka Kumar, Bhavika Mathur, Scarlett O'Hara, Susie Peachey, Alice Powers, Rada Radojicic, Erin Richards, Avijit Sengupta, Beverly Smart, Ajay Verma

**Cartography**
Maps on pages 216 and 218 are derived from © www.openstreetmap.org and contributors, licensed under CC-BY-SA, see www.creativecommons.org for further details.

**Photographic Reference**
The London Aerial Photo Library, and P F James.

**Photography Permissions**
Dorling Kindersley would like to thank the following for their assistance and kind permission to photograph at their establishments.

Arthur M. Sackler Gallery; The B&O Railroad Museum; Baltimore's Inner Harbor; Busch Gardens®; Center Café in Union Station; Dumbarton Oaks; Garland Scott at Folger Shakespeare Library; Franklin Delano Roosevelt Memorial; Frederick Douglass Houses; Freer Gallery of Art; Harpers Ferry National Historical Park; The International Spy Museum; Jamestown Settlement; Library of Congress; Lincoln Memorial; Madame Tussauds; Mandarin Oriental; Maryland Science Center; Mitsitam Café; Monticello; Mount Vernon; National Air and Space Museum's Steven F. Udvar-Hazy Center; Jen Bloomer at National Aquarium; Miriam Kleiman at National Archives; Sara Beth Walsh at National Gallery of Art; National Geographic Museum; National Museum of African Art; National Museum of American History; National Museum of American Indian; National Museum of Natural History; National Portrait Gallery; National Postal Museum; Jonathan Thompson at Newseum; The Phillips Collection; Port Discovery Children's Museum; Red Hot & Blue Restaurant; Sewall-Belmont House and Museum; Smithsonian's American Art Museum; Mandy Young at Smithsonian American Art Museum's Renwick Gallery; Amy Giarmo at Smithsonian's Hirshhorn Museum and Sculpture Garden; Smithsonian's National Air and Space Museum; Jennifer Zoon at Smithsonian's National Zoological Park; Thomas Jefferson Memorial; US Botanic Garden; US Capitol; US Holocaust Memorial Museum; The Walters Art Museum, Baltimore; Washington National Cathedral; Washington Union Station; Woodrow Wilson House; Wright Place Food Court.

Works of art have been reproduced with the permission of the following copyright holders: *Walking Man* 59tl & *The Burghers of Calais* 62bc by Auguste Rodin, Hirshhorn Museum and Sculpture Garden, Smithsonian Institution, Gift of Joseph H. Hirshhorn, 1966; *Family of Saltimbanques* © Succession Picasso/DACS, London 2012 77tc, Bas-relief at World War II Memorial © Kaskey Studio 2004 86cr; The Albert Einstein Memorial 1979 © Robert Berks 91cla; *Roosevelt and his wife* 92tl, *Roosevelt* 92 cr © Neil Estern; *The Lone Sailor* © Stanley Bleifeld 142bc; *Electronic Superhighway: Continental US., Alaska, Hawaii* © Nam June Paik 146crb; Alex Haley/Kunte Kinte Memorial © Ed Dwight 216cl.

**Picture Credits**
Key: a-above; b-below/bottom; c-centre; f-far; l-left; r-right; t-top.
The publisher would like to thank the following for their kind permission to reproduce their photographs:

ALAMY IMAGES: AF Archive 111c, 145tc; David Coleman 72cl; Danita Delimont 73c; Blaine Harrington III 29bl; William S. Kuta 80cr; Keystone Pictures USA 45cl; Morey Milbradt 198 cra; North Wind Picture Archives 43tl, 43c, 44tc, 44clb, 46cr; Kumar Sriskandan 10br; World History Archive 47bc. ARENA STAGE AT THE MEAD CENTER FOR AMERICAN THEATER: Nick Lehoux courtesy of Bing Thom Architects 34–35bc. BUSCH GARDENS®: © 2011 SeaWorld Parks & Entertainment. Reproduced by permission of SeaWorld Parks & Entertainment, 214c. CORBIS: 47tl; Demotix/Evan Golub 16br. DC UNITED: 41tl. DAUGHTERS OF THE AMERICAN REVOLUTION: 121br, Courtesy of NSDAR 118cr, 125cl. DREAMSTIME.COM: Chrisdodutch 126br; Lunamarina 50; Olivier Le Queinec 142tl; Timehacker 126br. THE FAIRMONT WASHINGTON, DC: 229bl. FOLGER SHAKESPEARE LIBRARY: John Gregory. A Midsummer Night's Dream bas relief, 1932 99cl, James Kegley 112tr, Lloyd Wolf 15bl. FOUR SEASONS HOTEL WASHINGTON, DC: 230bl. PAUL FRANKLIN: 13tr, 16bl, 34bl, 38bl, 38br, 39tl, 52cl, 53t, 83tr, 84tr, 86crb, 93tl, 94tl, 95bl, 96cl, 96cr, 101t, 102cl, 106br, 109bl, 127c, 151c, 156c, 156cr, 156clb, 160cb, 162–163, 164cr, 165t, 173cb, 176bl, 186cla. GOOD STUFF EATERY: 31bc; 111tl. HBO: Paul Morigi 37br. HELLO CUPCAKE: 30bc. HYATT REGENCY WASHINGTON, DC: 28bl, 227bl. IMAGINATION STAGE: Imagination Stage's Annette M. and Theodore N. Lerner Family Theatre 36br, Imagination Stage's world premiere musical – George and Martha: Tons of Fun (2011); photo by Scott Suchman 35br. INDIQUE: 169bl. INTERNATIONAL SPY MUSEUM: 135tr, 141cb. JALEO: 193clb. THE JACKSON ROSE BED & BREAKFAST: 233tl. AMIT KAPIL: 13tl, 24br, 36bl, 149cl, 152cl, 153t. MARYLAND AVIATION ADMINISTRATION: 18br, 19bl. NATIONAL CHERRY BLOSSOM FESTIVAL: Nick Eckert 15br, Ron Engle 14bl. NATIONAL GALLERY OF ART, WASHINGTON, DC: Auguste Renoir, A Girl with a Watering Can, 1876, oil on canvas, Chester Dale Collection 76cr; Claude Monet, Rouen Cathedral, West Façade, Sunlight, 1894, oil on canvas, Overall: 100.1 x 65.8 cm (39 3/8 x 25 7/8 in.), framed: 127.6 x 91.4 cm (50 1/4 x 36 in.), Chester Dale Collection 76clb; Edgar Degas, The Dance Lesson, c. 1879, oil on canvas, Collection of Mr. and Mrs. Paul Mellon 76br; Pablo Picasso, Family of Saltimbanques, 1905, oil on canvas, Overall: 212.8 x 229.6 cm (83 3/4 x 90 3/8 in.), framed: 240.4 x 256.3 cm (94 5/8 x 100 7/8 in.), Chester Dale Collection 77tc; Mary Cassatt, Girl Arranging her Hair, 1886, oil on canvas overall: 75.1 x 62.5 cm (29 9/16 x 24 5/8 in.), framed: 96.5 x 83.2 cm (38 x 32 3/4 in.), Chester Dale Collection 77cl; Edgar Degas, Little Dancer Aged Fourteen, 1878–1881, wax, Collection of Mr. and Mrs. Paul Mellon 77c; Byzantine, Enthroned Madonna and Child, 13th century, tempera on panel, Gift of Mrs. Otto H. Kahn 78c; James McNeill Whistler, Wapping, 1860–1864, oil on canvas, John Hay Whitney Collection 78crb; Thomas Moran (American, 1837–1926), Green River Cliffs, Wyoming, 1881, oil on canvas, overall: 63.5 x 157.5 cm (25 x 62 in.), framed: 109.22 x 203.2 x 15.24 cm (43 x 80 x 6 in.), Gift of the Milligan and Thomson Families 78br. NATIONAL GEOGRAPHIC SOCIETY: Mark Thiessen 175tl. BOB OGREN: 174br. PHOTOLIBRARY: Age fotostock/José Fuste Raga 8–9,/Kordcom 14br; Alamy/Irene Abdou 172clb,/ David Coleman 17bl, 40bl, 74bl,/Rob Crandall 153br,/ dbimages 74cla,/DC Stock 41cl,/Randy Duchaine 138tr,/ Michele and Tom Grimm 213c,/Nikreates 98–99,/Photos 12 195tc,/Aurice Savage 212tc,/Philip Scalia 220tl,/Lana Sundman 20bl,/Visions of America, LLC 18bl,/Wiskerke 17br; Glow Images 147cb,/Lite Productions 236–237,/ Superstock 2–3; Ticket/Barry Winiker 116–117; White/ VisionsofAmerica/Joe Sohm 1c. SMITHSONIAN AMERICAN ART MUSEUM'S RENWICK GALLERY: Ron Blunt 117c. SMITHSONIAN NATIONAL AIR AND SPACE MUSEUM: 194br. SMITHSONIAN NATIONAL MUSEUM OF AMERICAN HISTORY: 70cr; 71cl. SMITHSONIAN NATIONAL MUSEUM OF THE AMERICAN INDIAN: 60tr. SMITHSONIAN'S NATIONAL ZOOLOGICAL PARK: 168cl, 168cr; Sodexo 168cb. USDA FOREST SERVICE: Dominic Cumberland 97c. WHITE HOUSE HISTORICAL ASSOCIATION: Erik Kvalsvik 122cl, 122cr. WILLARD INTERCONTINENTAL: 228tr. WOLF TRAP: 197bl.

JACKET IMAGES: Front: 4CORNERS: Massimo Borchi c; ALAMY IMAGES: incamerastock tr; DREAMSTIME.COM: Valentin Armianu tc; ROBERT HARDING PICTURE LIBRARY: Chris Grill tl; Back: ALAMY IMAGES: Art Kowalsky tr; GETTY IMAGES: National Geographic/Paul Sutherland tl; PHOTOLIBRARY: We Shall Be as Relatives exterior ceramic mural for the entrance to the Admin.-Ed Building, National Zoological Park, Washington DC, 1978 by Judith Inglese/Age fotostock/Susan Isakson/ tc; Spine: CORBIS: Visions of America/Joseph Sohm t.

All other images © Dorling Kindersley
For further information see: www.dkimages.com

**SPECIAL EDITIONS OF DK TRAVEL GUIDES**

DK Travel Guides can be purchased in bulk quantities at discounted prices for use in promotions or as premiums. We are also able to offer special editions and personalized jackets, corporate imprints, and excerpts from all of our books, tailored specifically to meet your own needs.
To find out more, please contact:
(in the US) specialsales@dk.com
(in the UK) travelguides@uk.dk.com
(in Canada) specialmarkets@dk.com
(in Australia) penguincorporatesales@ penguinrandomhouse.com.au

# M metro
## System Map

wmata.com
Customer Information Service: 202-637-7000
TTY Phone: 202-638-3780
Metro Transit Police: 202-962-2121

## Legend

**RD** Red Line • Glenmont / Shady Grove
**OR** Orange Line • New Carrollton / Vienna
**BL** Blue Line • Franconia-Springfield / Largo Town Center
**GR** Green Line • Branch Ave / Greenbelt
**YL** Yellow Line • Huntington / Fort Totten
**SV** Silver Line • Wiehle-Reston East / Largo Town Center

### Station Features
🚌✈ Bus to Airport
P Parking
H Hospital
✈ Airport

### Connecting Rail Systems
AMTRAK • VRE • MARC

Station in Service
Transfer Station
Under Construction
Full-Time Service

Rush-Only Service: Monday-Friday
6:30am - 9:00am  3:30pm - 6:00pm

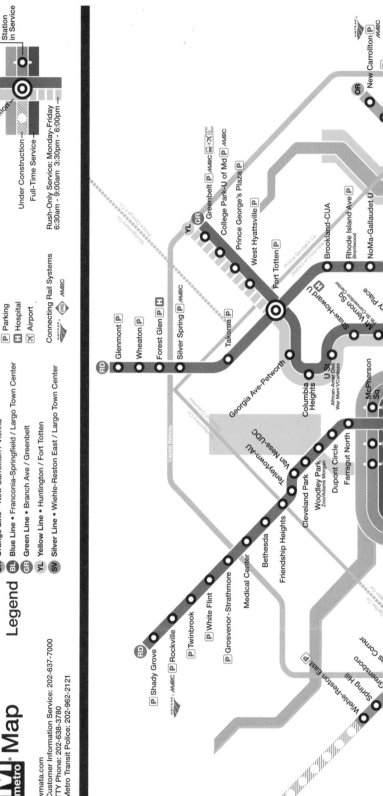